Environmental Policy
and
NEPA

Past, Present,
and Future

Environmental Policy and NEPA

Past, Present, and Future

Edited by

Ray Clark and Larry Canter

S^t_L

St. Lucie Press
Boca Raton, Florida

Phone: (561) 994-0555
E-mail: information@slpress.com
Web site: http://www.slpress.com

S^{t}L

Published by
St. Lucie Press
2000 Corporate Blvd., N.W.
Boca Raton, FL 33431-9868

CONTENTS

Preface ix

Contributors xiii

I. HISTORICAL TRENDS

1 The Historical Roots of NEPA 3
   R.B. Smythe

2 NEPA: The Rational Approach to Change 15
   R. Clark

3 Implementing NEPA: A Non-Technical Political Task 25
   L.K. Caldwell

4 The Rationality and Logic of NEPA Revisited 51
   R.V. Bartlett

5 Basic Purposes and Policies of the NEPA Regulations 61
   K.S. Weiner

6 The Unfinished Business of National Environmental Policy 85
   R.N.L. Andrews

7 What Has NEPA Wrought Abroad? 99
   C. Wood

II. CURRENT TRENDS

8 Cumulative Effects and Other Analytical Challenges of NEPA 115
   L.W. Canter

9 Can NEPA Prevent "Ecological Train Wrecks"? 139
   N.B. Dennis

10 The Case for Continuous Monitoring and Adaptive Management Under
   NEPA 163
   R.A. Carpenter

11 Highlights of NEPA in the Courts 181
        W.M. Cohen and M.D. Miller

12 The CEQ NEPA Effectiveness Study: Learning from Our Past and
        Shaping Our Future 193
        H. Welles

13 Increasing the Efficiency and Effectiveness of NEPA Through the
        Use of Technology 215
        R. Webster

14 Putting People in the Environment: Principles for Social Impact
        Assessment 229
        *Interorganizational Committee on Guidelines and Principles for Social
        Impact Assessment*

III. FUTURE OPPORTUNITIES

15 The Missing Link: Effects on Communities, Neighborhoods, and
        Individuals 251
        E.W. Cleckley

16 Public Involvement Under NEPA: Trends and Opportunities 261
        R.M. Solomon, S. Yonts-Shepard, and W.T. Supulski II

17 Alternative Dispute Resolution in the NEPA Process 277
        G. Bingham and L.M. Langstaff

18 Creating a User-Friendly NEPA 289
        P. Offringa

19 NEPA and Tribal Matters 299
        G. Mittelstaedt, T. Williams, and K. Ordon

20 The Role of NEPA in Sustainable Development 313
        H. Kaufman

21 NEPA's Interdisciplinary Mandate: Redirection for Sustainability 321
        A.F. Euston

22 Forum 335
        R. Clark, L. Caldwell, D. Bear, and D. Mandelker

INDEX 341

PREFACE

Converting great ideas into commonplace actions often takes hundreds of years. Environmental impact analysis and the quest to scout the future for the sake of the environment was urged by George Perkins Marsh in the 1960s. His idea took root only 100 years later with the passage of the National Environmental Policy Act (NEPA). Still, we have much to do to make NEPA the integrating and balancing tool its framers envisioned.

This book highlights historical trends, current issues, and future opportunities from the development of environmental policy resulting from the passage of NEPA. This act was signed into law in the United States on January 1, 1970, and this book represents both a retrospective and prospective synthesis of the effects that NEPA has had on environmental policy and governmental decision making. It has been prepared to coincide with the 25th anniversary of the passage of NEPA. The book is an outgrowth of initiatives taken by the Council on Environmental Quality (CEQ) to determine the effectiveness and efficiency of the implementation of NEPA. During the conduction of this study, it was realized that an opportune time existed for a careful review and assessment of environmental policy and this environmental law, which many have referred to as the Magna Carta for the environment in the United States.

The book has been prepared by multiple authors who have unique expertise in the topical areas they have addressed. A total of 28 authors or co-authors participated in the development of the 22 chapters included.

The 22 chapters in the book are grouped into three broad topical themes: historical trends, current issues, and future opportunities. Some chapters could have been placed in more than one theme grouping; thus, the reader should be aware of possible topical and chapter overlaps among the themes. Chapters 1 to 7 encompass the section on historical trends, with emphasis given to environmental policy and NEPA's effects on agency decision making (Chapters 2 and 4), the history of the development of NEPA (Chapters 1 and 3), regulations promulgated because of NEPA (Chapter 5), and the unfinished business of NEPA in terms of environmental management (Chapter 6). This section also includes one chapter (Chapter 7) related to the passage of laws similar to NEPA in numerous countries throughout the world.

The second section, which encompasses Chapters 8 to 14, is related to current substantive and conceptual issues associated with the environmental impact assessment

(EIA) process. Chapters in this grouping are primarily focused on methodologies and their usage in the EIA process. Included are chapters on cumulative effects and other analytical challenges (Chapter 8), approaches for avoiding ecological disasters (Chapter 9), and the use of adaptive management in conjunction with continuous monitoring (Chapter 10). The highlights of several court cases related to NEPA are the subject of Chapter 11; particular emphasis is given to landmark cases that have shaped EIA practice to date and are anticipated to influence future practice. Chapter 12 provides a summary of the 1994–95 CEQ effectiveness study, and emphasis is given to issues that represent positive accomplishments of NEPA as well as continuing concerns. Chapter 13 focuses on the use of emerging technologies in the NEPA process, with particular attention given to Geographic Information Systems (GIS), imaging, and the Internet. Finally, Chapter 14 emphasizes the importance of social impact assessment and associated methodologies as components in the EIA process.

The third section relates to future opportunities; it highlights relationships with various publics and the incorporation of sustainability considerations in the EIA process. Chapters 15 and 16 primarily address the importance of considering impacts on humans in the EIA process and the need for effective public involvement techniques to facilitate participation in project planning and decision making. Chapter 17 focuses on an emerging tool for resolving conflicts; the umbrella term for the tool is "alternative dispute resolution." Chapter 18 is related to the need for systematic presentation of information to decision makers in order to facilitate effective decision making in the EIA process. The special relationships that exist between the requirements of NEPA and Indian tribes and the management of environmental resources on reservation lands are the subject of Chapter 19. Chapters 20 and 21 highlight features of sustainability considerations as they relate to an expanded emphasis within the EIA process. The specific role of NEPA is addressed in Chapter 20, and the need for interdisciplinary perspectives in sustainability is the subject of Chapter 21. The final chapter (Chapter 22) is a forum of three of the most respected professionals in the environmental policy field.

The emphasis on historical trends, current issues, and future opportunities provides useful information for both practitioners and academicians associated with the EIA process. The book could be used as a textbook or supplemental reading in upper-division or graduate-level courses focused on environmental policy and/or the EIA process. The orientation of the information in this book is toward policy and procedural matters and less toward biophysical sciences and engineering. Individuals trained in many disciplines should find this book useful.

Although the book is oriented toward EIA practice in the United States, with only one chapter (Chapter 7) containing information on EIA practices in other countries, it should be of value to EIA practitioners throughout the world in that fundamental issues related to implementation, conceptual frameworks, and public participation in the EIA process are all matters of current concern, irrespective of country.

While the 22 chapters address a variety of topics, the book is not intended to encompass every possible consideration in the EIA process. Using this book in conjunction with other textbooks or materials more closely related to the scientific aspects of the EIA process would represent a good combination for comprehensive usage.

It should also be noted that both environmental policy and the practice of EIA are dynamic; even though 25 years has elapsed since the passage of NEPA, and a much greater uniformity in process and methodology now exists, there are still numerous anticipated changes that will occur in environmental policy and the EIA process in the next quarter century.

Finally, the editors are appreciative of the efforts of many persons. First, they wish to express their profound appreciation to their colleagues who participated in the assemblage of the chapters included herein. The timeliness of submittals is greatly appreciated, as is the analysis and synthesis included in the chapters.

The editors particularly express their appreciation for the positive attitude and helpfulness of Ms. Ginger Geis and Ms. Mittie Durham of the Environmental and Ground Water Institute, University of Oklahoma, in typing the manuscript and cross-checking on a variety of editorial issues. Their technical abilities and pleasant attitudes facilitated the timely generation of this manuscript.

The editors also express their gratitude to the Council on Environmental Quality and the College of Engineering, University of Oklahoma, respectively, for their support during the preparation of this manuscript. Included in these acknowledgments are Kathleen McGinty, Chairman of CEQ; Dr. Ronald Sack of the School of Civil Engineering and Environmental Science; and Dean Billy Crynes of the College of Engineering at the University of Oklahoma. Finally, Larry wishes to express thanks to his wife for her support and encouragement in the process of the development of this manuscript. Ray wishes to thank Taylor, who had less time with her dad than she deserves.

Ray Clark
Council on Environmental Quality

Larry Canter
University of Oklahoma

CONTRIBUTORS

Richard N.L. Andrews
Department of Environmental Science
University of North Carolina
Chapel Hill, North Carolina 27599-7400

Robert V. Bartlett
Department of Political Science
Purdue University
1363 Liberal Arts and Education Building
West Lafayette, Indiana 47907-1363

Gail Bingham
RESOLVE
2828 Pennsylvania Avenue, N.W., Suite 402
Washington, D.C. 20007

Rabel Burdge
Social and Natural Resources Section
Environmental Assessment Division
Argonne National Lab
370 L'Enfant Promenade, S.W., Suite 702
Washington, D.C. 20024

Lynton K. Caldwell
Woodburn Hall 406
Indiana University
Bloomington, Indiana 47405

Larry W. Canter
Environmental and Ground Water Institute
University of Oklahoma
200 Felgar Street, Room 127
Norman, Oklahoma 73019-0470

Richard A. Carpenter
State Route 676
Route 5, Box 277
Charlottesville, Virginia 22901

Ray Clark
Council on Environmental Quality
722 Jackson Place, N.W.
Washington, D.C. 20503

Eugene W. Cleckley
Environmental Operations
U.S. Department of Transportation
Federal Highway Administration
400 7th Street, S.W.
Room 3232
Washington, D.C. 20590

William M. Cohen
Environmental Litigation Branch
Department of Justice
601 Pennsylvania Avenue, N.W.
Washington, D.C. 20004

Nona B. Dennis
Environmental Science Associates
301 Brannon Street
Suite 200
San Francisco, California 94107

Andrew F. Euston
Urban Design and Energy Program
U.S. Department of Housing and Urban
Development
451 7th Street, S.W.
Washington, D.C. 20410

Holly Kaufman
Environmental Policy and Project
Management
1757 Q Street, N.W., No. F
Washington, D.C. 20009

Lee M. Langstaff
RESOLVE
2828 Pennsylvania Avenue, N.W.
Suite 402
Washington, D.C. 20007

Margo D. Miller
Environmental Litigation Branch
Department of Justice
601 Pennsylvania Avenue, N.W.
Washington, D.C. 20004

Gillian D. Mittelstaedt
7615 Totem Beach Road
Marysville, Washington 98271

Peter Offringa
ICF Kaiser Engineers, Inc.
1800 Harrison Street
Oakland, California 94612-3430

Kimberely Ordon
7615 Totem Beach Road
Marysville, Washington 98271

Robert B. Smythe
Potomac Resources Consultants
4807 Wellington Drive
Chevy Chase, Maryland 20815

Rhey M. Solomon
Resource Planning Staff
USDA Forest Service, 3 Central
P.O. Box 96090
Washington, D.C. 20090-6090

William T. Supulski II
Resource Planning Staff
USDA Forest Service, 3 Central
P.O. Box 96090
Washington, D.C. 20090-6090

Ron Webster
U.S. Army Environmental Policy Institute
Georgia Institute of Technology
430 Tenth Street, N.W.
Suite S-206
Atlanta, Georgia 30318-5768

Kenneth S. Weiner
5000 Columbia Center
701 5th Avenue
Seattle, Washington 98104-7078

Holly Welles
54 Tamalpais Road
Berkeley, California 94708

Gary Williams
Social and Natural Resources Section
Environmental Assessment Division
Argonne National Lab
370 L'Enfant Promenade, S.W.
Suite 702
Washington, D.C. 20024

Terry Williams
7615 Totem Beach Road
Marysville, Washington 98271

Christopher Wood
EIA Centre
Department of Planning and Landscape
University of Manchester
Oxford Road
Manchester, M13 9PL, U.K.

Susan Yonts-Shepard
Resource Planning Staff
USDA Forest Service, 3 Central
P.O. Box 96090
Washington, D.C. 20090-6090

HISTORICAL TRENDS

I

THE HISTORICAL ROOTS OF NEPA

R.B. Smythe

In every deliberation, we must consider the impact of our decisions on the next seven generations.
—Iroquois Confederation, 18th century[1]

Man is everywhere a disturbing agent. Wherever he plants his foot, the harmonies of nature are turned to discord.
—George Perkins Marsh, 1864[2]

But there must be the look ahead, there must be a realization of the fact that to waste, to destroy, our natural resources, to skin and exhaust the land...will result in undermining in the days of our children the very prosperity which we ought by right to hand down to them amplified and developed.
—Theodore Roosevelt, 1907[3]

By and large, our present problem is one of attitudes and implements. We are remodeling the Alhambra with a steam-shovel, and we are proud of our yardage. We shall hardly relinquish the shovel, which after all has many good points, but we are in need of gentler and more objective criteria for its successful use.
—Aldo Leopold, 1949[4]

I n late 1969, while environmental activists on several university campuses were organizing for the first Earth Day celebration, Congress completed and sent to President Nixon a short bill entitled the National Environmental Policy Act (NEPA) of 1969. The political and legal history of NEPA's enactment is discussed in detail by Caldwell in this volume (Chapter 3) and others.[5] This chapter instead examines the scientific and philosophical foundation for the policy goals articulated in NEPA, elements of which extend back in time at least to the beginning of the republic.[6]

THE RISE OF PUBLIC CONCERN FOR ENVIRONMENTAL VALUES

In the United States, the origins of public concern for the natural environment can be traced at least as far back as the 18th century. In his now-classic book, *Wilderness and the American Mind,* Roderick Nash observed that the European settlers of North America brought with them a largely hostile, Old Testament view of wilderness as something to be feared, endured, and subdued. The Puritans in particular viewed the dark forests, wild animals, and native Indians of the New England frontier as being under the influence of Satan himself. They labored relentlessly to clear the land, plant crops, build towns, and thereby achieve dominion over this uncivilized chaos.

But along with these grim and unyielding immigrants came others who were more tolerant of and more curious about the "state of nature" in the New World. From England and Europe, they were familiar with the writings and observations of the scholars of the Enlightenment: Locke, Newton, Galileo, Descartes, and Linnaeus. In *Nature's Economy: A History of Ecological Ideas,* Donald Worster says of the great Swedish botanist, "Though a national hero in Sweden, Linnaeus found his greatest following in England and America, especially among parson-naturalists such as Gilbert White and the Quaker botanists John and William Bartram of Philadelphia. These men shared his love of the Creator's handiwork as well as his scientific interest in nature."[7] The work of Linnaeus and other naturalists of the 18th century helped to support the argument, made by both deist and romantic philosophers, that the universe was governed by natural laws, from which followed natural rights that should be respected by all human beings.

The Bartrams, father and son, traveled extensively throughout eastern North America in the latter half of the 18th century, publishing their observations on the natural history, climate, landscape, and inhabitants they encountered. Thomas Jefferson made his own contributions to the natural history literature; his *Notes on the State of Virginia,* written in 1784, described the scenic beauty of the region. Jefferson, also a student of the Enlightenment, later invoked "the laws of nature and of nature's God" in the Declaration of Independence. In 1804, as president, Jefferson sent Lewis and Clark on their epic exploration of the newly acquired Louisiana Purchase; the journals of their trip gave citizens of the new nation the first direct account of much of the vast territory west of the Mississippi River.

Concurrent with these early records of America's flora, fauna, and physical features, expressions of concern for their protection began to emerge, often couched in philosophical or religious principles. Roderick Nash noted that in 1793 the American Philosophical Society published a paper by the Reverend Nicholas Collin that asked the society "to support the protection of little-known birds, apparently on the verge of extinction, until naturalists discovered 'what part is assigned to them in the oeconomy of nature.'"[8] Some of the states had already adopted ordinances that placed restrictions on hunting and timber harvesting in populated areas, but as yet there were no state or federal plans to designate natural areas or wildlife reserves.

In the first part of the 19th century, several American writers combined the themes of romanticism and nationalism to acclaim the values of the American wilderness and the beauty of its flora and fauna. The poetry of William Cullen Bryant, the Leatherstocking novels of James Fenimore Cooper, and the paintings and writings of Thomas Cole, John James Audubon, and George Catlin were all indicative of this trend.

This perspective was soon reflected and expanded in the writings and activities of the conservation philosophers Ralph Waldo Emerson and Henry David Thoreau, who found deep spiritual values in nature and who both expressed concern that commerce and technology were threatening those values. Catlin, Cole, Thoreau, and Horace Greely, among others, began to call for preservation of some natural areas as parks and preserves, complete with forests, buffaloes, and Indians, as places to restore mankind's vitality and inspiration.[9] Thoreau, in a lecture at the Concord Lyceum in April 1851, went so far as to state his view in eight famous words: "in Wildness is the preservation of the World."[10]

This opinion certainly ran counter to the dominant view that the American wilderness was, as Hawthorne's novels portrayed it, the sinister habitat of dark forces; nor was this opinion widely shared by those seeking to encourage westward expansion. A more popular view was expressed by Illinois Congressman Orlando Ficklin, who stated in 1845:

> Unless the government shall grant head rights, or donations of some kind, these prairies, with their gorgeous growth of flowers, their green carpeting, their lovely lawns and gentle slopes, will for centuries continue to be the home of the wild deer and wolf; their stillness will be undisturbed by the jocund song of the farmer, and their deep and fertile soil unbroken by the ploughshare. Something must be done to remedy this evil.[11]

Thoreau, however, continued to articulate his transcendentalist philosophy in *Walden,* published in 1854, and in his subsequent journals. In 1858, Thoreau wrote an article for the *Atlantic Monthly,* based on his travels in the Maine woods, in which he decried the consequences of indiscriminate logging and asked, "why should not we…have our national preserves…in which the bear and panther, and some even of the hunter race, may still exist…for inspiration, and our own true recreation?[12] Thoreau died in 1862, the year Congress passed the Homestead Act to encourage settlement of the vast western public lands.

Two years later, George Perkins Marsh brought complementary but more utilitarian arguments to the case for conserving and managing the nation's natural endowment. Marsh, a lawyer and diplomat from Vermont, described the multiple adverse effects of extensive logging operations in the Northeast and argued that preserving forest wilderness areas had long-term economic as well as philosophical value. Marsh's book *Man and Nature; or Physical Geography as Modified by Human Action* helped initiate efforts to establish a forest preserve in New York's Adirondack Mountains.

During that same year, in the midst of the Civil War, Congress was persuaded to grant ten square miles of Yosemite Valley to the state of California to be managed as a park "for public use, resort, and recreation."[13] The eminent landscape architect Frederick Law Olmstead, who had designed New York City's Central Park, served briefly as a commissioner of Yosemite; his report on the area's scenic and natural values laid the groundwork for its later expansion into a national park.

The world's first national park, however, resulted from the well-publicized Yellowstone River expeditions of Nathaniel Langford, Cornelius Hedges, and Ferdinand Hayden in 1870 and 1871. These three, with the help of artist Thomas Moran and photographer William Henry Jackson (and the self-interested support of the Northern Pacific Railway), employed a combination of philosophical and utilitarian arguments to persuade the Congress and President Grant to enact, in March 1872, a federal law that designated over two million acres of public land in northwestern Wyoming Territory as Yellowstone National Park—the world's first place in which "all timber, mineral deposits, natural curiosities, or wonders" were to be preserved "in their natural condition."[14]

To be sure, Congress was not solely, or even largely, occupied with preservation; that year it also enacted the General Mining Law, still in effect today, which allowed citizens unrestricted entry to public lands to prospect for and develop "valuable mineral deposits" unconstrained either by payment of royalties or by effective environmental controls. In general, federal laws and policies of the late 19th century continued to reflect the nation's post-Civil War enthusiasm for western expansion and settlement.

In New York, however, there was growing public interest in preserving the Adirondack forests before they were destroyed by lumber mills and iron foundries. A state park commission was created in 1872 to make recommendations that eventually led, in 1885, to a state law establishing a 715,000-acre forest preserve, to be protected both for its intrinsic natural value and for its importance as a source of water for the state's extensive system of canals. By 1892, this preserve had been expanded to over three million acres and redesignated as a state park to provide for recreation as well as for watershed protection and a future source of commercial timber. In 1894, permanent protection for the Adirondack State Park was approved by New Yorkers as a part of the state's constitution.[15]

PRESERVATION VERSUS CONSERVATION

In 1864, a young Scottish immigrant named John Muir left his family's Wisconsin farm for Canada, initially to avoid being drafted into the Union Army (a route followed by other Americans for similar reasons a century later). There he developed an amateur's interest in botany and a spiritual devotion to nature that led him to travel, mostly on foot, from Indiana to Florida and eventually to explore the wonders of the California wilderness, especially the Sierra Nevada mountain range. Muir, who was captivated by the writings of Emerson and Thoreau, turned their philosophy into activism in a campaign to preserve as wilderness the high ground around Yosemite Valley. Muir lectured, wrote articles, and led camping expeditions into the mountains to enlist political support and eventually saw Yosemite National Park created by an act of Congress on September 30, 1890.[16] But Muir and others who were concerned about the adverse effects of indiscriminate logging of the public lands also urged Congress to pass a law giving the president the power to create new forest reserves by declaration. In March 1891, Congress did so, and President Benjamin Harrison soon proclaimed 15 such reserves, totaling more than 13 million acres. The following year, Muir and others founded the Sierra Club, with Muir as its first president, in part to continue their efforts to protect the forests of the Sierra Nevada.[17]

The new forest reserves, however, received little actual protection, and their purpose was subject to debate. Secretary of the Interior Hoke Smith asked the National Academy of Sciences to form an advisory commission to consider options for managing the reserves. One of the commission members, a Yale graduate recently returned from advanced forestry training in Europe, was Gifford Pinchot. Pinchot and Muir agreed that the preserves could benefit from active management, but Pinchot's emphasis was on obtaining a steady supply of timber. Here the differences between conservation, as later defined by Pinchot in utilitarian terms, and preservation, as championed by Muir in philosophical terms, first became evident and still persist today. Muir and Pinchot grew increasingly critical of each other's positions. Pinchot's view prevailed in the language of the 1897 Organic Administration Act for the Forest Service, which declared that one of the main purposes of the reserves was "to furnish a continuous supply of timber for the use and necessities of citizens of the United States."[18]

Thereafter, Muir concentrated on the establishment of national parks and monuments, including the Grand Canyon, in which timber harvesting, mining, and other extractive commercial activities would be prohibited.[19] Pinchot went on to become a key advisor to President Theodore Roosevelt (who in 1905 made Pinchot chief forester of the newly established U.S. Forest Service) and an effective advocate for making efficient use of the nation's forests and other natural resources.

Muir and Pinchot clashed again over the city of San Francisco's request to the Interior Department for permission to dam the Tuolumne River and build a reservoir that would flood the Hetch Hetchy Valley within Yosemite National Park. Muir and the Sierra Club waged a national campaign against the city and pro-reservoir members of Congress, who were supported by Pinchot. The controversy ran for several years and encompassed arguments that presaged the topics to emerge in environmental impact statements (EISs) 60 years later—the importance of recreation versus development, the availability of alternatives, costs versus benefits, the values of wilderness, and the integrity of national parks. In the absence of any formal decision-making process for such a controversial proposal, a variety of conflicting claims, pro and con, were made about the merits of the project. Presidents Roosevelt, Taft, and Wilson all equivocated, leaving the decision to Congress, which finally enacted legislation in December 1913, which President Wilson signed, permitting the city to flood the Hetch Hetchy Valley. Though devastated by this defeat, Muir took some satisfaction in seeing that the preservation of Yosemite, and of wilderness in general, had become a matter of national concern.

Muir died in 1914, the same year that the last passenger pigeon died in a Cincinnati zoo. Two years later, an act of Congress established the National Park Service; its first director was Stephen Mather, a Sierra Club member who had been an opponent of the Hetch Hetchy project. Mather and his colleagues made the Park Service into a formidable agency for the protection of natural and scenic areas, thus providing a counterweight to the utilitarian conservation policies represented by Pinchot and the Forest Service.[20]

FEDERAL AUTHORITY FOR WILDLIFE PROTECTION

The Muir–Pinchot conflict had been focused largely on the protection and management of public forest reserves and park lands, but there was also a growing movement to protect wildlife, and birds in particular, from excessive hunting and commercial exploitation. The movement had humanitarian, utilitarian, and scientific factions. The deliberate destruction of the great bison herds, the overhunting of elk and bighorn sheep in the West, and the slaughter of hundreds of thousands of non-game birds to provide feathers for women's hats all helped to generate calls for state and federal protection. The American Ornithologists Union (AOU), a professional society founded in 1883, drafted a model state law to prohibit the killing of certain endangered species. The Massachusetts Audubon Society and 15 other state Audubon societies established in the 1890s encouraged Iowa Representative John Lacey to sponsor a bill that outlawed the interstate shipment of any "wild animals and birds" killed in violation of state laws and gave the Bureau of Biological Survey (BBS), then a part of the Agriculture Department, the authority to enforce the law. This legislation, known as the Lacey Act, was enacted in 1900. The AOU and the state Audubon societies worked with the BBS and the states to implement the Lacey Act; in 1905, 36 state Audubon groups formed the National Association of Audubon Societies to pursue further protection for birds and other wildlife.[21]

The effectiveness of the Lacey Act was limited by its reliance on state wildlife laws, which varied from state to state. President Theodore Roosevelt initiated wildlife protection on federal lands in 1903 when he declared Pelican Island in Florida a federal bird reservation, but this authority could only be applied to land that was federal property. Pressure on the federal government to provide more comprehensive and consistent wildlife protection led to passage of the Migratory Bird Act of 1913, which declared all migratory and insect-eating birds "to be within the custody and protection of the United States" and directed the federal government to regulate their hunting. This law was followed by a migratory bird treaty with Great Britain, on behalf of Canada, in 1916 and a law to implement that treaty, the Migratory Bird Treaty Act, in 1918. A challenge by Missouri to the constitutionality of the treaty and the act was rejected by the U.S. Supreme Court, which effectively confirmed the federal government's legal authority to protect and regulate wildlife.[22]

Naturalists and wildlife preservationists initially paid less attention to fish and other aquatic species than to terrestrial forms of life. However, by 1871, marked declines in the catch of several food-fish species led Congress to create a Commission on Fish and Fisheries to investigate the situation, determine the causes for those declines, and make recommendations regarding "protective, prohibitory, or precautionary measures" that might be needed to protect these fisheries. Congress also established the first federal fish hatchery in 1872. In 1903, the fish commission was renamed the Bureau of Fisheries and placed in the new Department of Commerce, where its principal mission was to assist and promote commercial fishing.[23] During the 1920s and 1930s, Congress passed several laws intended to reduce the devastating effects on freshwater and anadromous fish populations of major dams and hydropower projects. The Fish and Wildlife Coordination Act, first passed in 1934 and subsequently strengthened by several amendments, required other agencies to consult with the Bureau of Fisheries before constructing dams and to consider the feasibility of providing for fish migration. As later expanded, this statute became the principal federal interagency environmental planning requirement prior to passage of NEPA.

ECOLOGY, ETHICS, AND NATURAL RESOURCE MANAGEMENT

In 1909, another Yale Forestry School graduate joined the U.S. Forest Service, one who had read Thoreau and Darwin and was acquainted with the perspectives of both Muir and Pinchot. Assigned to work in the Territories of Arizona and New Mexico, Aldo Leopold perceived a need for conservation programs to address the declining numbers of big game animals, fish, and waterfowl. He began working with other foresters and local sportsmen to develop such programs and became an advocate within the Forest Service for giving greater consideration to wildlife conservation and recreation. He concluded that the designation of wilderness preserves within national forest units was an effective way to achieve these goals, and he became a persistent and articulate advocate for wilderness preservation.

Leopold's special contribution was the application of science, in the form of the emerging discipline of ecology, to both define and articulate his views. He was supported by others with scientific training, such as Victor Shelford, Bob Marshall, Sigurd Olson, and Steven Mather.[24] Although Leopold wrote professional texts on wildlife and game management and served a term as president of the Ecological Society of America, he also spoke, taught, and wrote about natural phenomena from aesthetic, historical, and ethical perspectives. In doing so, he was able to advocate an environmental strategy that integrated elements of scientific theory with the philosophical views of utilitarian conservationists and the moral arguments of preservationists. A paper Leopold presented in 1933 (the year he left the Forest Service to join the University of Wisconsin faculty), entitled "The Conservation Ethic," was later modified into "The Land Ethic," and he included it as the last chapter of his famous collection of essays, *A Sand County Almanac,* which was published in 1949, the year after his death.

Leopold, Marshall, and other government employees concerned about protecting environmental values had worked within their agencies to persuade presidents, cabinet officers, and other decision makers to give greater consideration to the protection of natural habitats, particularly those rich in unusual flora and fauna or with other recreational or scientific potential. Although they succeeded in having numerous tracts of public lands designated as wilderness preserves, there was no unifying legal authority for the designation and management of such areas. In part to address this problem, in 1935 Leopold, Marshall, Robert Sterling Yard, and others founded the Wilderness Society to be a permanent national voice for the protection of wilderness.

Although Marshall died in 1939 and Leopold in 1948, their advocacy was continued by others. In the early 1950s, Howard Zahniser, director of the Wilderness Society, proposed that a national wilderness preservation system be established by an act of Congress. At that time, the Sierra Club, led by David Brower, was engaged in a battle to prevent the construction of a dam that would flood the Dinosaur National Monument, which Brower saw as a second Hetch Hetchy. After joining forces with the Sierra Club and other organizations to defeat the Echo Park Dam bill in 1956, Zahniser used the momentum of that campaign to obtain broad support from environmental organizations for a national wilderness bill that he had drafted. He persuaded Senator Hubert Humphrey and Representative John Saylor to introduce the bill in Congress and then led a seven-year national campaign to secure its enactment, invoking the names and ideas of Thoreau, Muir, Marshall, and Leopold at every opportunity.[25] Zahniser died in May 1964, four months before President Lyndon Johnson signed the final version of the bill into law.

As enacted, the bill protected 54 areas encompassing only 9 million acres of federal land, all in the national forests, instead of the 60 million acres of federal lands then being managed as wilderness. However, the system was firmly established and has been greatly expanded by subsequent legislation. As Stephen Fox put it, "Seen in the light of history, Echo Park and the Wilderness Act of 1964 reversed the verdict of Hetch Hetchy. The utilitarian notion of nature for man's use gave way to a preservationist forbearance."[26]

During the 1960s, Congress, responding to growing scientific evidence of diminishing natural areas and declining wildlife, also passed several other laws to protect species and habitats at risk and to expand recreational opportunities. These laws included the Land and Water Conservation Fund Act (1965), the first Endangered Species Act (1966, and rewritten and greatly strengthened in 1973), the Wild and Scenic Rivers Act (1968), and the National Trails Act (1968).

Although these laws provided protection for designated organisms and areas with recognized natural, recreational, aesthetic, or scientific value, they did not establish an integrated strategy for the consideration and protection of such value by government agencies. Nor did they address other threats to that value which became increasingly evident during the post-World War II wave of economic development that included the "baby boom" and widespread residential and industrial expansion.

Although air and water pollution problems had been recognized in the 19th century, they were generally considered matters for local governments to address if necessary to protect public health and safety. For example, some cities had begun to treat their sewage, and Chicago and Cincinnati adopted smoke control ordinances in 1881. The Rivers and Harbors Act of 1899, often cited as the first federal pollution control law, prohibited the discharge into navigable waters of the United States of "any refuse matter of any kind or description whatever other than that flowing from streets and sewers and passing therefrom in a liquid state" without a permit from the Secretary of the Army.[27] However, the Army Corps of Engineers, charged with implementing the law, declined to apply it to any refuse smaller than building materials, large animal carcasses, or other objects big enough to pose clear obstructions to commercial navigation.

California began efforts to control industrial sources of smog in the 1940s. The Federal Water Pollution Control Act of 1948 and the Air Pollution Control Act of 1955 provided small federal grants to state agencies to develop monitoring and control programs, but no federal standards were proffered. The existence of toxic chemicals and hazardous wastes was hardly recognized as the nation thrived on a booming economy.

Between 1950 and 1970, the U.S. population grew by 37%, to 200 million, while both the gross domestic product and per capita income rose by more than 50% in real (inflation-adjusted) dollars. These gains were accompanied by a doubling of gross energy consumption (from 35 to 70 quadrillion Btus) and by the generation of massive amounts of air and water pollutants and other toxic chemicals with adverse effects on human health and the environment.[28]

Among the new industrial products to emerge from World War II were synthetic organic pesticides such as DDT. Initially highly effective against a variety of insect pests, these chemicals were widely used with little regard for their effects on non-target organisms. As the toxicity of these pesticides to fish and wildlife and their persistence in the environment became evident, criticism of their careless use began to mount.

One of those concerned about the unintended effects of pollutants in general, and chemical pesticides in particular, was Rachel Carson, a marine biologist and award-winning writer who had spent most of her professional career with the U.S. Fish and Wildlife Service. In 1958, she began research on a book that would document and dramatize the dangers of DDT and other chlorinated hydrocarbon pesticides. Although Carson was soon diagnosed with breast cancer, for which she underwent radiation treatments and surgery, she completed the book, entitled *Silent Spring*, in 1962. In the preface, she cited Albert Schweitzer's warning: "Man has lost the capacity to foresee and to forestall. He will end by destroying the earth."[29]

Carson and her book were praised by environmental scientists, President Kennedy, and most of the environmental community. The book won several awards, but she was harshly criticized by the chemical and agricultural industry as being hysterical and unprofessional. Excerpts from the book were published in *The New Yorker*. In a letter to the magazine's editor (not published by *The New Yorker* until February 1995), one reader responded:

> Miss Rachel Carson's reference to the selfishness of insecticide manufacturers probably reflects her Communist sympathies, like a lot of our writers these days. We can live without birds and animals, but, as the current market slump shows, we cannot live without business. As for insects, isn't it just like a woman to be scared to death of a few little bugs! As long as we have the H-bomb everything will be O.K.[30]

Silent Spring generated a nationwide reexamination of the use of chemical pesticides, which led to the passage in 1972 of a much-strengthened Federal Insecticide, Fungicide, and Rodenticide Act. Carson saw only the beginning of this process; she died of cancer in 1964, at age 56.

By the late 1960s, despite the enactment of numerous environmental laws, U.S. citizens had seen the spread of strontium-90 and other radioisotopes from nuclear weapons testing, habitat loss and soil erosion from widespread clear-cutting in the national forests, a proposal to dam the Grand Canyon for hydropower, an oil spill in the Santa Barbara Channel along the coast of California that killed thousands of seabirds, a river in Ohio so polluted that it caught fire, and the loss of nearly half of the nation's original wetlands from drainage and other development activities.

Some scientists, economists, and citizen activists began to identify several common underlying causes of many of the nation's growing environmental problems, including the following:

- A propensity to emphasize and value quantitative measures of growth over qualitative measures of well-being
- A failure of economic theory to internalize social and environmental costs in benefit–cost analyses
- The inadequacy of government institutions in dealing with problems that cut across political boundaries
- A lack of understanding of the fundamental interdependence of human populations and their environment
- A failure of both governmental and private institutions to take environmental factors into account as an essential part of planning and decision making
- A recognition that the U.S. government's narrow, mission-oriented approach to programs and projects and the lack of consideration given by federal agencies to environmentally preferable alternatives were contributing to these problems

A NATIONAL POLICY FOR THE ENVIRONMENT

Responding to growing public pressure for action to correct this situation, Congress in 1968 and 1969 held joint and separate House and Senate committee hearings to consider how to legislate a national policy for the environment. Testimony was taken from witnesses who represented a cross-section of government agencies, academic institutions, and national and regional environmental organizations. The issue was how to change agency decision making to ensure the timely consideration of environmental values. The objective was later described in one article as follows:

> The challenge was to approach environmental management in a comprehensive way. The new values of environmental policy had to intrude somehow into the most remote recesses of the federal administrative machinery and begin to influence the multitude of decisions being made by thousands of officials.[31]

The House drafted a bill to establish a Council on Environmental Quality within the Executive Office of the President, similar in structure and function to the Council of Economic Advisors, with the responsibility to prepare an annual report on the state of the nation's environment. Some witnesses called for stronger language, such as a constitutional amendment to add a "conservation bill of rights." The Senate bill contained a strong declarative statement of national environmental policy, and also an "action-forcing" provision to compel agencies to document their efforts to comply with the policy set forth in the law.

These House and Senate provisions were later combined by a conference committee into the bill that became NEPA when it was signed into law on January 1, 1970 by President Richard Nixon. Often subsequently referred to as the nation's environmental Magna Carta, NEPA articulated a concern for environmental quality that was firmly rooted in the values of America's earlier conservation philosophers, but also tempered by more recent utilitarian and scientific perspectives.

Much has been written over the intervening 25 years about the extent to which NEPA has achieved or fallen short of its stated purposes and the goals of its drafters.[32] Since compliance with NEPA is an ongoing federal activity, that issue remains subject to examination and debate, but the law's language and its objectives are strongly rooted in and reflective of two centuries of evolving American environmental values, experiences, and aspirations.

NOTES AND REFERENCES

1. As quoted in Rodes, Barbara and Rice Odell. 1992. *A Dictionary of Environmental Quotations.* Simon and Schuster, New York.
2. Marsh, George Perkins. 1864. *Man and Nature; or, Physical Geography as Modified by Human Action,* as quoted in Nash, Roderick Frazier. 1990. *American Environmentalism: Readings in Conservation History,* third edition. McGraw-Hill, New York.
3. Theodore Roosevelt, seventh annual message, December 3, 1907, as quoted in Rodes and Odell, 1992 (note 1).
4. Leopold, Aldo. 1949. *A Sand County Almanac and Sketches Here and There.* Oxford University Press, Oxford, England (reprinted 1968), pp. 225–226.

5. For example, Anderson, Frederick. 1973. *NEPA in the Courts: A Legal Analysis of the National Environmental Policy Act.* Johns Hopkins University Press, Baltimore; Liroff, Richard. 1976. *A National Policy for the Environment: NEPA and Its Aftermath.* Indiana University Press, Bloomington; and Grad, Frank. 1978. *Environmental Law,* second edition, Vol. 2. Matthew Bender, New York.

6. Only a few of the major federal environmental laws are mentioned in this chapter. For a historical review of U.S. environmental law, see Futrell, J. William. 1993. The History of Environmental Law. In *Sustainable Environmental Law.* Celia Campbell-Mohn, Barry Breen, and J. William Futrell, Eds. West Publishing, St. Paul, Minnesota, Chapter 1. For a chronological tabulation of key federal environmental laws, see Rodgers, William H. Jr.. 1994. *Environmental Law,* second edition. West Publishing, St. Paul, MN, p. ix.

7. Worster, D. 1977. *Nature's Economy: A History of Ecological Ideas.* Cambridge University Press, Cambridge, England, p. 33.

8. Nash, Roderick Frazier. 1989. *The Rights of Nature: A History of Environmental Ethics.* University of Wisconsin Press, Madison, p. 36. The quote from Collin is referenced as Collin, Nicholas. 1793. An Essay on Those Inquiries in Natural Philosophy, Which Are at Present Most Beneficial. *Transactions of the American Philosophical Society* 3:xxiv.

9. Roderick Nash credits George Catlin, best known for his dramatic paintings of American Indians, with originating the concept of a national park, which Catlin proposed in an article first published in a New York newspaper in 1832. Part of Catlin's article is reprinted in Nash, 1990 (note 2), pp. 31–35.

10. Thoreau, Henry David. 1851. Walking. reprinted in part in Nash, 1990 (note 2).

11. Congressional Globe, 28th Congress, 2nd Session, 52 (1845), quoted in Council on Environmental Quality. 1981. Environmental Quality—1980: The Eleventh Annual Report of the Council on Environmental Quality. U.S. Government Printing Office, Washington, D.C., p. 295.

12. Thoreau, Henry David. *Maine Woods, Writings,* as quoted in Nash, R. 1973. *Wilderness and the American Mind,* revised edition. Yale University Press, New Haven, Connecticut, p. 102.

13. U.S. Statutes at Large, 15, p. 325, as quoted in Nash, 1973 (note 12). Nash points out that the much larger Yosemite National Park was not created until 1890.

14. U.S. Statutes at Large, 17, p. 32, as quoted in Nash, 1973 (note 12), p. 102.

15. Nash, 1973 (note 12), pp. 116–121.

16. For a more detailed treatment of John Muir's life and his campaigns to protect the Yosemite Valley and the Sierra Nevada, see Fox, Steven R. 1981. *The American Conservation Movement: John Muir and His Legacy,* University of Wisconsin Press, Madison.

17. Nash, 1973 (note 12), pp. 133–136.

18. U.S. Statutes at Large, 30, p. 35, as quoted in Nash, 1973 (note 12), p. 137.

19. Nash, 1973 (note 12), pp. 137–140.

20. Fox, 1981 (note 16), p. 146.

21. Fox, 1981 (note 16), p. 152.

22. Bean, Michael J. 1978. Federal Wildlife Law. In *Wildlife in America.* H.P. Brokaw, Ed. Council on Environmental Quality, Washington, D.C., pp. 281–283. See also generally Bean, Michael J. 1983. *The Evolution of National Wildlife Law.* Praeger Publishers, New York.

23. Chandler, W.J. 1985. The U.S. Fish and Wildlife Service. *The Audubon Wildlife Report 1985, Part I.* National Audubon Society, New York.

24. Nash, 1973 (note 12), pp. 185–199; see also Stewart, Frank. 1995. *A Natural History of Nature Writing.* Island Press, Washington, D.C., pp. 142–149.

25. Nash, 1973 (note 12), pp. 220–226.

26. Fox, 1981 (note 16), p. 289.

27. 33 U.S. Code § 407, as quoted in Rodgers, 1994 (note 6), p. 254.

28. Council on Environmental Quality. 1979. Environmental Quality—1979: The Tenth Annual Report of the Council on Environmental Quality. Washington, D.C., pp. 2–5, 322.

29. Carson, R. 1962. *Silent Spring.* Houghton Mifflin, Boston.

30. Davidson, H., June 29, 1962, San Francisco, California, in *The New Yorker,* February 20 and 27, 1995, p. 18.
31. Dreyfus, D. and J. Ingram. 1976. The National Environmental Policy Act: A View of Intent and Practice. *Natural Resources Journal* 15:243, as quoted in Anderson, Frederick R., Daniel R. Mandelker, and A. Dan Tarlock. 1984. *Environmental Protection: Law and Policy,* Little, Brown. Boston, p. 684.
32. See, for example, Hildebrand, Stephen G. and Johnnie B. Cannon, Eds. 1993. *Environmental Analysis: The NEPA Experience.* Lewis Publishers, Boca Raton, Florida.

NEPA: THE RATIONAL APPROACH TO CHANGE

2

R. Clark

The process of environmental impact assessment (EIA) has been in existence for 25 years. For many national and regional governments and most international development organizations, EIA is now a required component of planning and decision making, and influences the design and execution of major projects and programs around the world. It is often one of the first reforms of emerging democracies. EIA provides, quite simply, a rational approach to change.

Why have so many countries developed EIA procedures? One reason is that the EIA process provides a way to make common and deeply held concerns operational for protecting the quality of the human environment. These concerns have many roots that can be found in the writings of Western philosophers, in the teachings of Eastern religions, in the cultural practices of diverse traditional societies, and increasingly in the laws and policies of national and local governments.

The late 20th century finds mankind with enormous technological capabilities for altering its surroundings and harnessing the power of the natural environment and communities. This ability has interfered with what some citizens have mapped as their vision of their own future. It is now possible to better express personal goals; thus, we are less sanguine about unintended consequences and are frustrated, even cantankerous, because we do not know who to blame for our goals and visions being shattered. As we come upon the metaphorical fork in the road, we often find several unlighted paths which nations can take. How much do we value wetlands? What are we willing to trade off to achieve more economic growth? How do we know what the trade-off options are? While all possible paths are scattered with uncertainties, there are ways and means for EIA practitioners to scout the future and to assist their leaders to take them down the path communities desire to travel. We are all in the scouting business—a profession with only 25 years of experience which began with the passage of the National Environmental Policy Act (NEPA) in the United States.

©CRC Press LLC CCC 1-57444-072-1 5/97/$100/$.50
St. Lucie Press is an imprint of CRC Press

This chapter focuses on experience in the U.S. with NEPA, frequently referred to as the Magna Carta of U.S. environmental law. This prescient law was designed to help light all possible paths so we may be enlightened decision makers. NEPA has not prevented us from making bad decisions, but it has done its job of providing plenty of advance notice of the consequences of that decision. This chapter outlines NEPA's origins, its track record, and some of the strengths and weaknesses that have been attributed to it and to the EIA process it has engendered since its enactment in 1970. Information is included on how this process might be made more efficient and more effective in the future, based on the considerable experience to date.

THE RISE OF PUBLIC CONCERN FOR ENVIRONMENTAL QUALITY

In the United States, the origins of public concern for environmental quality can be traced at least as far back as the 19th century, in the writings and activities of conservation philosophers such as Henry David Thoreau, George Perkins Marsh, and John Muir, and into the 20th century with such spokespersons as Theodore Roosevelt, Gifford Pinchot, Aldo Leopold, and Rachel Carson. Their thoughtful, sometimes passionate, expressions of concern for the preservation of natural habitats and wild creatures were in large part responsible for the passage of numerous laws by Congress to protect these resources. Examples include creation of the world's first national park (Yellowstone, in 1872), the Forest Preservation Act of 1891, the National Park Service in 1916, the Wilderness Act in 1964, the Wild and Scenic Rivers Act in 1968, and the Endangered Species Act of 1973.

Throughout the last 25 years, environmental threats have been addressed by enacting new federal laws to regulate air and water pollution, the use of pesticides, and the handling of toxic chemicals and hazardous wastes. However, these individual laws, with their requirements for detailed industry-specific standards and regulations, still do not provide a government-wide strategy or process for an integrated multidisciplinary consideration of environmental values during the development of projects, programs, and policies by government agencies or during the review by those agencies of permit applications submitted by private parties.

Rational people armed with good information will not let their home become so spoiled that its rivers catch fire, its wild animals have to jump chain-link fences to find food, and its wetlands are valued only for good landfill sites. The following are possible reasons. Rationality allows decision makers to value qualitative well-being as well as quantitative. It forces our extant economic theories to internalize social and environmental costs in benefit–cost analyses and to take environmental factors into account as an essential part of planning and decision making. An integrated approach to environmental planning would force government institutions to deal with problems that cut across political boundaries and recognize the fundamental interdependence of human populations and their environment.

Fundamentally, efforts are being made in many ways to account for the environmental costs of development, and EIA is one of the important analytical tools in these efforts.

CONGRESS ENACTS A NATIONAL POLICY FOR THE ENVIRONMENT

Responding to growing public pressure for action to correct minimal environmental emphasis, Congress in 1968 and 1969 held joint and separate House and Senate hearings to consider a national policy for the environment. Finally, a recognition that the government's actions make large and sometimes indelible footprints on the environment prevailed. Further, there was a growing recognition that the narrow, mission-oriented approach of federal agencies to programs and projects and the lack of consideration given by federal agencies to environmentally preferable alternatives were contributing to these problems. Additionally, it was realized that environmental concerns should be treated equally and contemporaneously with economic and technical considerations.

In 1969, Congressman John Dingell of Michigan sponsored a bill to establish a Council on Environmental Quality (CEQ) within the Executive Office of the President; the council was to be similar in structure and function to the Council of Economic Advisors already at the White House. Senator Henry Jackson of Washington provided a strong statement of national policy insisting that the federal government take no action that would significantly affect the quality of the human environment until the proponent agency understood the consequences of that action.

The legislation that became NEPA in January 1970 established the framework for environmental impact assessment as it is known today. NEPA declares that "it is the continuing responsibility of the Federal Government…to improve and coordinate federal plans, functions, programs, and resources" so as to "fulfill the responsibilities of each generation as trustee of the environment for succeeding generations"; to "attain the widest range of beneficial uses of the environment without degradation, risk to health or safety, or other undesirable and unintended consequences"; and to "preserve important historic, cultural, and natural aspects of our national heritage, and maintain, wherever possible, an environment which supports diversity, and variety of individual choice…." The language had antecedents and was rooted in the conservation writings of the early 20th century, the economic efficiency and public health lexicon in the 1950s, and the environmentalism of the 1960s.

NEPA also provides the tools for changing the ethic called for in the rhetoric. With a realization that late 20th century life had become complex, NEPA directed all federal agencies to use a systematic, interdisciplinary approach that will ensure the integrated use of the natural and social sciences and the environmental design arts in planning and decision making. NEPA provided the goals and the tools, and it promised the American people that in all future proposals for "major Federal actions significantly affecting the quality of the human environment, a detailed statement…" on the environmental impact of the proposed action must be prepared. NEPA also provided the public with an opportunity to influence the shape and breadth of a proposal. Agencies must also include in this statement a discussion of any adverse environmental effects of the proposed action, of alternatives to the proposed action, of the relationship between local short-term uses of the environment and long-term productivity, and of any irreversible and irretrievable commitments of resources that the project would involve. NEPA was, in most cases, the impetus for federal agencies to hire environmental professionals; that fact alone allows NEPA to claim that it began a cultural change in federal agencies. In short, NEPA changed the relationship of government to its people.

THE EVOLUTION OF NEPA

In 1970, the agencies, the public, and the federal courts had nothing but the very eloquent but general language of NEPA itself and its ambiguous legislative history upon which to act. As NEPA scholars have pointed out, the law was intended to produce changes in the diverse internal planning and decision-making processes of the federal agencies. Its drafters assumed that this could be done without amending the original missions of these agencies. They also assumed that the agencies would turn to the environmental and social sciences for the tools needed to produce the required environmental analyses; therefore, NEPA contained no quantitative standards or rigid methodologies for compliance.

But NEPA also contained no exemption for proposals that were in the planning stages before passage of the act. This fact was soon discovered by many environmental advocates who had long sought ways to stop or to modify federal projects that they felt were environmentally destructive. These groups promptly went to the courts to seek immediate application of NEPA to scores, even hundreds, of federal projects in various stages of planning, construction, and implementation. To the surprise of many, the courts enjoined federal agencies from proceeding with many of these actions pending completion of the required "detailed statement."

This requirement for a detailed statement, more commonly known as an environmental impact statement (EIS), was first fully examined shortly after NEPA's enactment, when the Atomic Energy Commission failed to comply with NEPA for the promulgation of its licensing regulations. A federal court held that NEPA's requirements apply to all federal agencies, that NEPA requires agencies to consider to the fullest extent possible alternatives to its proposed action that would reduce environmental damage, and that while delay may be inherent in complying with NEPA, it was far more consistent with the act to delay operation at a stage when real environmental protection could occur rather than at a stage when corrective action could be extremely costly.

This early case set the tone for subsequent NEPA cases. By the mid-1970s, it became clear that courts would be adding shape to the intent of the legislation; in fact, by June 1975, 654 NEPA cases had been filed in U.S. courts, resulting in 119 injunctions.

Thus, agency officials suddenly found themselves needing to find the funds and technical resources necessary to produce EISs pursuant to court orders, in order to complete projects that had been planned and designed months or years earlier, when no explicit consideration had been given to "adverse environmental effects," environmentally preferable alternatives, or "presently unquantified environmental amenities and values." As a consequence, compliance with NEPA became as much a matter for lawyers as for scientists and planners. The Supreme Court made it clear that lower courts were to enforce only the procedural requirements of NEPA and not second guess agency decision makers. Priority was then placed on producing documents that would fulfill NEPA's procedural requirements as interpreted by federal judges, rather than on whether the decisions were actually consistent with NEPA's policies (NEPA's substantive mandate). When the courts rejected some agencies' early attempts to comply with the detailed statement requirement in a few pages, senior agency officials, often under pressure from members of Congress who wanted to see their public works projects completed without delays, tried another approach. They expanded the EIS to include all available studies and other information of even marginal relevance to the proposed action, result-ing in voluminous documents that often relied on weight rather than analytical content to prevail. Although these attempts received mixed reviews in the courts, the pattern of viewing NEPA compliance as a defensive exercise rather than an aid to decision making was established in many agencies. This situation has been and still is one of the most difficult barriers to making the EIA process more effective in achieving the fundamental purposes of NEPA. A secondary problem for some agencies has been their continued reliance on outside contractors for preparing their EISs, which may have inhibited devel-opment of their own in-house NEPA expertise.

Within two years of the passage of NEPA, federal agencies had produced 3,635 EISs and had been sued in 149 separate litigations. In 1979, CEQ reported that by December 31, 1978, nine years after NEPA's enactment, more than 11,000 EISs had been filed by 70 different federal agencies. During that same period, 1,052 suits were filed by a variety of plaintiffs. The courts issued injunctions related to NEPA matters in 217, or about 20%, of those cases, or for about 2% of all projects involving the preparation of an EIS.

By the mid-1970s, federal agencies had cleared most of their backlog of EISs for projects and programs begun prior to NEPA, and many agencies had also developed their own NEPA guidance, training programs, and environmental planning and assessment offices. A 1976 CEQ study of EISs analyzed the cost of agency compliance with NEPA, particularly regarding the preparation of EISs. Although no standard or exact method was available to isolate the costs of NEPA compliance from other related planning and evaluation costs, data submitted by more than 20 agencies indicated that the federal costs of EIS preparation, review, and commenting averaged between 1 and 2% of the agencies' annual project costs. The agency with the highest EIS cost estimate was the Department of Transportation; its fiscal year 1974 estimate of nearly $32 million was slightly less than 2% of its total project budget for that year.

Many external reviews and commentaries on the theory and practice of NEPA were also published during the 1970s. At a 1975 workshop, one scholar concluded that NEPA had proven far more significant as an administrative reform statute than as a substantive policy mandate, and that in the former capacity, though not the latter, it had proven extraordinarily effective. Richard Carpenter with the Congressional Research Service examined the scientific basis of NEPA and argued that the state of knowledge in envi-ronmental sciences fundamental to NEPA was unsatisfactory compared to the magnitude of the management decisions being made and the values at stake. Carpenter observed that the agencies could make better use of existing data, could devote more of their budgeted ecological research funds to ecosystem analysis, and should begin regular follow-up assessments of environmental impact after projects have been implemented to provide a measure of the accuracy of predictions and an improved basis for future EISs in similar situations.

In 1977, President Carter directed CEQ to convert its 1973 EIS guidelines into formal regulations for implementing all the procedural requirements of NEPA. Subsequently, CEQ published regulations in November 1978. The stated purpose of the regulations was to reduce excessive paperwork associated with NEPA, to better integrate NEPA with other planning and environmental review procedures, to encourage more effective public involvement, and to reduce unnecessary delays in completing the NEPA process. Among other provisions, these regulations:

1. Required federal agencies to issue or revise their own procedures, consistent with the CEQ regulations, to achieve these purposes
2. Established a "scoping process" for making an early and open determination of the scope and significant issues to be addressed in EISs
3. Established a default standard format and page limits for EISs to improve their utility and readability
4. Provided clearer instructions for inviting and responding to comments on EISs
5. Set forth formal criteria and procedures for referring to CEQ federal interagency disagreements on proposed actions
6. Articulated other specific agency responsibilities for compliance with NEPA and defined limitations on agency actions during the NEPA process

The regulations also required each agency, for actions requiring an EIS, to publish a record of its decision, stating what the decision was, identifying all alternatives considered, stating what means have been adopted to minimize environmental harm, and summarizing any monitoring and enforcement program adopted for mitigation measures. The regulations also included an extensive set of definitions of the EIA terminology used, much of which has been adopted by the EIA community throughout the world.

CEQ's NEPA regulations were designed to address many of the problems with the NEPA process that had been identified by prior studies and critics and by the governmental agencies themselves. The regulations were widely praised by groups as diverse as the business and commerce sector, the governors of various states, and several national environmental organizations. Perhaps the best indication of the success of the regulations is that they have remained in effect, with only one change, for nearly 25 years. During that period, the number of NEPA lawsuits filed has declined substantially, and many excessive costs and delays have been brought under control. Nevertheless, constraints on the effectiveness of the NEPA process remain, and new issues have arisen in recent years which deserve attention.

The principal ongoing technical issues associated with the EIA process mandated by NEPA include:

1. ***Undertaking the analyses required by NEPA early enough in the planning process to be useful to agency decision makers and before planners get so wedded to an alternative that it is difficult to change***—An associated issue is the level at which proposals are analyzed. The analysis may be for a project where key and critical decisions have already been made. Therefore, it may be desirable to move the environmental analysis upstream, preferably to the level of strategic environmental impact analysis.
2. ***Determining the proper scope of analysis (including the analysis of "reasonable" alternatives)***—In the United States, as perhaps in many countries, the trend is toward an ecosystem approach to managing resources. Certainly that is also the scale at which proposals should be assessed. An issue related to determining the appropriate scope is the assessment of cumulative effects. Without appropriate scoping, there is little hope for assessing cumulative effects. Analysts treating scoping as an analytic task will draw the boundaries of a study more appropriately.

3. *Encouraging and accommodating informed, timely, effective public review of and comment on NEPA analyses*—The public should not be an afterthought; it should be a partner, involved early and often. For example, the EIS can serve as a negotiating document and a place to resolve disputes.
4. *Limiting the length, ensuring the objectivity, and taking out the jargon*—You do no damage to science by explaining cause and effect in plain language. Einstein once said that "everything must be as simple as possible; but no simpler."
5. *The adequacy of post-decision monitoring of predicted impacts and promised mitigation measures must be improved*—EIA can be a learning tool upon which we base our environmental management programs and policies. It is not an effective learning vehicle yet.

One issue not anticipated when the NEPA regulations were issued is the reduction in the number of EISs prepared for proposed agency actions and the dramatically increased reliance of agencies on less rigorous (and less public) environmental assessments (EAs) and findings of no significant impact (FONSIs), along with the liberal use of "categorical exclusions" as defined in the agencies' own NEPA procedures. In the United States, federal agencies currently produce about 400 to 500 draft, final, and supplemental EISs per year, but they produce about 50,000 EAs. This development is one of the most fruitful areas for research to determine if the purposes of NEPA are being served by this clearly unintended consequence.

Another general issue is the extent to which the EIA process mandated by NEPA can or should be used to integrate other federal laws, rules, or policies. For example, in February 1994, President Clinton issued an executive order on environmental justice, directing all federal agencies to evaluate the effects of their proposed actions on low-income and minority communities and to take steps to assure that such communities do not experience disproportionate health and environmental effects from federal actions. The White House called the attention of agencies to the NEPA process as a powerful tool available to decision makers to better understand these consequences. Some agencies' approach to EIA, however, excludes examination of social impacts in EAs, thus stripping the decision makers of the value of integrating social, economic, and environmental considerations into one analysis.

NEPA also has the potential to be a very effective dispute resolution tool. However, as indicated previously, many disputes in the United States are still resolved the old-fashioned way: via litigation! Still, the developing techniques of alternative dispute resolution can be used more frequently to deal with interagency disagreements and public controversies that arise during the NEPA process. Such techniques, employed by trained professionals, might further diminish the number of NEPA-related lawsuits and in other ways reduce the time and costs associated with NEPA analyses.

THE CURRENT SITUATION: NEPA'S STRENGTHS AND WEAKNESSES

To address both the ongoing and emerging issues associated with the NEPA process, CEQ has been taking steps to improve the efficiency and effectiveness of the process.

First, the United States has published a study of the effectiveness of the EIA process in achieving NEPA's stated goals. Comments and suggestions from the federal agencies and representatives of business, academia, the legal profession, state governments, and the environmental community were solicited and a NEPA re-invent project is underway.

One of the most difficult aspects of environmental impact analysis is the assessment of the cumulative effects of a proposal. A cumulative effects analysis initiative has been ongoing to identify the current state of the science, to recommend steps for improving such analyses in the NEPA process, and to make the best current thinking on this subject available to NEPA practitioners. A handbook was published in January 1997.

As consideration is given to 25 years of experience with NEPA, an appropriate question is whether or not it can make a difference in planning outcomes and whether that difference is significant. The EIA process established by NEPA's drafters over 25 years ago is vibrant and functioning on the whole rather well, though sometimes in ways that were not envisioned at that time. Further, with the perspective provided by those years, one can identify several overall strengths and weaknesses associated with agencies' management of the NEPA process. For example, the accomplishments include:

1. NEPA has produced a positive revolution in the consideration by government agencies of the environmental effects of their projects and programs.
2. NEPA has generated an international, interdisciplinary profession dedicated to EIA, which now includes professional organizations, peer-reviewed journals, academic programs and other training courses, and a broad range of statutes and other formal requirements for EIA at the international, national, state, and local levels of government.
3. NEPA's EIA process has caused the modification of thousands of proposed actions in ways that have reduced or avoided such impacts and in many cases saved money associated with the project.
4. NEPA has been and still is the principal avenue for public involvement in the planning and decision-making processes of federal agencies, and the public has thus played a major role in maintaining the viability and importance of NEPA.
5. As a strategic emphasis and analytical framework, NEPA's broad mandate allows it to incorporate and integrate other regulatory requirements and emerging objectives such as biodiversity, conservation, environmental justice, and risk analysis.

Management weaknesses that still need to be addressed are:

1. Effectively integrating into agency planning and decision making and moving it to a strategic decision-making level.
2. Improving the science of EIA and developing the environmental baseline data required to support analyses.
3. The NEPA process has been more effective in preventing environmentally destructive actions than in developing environmentally beneficial actions, in large part because senior government officials often do not make effective use of NEPA in evaluating alternatives or reaching decisions.
4. The NEPA process has not been effectively pursued into the project implementation phase; thus, the reality and accuracy of environmental effects projected in EISs and EAs have rarely been put to the ultimate test—nor has the imple-

mentation or effectiveness of promised mitigation measures been objectively evaluated.

5. The public, and indeed those within the government who are responsible for the EIA process, often appear to treat the NEPA process as a rigid paperwork exercise designed to meet legal requirements rather than as a way to maintain or achieve environmental objectives.

6. Finally, and perhaps most importantly, the power of NEPA as a strategic decision-making tool has not been realized. EIA is accomplished long after strategic decisions have been made and alternatives have been foreclosed.

SUMMARY

The field of EIA represents a very young professional discipline. Current practitioners represent the first generation of professionals working in the EIA field. Pioneers are often left wondering whether or not the right path was taken. During the next 25 years, it is envisioned that NEPA and the EIA process will continue to evolve in the direction of preparing EIAs for strategic-level decision making, fostering ecosystem-level analysis, incorporating biodiversity conservation and pollution prevention into the routine planning and decision-making processes of government agencies, and serving as a valued analytical tool around the world, illuminating the choice between alternative paths. EIA is not a perfect science; however, a perfect science is not necessary to help leaders in the decision-making process. The EIA process can help define what sustainability is; it can also help in delineating environmental threshold concepts like carrying capacity. Practitioners of EIA must continue to hone their abilities, but policymakers must understand the value of EIA as a tool to make change rational.

IMPLEMENTING NEPA: A NON-TECHNICAL POLITICAL TASK

3

L.K. Caldwell

F ew statutes of the United States are intrinsically more important and less understood than the National Environmental Policy Act of 1969 (NEPA).[1] This legislation, the first of its kind to be adopted by any national government and now widely
emulated throughout the world, has achieved notable results yet has not fully achieved
its basic intent. Its purpose and declared principles have not yet been thoroughly internalized in the assumptions and practices of American government. Nevertheless, there
appears to be a growing consensus among the American people that environmental
quality is a public good, and development of the economy does not require a trade-off
between environmental quality and economic well-being. Voluntary compliance with
NEPA principles may one day become standard operating procedure for government and
business. Meanwhile, it is in the national interest to understand the historical developments that led to NEPA and the subsequent course of its implementation.[2] Numerous and
often contradictory evaluations of its intent and effectiveness have followed its enactment.

The legislative history of NEPA and the concepts it has sought to internalize in the
priorities and performance of the federal agencies are far more numerous and accessible
than some of its critics concede. A substantial part of the criticism follows from an
unduly narrow judicial interpretation of the act. Treating NEPA as if it were a special
application of the Administrative Procedures Act of 1946 misreads its principal purpose
and misdirects criticism. A decade of thought, advocacy, and negotiation in and out of
Congress preceded the legislation of 1969. Dissatisfaction with NEPA and its implementing institution, the Council on Environmental Quality (CEQ), should not be directed
against this innovative and well-considered statutory declaration of policy, but toward
those authorities who have failed in their responsibilities to support its declared intent.

Through the judicially enforceable process of impact analysis, NEPA has significantly modified the environmental behavior of government agencies and, indirectly, of private enterprises. Relative to other statutory policies, NEPA must be accounted an important success. But implementation of the substantive principles of national policy declared in NEPA requires a degree of political will that has not yet been evident in either Congress or the White House—nor audibly demanded by a public at-large that has received little help in understanding the purpose of the act or the requirements for its implementation.

A quarter century, however, is a very short time for a new area of public policy to attain the importance and priority accorded such century-old political concerns as taxation, defense, education, civil liberties, and the economy. The goals declared in NEPA are as valid today as they were in 1969—indeed perhaps more so as the consequences and costs of environmental mismanagement become more evident. Shortfalls in achieving the NEPA intent are not likely to be overcome (except in minor ways) by technical remedies or changes in the statute or by administrative reorganization. For example, substitution of a single administrator for the deliberative functions of a council would repudiate ten years of consideration in the Congress and would misconstrue the intent of NEPA and the role of the CEQ. However, the council and NEPA could benefit from an administrative officer, especially in communication with other divisions of the Executive Office of the President (EOP) and the environmental officers of the agencies.

If, however, interpretation of NEPA continues to be administered by the courts, statutory amendment to give its substantive provisions juridical status might further realization of the act's intent. As to the statute, some defenders of NEPA fear that opening it to amendment might result in its being weakened in, for example, its applicability to federal action having an environmental impact beyond U.S. territorial limits. A constitutional amendment could strengthen the applicability of substantive provisions in the courts, but at the present time this possibility lacks political feasibility.

For the intent of NEPA to be more fully achieved without these reinforcing measures, two developments will be necessary:

1. A greatly increased comprehension and appreciation of the purpose and principles of NEPA by the organized non-governmental sectors of society, especially by conservation and environmental groups, by religious denominations, and by political parties at the grass roots. There is also needed recognition, now beginning to appear in the world of business, that economic and environmental objectives need not be incompatible. Application of NEPA principles would help sustain the future health of the economy and the environment.

2. Appreciation by the Congress, the executive branch, and the news media of the political relationships and institutional arrangements necessary to fulfill the NEPA mandate. Beyond institutional structure, a commitment is needed, notably in the White House and EOP, to honor the national policy through action.

NEPA contains within its provisions means intended to achieve its purpose. Institutional arrangements were established after extensive consultation over at least a decade within and between both houses of Congress, with federal agencies, and with non-governmental representatives of public interests. The advisory and overview functions of a council have characterized every major proposal to establish an implementable policy for resource conservation or the environment since 1959. What has been lacking and what is needed has been the political will to enable NEPA to achieve its declared intent.

The preamble to NEPA declares it to be "an Act to establish a national policy for the environment, to provide for the establishment of a Council on Environmental Quality, and for other purposes." Although the implications of NEPA are far-reaching and complex, the language of the act is simple, straightforward, and brief. The following analysis of purpose, substance, and implementation falls logically into six parts:

- Part I: Historical Background
- Part II: Declaration of National Policy
- Part III: Intentions of the Framers
- Part IV: Purpose and Functions of the CEQ
- Part V: Implementing Action-Forcing Provisions
- Part VI: Administration of NEPA within the Executive Office of the President

Implementation in the context of this chapter deals almost wholly with policy and action at the presidential and congressional levels. With few exceptions, it does not report or analyze the numerous interpretations of NEPA in the federal courts. It is the author's "Jeffersonian" contention that an appropriate balance among the legislative, executive, and judicial branches in the interpretation of constitutional intent has not yet been found.

PART I: HISTORICAL BACKGROUND

To better understand the purpose, politics, and potential of the National Environmental Policy Act of 1969 (PL 91-190), a brief retrospective of its origins and legislative history is necessary. Terence T. Finn, the author of the most detailed account of the enactment of NEPA, writes that "for over ten years the concepts incorporated in Public Law 91-190 were developed, expressed, explained, forgotten, revised, advocated, opposed, and finally accepted" (Finn, 1972). Although the focus herein is primarily on the implementation of NEPA, the circumstances under which this legislation took shape decisively influenced both the timing of its enactment and its subsequent history. The historical record of all innovative ideas or changes in popular perceptions show a lag time between the emergence of new ways of thinking and their ultimate acceptance. The decade between the introduction of Senator James Murray's Resources and Conservation Act of 1959 and the congressional passage of NEPA was a relatively short interval for a major change in law and government. A basic factor in this pace of change was the emergence of the environmental movement as a popular political force.

A conceptual foundation for the environmental movement had been building for several decades. Parallel to and to some extent within the conservation movement, an ecological concern was growing. Unlike the conservation movement, the concerns of which were essentially those of economy and efficiency, the emphasis of the environmental movement was on ecological relationships between man and nature and the protection and preservation of the life-support system of the biosphere. The concept of the biosphere—although of earlier origin—had become barely current in the 1920s. Few

Americans were aware of the term or concept. "Environment," as understood today, had very limited meaning prior to the 1960s. To Americans in general, the natural world was seen as a storehouse of raw materials, intended for human economic purposes.

The conservation movement sought to ensure the "wise use" of the potential wealth of nature. Although their assumptions and objectives differed, there was some overlap between the two movements. In the absence of the term "environment" to identify the new ecological perspective, President Lyndon Johnson spoke of "the new conservation," and his 1965 White House Conference on Natural Beauty was essentially concerned with environmental quality without using the name.[3]

From the 1930s through the 1960s, a science-based literature began to lay a foundation for political action leading to the legislation. In 1956, an 1,193-page report of an international symposium, *Man's Role in Changing the Face of the Earth,* was published,[4] and in 1964 the nearly forgotten book *Man and Nature* by George Perkins Marsh was reprinted by Harvard University Press (Marsh, 1864). In 1965, the Conservation Foundation convened a conference on Future Environments of North America, the proceedings of which were published in 1966 (Conservation Foundation, 1966). Books by Paul Sears (1935), William Vogt (1948), Fairfield Osborn (1948), Aldo Leopold (1949), and especially by Rachel Carson (1962) and Stewart Udall (1963) contributed cumulatively to a heightened public awareness of an endangered environment. Although aesthetic and ethical values tended to dominate the popular literature of environmental protest, science was more frequently invoked, as scientific instrumentation and methods permitted increasingly refined analyses of environmental effects, notably measurements of contaminants and carcinogens in air, water, soil, and food. All of the foregoing values were enhanced by the Apollo VIII astronauts, providing humanity on Christmas Eve of 1968 with the first view of planet Earth from outer space. The concept of Earth as a spaceship, although oversimplified, had a powerful psychological effect upon public attitudes.

Personal experience was also a factor that stimulated a public demand for the reduction of air and water pollution. During the 1950s and 1960s, Congress enacted and amended laws intended to reduce air and water pollution.[5] By the 1960s, environmental pollution had become a major public health concern. Reports to the Public Land Law Review Commission (1964) and the Outdoor Resources Recreation Commission (1958–62) stimulated popular concern for the declining quality of the American environment. Between 1964 and 1969, the American Medical Association sponsored six major conferences on environmental health. Here was an issue that had personal impacts translatable into political action. Sportsmen's groups such as the Isaac Walton League were angry over contamination and unsightliness of lakes and streams and declining populations of waterfowl. To a large number of people, including many congressmen, environment was a surrogate term for anti-pollution measures. It seems probable that many congressional votes for NEPA were cast on the assumption that the Act was essentially an anti-pollution statute. The news media generally shared in this misconception. Not until after NEPA came into effect in the 1970s did some members of Congress, the federal agencies, and the public discover its larger dimensions and implications.

The legislative history of NEPA begins in 1959 with the effort of Senator James E. Murray (Montana) to obtain consideration of his Resources and Conservation Act of 1960 (S2549). The Murray Bill contained several elements ultimately incorporated in NEPA—a declaration of policy, an advisory council in the EOP, an annual report, and a structure following that of the Council of Economic Advisors. A joint committee of Congress was included in this and several subsequent bills. It was considered in the drafting of NEPA, but was unable to overcome objections by the several committees of Congress claiming jurisdiction over all or parts of the statute. Hearings on the Murray Bill were held in January 1960, and although the bill had 30 co-sponsors, it was opposed by the Eisenhower administration, many federal agencies, and organized business. Republican Vice President Richard M. Nixon, then a candidate for the presidency, proposed the alternative of a council composed of cabinet secretaries—a forecast of his action as president in 1969.

Senator Murray did not seek reelection in 1960, but his bill was reintroduced in the 87th Congress by Senator Clair Engle (California). A similar bill (S1415) was introduced by Senator Gale McGee (Montana) but did not include provision for a joint committee. Hearings on these bills were held in April 1961; the Kennedy administration and the federal agencies opposed both measures. Neither bill was reported out of the Senate Interior Committee. Similar bills introduced by Senator McGee in 1963 and Senator George McGovern (South Dakota) in 1965 received hearings. The "environmental problem" was widely acknowledged during these years, but dissatisfaction with worsening conditions was not yet firmly linked to political solutions. Because the problem was defined as conservation of natural resources and pollution caused by mismanagement of the externalities of material production, the solution was seen as economic. The economic perspective was present in the 1962 summary report of the National Academy of Sciences–National Research Council to President Kennedy.[6] This document, however, introduced the concept of "environment" as a natural resource, observing that "perhaps the most critical and most often ignored resource is man's total environment."

Heretofore, ecology as a science had not been regarded seriously by most "mainstream" scientists. During the 1960s, however, the relevance, volume, and influence of ecological studies increased.[7] Environmental science became a major factor in legislative proposals beginning in 1965 with the introduction of Senator Gaylord Nelson's Ecological Research and Survey Bill (S2282). This bill did not come to a vote, but many of its principles were incorporated in Title II of NEPA. In 1966, both Senator Henry Jackson and Representative John Dingell, among others, introduced legislation to establish an environmental advisory council. A council of ecological advisors was recommended to the Department of Health, Education, and Welfare by a task force report on A Strategy for a Livable Environment (1967).[8] The task force, chaired by Ron Linton, urged that the president submit to Congress a proposal for an Environmental Protection Act.

By the years 1967 and 1968, the environment had become a major legislative issue as distinguished from natural resources and conservation. During the 90th and 91st Congresses, as many as 30 separate proposals for environmental advice and protection were introduced. Meanwhile, a number of reports on environmental policy were issued by congressional committees.

The House Subcommittee on Science, Research, and Development, chaired by Emilio Q. Daddario, transmitted a report on June 17, 1968 to the Committee on Science and Astronautics, chaired by George P. Miller, on Managing the Environment.[9] The report did not propose specific legislation but summarized previous hearings, comments of staff and advisors, and listed the principal relevant legislative proposals before the Congress. On July 11, 1968, a report to the Senate Interior Committee on A National Policy for the

Environment,[10] which this author prepared as consultant to the committee, made the case for a national policy as expressed primarily in Senator Jackson's bill S2805 (subsequently reintroduced as S1075).

On July 17, 1968, a joint House–Senate colloquium was held on a National Policy for the Environment.[11] Its purpose was to avoid conventional committee jurisdiction limitations and bring together members of the Congress with executive branch heads and leaders of industrial, commercial, academic, and scientific organizations. The colloquium helped to raise congressional awareness of the environmental policy issue and to legitimize it as a concern of the entire Congress as contrasted with the exclusive jurisdictional interests of specific committees. A Congressional White Paper[12] reported in October 1968 the proceedings of the colloquium and documented the broadening of legislative concern.

In 1969, Senator Jackson's S2805 was reintroduced in the 91st Congress as S1075. The only Senate hearing on this bill occurred on April 16.[13] In retrospect, the notable event on this occasion was the introduction of the concept of an environmental impact statement. The need for an action-forcing provision to obtain compliance from the federal agencies had been recognized by other commentators on environmental protection legislation. As consultant to the committee and a committee witness, this author said, in response to a question by Senator Jackson, that a declaration of environmental policy to be effective must be operational, written so that its principles could not be ignored. It was proposed that "a statement of policy by the Congress should at least consider measures to require Federal agencies, in submitting proposals, to contain within those proposals an evaluation of their effect upon the state of the environment."[14] This action-forcing provision (Section 102(2)(c)) could be reviewable by the courts, providing an alternative to exclusive enforcement of NEPA in the executive branch, the reliability of which was doubted. Detailed language for the impact statement requirement was drafted by Interior Committee staff member Daniel A. Dreyfus.

During 1969, complex strategies and maneuvers occurred in both the House and Senate between competing legislative proposals and jurisdictional rivalries. In the Senate, conflict between Jackson and Muskie and staffs of the Committee on Public Works and the Committee of Interior and Insular Affairs threatened delay and possible defeat of Jackson's bill S1075, which was moving into a lead position. Senator Jackson and his principal counsel on environmental policy, William Van Ness, proved to be the better legislative tacticians. On July 9, 1969, S1075 was reported by the Interior Committee and placed on the Senate calendar. With swiftness not anticipated by most members of the Senate, S1075 was called up the very next day, July 10, under the "consent calendar" during the "morning hour," a period set aside for routine matters before the beginning of the principal business of the day. The act was passed without debate and no amendments were offered. Meanwhile, similar legislation sponsored by Congressman John Dingell was pending in the House but encountering procedural delays.

A House–Senate Conference Committee meeting in December 1969 resolved differences between Jackson's and Dingell's bills.[15] On December 20, the conference report on S1075 passed the Senate, and on December 22, one day before the House adjourned *sine die,* the conference report passed the House. NEPA as enacted closely resembled the original S1075. Similar legislation introduced by Congressman Dingell might have been the bill enacted but for jurisdictional conflict in the House that delayed action on his proposals. In May and June 1969, Dingell had held hearings on bills to establish a Council on Environmental Quality.[16] In subsequent negotiations and the House–Senate Conference on S1075, a number of Dingell's ideas were incorporated in Public Law 91-190 (NEPA).

On January 1, 1970, President Nixon signed NEPA into law, an act that with remarkable coherence embodied the principles and institutional arrangements that had been proposed, debated, and redefined during the preceding decade. Of the leading proposals during these years, only the Joint Committee of the Congress failed to be included. A new element, however, was added in the requirement of an environmental impact statement for all federal legislative proposals or actions having a significant impact upon the environment. This provision became the most influential and widely emulated feature of the act. Its effectiveness in the United States, however, depended upon judicial review of agency compliance. As a mandatory procedure required of all federal agencies in actions having a major impact upon the environment, the courts could hold them to strict compliance with the law, whereas on the policy or substantive provisions of NEPA, the courts have generally deferred to agency discretion.

PART II: DECLARATION OF NATIONAL POLICY

The most important and least understood provision of NEPA is the congressional declaration of national policy under Title I, Section 101. The statute declares:

> that it is the continuing policy of the Federal government, in cooperation with State and local governments, and other concerned public and private organizations, to use all practicable means and measures, including financial and technical assistance, in a manner calculated to foster and promote the general welfare, to create and maintain conditions under which man and nature can exist in productive harmony, and fulfill the social, economic, and other requirements of present and future generations of Americans.

Seven specific aspects of policy are enumerated, and while necessarily stated in general terms, they are hardly vague in purpose (as alleged by some commentators). Section 101b states that:

> in order to carry out the policy set forth in this Act, it is the continuing responsibility of the Federal Government to use all practicable means, consistent with other essential considerations of national policy, to improve and coordinate Federal plans, functions, programs, and resources to the end that the nation may
>
> 1. fulfill the responsibilities of each generation as trustee of the environment for succeeding generations;
> 2. assure for all Americans safe, healthful, productive, and aesthetically and culturally pleasing surroundings;
> 3. attain the widest range of beneficial uses of the environment without degradation, risk to health or safety, or other undesirable and unintended consequences;
> 4. preserve important historic, cultural, and natural aspects of our national heritage, and maintain, wherever possible, an environment which supports diversity, and variety of individual choice;

5. achieve a balance between population and resource use which will permit high standards of living and a wide sharing of life's amenities; and
6. enhance the quality of renewable resources and approach the maximum attainable recycling of depletable resources.

In addition, the Congress recognized that "each person should enjoy a healthful environment and that each person has a responsibility to contribute to the preservation and enhancement of the environment."

The declaration clearly implies that economic and environmental quality are or should be compatible. A key to understanding NEPA may be found in the phrase "...to create and maintain conditions under which man and nature can exist in productive harmony, and fulfill the social, economic, and other requirements of present and future generations of Americans." This statement has often been interpreted to require a balancing of equities, primarily economic and environmental, but the intent of NEPA would not be achieved by offsetting (but still retaining) an economic "bad" with an environmental "good," as mitigation measures often attempt. More consistent with the spirit of the act would be a synthesis in which "productive harmony" is attained and transgenerational equity is protected.

Beneath the language of the declaration there are fundamental questions of jurisprudence and constitutional responsibility that have been largely unrecognized and unaddressed. Does the declaration establish a policy by law? If the statute, in fact, is a declaration of law as well as policy, what then are the responsibilities of the president under Article II of the Constitution that "he shall take care that the laws be faithfully executed"? And what are the responsibilities of the Congress to see that a policy declared by Congress, and not repealed, is not sabotaged or neglected in the executive branch?

Critics of NEPA have found its substantive provisions non-justiciable and by implication not positive law. Although the courts have generally refrained from "overturning" administrative decisions involving any of these substantive provisions, in the case of *Calvert Cliffs Coordinating Committee v. Atomic Energy Commission*, Judge Skelly Wright of the U.S. Circuit Court of Appeals of the District of Columbia declared that:

> The reviewing courts probably cannot reverse a substantive decision on its merits, under Section 101, unless it can be shown that the actual balance of costs and benefits that was struck was arbitrary or clearly gave insufficient weight to environmental values. But if the decision was reached procedurally without individualized consideration and balancing of environmental factors—conducted fully and in good faith—it is the responsibility of the courts to reverse.[17]

The generally recessive posture of the courts on the policy provisions of NEPA contrasts markedly with their aggressive actions in constitutional rights cases. Federal judges have not hesitated to assert sweeping jurisdiction over all levels of government in which actions by legislative and administrative authorities are at variance with judicial opinion. A plausible explanation for this contrast is the absence of any direct provision in the Constitution for environmental policy or protection, in contrast to explicit provisions for property rights and civil rights in the Fifth and Fourteenth Amendments. Where the Congress, for example, has mandated or prohibited specific actions affecting air and water pollution or endangered species, and provided penalties for violations, the courts do enforce. Presumably they would do so for any of NEPA's substantive policy mandates for which Congress provided specific procedures and penalties not subject to judicial reversal as contrary to the Constitution. An environmental protection amendment to the Constitution could clarify equities between private rights and public interests. It could reduce litigation in environmental affairs and reduce arbitrary and unpredictable policy making by the federal courts. Section 101 establishes the principles and goals of environmental policy. Implementation of these provisions can be and has been affected by other legislation reviewable by the courts. The National Historic Preservation Act and the Endangered Species Act are examples. Substantive mandates in these and other statutes are reinforced by the substantive and procedural provisions of NEPA.

Beyond the judiciary, there is another recourse to enforcement of the principles of NEPA in the constitutional obligation of the president "to take care that the laws be faithfully executed." The president rarely needs a court opinion to use residual executive power to apply the law. The president enjoys broad executive discretion over implementation of the laws by the federal agencies. A president whose priorities coincided with NEPA's declared principles could—absent blocking in the Congress—go a long way toward fulfilling the NEPA mandates. How presidential power has been applied to execute the policy provisions of NEPA (or more often not applied) will be considered in Part VI.

As previously observed, broad statements of policy and principle seldom arouse much public interest or positive response. Policies that do elicit popular concern almost always affect the personal advantages or apprehensions of people. Attitudes relating to the environment in modern American society have been largely issue specific and subjective, as in the NIMBY (not in my back yard) syndrome. Effective response to the larger societal and biospheric environment necessarily must be collective—with whole communities or a "critical mass" of the society activated. And while non-governmental organizations may help in many ways to assist environmental protection, the ultimate agent of public interests affecting the whole nation is the federal government. State boundaries are notoriously artificial and do not correspond to ecosystems, bioregions, or economic activities.

NEPA, plus the legislative powers of the federal government over interstate commerce, navigable waters, and public lands, creates an obligation to apply federal environmental requirements where relevant. Thus, federal permits, licenses, purchases, and grants may become instruments for applying federal environmental policies. The president, through executive orders, may instruct the agencies in the performance of their administrative functions, including observance of non-self-enforcing NEPA mandates (e.g., interdisciplinary use of science and consideration of non-quantified environmental values). In general, the citizen conservation and environmental organizations have not made effective use of the declaration and Section 101. It is probably not unfair to conclude that the officers of these organizations have not fully understood the act or appreciated its potential beyond the impact statement requirement.

Environmental organizations have played a major role in protecting environmental quality. Without reference to NEPA, their actions have often promoted NEPA objectives. However, as voluntary membership organizations, they depend upon membership support for their ability to act. Their appeals for membership and money are based on specific threats and issues that appear to be easily understood. The principled, generalized, and (to some) abstract provisions of the declaration do not rally constituents, who more readily respond to appeals to "stop that dam, ban timbering in the Tongass, save the Everglades, preserve the rain forests, and prevent global climate change."

This issue-specific focus on environmental policy is at least a partial explanation for the initial support by most of the nation's large volunteer environmental organizations for the Clinton–Gore intention to abolish the CEQ and transfer oversight of the environmental impact statement (the NEPA process) to a cabinet-level Department of Environmental Protection. Alternatively, a non-statutory office administered by White House staff was proposed, presumably eliminating most of the functions specified for the CEQ under Title II of the act.

Although speculative, the proposal to abolish the CEQ can be explained by a reliance by the president and vice president on an overly ambitious and underinformed White House staff. The effect, however unintended it may have been, would have repealed Title II of NEPA, and implementing the declared national policy would have relied upon a White House staff generally lacking the qualifications that NEPA specified for the CEQ. The CEQ was absolutely integral to the purpose and the intended implementation of NEPA. The legislative history of NEPA and its antecedents shows clearly that an advisory council with powers of initiative was regarded as essential to the shaping and monitoring of a national policy for natural resources and the environment. The reasons for a highly qualified council rather than a single non-statutory administrator were spelled out repeatedly. They appear to have been overlooked by the Clinton–Gore proposal to replace the CEQ with a non-statutory White House appointee. A liaison officer to strengthen relationships between the White House and the CEQ might facilitate implementation of NEPA provided that respective functions were clearly delineated. Indifference to the CEQ and disregard for Title II appear to be an unfortunate consequence of a widespread misconception that the purpose of NEPA was the writing of impact statements.

The "mainline" non-governmental environmental organizations generally supported Senator Jackson's bill at the time of its enactment; they showed interest in NEPA primarily as the environmental impact requirement (Section 102(2)(c)) enabled them to stop or delay specific government programs or projects to which they objected. But it is not apparent that the CEQ consistently reached out to these organizations or undertook to explain its purpose or functions to them. Accordingly, when the Senate Committee on Environment and Public Works held a hearing on April 1, 1993 on Abolishing the Council on Environmental Quality,[18] no environmental organization appeared in protest, and statements from them were introduced in support of the president's action. Had the CEQ met together periodically with the heads of the principal environmental organizations (and also with representatives of the news media), the purpose of NEPA and the role of the CEQ might have been better understood. It seems a fair inference that such a public outreach by the CEQ would not have been approved by the White House and in particular by White House staffers who were assigned the function of "shepherding" the CEQ.

Although the principles of NEPA appear to have wide popular support, appreciation of the action required for its implementation has not been firmly internalized in American political ethos. Opinion polls give a deceptive impression of the concern of most Americans for broad environmental policy. The polls have not been very informative about what most respondents have in mind when they appear to give a high priority to environmental protection. Their response may reflect concern about a very specific and localized issue (e.g., a toxic landfill, air pollution, an endangered species, forestry practice, etc.). The most convincing test for the nation's concern for the purposes and principles of NEPA would be a positive response to a proposed environmental amendment to the Constitution.[19] A widely held opinion among lawyers and politicians that no constitutional provision could be adopted today makes effective statutory implementation of NEPA all the more important. There is no inadequacy or impracticality in the language of NEPA, but no statute is stronger than the will to enforce it. NEPA has been as effective as political circumstances have permitted. It could be more effective if the intentions of its framers as declared in Title I were realized through a fuller performance of the statutory functions of the CEQ as detailed in Title II and through a reinforcement of its status in the EOP. As overseer of an important national policy, the enumerated functions of the CEQ as declared in NEPA make it more than merely advisory to the president.

PART III: INTENTIONS OF THE FRAMERS

It would hardly be possible to establish that there was a unanimity of intention among all of the persons involved in the drafting and enactment of a national policy for the environment. Even so, there was sufficient agreement on basic principles to certify a general intent among the framers regarding the purpose of NEPA and the means toward achieving its precepts. As previously reported, the basic purposes of NEPA had been considered in the Congress over the preceding ten years, and there was substantial agreement regarding the principles to be declared, if not in all of the details of implementation.

The argument for a national policy, and hence an indicator of intent, was set forth in the report on A National Policy for the Environment, which this author prepared in the summer of 1968 at the request of Senator Jackson for the Senate Committee on Interior and Insular Affairs. This document was reprinted in the report on the Joint House–Senate Colloquium to Discuss the Need for a National Policy for the Environment (July 17, 1968).[20] At that time, there were three options for establishing a national policy for the environment: (1) a joint resolution of the Congress, (2) a statute, and (3) a constitutional amendment. A statute appeared to be the most effective and attainable choice, and bills were already being drafted in the House and Senate.

A constitutional amendment (several had been proposed) was rejected as requiring a protracted process of uncertain result—a priority for which the nation was not yet ready. A joint resolution would not bind government agencies to compliance, although a suggested draft was appended to the Senate report on A National Policy for the Environment.[21] The strategy for a realizable national policy was perforce through control over the actions of the federal agencies. The Congress had no explicit constitutional authority to legislate environmental policy per se, but Congress and the president did have authority to define and direct the policies and actions of the federal agencies. Because agency missions impinged directly or indirectly upon almost every aspect of American society, a statutory law could be enacted that would be both effective and constitutional. Moreover, a statutory declaration of national policy could be binding upon both the legislative and executive branches.

NEPA was thus conceived as national policy, rather than merely a congressional or presidential policy. This intent was significant in establishing the Council on Environmental Quality in the EOP. The subject area of environmental policy was understood to be broad, complex, and subject to unforeseeable change in information and circumstances. Environmental policy required a continuity and deliberative capability that might best be obtained through guidance by a multidisciplinary council of high competence.

In various ways and degrees, many members of the Congress participated in the framing of NEPA. Critical roles were those of Senators Jackson, Nelson, and Muskie and Representatives Miller, Daddario, and Dingell. Legislation in the House was complicated by rivalries over committee jurisdiction. Faced with these complications and procrastination by House leadership, Dingell, through rigorous perseverance, obtained jurisdiction over a bill (H.R. 6750) that would establish an independent Council on Environmental Quality, "free from partisan politics, free from Cabinet imperatives, and free from sectional viewpoints." The subcommittee in the House, which Dingell chaired, subsequently undertook the principal oversight hearings on the administration of NEPA.

The framers of NEPA did not assume that placing the CEQ in the Executive Office would cause the president to embrace NEPA principles or to give the environment a prominent place on his agenda. President Nixon had opposed locating the CEQ in the Executive Office and had appointed a cabinet-level council to head off NEPA. Defeated in the effort, he accepted NEPA with good grace and appointed council members whose qualifications matched those specified in Title II of the statute. Neither the Congress nor the law can determine the president's interests or priorities, but Article II of the Constitution specifies among his duties that "he shall take care that the laws be faithfully executed." Thus, the future of NEPA depends upon the accepted interpretation of the roles of the EOP and the president (White House) as executors of the nation's laws.

Indeed, the language of the act and location of the council in the Executive Office were intended to ensure that the national policies declared by the Congress were not ignored or sabotaged by successive presidential incumbents or their White House staffs. An unsympathetic president may nevertheless diminish the effectiveness of NEPA and the CEQ by use of the presidential powers of appointment and budgetary initiative. The framers appeared to have assumed that a Congress that enacted the provisions of NEPA would be vigilant in their defense, but appointees to the council have often fallen short of the qualifications stated in Title II of the act. Diminishing budget allocations to the CEQ seem intended to marginalize its effectiveness. A long-practiced political strategy to rid an administration of an unwanted agency is to deny it adequate personnel and funding, to veto its initiatives, and then to call for its abolition because it has been ineffective. It is a transparent policy that often works.

The framers of NEPA thus intended a stable but evolving national policy, nonpartisan and drawing upon the best available science. To realize this intention, a statutory agency was necessary. The 91st Congress, by its own declaration, established principles of environmental policy and administration with which subsequent Congresses and future presidents would be expected to comply. However, it is beyond the competence of any Congress to ensure that subsequent Congresses or successive presidents will honor commitments that they have inherited but not themselves made.

Upon enactment, NEPA was widely misconstrued as an anti-pollution law. The *New York Times* headlined its report of the signing of NEPA by President Nixon as

"Nixon Promises an Urgent Fight to End Pollution."[22] Few news media reporters appear to have even read the law despite its extraordinary brevity. Popular opinion, seldom well informed, shifted with judicial review of the NEPA action-forcing provisions and the declaration by lawyers and judges that the act was essentially procedural. With judicial enforcement of Section 102(2)(c), widespread opinion developed and proliferated that the writing of impact statements was the primary purpose and intent of NEPA. Even the editors of the prestigious journal *Science* appeared to concur with this misinterpretation.[23]

Commentaries in many law journals and in many judicial opinions have described NEPA as essentially procedural (Bear, 1993). The concept of a policy act—as distinguished from regulatory legislation—appears to have been lost on these writers. The substantive provisions of Section 101 were dismissed, in effect, as harmless rhetoric and as judicially inoperable. Yet the language of Section 101 was explicit and mandatory. Although the courts have generally conceded the interpretation of the substantive provisions to the executive agencies, this judicial concession in no way removed these provisions from the status of law or the responsibilities of the president. The substantive provisions of NEPA are enforceable through executive orders and judicially reviewable statutes (as is presently the case with acts establishing mandatory obligation upon the agencies, e.g., protection of endangered species and wetlands). If the courts are the only executors of law, of what significance is the declaration in Article II of the Constitution that "he shall take care that the laws be faithfully executed"? If national policy were no more than presidential policy, the three departments of government—legislative, executive, and judicial—and the doctrine of the separation of powers, as commonly understood, would be inoperative.[24] The distinctions are, of course, basic to the Philadelphia Constitution of 1787 and to the way the United States has generally been governed since ratification in 1789.

PART IV: PURPOSE AND FUNCTIONS OF THE CEQ

The Council on Environmental Quality is integral to the National Environmental Policy Act of 1969. To ignore or to eliminate the role of the CEQ in relation to NEPA would be, in effect, to repeal the act as an instrument of national policy. As adopted in 1969, NEPA initiated an unprecedented and comprehensive innovation in public policy. No other nation had enacted such a statute. No experience provided guidance in its implementation. Popular concern for the environment had grown rapidly during the late 1960s and had been expressed most frequently in demand for a council of ecological or environmental advisors to guide the development and implementation of government policy for the environment.

Public expressions of dissatisfaction had been growing since publication of Rachel Carson's *Silent Spring* (1962) and Lyndon Johnson's White House Conference on Natural Beauty (1965). Degradation of the environment—urban and rural—was featured widely in the news media. Congress was being importuned to "do something" about the environment, and as many as 30 bills were introduced to this effect in the 90th and 91st Congresses (1967–71). Environmentally concerned organizations opposed locating so comprehensive a function in a single cabinet-level department—especially in the Department of Interior. The environmental agenda was conceived as broader than the jurisdiction of any one department, and Interior had an unsavory reputation for domination by environmentally insensitive natural resource interests.

The Council of Economic Advisors (CEA) was the model most often suggested, and (as previously noted) numerous bills were introduced in the 90th and 91st Congresses to establish such a body. Thus, the idea of a high-level council comparable to the CEA preceded consideration of a statutory declaration of national policy. It was intended that the council identify important environmental issues, monitor environmental performance, and advise the president and the Congress on appropriate action.

Although most prior proposals for establishing a policy for natural resources and environment adopted the concept of an advisory council, the CEA provided the immediate model for the CEQ. On certain critical points, the language of NEPA is identical to the language of Section 4 of the Employment Act of 1946.[25] The requirement "with the advice and consent of the Senate" implies a congressional concern for the actions of the councils. Neither was constituted as the exclusive agent of the president. Most pertinent in relation to the congressional intent as subsequently expressed in NEPA are the following provisions of the Employment Act of 1946.

COUNCIL OF ECONOMIC ADVISORS TO THE PRESIDENT

Sec. 4. (a) There is hereby created in the Executive Office of the President a Council of Economic Advisors (hereinafter called the "Council"). The Council shall be composed of three members who shall be appointed by the President, by and with the advice and consent of the Senate, and each of whom shall be a person who, as a result of his training, experience, and attainments, is exceptionally qualified to analyze and interpret economic developments, to appraise programs and activities of the Government in the light of the policy declared in section 2...

(c) It shall be the duty and function of the Council—
(1) to assist and advise the President in the preparation of the Economic Report;
(2) to gather timely and authoritative information concerning economic developments and economic trends, both current and prospective, to analyze and interpret such information in the light of the policy declared in section 2 for the purpose of determining whether such developments and trends are interfering, or are likely to interfere, with the achievement of such policy, and to compile and submit to the President studies relating to such developments and trends...

A significant difference between the two councils is the establishment of a congressional Joint Committee on the Economic Report (of the CEA) and the absence of such a council in NEPA. A Joint Committee on the Environment was urged by some of the drafters of NEPA but was opposed by the chairmen of existing committees with claims to jurisdiction over all or parts of NEPA and environmental policy. The two councils also differ in that members of the CEQ serve at the pleasure of the president, whereas no such qualification applies to members of the CEA. Since 1980, presidents have not treated the CEQ as a council, appointing only a chairman; from 1993 to 1995, there was no chairman. Inasmuch as the CEQ serves at the pleasure of the president and has no joint oversight committee in the Congress, there appears to be no institutional means to compel the president to appoint a full council.

The obvious inference to be drawn from a comparison of the CEA and the CEQ is that the former represents a high presidential priority and the latter has been relatively low on the scale of presidential attention. Great disparities in budget requests for Executive Office agencies show where presidential priorities lie. No president would think of abolishing the CEA, even where its members do not view the economy from precisely the same perspective as the president. But abolition of the CEQ was attempted in the Carter and Clinton administrations, and budgetary starvation severely limited its functions during the Reagan years.

The placement of the statutory CEQ in the EOP was motivated by two considerations:

1. NEPA applied to all federal agencies, cutting across departmental jurisdictions. It could not appropriately be administered by any one department which would be expected to apply its provisions to other, presumably co-equal, departments. Interagency conflict would be almost inevitable.
2. The president is the constitutional executor of federal law. The president has the powers needed to direct compliance with the law by agencies within the executive branch. But a controversy over constitutional interpretation has created ambiguity concerning how the president fulfills his obligation to take care that laws be faithfully executed. The significance of this ambiguity will be addressed in Part VI.

It is sufficient here to observe that locating the CEQ in the EOP was intended to facilitate the advisory role of the CEQ to the president, the agencies, and the Congress. The EOP was established as an outgrowth of the President's Committee on Administrative Management (Brownlow Committee), appointed in 1936 by Franklin D. Roosevelt to advise on ways to assist the performance of the president's institutional managerial functions.[26] Those agencies comprising the Executive Office were regarded by the President's Committee on Administrative Management as the central managerial and coordinative agencies of the federal government encompassing budget, personnel, planning, and administrative management. Although intended to facilitate performance of the executive functions of the president in the implementation of national policies, appointees to the central managerial agencies were not regarded as his personal political aides. The White House staff was "invented" by the committee for that function.

In recent years, this distinction between the White House staff and the EOP appears to have been lost. Although intended to assist the president in the discharge of his managerial duties through institutions established by the Congress, a broader governmental responsibility was implied in the statutory specification of qualifications for appointment as the principal officers of these central agencies. For appointment to the CEQ (subject to confirmation by the Senate), Title II of NEPA requires that:

> Each member shall be a person who, as a result of his training, experience, and attainments, is exceptionally well qualified to analyze and interpret environmental trends and information of all kinds; to appraise programs and activities of the Federal government in the light of the policies set forth under Title I of

this Act; be conscious of and responsive to scientific, economic, social, and cultural needs and interests of the Nation; and to formulate and recommend national policies to promote the improvement of the quality of the environment.

This language, as previously noted, closely follows that establishing the CEA. No comparable standards are required for appointment by the president to the White House staff.

Title II specified a council of high intellectual and professional qualifications capable of formulating and recommending "national policies to promote the improvement of the quality of the environment." The White House staff as conceived by the Brownlow Committee had no such authorization and was specifically enjoined from making policy decisions. In brief, the White House staff was to serve the president in such matters as he might choose. The CEQ was to serve the nation through action taken by the president and Congress. The White House staff could assist the president in the formulation of policy, but was not intended to play a role in the decision process.

Unlike the council members, the White House staff (the chief of staff excepted) were truly anonymous—as the Brownlow Committee recommended. The background and qualifications of council members were (or could be) known to the Congress and the public, at least through the process of senatorial confirmation. Their responsibilities could be fixed and their performance assessed, regardless of whether this was in fact done. But use of the metonym "the White House" (especially by the news media) as an ambiguous source of presidential policy provides no indication of whether a policy represents the personal agenda of the president or is a matter of secondary priority that the president tacitly (or inadvertently) turns over to White House staffers whose identity and capabilities are generally unknown. From the date of President Nixon's signature of NEPA, The *New York Times* led the media misconstruction of the role of the CEQ by referring to its location not in the EOP but in the White House.

PART V: IMPLEMENTING ACTION-FORCING PROVISIONS

This and the following section deal with administrative implementation of NEPA policy and intent, at the level of the EOP. They do not deal with judicial interpretations of NEPA except where very basic constructions of the act have been made, as in the *Calvert Cliffs* case. The implementing and action-forcing provisions of NEPA are primarily in Section 102 of Title I. Implementation is also provided in Sections 103 and 105[27] and in the functions specified for the CEQ under Sections 204 and 205.[28] The provision requiring the president's annual Environmental Quality Report (Section 201) underscores NEPA as national policy. Implementation is not discretionary presidential policy, although whether or how the president fulfills his constitutional responsibility under the act is largely, but not exclusively, a matter for his decision. Article I of the Constitution vests legislative power in the Congress, and this would imply congressional power to see that the legislative intent was not ignored or transgressed.

Because Section 102(2)(c) imposes a mandatory performance requirement on federal agencies, its implementation is reviewable by the courts. This action-forcing provision—the environmental impact statement (EIS)—was not present in earlier drafts of this legislation. The concept was introduced in a public hearing on April 16, 1969 before the Senate Committee on Interior and Insular Affairs. Senator Jackson, committee chairman and principal sponsor of the Senate bill, agreed with committee staff that without a justiciable provision the act might be no more than a pious resolve that the federal bureaucracy could ignore with impunity. There was also well-founded doubt that the president could be relied upon to enforce the act.

Recognizing the novelty of the EIS, and lack of experience with its implementation, some committee staff urged that provision be made and funds provided to help the agencies learn how to fulfill their responsibilities under Section 102. This proposal was not accepted by Senator Jackson, who held that the agencies should meet this obligation within their own funds by re-ordering their priorities. The CEQ undertook to remedy this lack of experience with impact analysis by issuing guidelines after consultation with the agencies, but effective implementation of Section 102 was never built into the agencies as integral to their missions and responsibilities. As a consequence, agency action relating to the EIS was too often misdirected, inadequate, and irrelevant to agency planning and decision making. Lacking effective interpretation, the purpose of NEPA was widely construed in the agencies to be preparation of impact statements. This was notably so after the judicial decision in the *Calvert Cliffs* (1971) case. The agencies were to be held to strict compliance with the mandatory procedures specified by NEPA. These mandates applied to all actions of major environmental significance subsequent to the date upon which NEPA became effective, January 1, 1970, and to projects and policies in effect as of that date, regardless of their previous authorization or state of completion.[29]

Some observers hailed NEPA as an environmental Magna Carta; others ridiculed the EIS as a "boondoggle" for underemployed ecologists and, without showing evidence of familiarity with the scope and intent of the act,[30] and in obvious ignorance of its legislative history and intent, declared it to be a disaster to the environmental protection movement.[31] After 25 years of experience, NEPA is still widely perceived as a procedural law requiring impact statements. Following further experience with the EIS, Executive Order 11991 (1977) was issued by President Carter, enabling the CEQ to adopt uniform regulations to enhance the informative value of the EIS, to coordinate its implementation across agency lines, and to remedy earlier inadequacies and misuse—many of which resulted from inexperienced fumbling attempts to meet the NEPA mandate.

Some agencies made an early show of compliance; others sought to evade EIS requirements or to satisfy the courts through minimal pro forma procedures. Unequivocal White House and Office of Management and Budget (OMB) support for NEPA might have moved the agencies to more serious efforts toward conformity with NEPA principles. However, as often happens when a presidential administration is presented with a policy for which it lacks enthusiasm, enforcement is largely left to the courts. Nevertheless, agency pro forma compliance with the EIS requirement was generally attained. Not all agency personnel were indifferent or opposed to NEPA principles. Some, notably younger employees, welcomed NEPA objectives. Even though agency compliance often fell short of the intentions of the framers, a significant reform in agency project planning and policy was recorded.[32] Some shortfalls in performance were less attributable to agency resistance than to inadequate science or faulty methodology in impact analysis. Relative to the enforcement of other federal statutes, the EIS provision of NEPA has been a success. It has been estimated to be the most emulated provision of any U.S. law, with adoptions in some form in more than 80 other countries (Yost, 1992).

As experience with impact analysis grew, it was inevitable that technique would gain emphasis, often with a view to avoid overruling by the courts. However, technical procedures tend to generate lives of their own at risk of displacing the larger purpose of policy. Nevertheless, learning how to apply new techniques of impact assessment is necessary for their reliability. There is now an International Association for Impact Assessment (IAIA), and improvements in the art and science of impact analysis have been made.

Preparation of an environmental impact statement or assessment, often called "the NEPA process," is vulnerable to several risks: (1) to the inadequacy of reliable scientific information; (2) to the changing character of the environment and the effects of unforeseen interposing forces; and (3) to biases among agency administrators, among impact assessors, and in arbitrary legal requirements (e.g., the Delaney amendment regarding carcinogens in food and drugs). Oversight functions, independent of agency administration, are needed if NEPA is to be effective. The CEQ was established to provide this independent oversight. A NEPA compliance office in a cabinet-level department could hardly succeed in overseeing performance in co-equal departments, and "political" considerations would likely influence oversight in a White House office. A greater handicap to achieving NEPA objectives than overemphasis on technique has been a too frequent failure—inadvertent or deliberate—to integrate NEPA policy into agency planning and decision making. The CEQ and several agencies have addressed the integration problem, but these efforts could be assisted significantly by the OMB and congressional committees exercising appropriate jurisdiction over decisions in which NEPA principles are involved.

Integration of NEPA principles and agency policies could be assisted by oversight hearings in the Congress, by General Accounting Office reviews, and by the inquiries of OMB examiners. Under Title II, the CEQ appears to have the statutory authority to undertake performance inquiries and make recommendations, but it is probably unable to do so without unequivocal support of the president.

The location of a NEPA compliance office within the structure of an agency has often been an indicator of agency receptivity to the purposes of the act and its willingness to implement its provisions. A National Science Foundation funded study of ways to improve the scientific method and content of the EIS[33] found that the principal problem of implementing NEPA objectives within the agencies was attributable not only to the perceived burden of impact analysis but also to agency indifference, impatience, or opposition to NEPA principles, which conflicted with an agency's sense of mission. NEPA does not require the agencies to conform their decisions to the findings of an EIS, although the act implicitly requires that they be given weight. Such action would be a function of the president, who might do so through an executive order, or the Congress, which could require it by law. To require conformity to an EIS would be unwise because of the limited predictability of many impact assessments and because other than environmental considerations may be important. If the president chose to intervene short of an executive order, he could not invariably obtain agency compliance in a specific decision. Some agencies regard the authorizing and appropriating committees of the Congress as their de facto authorities, and a president may have motives for accommodating these committees for reasons unrelated to NEPA compliance. Of course, some agency decisions not contrary to NEPA may be bound by other statutory laws.

PART VI: ADMINISTRATION OF NEPA WITHIN THE EXECUTIVE OFFICE OF THE PRESIDENT

Although NEPA declared a national policy for the environment and created the CEQ to facilitate its implementation, this statute alone could not enable the CEQ to carry out its mandates. Constitutional responsibility for action by government is placed in the three branches—legislative, executive, and judicial. The presidency was established to oversee administration of the executive branch and the execution of the laws, but the status of the incumbent of the presidential office—of the elected president—has received two dissimilar interpretations. These differences are matters of emphasis, for both are inherent in the office. The first sees the presidential role as importantly institutional—performing the chief managerial function within an interrelating system of public law, policy development, and governance.[34] The second emphasizes the role of the president as political leader—articulating goals and persuading action—largely independent of the legislative branch and with broad discretion in his selective attention to the multiplicity of federal laws.[35] When news of the Philadelphia Convention of 1787 reached Thomas Jefferson in Paris, he remarked with dismay that the president would be an elective monarch, a personal head of state comparable to the King of Poland. In fact, the primary intention of the convention appears to have been to establish an institutional presidency. The personal presidency emphasizes political leadership and decision making by the man; the institutional presidency subordinates the man to the office and to the functions and duties specified under Article II of the Constitution.

With few exceptions, the concept of an institutional presidency prevailed in American politics prior to the election of John Kennedy. Thereafter, a tacit assumption of a personal presidency gained ascendancy in the news media, in popular perception, and even in the Congress. Neither perception eliminates the other; the dominant perception at any one time has tended to reflect the preferred style of the incumbent president. Placing oversight of NEPA in the EOP rather than in the White House appeared tacitly to assume an institutional president. Accordingly, the president could be expected to reinforce the implementation of NEPA regardless of his personal attitudes toward environmental policy. However, the personal style of a president is reflected in his emphasis on either the political or the managerial aspects of the office. The agencies of the EOP are intended to assist the president in performance of his constitutional duties, but they cannot assume his political powers or responsibilities.

The decision taken by President Clinton to restructure the administration of environmental policy illustrates the significance of the dichotomy. The 1993 proposal to abolish the CEQ and to move the administration of NEPA to a cabinet-level Department of Environmental Protection, while creating an Office of Environmental Policy in the White House, was consistent with the Clinton–Gore "reinvention of government." The philosophic assumption underlying this action appears to be that the functions of administrative management, which the EOP was intended to assist, should devolve upon the cabinet-level agencies, thus freeing the president for a role of primarily policy formulation and persuasion. The coordinative functions that the management section of the OMB and the CEQ were intended to perform would be replaced by interdepartmental committees.

The reasons for placing central managerial agencies in the EOP were set out in the

Brownlow Report. Not the least of these was interdepartmental rivalry, competition, and non-cooperation. Conflicts between the Corps of Engineers and the Bureau of Reclamation, between the National Park Service and the Forest Service, and between separate armed services were reported in the press. Observers closer to the Washington scene also noted a parallel tendency among departments and interagency committees to accommodate competing interests by compromises, protecting each party's projects and programs but not necessarily the broader, longer range public interest.

It appears that neither Congress nor the courts can directly compel the president to enforce a particular interpretation of the law—as through a writ of mandamus. Indirectly the Congress might influence presidential action. Congress does possess powers (e.g., appropriation, confirmation, investigation) to persuade the president to take NEPA more seriously, but popular apathy on non-specific issues of principle and the well-organized pressures of groups whose economic interests conflict with environmental protection diminish the prospect of effective congressional oversight of NEPA. Nevertheless, such oversight hearings as have been held have resulted in an affirmation of NEPA and the CEQ.[36]

It would be erroneous to believe that altering or amending the text of NEPA would in itself result in its enhanced effectiveness, all other things being unchanged. When problems of policy implementation arise, there is a tendency characteristically, but not exclusively American, to seek technical solutions. The real difficulties, however, often lie elsewhere, usually in political circumstances, which technical remedies cannot fix. Implementation of NEPA cannot realistically be separated from the constitutional responsibilities of the institutional presidency. Conflict over the administration of NEPA leads to the suggestion that the status and significance of the EOP need reexamination—a non-technical political and constitutional issue.

Is the institutional role of the EOP in assisting the president to implement national policies as envisaged by the Brownlow Committee in accord with present assumptions in the Congress and among students of the presidency? Should opinion that regards the Executive Office as practically indistinguishable from the White House staff now be acknowledged as politically and constitutionally correct? Insofar as the members of Congress and the courts regard the personnel of the EOP, and consequently of the CEQ, as White House staff—as personal aides to the president rather than as national institutions—NEPA's full implementation is unlikely to be achieved. It must await a genuine conviction in the federal political leadership that the Congress was indeed serious in the declaration of a national environmental policy. Most members of Congress and probably most informed Americans would agree that presidential action ought to be consistent with declared national policy, but they appear to be far from clear about the intent and substance of NEPA.

The intrinsic importance of the goals and principles of NEPA is confirmed by events, by scientific information, by general public sentiment, and by widespread emulation around the world. In comparison with the administration of other statutes, NEPA should be considered a success, but that success and attainment of NEPA's yet to be fulfilled mandate depend upon the active oversight of a body like the CEQ. The appropriate task in relation to NEPA is to bring political action up to the level of the national policy which NEPA declares. In evaluating the performance of the CEQ (and coincidentally of NEPA) in 1976, a Senate oversight report concluded "that by statutory design, CEQ is part of the Office of the President. Therefore its strength and ability to control environmental policies are primarily determined by the sympathies and beliefs of the President and his staff."[37] Such problems as may be alleged regarding the effectiveness of NEPA are found not within the text of the statute but with its administration.

The president cannot possibly encompass his institutional responsibilities in the world of today. No one can be omnicompetent. The office of the president must encompass more than the personal presidency. The EOP was created to serve this institutional purpose. The leadership role of the personal presidency, among other things, activates the institutional role in bringing coherence, consistency, and an articulation of purpose to the office, which is larger than the personal presidency. The future of NEPA and the CEQ will demonstrate societal will and capability in realizing a fundamental national purpose.

CONCLUSIONS

The future of NEPA depends upon more than a popular commitment to environmental quality and protection. The status of the CEQ and the administrative implementation of NEPA involve an unresolved constitutional question. Is the executive power detailed under Article II of the Constitution conferred upon the office of the president or upon the occupant of that office? Without question there is a synergistic relationship between the person of the president and the executive power specified in the Constitution, but scholars and legalists have differed over the role of the president as executor of the power conferred upon the office. The language of Article II is ambiguous. Section 1 declares that "the executive power shall be vested in a president," but Article II also refers to the office of the president (e.g., term of office, eligibility for the office, and execution of the office). The office may be presumed to exist even without an incumbent. The relevant question upon which opinion is divided is this: Does the power of a president reside primarily in the person or the office?

Obviously, the presidential role is both personal and institutional. Inevitably, they combine in the execution of the office. Opinions differ concerning the degree or emphasis accorded the personal agenda of a president and his institutional responsibilities as chief executor of the nation's laws. In recent years, the role of the president as primary political leader and initiator of policy has gained advocates. Beginning with the Kennedy administration in 1960, the institutional presidency has been displaced by the personal presidency, with the apparent acquiescence of the news media, the Congress, and the public. The purpose of NEPA has been poorly understood by successive presidents and has not occupied a significant place on their political agendas. The managerial functions of the presidential office have often been either politicized or neglected.

The managerial responsibilities of the president have grown enormously since the early decades of this century. In 1937, the President's Committee on Administrative Management was charged with finding ways to allow the president to perform both roles—political and administrative. The committee recommended two institutional innovations—a White House staff to assist the political functions of the presidency and a group of central managerial agencies to assist the administrative functions of the presidential office. The responsibilities of the White House staff and the EOP were intended to serve distinctly different functions; the White House staff served the personal president, whereas the Executive Office assisted the president to "take care that the laws be faithfully executed" beyond but encompassing the jurisdictions of the cabinet-level executive agencies.

Successive proposals for declaring and implementing a national policy for the environment have almost uniformly included a council for policy advice and oversight. The great breadth and complexity of environmental issues and the objective of "balancing" or integrating economic and environmental values exceed the probable competence of any single administrator. The 1993 presidential proposal to abolish the CEQ and place the implementation of NEPA in a single partisan appointee evidenced incomprehension of NEPA and its declared purpose.[38] The CEQ is not and was never intended to be an enforcement agency. The long-standing objection to administration by boards is not applicable to the functions of the CEQ, which are spelled out in Title II of NEPA. In principle, its advisory functions resemble those of the CEA, but the CEQ has responsibilities under Title II to foster and assist development of the information needed for sound environmental policy. The CEQ has only partially performed its intended functions, but responsibility for its failure to fulfill the expectations of the framers of NEPA lies primarily on successive presidents and secondarily on the Congresses that were either indifferent to the NEPA intent or on senators that acquiesced in the appointment of inappropriate nominees to the council.

NEPA is potentially a powerful statute—well integrated, internally consistent, and flexible. Its history reflects poorly not on the act itself but upon the quality and responsibility of public administration in the federal government. NEPA was not a sudden inspiration, nor was it put over on an unsuspecting Congress and public by an environmental lobby. Its purpose was never the writing of impact statements, but this action-forcing procedure has been a great inducement to ecological rationality in federal actions which traditionally had largely ignored environmental consequences. No technical fix or administrative reorganization will achieve the NEPA intent. To implement NEPA as intended requires a president committed to its objectives and using his appointive, budgetary, and leadership powers to that end.

The argument that the president cannot be realistically expected to support policies and agencies forced on him by the Congress misstates the issue. Laws are enacted by the Congress, not by the president alone. As with "the Crown" in Great Britain, the presidency is more than the personal president. The constitutional duties of the president, prescribed in Article II, preclude lawful neglect of a statutory agency because its functions do not serve the president's personal agenda, but the Congress, and especially the Senate, needs to more effectively use its confirmation and oversight responsibilities to take care that national policies are not neglected. It is the duty not only of the courts, but equally of the president and the Congress "...to see that important legislative purposes, heralded in the halls of Congress, are not lost or misdirected in the vast hallways of the federal bureaucracy."[39]

NOTES

1. The National Environmental Policy Act of 1969, Pub.L. 91-190, 42 U.S.C. 4321–4347, January 1, 1970, as amended by Pub.L. 94-52, July 3, 1975 and Pub.L. 94-83, August 9, 1975. 42 U.S.C.

Sec. 4371 (1976). Executive Office of the President, *Regulations for Implementing the Procedural Provisions of the National Environmental Policy Act,* 43 Fed. Reg. 55978–56007 (November 29, 1978).

2. For background on NEPA and rulings in the federal courts, the following publications are representative of a much larger bibliography. Lazear, Robert. 1978. *The National Environmental Policy Act and Its Implementation: A Selected, Annotated Bibliography.* Wisconsin Seminars on Resource and Environmental Systems, Institute for Environmental Studies, University of Wisconsin, Madison; Anderson, Frederick. 1973. *NEPA in the Courts: A Legal Analysis of the National Environmental Policy Act.* Johns Hopkins Press, Baltimore, Maryland; Andrews, Richard N.L. 1976. *Environmental Policy and Administrative Change.* Lexington Books, Lexington, Massachusetts; Liroff, Richard A. 1976. *A National Policy for the Environment and its Aftermath.* Indiana University Press, Bloomington; Caldwell, Lynton K. 1982. *Science and the National Environmental Policy Act: Redirecting Policy Through Procedural Reform.* University of Alabama Press, University.

A five-article symposium on environmental impact statements was published in the *Natural Resources Journal* 16(2) (April 1976). Note especially Dreyfus, Daniel A. and Helen M. Ingram. The National Environmental Policy Act: A View of Intent and Practice. pp. 243–262. Arguments for clarifying amendments to NEPA to enable courts to review the merits of agency treatment of substantive provisions have been advanced in Ferester, Philip Michael. 1992. Revitalizing the National Environmental Policy Act: Substantive Law Adaptations from NEPA's Progeny. *Harvard Environmental Law Review* 19:207–269.

Although this chapter deals only peripherally with judicial interpretations of NEPA, there are chapters on the origins and intent of NEPA in numerous casebooks on environmental law. For example, NEPA is treated extensively in Hanks, Eva, A. Dan Tarlock, and John Hanks. 1974. *Environmental Law and Policy.* West Publishing, St. Paul, Minnesota. Other casebooks authored in the first decade of NEPA include history and analysis by Erica L. Dolgin and Thomas G.P. Guilbert, 1974; Frank Grad, 1978; Oscar S. Gray, 1971; James E. Krier, 1971; Norman J. Landau and Paul Rheingold, 1971; Neil Orloff and George Brooks, 1980; Arnold W. Reitze Jr., 1972; and Edwin Wallace Tucker, 1972. More recent publications include: Bonnie, John E. and Thomas Owen McGarity. 1992. *The Law of Environmental Protection: Cases, Legislation, Policies.* West Publishing, St. Paul, Minnesota; Breen, Barry, Celia Campbell-Mohr, and S. William Futrell. 1993. *Handbook on Environmental Law: From Resources to Recovery.* West Publishing, St. Paul, Minnesota; Findley, Roger W. and Daniel A. Farber. 1991. *Cases and Materials on Environmental Law,* third edition. West Publishing, St. Paul, Minnesota; Plater, Zygmunt J.B., Robert H. Abrams, and William Goldfarb. 1992. *Environmental Law and Policy: Nature, Law, and Society.* West Publishing, St. Paul, Minnesota; Rogers, William H. Jr. 1994. *Roger's Handbook on Environmental Law,* second edition. West Publishing, St. Paul, Minnesota; Schoenbaum, Thomas J. and Ronald H. Rosenberg. 1991. *Schoenbaum and Rosenberg's Environmental Policy Law.* Foundation Press, Westburg, New York.

3. Beauty for America: Proceedings of the White House Conference on Natural Beauty, May 24–25, 1965. U.S. Government Printing Office, Washington, D.C., 1965.

4. *Man's Role in Changing the Face of the Earth, International Symposium on Man's Role in Changing the Face of the Earth.* University of Chicago Press, Chicago, 1955.

5. Advisory Commission on Intergovernmental Relations (ACIR). 1981. *The Federal Role in the Federal System: The Dynamics of Growth—Protecting the Environment: Politics, Pollution, and Federal Policy,* ACIR, Washington, D.C., March.

6. U.S. National Academy of Sciences–National Research Council, Committee on Natural Resources. 1962. Natural Resources: A Summary Report to the President of the United States. NRC Publication 1060. Washington, D.C.

7. Worthington, E.B. 1977. *The Ecological Century: A Personal Appraisal.* Oxford University (Clarendon) Press, Oxford. Worster, Donald. 1977. *Nature's Economy: A History of Ecological Ideas.* Cambridge University Press, Cambridge.

8. U.S. Department of Health, Education, and Welfare. 1967. A Strategy for a Livable Environment: A Report to the Secretary of Health, Education, and Welfare by the Task Force on Environmental Health and Related Problems, Washington, D.C., June.

9. Managing the Environment. Report of the Subcommittee on Science, Research, and Development to the Committee on Science and Astronautics, U.S. House of Representatives, 1968.

10. A National Policy for the Environment: A Report on the Need for a National Policy for the Environment: An Explanation of Its Purpose and Content; An Explanation of Means to Make It Effective; and a Listing of Questions Implicit in Its Establishment. Special Report to the Committee on Interior and Insular Affairs, United States Senate, 90th Congress, Second Session, July 11, 1968.

11. Joint House–Senate Colloquium to Discuss a National Policy for the Environment. Hearing Before the Committee on Interior and Insular Affairs, United States Senate, and the Committee on Science and Astronautics, U.S. House of Representatives, 90th Congress, Second Session, July 17, 1968.

12. Congressional White Paper on a National Policy for the Environment. Submitted to the United States Congress under the auspices of the Committee on Interior and Insular Affairs, United States Senate and the Committee on Science and Astronautics, United States House of Representatives, 90th Congress, Second Session, October 1968.

13. National Environmental Policy: Hearing Before the Committee on Interior and Insular Affairs. United States Senate, 91st Congress, First Session on S.1075, S.237, and S.1752, April 16, 1969.

14. Ibid., p. 116.

15. U.S. House of Representatives, Conference Report, National Environmental Policy Act of 1969, H. Report 91-765. 91st Congress, First Session, 1969.

16. Environmental Quality: Hearings Before the Subcommittee on Merchant Marine and Fisheries. United States House of Representatives, 91st Congress, First Session—on Bills to Establish a Council on Environmental Quality, and for Other Purposes. May 7 and 26 and June 13, 20, 23, 26, and 27, 1969.

17. *Calvert Cliffs Coordinating Committee v. Atomic Energy Commission.* United States Circuit Court of Appeals of the District of Columbia Circuit, 1971, 449 F.2d. 1109.

18. Abolishing the Council on Environmental Quality: Hearing Before the Committee on Environment and Public Works. United States Senate, 103rd Congress, First Session, Section 112 of S.171—Termination of the Council on Environmental Quality and Transfer of Functions, April 1, 1993.

19. Caldwell, L.K. 1989. A Constitutional Law for the Environment: 20 Years with NEPA Indicates the Need. *Environment* 31(3):6–11, 25–28 and Commentaries, 2–5, 31–32. See also *Duke Environmental Law and Policy Forum* I(1991):1–10 and II(1992):1–3.

20. Supra, note 11.

21. Supra, note 19, Appendix D, p. 35.

22. Nixon Promises an Urgent Fight to End Pollution; Signs Measure to Establish a 3-Member Council on Environmental Quality. *New York Times,* January 9, 1970, p. 1; Nixon Appoints 3 in Pollution War. *New York Times,* January 30, 1970, pp. 1, 7.

23. Fairfax, Sally K. 1978. A Disaster in the Environmental Movement. *Science* 199:743–748. Although *Science* printed several letters of protest from well-informed students of NEPA, the editors declined a well-documented assessment of NEPA that corrected the biased misstatements of the Fairfax article. The so-called "peer reviews" of this article were protracted and curious, supporting an inference that attitudes of the editors of *Science* were far from objective on environmental legislation and NEPA in particular. An article countering the Fairfax piece was subsequently printed in the *Environmental Law Reporter* 9(1):50001–50007, January 1977.

24. This doctrine recognizes that each of the three exercises certain powers placed primarily in the others (e.g., presidential power of pardon and treaty making and the congressional power of impeachment). The separation doctrine provides that no one of the three is completely dominant over the others. The doctrine has been modified to some extent by a deference to the Supreme Court, which Thomas Jefferson, at least, regarded as contrary to the intention of the framers of

the Constitution. See Haines, Charles Grove. 1959. *The American Doctrine of Judicial Supremacy.* Russell and Russell, New York, reprint; Snowiss, Sylvia. 1990. *Judicial Review and the Constitution.* Yale University Press, New Haven, Connecticut.

25. Employment Act of 1946. Chapter 33-Public Law 304, February 20, 1946. U.S. Code Congressional Service. Laws of the 79th Congress, Second Session, pp. 20–22.

26. The President's Committee on Administrative Management in the Federal Government: Report of the Committee with Studies of Administrative Management. Submitted to the President and to the Congress in accordance with Public Law No. 739, 74th Congress, Second Session, 1937 (Note p. 5, I. The White House Staff and pp. 31–47, *V. Administrative Reorganization of the Government of the United States*).

27. Section 103 requires federal agencies to report anything in their statutory authority that would prevent "full compliance" with NEPA and to propose remedial measures when needed. Section 104 states that "the policies and goals set forth in this Act are supplementary to those set forth in existing authorizations." In effect, NEPA amended all relevant authorizing legislation.

28. Sections 204 and 205 specify ten functions and duties of the CEQ. Owing to White House parsimony and indifference, many of these functions have never been fulfilled. Proposals have been made to establish a capability for forecasting interactive trends in population, resources, and environment, overlooking the charge to the CEQ under Section 204 to undertake investigations in this area. See Grant, Lindsay. 1988. *Foresight and National Decisions: The Horseman and the Bureaucrat.* University Press of America, Lapham, Maryland, pp. 48–53.

29. *Environmental Defense Fund, Inc. v. Corps of Engineers*, U.S. Court of Appeals, Eighth Circuit, 1972, 470 F.2d. 289 (the Gillham Dam case). The court rules that the Corps must satisfy the requirements of NEPA before completing the dam even though "...the overall project was authorized by Congress eleven years prior to the passage of NEPA and was sixty-three percent completed at the date this action was instituted."

30. Shindler, W. 1976. The Impact Statement Boondoggle (editorial). *Science* 192:509. Contrary to the intentions of the framers and inconsistent with its proper administration, the impact statement requirement was seen as a bonanza by consulting firms around the Washington Beltway. This author warned against this perversion. See Caldwell, Lynton K. 1978. The Environmental Impact Statement, a Misused Tool. In *Environmental Impact Analysis: Emerging Issues in Planning.* Ravinder K. Jain and Bruce L. Hutchings, Eds. University of Illinois Press, Urbana-Champaign.

31. Supra, note 23.

32. Taylor, Serge. 1984. *Making Bureaucracies Think: The Environmental Impact Statement Strategy of Administrative Reform.* Stanford University Press, Stanford, California; Bartlett, Robert V. 1986. Rationality and the Logic of the National Environmental Policy Act. *The Environmental Professional* 8:105–111; Bartlett, Robert V. 1979. Environmental Impact Assessment and Administrative Theory. In *Managing Leviathan: Environmental Politics and the Administrative State.* Robert Paehlke and Douglas Torgerson, Eds. Broadview Press, Petersborough, Ontario; Mazmanian, Daniel and Jeanne Nienaber. 1979. *Can Organizations Change?: Environmental Protection, Citizen Participation and the Corps of Engineers.* Brookings Institution, Washington, D.C.

33. A Study of Ways to Improve the Scientific Content and Methodology of Environmental Impact Analysis. Final Report to the National Science Foundation on Grant PRA-79-10014. Indiana University School of Public and Environmental Affairs, Bloomington, 1982.

34. Moe, Ronald C. 1990. Traditional Organization Principles and the Managerial Presidency: From Phoenix to Ashes. *Public Administration Review* 50:129–140; Moe, Ronald C. and Robert S. Gilmour. 1995. Rediscovering Principles of Public Administration: The Neglected Foundation of Public Law. *Public Administration Review* 55. For the institution of the presidency in historical perspective, see Corwin, Edward S. 1941. *The President, Office and Powers: History and Analysis of Practice and Opinion,* second edition. New York University Press, New York.

35. For the president as personal leader, see Neustadt, Richard. 1960. *Presidential Power: The Politics of Leadership.* Wiley, New York.

36. Administration of the National Environmental Policy Act—Parts I and II: Hearings Before the Subcommittee on Fisheries and Wildlife Conservation of the Committee on Merchant Marine and

Fisheries, United States House of Representatives, 91st Congress, Second Session—on Federal Agency Compliance with Section 102(2)(c) and Section 103 of the National Environmental Policy Act of 1969. December 7–11, 16, 18, 21, and 22, 1970; Administration of the National Environmental Policy Act (PL91-190). Report by the Committee on Merchant Marine and Fisheries. United States House of Representatives, 92nd Congress, First Session, House Report No. 92-316, June 29, 1971; Administration of the National Environmental Policy Act—1972: Hearings Before the Subcommittee on Fisheries and Wildlife Conservation of the Committee on Merchant Marine and Fisheries, United States House of Representatives, 92nd Congress, Second Session on NEPA Oversight, February 17, 1972 [Federal Agency Compliance]; Administration of the National Environmental Policy Act—1972: Appendix to Hearings Before the Subcommittee on Fisheries and Wildlife Conservation of the Committee on Merchant Marine and Fisheries, United States House of Representatives, 92nd Congress, Second Session—Federal Agency Documents Which Outline Research and Evaluation Techniques Underlying the Preparation of Environmental Impact Statements. February 17 and 25, May 24, 1972; National Environmental Policy Act Oversight, Hearings Before the Subcommittee on Fisheries and Wildlife Conservation and the Environment of the Committee on Merchant Marine and Fisheries, United States House of Representatives, 94th Congress, First Session, September 8, 17, 18, 26, 1975; Implementation of the National Environmental Policy Act by the Council on Environmental Quality, Hearing Before the Subcommittee on Toxic Substances and Environmental Oversight, United States Senate, 97th Congress, Second Session, July 21, 1982; CEQ Authorization and NEPA Oversight, Hearing before the Subcommittee on Fisheries and Wildlife Conservation and the Environment of the Committee on Merchant Marine and Fisheries, United States House of Representatives, 100th Congress, First Session, April 9, 1987.

37. Council on Environmental Quality: Oversight Report. Committee on Interior and Insular Affairs, United States Senate, 94th Congress, Second Session, November 1976.

38. Clinton, William J. 1993. Remarks Announcing a New Environmental Policy, February 8, 1993. *Weekly Compilation of Presidential Documents* 29(6):159–160. Also Cushman, John H. Jr. 1993. A Clinton Cutback Upsets Environmentalists. *The New York Times* (National) September 26, 1993, p. 33.

39. Judge Skelly Wright in *Calvert Cliffs* opinion. See note 17.

SELECTED REFERENCES

Bear, D. 1993. NEPA: Substance or Merely Process? *Forum for Applied Research and Public Policy* pp. 86–88.

Carson, R. 1962. *Silent Spring.* Houghton Mifflin, Boston.

Conservation Foundation. 1966. *Future Environments of North America: Transformation of a Continent.* Natural History Press, Garden City, New York.

Finn, T.T. 1972. Conflict and Compromise: Congress Makes a Law: The Passage of the National Environmental Policy Act. Doctoral dissertation. Georgetown University, Washington, D.C.

Leopold, A. 1949. *Sand County Almanac.* Oxford University Press, New York.

Marsh, G.P. 1864. *Man and Nature.* Scribners, New York; reprinted in 1965 by Harvard University Press, Cambridge, Massachusetts.

Osborn, F. 1948. *Our Plundered Planet.* Little-Brown, Boston.

Sears, P. 1935. *Deserts on the March.* University of Oklahoma Press, Norman.

Udall, S. 1963. *The Quiet Crisis.* Holt, Rinehart, & Wilson, New York.

Vogt, W. 1948. *Road to Survival.* W. Sloane Associates, New York.

Yost, N.C. 1992. Rio and the Road Beyond. *Environmental Law American Bar Association* 11(4):6.

THE RATIONALITY AND LOGIC OF NEPA REVISITED

4

R.V. Bartlett

The National Environmental Policy Act (NEPA) is a complex and subtle piece of legislation, not susceptible to simple explanation or interpretation. The logic of NEPA and its environmental impact statement (EIS) requirement is best understood as institutionalization of a kind of mandatory, continuing, systematic, integrated, science-based policy analysis—thus altering the substantive outcomes of government activities by changing the rules and premises for arriving at legitimate decisions. Embodied in NEPA and this institutionalized policy analysis (environmental impact assessment, EIA) is a particular form of reasoning, ecological rationality, which NEPA requires in all federal policy and decision making. NEPA fosters and institutionalizes ecological rationality by a complex mix of political means—among others, by judicial enforcement of substantive and procedural mandates, by persuasive appeal of precepts and declarations, by opening policy and decision processes to external influences, by forcing changes in the values of agency personnel, and by stimulating the generation and use of new information.

The above key arguments were advanced in a 1986 article entitled "Rationality and the Logic of the National Environmental Policy Act" (Bartlett, 1986a). Ten years later, all of those arguments remain, in my view, perfectly sound. They are even possibly a bit more widely accepted than they were ten years ago. NEPA and EIA have been around long enough that perhaps, finally, they are a little less susceptible to simplistic understanding and evaluation. In ten years, the premise of ecological rationality has been further developed and analyzed conceptually, and it now sounds less exotic and farfetched (Dryzek, 1987; Bartlett, 1986b, 1990). Also, policy analysts in and out of government are now perhaps more accustomed to accounting for policy development in terms of multifaceted, indirect means for achieving policy change.

Because the above arguments are still not common wisdom, everywhere known and automatically accepted, some purpose is served in this chapter by restating them and reviewing misconceptions that are still being advanced. Moreover, in the last decade there have been several developments in the understanding of public policy generally that provide new perspectives on NEPA, perspectives that are fully consistent with the above arguments but provide additional insight into NEPA's rationality and logic. Particularly significant in this regard are the policy tools approach and the new institutionalism in policy research.

NEPA AND THE "RATIONALITY PROJECT"

"Rationality" was, and is, a term subject to much confusion and misinterpretation as used in connection with NEPA. This confusion has two sources. First, most persons with any exposure to the social or administrative sciences after World War II probably know about the many efforts of researchers to extend use of the rationality assumption to understand public policy. Second, many are also knowledgeable of the cogent criticisms other scholars have made of rational comprehensive decision making as a normative ideal. Likewise, persons whose backgrounds are primarily in the natural sciences tend to think of scientific methods as the epitome of rationality. Consequently, there have always been persons ready to interpret NEPA as an effort to make government more rational, part of a larger "rationality project" seeking to rescue "public policy from the irrationalities and indignities of politics, hoping to conduct it instead with rational, analytical, and scientific methods" (Stone, 1988, p. 4).

Given that a good part of my 1986 article involved grounding ecological rationality in the science provisions of NEPA, I had anticipated possible misinterpretation, but inadequately (Bartlett, 1986a). I had included a brief caveat to preempt such misinterpretation: "it is not just any conception of rationality that underlies NEPA—not some superficial and simplistic view of scientific rationality, nor some warmed over and disguised revisitation of the rational-comprehensive decision-making model of classic public administration" (Bartlett, 1986a, pp. 108–09). I argued that NEPA was, rather, a charter for a form of rationality distinct from instrumental scientific, technical, or economic rationality. This form of rationality, ecological rationality, is not a purely instrumental form of reason and is as applicable to ultimate ends as it is to means (Bartlett, 1986a,b, 1990; Dryzek, 1987). That which NEPA is not, however, apparently still requires further explanation.

The rationality project of the social sciences rests on three pillars: a model of reasoning based on calculation and optimal choices, a market model of society, and a production model of public policy (Stone, 1988). Policy issues consist of goals, problems, and solutions. NEPA, however, clearly does not incorporate a production model of public policy. This is why NEPA raised few alarms during its passage and has been so widely misunderstood and even, by policy scholars, ignored. It offers no predefinition of problems, nor any packaged solutions that can be implemented and the success of which evaluated. The implied assumption that NEPA, as a policy act, must produce something has given rise to an unproductive debate as to whether it is substance or procedure that NEPA produces. However, as James P. Boggs notes, "While NEPA does have both procedural and substantive aspects, its basic and most explicit intent reaches beyond this dichotomy" (Boggs, 1993, p. 25).

Given its substantive emphasis on trusteeship for succeeding generations, aesthetically and culturally pleasing surroundings, and preservation of important historic, cultural, and natural aspects of national heritage, it is clear that NEPA is not founded exclusively on a market model of society either. Rather than autonomous interactions to maximize self-interest, NEPA is based on presumptions about the public interest (Section 101: "overall welfare and development of man...foster and promote the general welfare...create and maintain conditions in which man and nature can exist in productive harmony"), about cooperation (Section 102: "the integrated use of the natural and social sciences and environmental design arts...consult with and obtain the comments of...maximize international cooperation"), and about the cultivation of important values (Sections 101 and 102: "each person has a responsibility to contribute to the preservation and enhancement of the environment...ensure that presently unquantified environmental amenities and values may be given appropriate consideration").

It is NEPA's requirement for environmental impact assessment, of course, that reminds critics of discredited prescriptions for rational comprehensive decision making, in particular the investigations NEPA demands of consequences and alternatives prior to taking action and the mandate to use a systematic, interdisciplinary approach to planning and decision making (Fairfax, 1978). But this is hardly the stuff of optimal decision making or wholly science-based decision making. NEPA's EIS requirement does not insist on the identification or specification of objectives in decision making, nor does it specify or recommend the ultimate selection of the best alternative. The requirements that alternatives be considered and consequences investigated have always been interpreted in common-sense ways by the courts and the Council on Environmental Quality (CEQ). Science and scientific concepts are pervasive in nearly every section of NEPA, but nowhere does NEPA preclude policy and decision making based on non-scientific information, ideas, or values. Indeed, several provisions require attention to non-scientific matters, such as historic and cultural aspects of national heritage, unquantified amenities and values, and a variety of individual choices.

The actual processes prescribed or implied by NEPA are, in fact, largely inconsistent with either scientific methods per se or rational comprehensive decision making. True, NEPA does require a systematic interdisciplinary approach, and it requires consideration of alternatives and environmental consequences among other things. It requires, in short, ecological reasoning from individuals and agencies. Also, it dictates that this process be documented in EISs, but then it specifies and implies that the resulting documentation and any ensuing decision be handled politically. Other agencies are to be consulted and the EIS is to be published and made available to state and local agencies, the president, the public, and, by implication, Congress and the courts. Since NEPA is silent about what is to happen next, the conclusion must be that decisions are expected to be made in political ways, by political persons, in political settings. The logic of NEPA is one of influencing that political process strategically, even to redirect it in significant ways, but not to replace it with scientific reasoning nor to require it to use rational comprehensive decision making.

Neither is there any evidence that NEPA assumes that agency decision making or government policy making corresponds with the rational comprehensive model of decision making. NEPA does not presume that policy and decision processes will be serial and linear, non-conflictual, or unaffected by power, passion, loyalty, habits, or contradictory values. Rather, NEPA recognizes a deficiency in the political system and prescribes integration of ecological rationality with other forms of rationality, notably technical, economic, social, and legal, through a process that is overtly and intentionally political. The institutionalized analysis required by NEPA must be understood as a "strategically crafted argument, designed to create paradoxes and resolve them in a particular direction" (Stone, 1988, p. 4; Majone, 1989). Rationality is central to the logic of NEPA, but not the narrow, simplistic, dated conception of rationality that some critics have alleged.

NEPA AND THE TOOLS OF POLICY

Although NEPA is not primarily a mandate for instrumental rationality, it does have what Lynton K. Caldwell has always called its "action-forcing provisions" (Caldwell, 1982). That is to say, it uses certain tools, instruments, or mechanisms to achieve policy change. In writing about the rationality and logic of NEPA today, account should be taken of an increasing emphasis by analysts on the tools of government in policy research (Hood, 1986; Salamon, 1989). Because NEPA does not employ any of the tools with which analysts are most familiar (exhortation, administrative reorganization, budgetary redistribution, financial inducements, regulatory rule making, public ownership, or creating markets), its primary tool, environmental impact assessment, has not been formally studied in relation to other tools. Also, because EIA is a particularly subtle and complex tool, it poses some challenges to analysis. Understanding EIA means understanding its catalytic character with respect to both ideas and to the opportunities it provides for administrative entrepreneurship:

> Catalytic controls require the bureaucracy to act and direct the bureaucracy towards certain goals but do not rob it of the capacity for creative problem-solving...They prod, stimulate, and provoke bureaucrats but also allow them to be both innovative and efficient (Gormley, 1987, p. 160).

Regarding ideas as policy instruments, Janet Weiss argues that they work

> by inviting people to think differently about their situation, by providing them with information about new alternatives or about the advantages or disadvantages of existing alternatives, making some perspectives more salient than others, directing attention toward some phenomena and away from others, or leading people to accept different values or preferences...Through ideas, government can animate and direct patterns of action and inaction to change policy outcomes (Weiss, 1990, p. 179).

Weiss's concern was with mental health policy, but a more cogent statement about the logic of NEPA could not be found.

This strategic use of ideas as a policy tool is at the core of Boggs's characterization of NEPA as aiming at cognitive reform: "NEPA legislatively establishes an essentially moral framework that gives direction to the links between knowledge and action that must be forged under NEPA's Section 102 mandate on a case-by-case basis" (Boggs, 1993, p. 27). Policy and decision analysis cannot be extracted from politics; both analysis and politics are fundamentally about the struggle over ideas. NEPA restructures environmental politics and policy making—the framework for political reasoning—so as to facilitate the greater use of ecological rationality in defining problems, defining ideals, and defining solutions.

NEPA implementation, of course, is not entirely non-coercive. To some extent, agencies and individuals are forced to think ecologically, or pretend to, by the federal courts and by CEQ in its oversight capacity. Intermittently, Congress, state and local governments, other agencies, and the public also may bring pressure to bear on agencies to operate more consistently with NEPA, but in the midst of these pressures and constraints, EIA as required under NEPA creates innumerable opportunities for learning and adaptation. The evolving nature of the theory and practice of EIA offers "opportunities for enterprising people to cause change" in rules, agency structures, or patterns of relationships. Wandesforde-Smith (1989, p. 162) points out that all EIA tasks are done by people acting as administrative entrepreneurs. Doing EIA demands the creative, constructive, and controlled exercise of discretion, including the central tasks of building coalitions, making a case on the merits, and developing and affirming environmental values (Wandesforde-Smith, 1989).

The ecological rationality that is institutionalized in American national government by NEPA is not a simple, fully developed algorithm for choice, but rather a form of reasoning based on principles derived from, among other sources, the still evolving environmental sciences. John Dryzek's five criteria for ecological rationality, for example, are feedback potential, coordinative capability, robustness, flexibility, and resilience (Dryzek, 1987). All of these criteria are amenable to further learning, especially in the context of the logic of NEPA-mandated EIA as "a self-regulating and self-sustaining learning process that, through analysis, adapts policy to a changing world" (Wandesforde-Smith, 1989, p. 155).

MODELS OF EIA

Thinking about EIA as an instrument of government forces consideration of how and why EIA works. How and why does EIA assure the practice and political efficacy of NEPA's ecological rationality? In 25 years, policy scholars have provided multiple answers to that question. Although EIA is not often analyzed explicitly as a tool or instrument, the kind of tool that it has been assumed to be has been determined by one of several models of policy or decision making, each of which has been accepted in different contexts without much question (Culhane et al., 1987; Murray, 1990; Kurian, 1993).

For example, the model underlying most assessments of NEPA before its passage was one of symbolic tokenism, a model which saw NEPA as neither substantive nor procedural reform, but mere words—"a symbolic statement of good intentions" (Caldwell, 1988, p. 75). Most of the scholarship on EIA, however, and the view of what EIA ought to be that is held by many scientists and environmental professionals, is founded on a technical information-processing model. This model suggests that EIA is effective because it provides better information to a decision process that presumably will use it well (that is, apolitically). This is a model that indeed sees EIA as one contribution to making policy processes more rational scientifically, comprehensively, and instrumentally.

A more overtly political model has focused on EIA as an instrument of "external reform." This pluralist politics model emphasizes the changes in policy that have resulted from the public participation and interest group involvement that NEPA and EIA have made possible. Alternatively, EIA has been interpreted by an organizational politics model as primarily an instrument of "internal reform," forcing changes in agency missions, structures, budgets, personnel, and procedures. To these two models must be added the perspectives on cognitive reform and administrative entrepreneurship, discussed earlier, which are different emphases of what is basically a catalytic model.

Some of these models are fundamentally flawed and can easily be discredited in part, notably the symbolic tokenism and technical information-processing models, but none by itself provides an adequate framework for understanding the rationality and logic of NEPA. To understand NEPA, and to exploit further its only partially tapped potential for environmental policy development, is going to require a better appreciation of the subtlety, complexity, and distinctiveness of EIA as a policy instrument, which will demand greater richness and correspondence in models and theories (Majone, 1986). Even after 25 years of learning and, one hopes, some reflection, it means a continuing struggle over the ideas that constitute NEPA; it also means there is a great deal more to learn.

Better explanations of NEPA will require the abandonment of a simple theory or model for classifying it into a neat, simple, preexisting category with readily agreed boundaries. This is increasingly recognized in some of the policy scholarship on NEPA and EIA, which tries to identify and draw upon the full range of factors that might affect how and why EIA works (Taylor, 1984; Wandesforde-Smith and Kerbavaz, 1988; Wandesforde-Smith, 1989; Culhane et al., 1987; Boggs, 1993; Gibson, 1993). Which is the one most important way that NEPA causes policy change is not the important question. Rather, what is needed is an understanding of how these alternative explanations are complementary and interactive and, if they collectively remain inadequate, what else should be considered?

My 1986 article (Bartlett, 1986a) accepted Taylor's integration of the internal reform–external reform models and his finding that the impact of NEPA and EIA was to make bureaucracies think, but Taylor (1984) had not really dealt with how or about what agencies ought to think or whether the injunction to think extended beyond the bureaucracy itself. EIA must be understood, I argued, in the context of NEPA, in that context EIA makes no pretense to be value neutral. Agencies, and others as they deal with federal agencies, were charged by NEPA to think in certain ways, and especially about certain things, in accordance with certain principles. Those ways, things, and principles collectively constitute ecological reasoning; ecological rationality is embodied in NEPA and the whole logic of NEPA revolves around advancing and fostering ecological rationality.

Ideas as policy tools, administrative entrepreneurship, and indeed the whole model of catalytic controls are concepts entirely consistent with the view of NEPA as a charter for ecological rationality. They further illuminate the rationality and logic of NEPA in several important ways not addressed earlier (Bartlett, 1986a).

But a problem with all of these models—symbolic tokenism, technical information processing, internal reform, external reform, and catalytic controls—is that they are all merely process models. Accordingly, they all underestimate both the stability and ultimate potential of NEPA and EIA to effect policy change. I addressed this inadequately in 1986 by emphasizing the "institutionalization" of ecological rationality—the ways NEPA attempts to build ecological rationality into not only processes and procedures but also the agencies themselves as well as their political environments (Bartlett, 1986a). The subsequent development of "new institutionalism" in political science and institutionalist approaches in other social sciences offers a framework for understanding and evaluating this significance of NEPA for environmental policy change (March and Olsen, 1989; Majone, 1989).

INSTITUTIONALISM AND THE LOGIC OF NEPA

Process models may have significantly influenced the thinking of the drafters of NEPA, but there is considerable evidence that they were centrally concerned with policy and decision structures and the development of values as guides for policy choices (Caldwell, 1968; U.S. Congress, 1968, 1969). Review of the legislative history of NEPA reveals ongoing concern by congressional sponsors, staff, and consultants with the dysfunctional consequences of narrow agency mandates, the segmented character of bureaucratic decision structures, the lack of coordination among agencies, specific organizational deficiencies with respect to research and environmental advice, and the inadequate legal basis for consideration of environmental values. Recognized as key difficulties that needed to be addressed by any prospective new legislation were the rules, routines, and traditional patterns of resource allocation that fostered or condoned environmental degradation but nevertheless were deeply entrenched politically. Policy change would have to occur in a complex multiorganizational and multipolicy political environment in which supporters of the old order, individually and collectively powerful, would remain and act. NEPA calls itself a policy act, and it prescribes procedural reforms aimed at achieving its policy aims, but if fully implemented, the procedural requirements of NEPA necessarily require extensive change to address some of the fundamental institutional inadequacies that the drafters of NEPA saw in the American political and economic system.

These induced changes in layers of rules, culture, values, meanings, and patterns of relationships could, of course, be expected to be difficult, painful, slow, and far from fully predictable in their specifics. The institutionalist approach to policy evaluation suggests that evaluation of the significance and impact of governmental reforms like NEPA and EIA will require the perspective of decades rather than years (Bartlett, 1994). The institutionalist approach also facilitates the avoidance of several pitfalls in understanding the rationality and logic of NEPA:

1. NEPA may appear to focus on individual decisions, but its ultimate (and intended) impact is on policies as interconnected with other policies (Bartlett, 1993).
2. NEPA may appear to be directed at one-pass problem solving, but the consideration of an EIS is really only a manifestation of a larger process, "a component of a larger, extended, iterative policy process through which the parameters of public policy, taken very broadly, are determined" (Peters, 1992, p. 178).
3. All policy and decision making is based on a socially constructed reality; the construction of this reality is done in institutions. The logic of NEPA is clearly aimed at restructuring rules and values, both in federal agencies and in the organizations that interact with them through the forced institutionalization of ecological rationality.

4. Policy change through NEPA will never be easy, even under ideal circumstances. Institutions embody values that will virtually always be vigorously defended. Yet this means that institutional change caused by NEPA is now also entrenched and will continue to produce future streams of outcomes.

5. Although policies are likely to be fairly persistent, the potential over time for significant policy change through institutional transformation is great. Perhaps, as Caldwell suggests, it is unrealistic to expect NEPA to accomplish with respect to Congress, the president, and the Supreme Court what only a constitutional amendment can do on a permanent basis (Caldwell, 1989). Yet even after a quarter of a century since NEPA's passage, the ramifications of the first institutional changes stimulated by NEPA are still playing out, creating opportunities and stimuli for further change while opportunities remain for agency executives and the CEQ to undertake initiatives to further facilitate the institutionalization of ecological rationality through EIA.

CONCLUSIONS

After 25 years of experience under NEPA, even if appreciation of its rationality and logic is still not widespread, there is no shortage of ideas for improving its implementation. Some of these, of course, are more feasible than others. A constitutional amendment for the environment is not a strong likelihood in the short run (although with advance preparation it might be adopted during some future great wave of environmental concern and attention). Nor is strengthening NEPA by amending it legislatively likely to be an option that NEPA's supporters will wish to risk in the next few years. To some extent, the evolving institutionalization of ecological rationality will always be influenced by unpredictable events and developments, including public opinion, fiscal constraints, international pressures, congressional sympathy, judicial receptivity, and presidential commitment, as well as by the availability of new techniques and new scientific knowledge.

The political health of CEQ, assuming it continues to survive in spite of recurrent presidential consideration of plans to reorganize it out of existence (under Presidents Carter, Reagan, and Clinton, so far), determines how many resources it can devote to its role in providing direction and guidance for the implementation of NEPA. Within the political and resource constraints imposed on it, CEQ continues to undertake initiatives to improve implementation of NEPA, ranging from studies of the use and misuse of environmental assessments (Blaug, 1993), to training initiatives (Clark, 1993), to general NEPA efficiency and effectiveness studies. With more resources, and stronger support of CEQ from the White House, bolder, more thoroughgoing initiatives could be forthcoming for extending the spirit and intent of NEPA throughout government. Although a great deal of effort continues to go into innovation and adaptation of agency policy processes by those federal employees and consultants who have responsibilities for NEPA, formally the agencies have tended to wait for CEQ to provide leadership or a push. However, there is no reason why individual agencies could not themselves undertake initiatives in this respect.

The 1979 NEPA regulations promulgated by CEQ required all agencies to adopt procedures to supplement those regulations, further mandating that "agencies shall continue to review their policies and procedures and in consultation with the Council to revise them as necessary to ensure full compliance with the purposes and provisions of the Act" (40 CFR 1507.3). To date, the procedures issued by virtually every agency have been extremely superficial and vague, mostly repeating phrases from NEPA and the CEQ regulations (Malik and Bartlett, 1993), but the opportunity remains for agencies to adopt a great deal more specific, meaningful, innovative guidance in their NEPA procedures.

In sum, the co-evolution of politics and policy stimulated by NEPA continues and will continue (Wandesforde-Smith and Kerbavaz, 1988). The intent of NEPA is to advance and foster social intelligence with respect to the human environment—not a narrowly instrumental intelligence, but an integrated political and ecological rationality, directed as much at the ends embraced as a society and a polity as at the means adopted in policy processes. This, and not rational comprehensive decision making or scientific rationality per se, is the rationality of NEPA. The logic of NEPA is that this ecological rationality should be built into all government structures and activities, particularly those of an administrative character, and fostered in the broader society. The catalyst for this institutional development is EIA. EIA is a policy tool, but a particularly complex, subtle one that forces reform of processes for making individual decisions and policy choices. More importantly, it also works by creating opportunities for advancing the ideas, developing the values, and recreating the institutions that will structure and shape future policy, decision making, and environments.

SELECTED REFERENCES

Bartlett, R.V. 1986a. Rationality and the Logic of the National Environmental Policy Act. *The Environmental Professional* 8(2):105–111.

Bartlett, R.V. 1986b. Ecological Rationality: Reason and Environmental Policy. *Environmental Ethics* 8:221–239.

Bartlett, R.V. 1990. Ecological Reason in Administration: Environmental Impact Assessment and Administrative Theory. In *Managing Leviathan: Environmental Politics and the Administrative State*. R. Paehlke and D. Torgerson, Eds. Broadview Press, Peterborough, Ontario, Canada, pp. 81–96.

Bartlett, R.V. 1993. Integrated Impact Assessment as Environmental Policy: The New Zealand Experiment. *Policy Studies Review* 12(3–4):162–177.

Bartlett, R.V. 1994. Evaluating Environmental Policy Success and Failure. In *Environmental Policy in the 1990s*, second edition. N.J. Vig and M.E. Kraft, Eds. CQ Press, Washington, D.C.

Blaug, E.A. 1993. Use of Environmental Assessment by Federal Agencies in NEPA Implementation. *The Environmental Professional* 15(1):57–65.

Boggs, J.P. 1993. Procedural vs. Substantive in NEPA Law: Cutting the Gordian Knot. *The Environmental Professional* 15(1):25–33.

Caldwell, L.K. 1968. A National Policy for the Environment. A special report to the Committee on Interior and Insular Affairs, United States Senate, 11 July. U.S. Government Printing Office, Washington, D.C.

Caldwell, L.K. 1982. *Science and the National Environmental Policy Act: Redirecting Policy Through Procedural Reform*. University of Alabama Press, University.

Caldwell, L.K. 1988. Environmental Impact Analysis (EIA): Origins, Evolution, and Future Directions. *Impact Assessment Bulletin* 6(3-4):75–83.

Caldwell, L.K. 1989. A Constitutional Law for the Environment: Twenty Years with NEPA Indicates the Need. *Environment* 31(10):6–11.

Clark, R. 1993. The National Environmental Policy Act and the Role of the President's Council on Environmental Quality. *The Environmental Professional* 15(1):4–6.

Culhane, P.J., H.P. Friesema, and J.A. Beecher, Eds. 1987. *Forecasts and Environmental Decisionmaking.* Westview Press, Boulder, Colorado.

Dryzek, J.S. 1987. *Rational Ecology: Environment and Political Economy.* Basil Blackwell, New York.

Fairfax, S.K. 1978. A Disaster in the Environmental Movement. *Science* 199(917):743–748.

Gibson, R.B. 1993. Environmental Impact Design: Lessons from the Canadian Experience. *The Environmental Professional* 15(1):12–24.

Gormley, W.T. 1987. Institutional Policy Analysis: A Critical Review. *Journal of Policy Analysis and Management* 6:153–169.

Hood, C.C. 1986. *The Tools of Government.* Chatham House, Chatham, New Jersey.

Kurian, P.A. 1993. Gender and Environmental Policy: A Feminist Critique of Environmental Impact Assessment Theories. Paper presented at the annual meeting of the American Political Science Association, September 2–5, Washington, D.C.

Majone, G. 1986. Analyzing the Public Sector: Shortcomings of Current Approaches—Part A. Policy Science. In *Guidance, Control, and Evaluation in the Public Sector.* F. Kaufman, G. Majone, and V. Ostrom, Eds. Walter de Gruyter, New York.

Majone, G. 1989. *Evidence, Argument, and Persuasion in the Policy Process.* Yale University Press, New Haven, Connecticut.

Malik, M. and R.V. Bartlett. 1993. Formal Guidance for the Use of Science in EIA: Analysis of Agency Procedures for Implementing NEPA. *The Environmental Professional* 15(1):34–45.

March, J.G. and J.P. Olsen. 1989. *Rediscovering Institutions: The Organizational Basis of Political Life.* Free Press, New York.

Murray, A.C. 1990. Environmental Assessment: The Evolution of Policy and Practice in New Zealand. M.Sc. thesis. University of Canterbury, Christchurch, New Zealand.

Peters, B.G. 1992. The Policy Process: An Institutionalist Perspective. *Canadian Public Administration* 35(2):160–180.

Salamon, L.M. 1989. *Beyond Privatization: The Tools of Government Action.* Urban Institute Press, Washington, D.C.

Stone, D.A. 1988. *Policy Paradox and Political Reason.* Scott, Foresman, Glenview, Illinois.

Taylor, S. 1984. *Making Bureaucracies Think: The Environmental Impact Statement Strategy of Administrative Reform.* Stanford University Press, Stanford, California.

U.S. Congress. 1968. Joint House–Senate Colloquium to Discuss a National Policy for the Environment: Hearings. Senate Committee on Interior and Insular Affairs and House Committee on Science and Aeronautics. 90th Congress, Second Session, July 17.

U.S. Congress. 1969. National Environmental Policy: Hearing on S. 1075, S. 237, and S. 1752. Senate Committee on Interior and Insular Affairs. 91st Congress, First Session, April 16.

Wandesforde-Smith, G. 1989. Environmental Impact Assessment, Entrepreneurship, and Policy Change. In *Policy Through Impact Assessment: Institutionalized Analysis as a Policy Strategy,* R.V. Bartlett, Ed. Greenwood Press, Westport, Connecticut, pp. 155–166.

Wandesforde-Smith, G. and J. Kerbavaz. 1988. The Co-Evolution of Politics and Policy: Elections, Entrepreneurship and EIA in the United States. In *Environmental Impact Assessment: Theory and Practice.* Peter Wathern, Ed. Unwin Hyman, London.

Weiss, J.A. 1990. Ideas and Inducements in Mental Health Policy. *Journal of Policy Analysis and Management* 9(2):178–200.

BASIC PURPOSES AND POLICIES OF THE NEPA REGULATIONS

5

K.S. Weiner

The National Environmental Policy Act (NEPA), the nation's environmental Magna Carta, stands out among federal laws as a model of brevity and simplicity. Yet NEPA takes on the profound challenge of redirecting the entire federal government, with its thousands of employees and trillion-dollar budgets, to act in a way that creates and maintains conditions under which people and nature can live in "productive harmony." This is no small task.

NEPA, the statute, provides a foundation and a framework for turning the ship of state. If the challenge appeared great 25 years ago, it is no less compelling as the next millennium approaches. To NEPA's credit, the term "environmental impact" has not only entered the lexicon but has been widely emulated. Awareness of the "undesirable or unintended consequences" of government-approved or -funded actions offers only a first step. NEPA's mandate and its promise lie in helping society to work together to determine how to move forward. NEPA's goal of "productive harmony" has yet to be realized, though the term in global usage today is "environmentally sustainable development."

Concise and to the point, NEPA reads more like a constitution than a typical statute. The NEPA regulations, adopted by the Council on Environmental Quality (CEQ) in 1978, are similarly concise and to the point for a set of federal regulations. Unlike most regulations which are considered "balanced" if every interest groups attacks them, the NEPA regulations were widely praised by business, labor, environmental, local, state, federal, and tribal officials and scientific communities. For over 15 years they have stood the test of time, including three consecutive regulatory reform commissions established by Presidents Carter, Reagan, and Bush to review federal rules. They continue to be used as one of the models for reinventing government under President Clinton and Vice President Gore. The CEQ NEPA regulations have been recognized as an extraordinary set of government regulations, both for their content as well as for being well written and readable.

To understand the purposes and intent of the NEPA regulations, it is essential to understand why NEPA was enacted in the first place. Among the primary reasons for the NEPA regulations' common sense and success in anticipating many of the same efficiencies being touted in regulatory reform efforts across the nation in the 1990s are:

1. Their focus on implementing the original legislative intent, rather than creating a regulatory process in reaction to agency misinterpretations or to early court cases that addressed egregious failures to comply with the law
2. The fact that they were developed by communicating with people around the country who had to use the regulations or were affected by them, rather than just federal officials or interest groups in the nation's capital

NEPA'S BASIC MANDATES

NEPA has several basic mandates, as the statute, its legislative history, and the NEPA regulations all reflect:

1. *Supplemental mandate*—To add to the existing authority of every federal agency the responsibility and power to protect the environment when carrying out other agency functions.
2. *Affirmative mandate*—Not only to preserve existing environmental quality, but to make decisions that restore and enhance the environment.
3. *Procedural mandate*—To use a planning and decision making process for developing or considering the approval of plans, policies, programs, or projects that gives "appropriate consideration to environmental values and amenities," which occurs mainly through the analysis of environmental impacts and alternatives, including mitigation measures.
4. *Substantive mandate*—To recognize that each person should have a healthful environment and a responsibility to contribute to environmental quality, and to require all federal agencies "to the fullest extent possible" to "interpret and administer all laws" in ways that implement the policy of serving as a trustee of the environment for present and future generations and the other policies set forth in NEPA; in other words, the responsibility to "act" to protect the environment.
5. *Balancing mandate*—To implement the substantive national environmental policy "to the fullest extent practicable" in a manner that is "consistent with other essential policy considerations;" in other words, to take the environmentally preferred course of action unless it poses a conflict with other essential policies, in which case the decision maker looks to the substantive policies of NEPA as guidance in balancing competing considerations and making decisions directed toward achieving a "productive harmony" between people and nature.

In fact, NEPA is really quite simple. It boils down to two concepts: (1) think about environmental quality and (2) act on the knowledge gained. In technical circles, the first concept is commonly called "environmental impact assessment." In legal circles, "thinking" is called "consideration," and this aspect of NEPA is called "procedural," including "full disclosure" of impacts. The NEPA regulations and judicial review of NEPA compliance address procedural compliance, which includes decisions to prepare environmental documents, the adequacy of the documents, public and agency review, and whether actual consideration was given to the studies in the decision-making process.

Many people, especially in academic circles, have misunderstood NEPA's purposes. NEPA and NEPA documents do not require scientific prediction or certainty about the environmental consequences or outcome of proceeding with a proposed action. NEPA and the NEPA regulations recognize that many decisions involve uncertainties or risks about the future and that perfect information is unlikely. They require decisions to be informed by thoughtful environmental analysis—rather than by definitive predictions of environmental outcomes—so that decision makers can take reasonable steps to manage risks and uncertainties.

Acting on the knowledge gained, the second concept of NEPA is commonly called "mitigation," which means avoiding or otherwise reducing environmental harm. In legal circles, this aspect of NEPA is called "substantive." Currently, the courts basically will not review and substitute their judgment for an agency's substantive decisions, such as whether to authorize, place mitigation conditions on, or deny a proposal. The NEPA regulations do not directly regulate substantive compliance, although they do include certain procedures for requiring agencies to think about the act's substantive policies, to disclose and implement any mitigation decisions, and to appeal to CEQ to mediate substantive disputes among federal agencies.

NEPA'S PRIMARY ROLE

In light of its basic mandates, NEPA's fundamental role in the regulatory process is to focus on the "gaps and overlaps" among environmental laws and other requirements that apply to a proposed federal action. When NEPA was adopted in 1970, several other laws governing environmental quality and natural resources already existed. By the time the NEPA regulations were adopted in 1978, the number of other environmental laws had increased dramatically. With the increasing shift in initiative from the federal to the state and local level in the past decade, there are relatively few areas of environmental quality that are not subject to some federal, tribal, state, or local law, regulation, plan, or policy.

By the same token, neither human knowledge nor environmental regulation is perfect. There are often gaps where existing laws do not anticipate or address how to mitigate an environmental impact. With the plethora of environmental requirements, there are often overlaps, where different policies or requirements may appear to conflict with one another or where "the whole is more than the sum of its parts," such as cross-media or cumulative impacts. Most other environmental laws—even broad laws addressing water, air, endangered species, hazardous waste cleanup, or land use—focus on a particular aspect of environmental quality and, unlike NEPA, do not deal effectively with either cross-media issues or a comprehensive view of the environment.

NEPA was not designed to substitute for other agency planning or regulatory processes. In fact, NEPA could only be enacted after a compromise that included assurance that NEPA would not substitute for or undermine other statutes, such as specific clean air and water standards. The NEPA process is meant to be integrated with and inform planning and decision making, not to substitute for it.

NEPA's own structure reflects its primary role in addressing gaps and overlaps. Section 101 specifies the nation's overall environmental goals and policies. Section 102 requires all agencies to interpret and administer their activities in accordance with these policies to the fullest extent possible. Section 103 requires all agencies to review their statutory authority and policies to remove impediments and to ensure their ability to implement this act. Section 104 recognizes the existence of other laws and makes clear that this act does not alter an agency's statutory obligations to comply with environmental standards in these other laws. Section 105 supplements an agency's authority if the agency's existing authority is insufficient to implement the policies of the act —in other words, the authority to deal with the gaps and overlaps. The NEPA regulations echo this role; see, for example, 40 CFR §§ 1500.2(c), 1501.1, 1501.2, 1502.25, and 1506.4.

At a time of great public skepticism and business frustration with complex regulatory and permitting processes, it is especially important that the role of NEPA and the NEPA regulations be understood and not perceived as duplicating the many other environmental requirements that already exist.

NEPA AND THE ORIGIN OF THE REGULATIONS

Unlike many other laws, NEPA does not dictate what decision a government official must make. For example, NEPA does not prescribe specifically how to control pollution, protect species, or manage land and natural resources to meet the needs of people in both the short and long term. In fact, NEPA could be an example for reinventing government and returning power to people. With its emphasis on thinking through the consequences of government decisions, finding better ways to do business, getting different agencies "on the same page" on the same issue, and being accountable to the public for government decisions and spending, NEPA provides a textbook example of an alternative to "command and control" environmental regulation.

NEPA was intended to provide a framework for public officials to use in making decisions that affect environmental quality. One of NEPA's primary purposes, often forgotten in the focus on its well-known environmental impact statement (EIS) requirement, is to make sure the president and other federal officials have environmentally knowledgeable staff and good information to conduct the work Congress has directed. NEPA recognized that people make decisions and that the capacity to make sensible, environmentally sound decisions relies far less on skilled people from the private and public sectors working together than on required studies or documents.

President Nixon signed NEPA into law on January 1, 1970 and issued an executive order in March 1970 requiring all federal agencies to protect and enhance environmental quality and directing CEQ to issue "guidelines" and other instructions to agencies to carry out NEPA. CEQ was also directed to coordinate federal programs related to environmental quality, to determine the need for new policies, to recommend to the president and agencies priorities for more effective protection and enhancement of environmental quality, and to seek resolution of significant environmental issues.

Against this background, in 1971 CEQ staff issued a set of "interim" guidelines to all federal agencies for complying with NEPA, followed by a more complete set of guidelines in 1973. The CEQ guidelines outlined the process for studying the environmental impacts of proposed federal actions. CEQ created approaches that have become widely accepted, such as an "environmental assessment" and a "draft" EIS for public comment, as tools to implement NEPA's directives. The federal courts soon upheld challenges against those agencies that did not make a serious effort to comply with the new law, warning that NEPA was not a "paper tiger."

By 1976, CEQ staff had worked closely with federal agencies to build their own environmental capabilities, completed a five-year review of NEPA's use in 70 federal agencies, and commenced a comprehensive review to update, upgrade, and simplify its guidelines. Soon after President Carter took office, he amended Executive Order 11514 to upgrade CEQ's guidelines to "regulations":

> designed to make the environmental impact statement process more useful to decision-makers and the public; and to reduce paperwork and the accumulation of extraneous background data, in order to emphasize the need to focus on real environmental issues and alternatives.

The resultant CEQ effort culminated in the adoption of the NEPA regulations in 1978. Shortly afterward, the Supreme Court affirmed the regulations and CEQ's role in interpreting and overseeing NEPA. From the opening sections, the NEPA regulations seek to shift the focus from producing documents to a renewed focus on the act's twin purposes of "thinking" about environmental quality and then "acting" on what is learned:

> Ultimately, of course, it is not better documents but better decisions that count. NEPA's purpose is not to generate paperwork—even excellent paperwork—but to foster excellent action. The NEPA process is intended to help public officials make decisions that are based on understanding of environmental consequences, and take actions that protect, restore, and enhance the environment (40 CFR § 1500.1(c)).

To achieve efficiency, the regulations require that the NEPA process be integrated and conducted concurrently with requirements of other environmental laws, listing nearly 30 specific tools available and required to be used to reduce paperwork and delay (see 40 CFR §§ 1500.2(c), 1500.4, and 1500.5). Many of these tools, such as "scoping," have been borrowed to improve the efficiency of other environmental laws.

The NEPA regulations reflected a fundamental shift from a focus on EIS preparation in the guidelines to the overall "environmental review process." This approach reflected one of the most profound realities and legacies of NEPA: that the dynamic process of thinking through alternatives and impacts—in-house; with consulting professionals; with other federal, state, local, and tribal governments; and with applicants and the citizens— is the key to NEPA's power and effectiveness.

THE BASIC DEFINITIONS: NEPA'S BUILDING BLOCKS

Any law rapidly acquires a "gloss," in legal terminology, of interpretations and misinterpretations. NEPA was no exception, given the limited focus of the CEQ guidelines and the flood of initial litigation. One measure of the success of the NEPA regulations is that litigation over NEPA's basic requirements has been reduced.

The drafters of the NEPA regulations rethought the key statutory and regulatory terms and concepts in an effort to simplify them, minimize legal fictions (terms of art with specialized meanings that do not comport with everyday usage), and use common meanings.

Rather than competing with courts and consultants to create a convoluted interpretation of the statutory phrase in Section 102(2)(C) —"proposals for legislation and other major Federal actions significantly affecting the quality of the human environment"—the NEPA regulations define each of these words based on original intent in a way that creates a set of building blocks for understanding the provision. Other key words and phrases, such as scope and mitigation, have become common definitions across a range of international, federal, state, and local environmental laws. The premise of the drafters, which has been proven out in practice time and time again since 1978, is that a user of NEPA who takes the time to understand each of the key phrases defined in the NEPA regulations will be able to interpret and answer the vast majority of questions that may arise.

In the early years, as the courts and agencies struggled with NEPA, distinctions were made in phrases where in fact no differences were intended or necessary—for example, the distinction between "major" and "non-major" federal actions (the regulations clarify that "major" and "significant" are synonymous, so that major actions are ones with significant environmental impacts); between "proposal" and "proposed action," which are also synonymous; and between "affecting," "effects," and "impacts," which are also synonymous and are separately defined from the term "human environment." Key concepts such as "mitigation," "scope," and "tiering" provide other basic building blocks.

Human Environment

Although NEPA regulations clarified the reach of NEPA and have been upheld by subsequent case law, the term "human environment" remains a source of some confusion and controversy. Two principal objections have been made, from opposing directions. One perspective maintains that the phrase perpetuates an anthropocentric view of the world, where people perceive themselves as separate from and exercise dominion over nature. In practical regulatory terms, this raises the question of whether preservation and enhancement of the environment under NEPA encompass aspects of nature and the universe that are not inhabited or used by humans.

Reviewing NEPA's purposes, Section 101(a) acknowledges both the "profound impact" of people on the natural environment and "the critical importance" of restoring and maintaining environmental quality to support human "welfare and development." This dual theme carries through to the end of Section 101(a), which recognizes the role of environment quality in fulfilling the "social, economic, and other requirements of present and future generations of Americans," while aspiring to "create and maintain conditions under which man and nature can exist in productive harmony."

In addition to several policies that discuss how people use their environment, Section 101(b)(4) of NEPA speaks simply of "preserving important historic, cultural, and natural aspects of our national heritage." Most directly, Section 101(c) echoes both people's use of the environment and the value of the environment in its own right by stating that "each person should enjoy a healthful environment and that each person has a responsibility to contribute to the preservation and enhancement of the environment."

The NEPA regulations included both concepts in stating that "human environment shall be interpreted comprehensively to include the natural and physical environment and the relationship of people to that environment" (40 CFR § 1508.14).

Some states, such as Washington, have refined the "natural and physical" distinction to the "natural" and "built" environment, which more closely approximates the concepts discussed above. This distinction mirrors the required content of impact analysis under the NEPA regulations, which likewise refers to the natural and built environment (40 CFR § 1502.16(f) and (g)). The natural environment includes the classic Greek elements (earth, air, water, and fire, or energy) plus plants and animals, while the built environment includes environmental health (toxics and noise), land use, and infrastructure (transportation, public services, and utilities). This approach also allows for easier cross-media analysis and the combining of related topics.

The second critical perspective is that the NEPA regulations should use the term in a more encompassing fashion, including relationships among people. If NEPA truly seeks environmentally sustainable development, the analysis cannot focus only on the natural or physical world, or even human interaction with that world. Rather, the entire human realm is within its scope. Given the broad perspective of Section 101(a) of NEPA, including population growth, urbanization, technology, and the "overall general welfare and development of man," the NEPA regulations addressed this issue, with three factors influencing the outcome:

1. The most common understanding of "environment" is in relation to the natural and physical environment. Although Section 2 of NEPA refers to the role of the environment in stimulating human health and welfare, Congress plainly understood the term in connection to the natural world, using terms such as "environment and biosphere" and "ecological systems and natural resources" in the statement of purpose.

2. NEPA has been controversial enough just trying to address agreed-upon issues. There appears to be even less uniformity and consensus on appropriate impact analysis in the social, economic, and other social science disciplines than in the environmental arts and sciences. There was considerable concern that the statute would collapse of its own weight with these additional analyses and with judicial scrutiny of their adequacy.

3. NEPA was enacted to correct a serious imbalance where economic, social, and political factors regularly outweighed concern for the physical and natural environment. To place substantial weight back on these other factors would undermine one of the fundamental purposes for enacting NEPA.

The NEPA regulations do not preclude integrating other analyses into the NEPA process and NEPA documents. EIS writers who take seriously the requirements in Section 102(2)(C)(iv) and (v) to analyze the effect of short-term uses of the environment and significant commitments of natural resources on the maintenance of long-term ecological productivity will come much closer to addressing both NEPA's original intent and global sustainability. However, the NEPA regulations may provide the best balance. Other analyses may always be included or combined with the environmental analysis and documents (40 CFR § 1506.4). The required NEPA analysis would be subject to accepted standards of quality and judicial scrutiny, in contrast to these other elements. This approach allows experimentation and time to develop good methods for evaluating sustainability and integrating the analysis with conventional environmental review.

Proposed Action

Two of the basic definitions in the NEPA regulations work in concert to define the "underlying governmental action" subject to environmental review: "major federal action" and "proposal." A third provision, discussed later under the scoping process, complements these two definitions by identifying the scope of the action that is receiving environmental review (40 CFR §§ 1508.18 and 1508.23).

One of the key aspects of NEPA regulations is the classification of four types of federal activities—the "4Ps"—subject to NEPA analysis: policies, plans, programs, and projects. The regulations provide specific criteria or examples of each, so that it is clear that these actions must reach a certain level of "formality" and do not refer to all internal thinking by or among federal officials.

The regulations consciously take this approach to recognize two inherent tensions posed by the idea of "compliance" with NEPA. First, NEPA and Section 2 of Executive Order 11514 require all agencies to carry out the national environmental policy set forth in NEPA (which includes acting consistently with "other essential considerations of national policy"); to think comprehensively about environmental quality in whatever they do; to assist and share information related to environmental quality with the public and all levels of domestic and foreign governments; and, perhaps most importantly, to develop, monitor, and improve federal programs to control pollution and enhance environmental quality. Viewed in this light, all of the activities, staffing, and expenditures directed toward environmental quality by every agency—ranging from recycling in federal offices to setting priorities and carrying out major environmental programs under other laws—are aspects of implementing NEPA.

Although this infusion of environmental awareness into the national government lies at the very heart of NEPA's purposes, most people do not think of NEPA in this way. A quarter century of federal environmental legislation on numerous issues, coupled with the dominance of the EIS process and the Supreme Court's narrowing of the scope of review under NEPA, has shaped the perception of NEPA as a limited-purpose statute. Most people now think of NEPA implementation in terms of the formal analyses or documents that are required for certain federal actions.

The NEPA regulations reflect this reality by requiring that "non-project" actions must be sufficiently recognizable as official policies, plans, and programs to trigger formal environmental analyses under NEPA. Even so, many agencies do not perform required environmental analyses on these non-project actions. This lack of compliance stems from agencies' lack of ability or competence to perform this type of study, from a fear of opening up the policy-making process to the public and to litigation (ironically, often from business interests wishing to stop changes in federal policy), from a belief that environmental laws enacted and patterned in part after NEPA (such as the Clean Air, Clean Water, Superfund, Endangered Species, and public lands management acts) provide for alternatives and environmental consequences to be examined, from practical difficulties in integrating the formal NEPA process with the iterative nature of planning and policy making, and, not least of all, from a lack of NEPA oversight and encouragement by the Executive Office of the President.

Just as the NEPA regulations developed an alternative process for legislative proposals, which was upheld by the Supreme Court (40 CFR § 1506.8; *Andrus v. Sierra Club,* 47 USLW 4676 (1979)), at some point CEQ will need to adopt an alternative process that allows strategic environmental assessment to be integrated with agency planning and policy making.

The second tension relates to timing rather than to the type of federal activity subject to NEPA review. NEPA requires that agencies evaluate proposed actions significantly affecting environmental quality. This "look-before-you-leap" mandate allows better actions to be developed that will promote "productive harmony" between people and nature in the short and long term and will avoid or otherwise mitigate environmental damage or "other undesirable or unintended consequences." By requiring public and intergovernmental review before making final decisions, the NEPA process also promotes the NEPA objective to "improve and coordinate Federal plans, functions, programs, and resources" (Section 101).

By establishing uniform criteria for determining whether a proposal exists, the NEPA regulations provide realistic and indispensable guidance on the timing of the formal environmental review process. The regulations state that:

> A proposal exists at that stage in the development of an action when an agency subject to the Act has a goal and is actively preparing to make a decision on one or more alternative means of accomplishing that goal and the effects can be meaningfully evaluated (40 CFR § 1508.23).

Most importantly, this definition recognizes that NEPA is not an academic exercise, but that it comes into play when an agency is actively preparing to make a decision. The definition recognizes the need to allow agencies to think, dream, "contemplate" actions (in the Supreme Court's words), or otherwise do early planning and environmental thinking without being required to prepare a formal NEPA document, such as an environmental assessment (EA) or EIS.

Because many federal actions occur over time or in phases, a series of "proposed" actions may occur. Since NEPA seeks to put good environmental information before federal officials and the public when the information can influence decisions, agency staff will need to make a judgment about the key points in the decision process when environmental analysis will be meaningful. The final requirement, therefore, is that a proposal only exists for NEPA purposes when the effects can be meaningfully evaluated.

Tiering, or the use of successive phases of environmental review, allows for different levels of detail or specificity of environmental analysis as a proposal moves from a broad or early stage to a narrower or subsequent stage (40 CFR § 1508.28). Assuming the public can accept less detail at broader or earlier phases, which may be a big assumption for controversial proposals, tiering (or phased review, as it is sometimes called) can promote efficiency and help to bridge the gap between initiating environmental review too early or delaying review until it is too late.

The definition of a proposal also recognizes that it is usually too late to integrate environmental values if one waits until an agency has settled on a single preferred course of action. A proposal exists, therefore, when alternatives are being actively considered, whether the "goal" is a direct federal project or a federal response to a permit or funding application from another government or from the private sector. The definition therefore recognizes that an agency may have developed a proposal even if the agency has not formally proposed an action or acknowledged its existence.

The parameters of "major federal action" (the "4Ps") and the timing dimension of "proposal" have been examined in some detail because these terms provide the foundation for understanding the scope of environmental review. In addition, from a policy perspective, these two terms are central to the future role of NEPA in strategic planning and in truly integrating environmental review under NEPA with other laws and agency mandates.

SCOPE OF ENVIRONMENTAL REVIEW

Perhaps the greatest practical genius of the NEPA regulations is in the simple, coherent, workable framework, based on nearly a decade of accumulated experience and court precedents, which consists of defining the "scope" of environmental review as three types of actions, three types of alternatives, and three types of impacts (the "3 by 3" rule) (40 CFR § 1502.4 and 1508.25). This construct has provided a powerful tool for organizing and preparing environmental documents, as well as for reviewing their adequacy. Equally important, it has helped the public to comprehend and participate constructively in environmental review through the "scoping" process (40 CFR § 1501.7). One area where the NEPA regulations might be updated would be to state explicitly that the definition of the scope of environmental review and the use of a scoping process are equally available to agencies when environmental studies other than EISs are prepared, as noted in CEQ's "Forty Most Asked Questions Concerning CEQ's National Environmental Policy Act Regulations" (46 Federal Register 18026, March 23, 1981).

Action

Although the term "action" is used to refer to the underlying decision or activity of a federal agency that brings NEPA into play, the term has a specific meaning and usage with regard to the "scope" of environmental review—namely, what range of federal activities will be included in the environmental analysis.

At its most basic level, as discussed in the previous section, "action" is part of the term "major federal action" and refers to federal activities that warrant environmental review, including new and continuing actions that fall into the four main categories (the "4Ps") discussed above: policy, plan, program, and project action (40 CFR § 1508.18). In this context, the applicability of NEPA itself hinges on whether a federal action exists. At the next level, "action" is part of the term "proposed action" or "proposal" and refers to the timing of when an action exists. In defining the scope of environmental review, as discussed below, the term "action" refers to which proposed federal actions will be studied.

The NEPA regulations identify three types of actions: connected, cumulative, and similar actions (40 CFR §§ 1502.4 and 1508.25(a)). This provision also identifies another kind of action: single actions, which are actions that are essentially so self-contained or apparent in scope that it is not necessary to apply the criteria in the section to determine their scope.

Since the inception of NEPA, agencies, applicants, citizens, and the courts have struggled with the issue of "piecemealing" or "segmenting" environmental review, where the alternatives and impacts of a part of a proposal are evaluated. Building on and clarifying the doctrine of "independent utility," the regulations articulate specific criteria for determining when proposed federal actions are related to one another closely enough to be, in effect, a "single course of action" that requires evaluation in the same environmental document (connected actions), in contrast to actions with similarities which, as a matter of public policy, an agency may wish to evaluate together (similar actions).

Connected actions are those proposed federal actions that automatically trigger other environmentally significant actions, will be implemented with other actions, or are interdependent parts of a larger proposal and depend on the larger proposal for their justification. In contrast, similar actions may have common timing, impacts, alternatives, or geographical locations, so that agencies will make better plans or decisions by considering them together, but the actions do not depend on each other for their justification or implementation.

The regulations also refer to cumulative actions, requiring that significant cumulative impacts be evaluated in the same EIS. This category does not define the nature of the proposal; it is not the "actions" that are "cumulative" but their impacts. Since the regulations require cumulative impacts to be evaluated (40 CFR §§ 1508.25(c)(3)), this category is somewhat confusing and possibly redundant. Some state mini-NEPAs have clarified this provision by listing the three types of actions as "single," "connected," and "similar." These regulations logically use the "cumulative impact" category (under the three types of impacts) to make sure that cumulative impacts are addressed, regardless of whether these impacts are caused by proposed actions that are the subject of the environmental document or by similar or even other actions.

Alternatives

The preeminent mandate of NEPA is the attainment of "productive harmony between people and nature." NEPA's central procedural requirement remains the search for alternatives to achieve this goal. The examination of alternatives not only permeates NEPA but is required independently of the EIS requirement (see Section 102(2)(E)).

The point of analyzing impacts is not to fix the status quo but to stimulate decision makers to find environmentally better ways to conduct their business. Environmental impact assessment should be used, in NEPA's words, to find ways to fulfill the "social, economic, and other requirements of present and future generations," to "fulfill the responsibilities of each generation as trustee of the environment for succeeding generations," and to "attain the widest range of beneficial uses of the environment, without degradation, risk to health or safety, or other undesirable and unintended consequences." It would be difficult to find a plainer statement of the goal of environmental sustainability.

Not surprisingly, the NEPA regulations recognize the analysis and comparison of alternatives as the "heart" of the EIS process. The decision maker can choose only from among the range of alternatives in the environmental document, the agency cannot limit the choice of reasonable alternatives before a decision is made, and the alternatives must be judged against the substantive environmental policies set forth in NEPA and other laws (40 CFR § 1502.1, 1502.2(d)–(g), and 1502.14).

The NEPA regulations create an important conceptual framework for the analysis of alternatives by identifying three types: the no-action alternative, other reasonable courses of action, and mitigation measures. Typically, an alternative would be considered as a different course of action than the proposed action. In order to make sure there is a baseline to compare environmental quality with and without the proposed action, one alternative course of action—the no-action alternative—is always required to be evaluated. By predefining and requiring the inclusion of the no-action alternative, the NEPA regulations implicitly recognize that the no-action alternative may not be "reasonable" either because the legislature or courts have directed that some action occur or because of the environmental harm that would result from a failure to take some action. The regulations also give latitude to agencies to define a no-action alternative that makes sense in the context of the decision. Sometimes the no-action alternative reflects a continuation of existing conditions, because the future course of events cannot be reliably evaluated. At other times, the no-action alternative may reflect degradation or less well-managed development.

Mitigation measures lie at the other end of the spectrum of the three types of alternatives. Mitigation measures are variations on a course of action that avoid or otherwise reduce adverse environmental impacts and are usually required as conditions of a governmental approval. One of the most widespread and lasting legacies of the NEPA regulations has been the establishment of a uniform definition of mitigation, which has been widely adopted in numerous federal, state, and local laws and regulations. This definition is addressed in the next section.

For purposes of understanding the three types of alternatives, the concept of mitigation measures lies on a continuum with alternative courses of action. Alternative courses of action may be formulated for the purpose of avoiding or otherwise mitigating the environmental impacts associated with a proposed action. For EISs, the NEPA regulations require a brief statement of the underlying purpose and need to which the agency is responding (40 CFR § 1502.13). This crucial statement allows a reviewer to consider and suggest whether there might be other reasonable courses of action to accomplish this purpose and need.

In siting a project, for example, environmental impacts might be avoided or otherwise mitigated by relocating the project to a different site or by redesigning the site plan to use a smaller portion of the site. Generally speaking, an alternative course of action reflects a different approach to meeting the proposal's objectives, while alternative courses of action, including the proposal (other than no action), will each have mitigation measures associated with them as well. The NEPA regulations do not require a rigorous classification; they require rigorous thinking about how to accomplish a proposal's objectives in a way that avoids or otherwise mitigates environmental harm.

The three principal tensions in developing reasonable alternative courses of action pertain to the relationship to the proposed action, the number of alternatives, and the timing of the NEPA process. The NEPA regulations help create a framework for thinking about these issues but are largely silent about how to resolve them.

The NEPA regulations intentionally use the phrase "alternatives including the proposed action" and require that a preferred alternative be identified in a draft EIS only if one exists (a preferred alternative must be identified in a final EIS so that it can be used to make a final decision) (40 CFR § 1502.14). By using the term "including," the regulations make clear that even if an agency has a proposed action, it must be considered as one of several alternative courses of action. A further intention of these provisions is to allow an agency to propose more than one course of action to meet the identified purpose and need, rather than force an agency to develop one "proposal" and a set of "alternatives" to it.

As environmental planning and data have become more sophisticated and NEPA review more routine, the number of potential alternatives has often multiplied, while at the same time the number of serious alternatives that emerge from the scoping process have become fewer. This phenomenon tends to occur because many bad ideas and dead ends are eliminated during the scoping process, as well as the fact that limited resources have been focused on improving the agency's preferred option.

Although it has become a rule of thumb that environmental documents should contain three alternatives, including no action, to be found adequate, the best environmental documents have resulted from a serious effort to include the public in an influential way early and often. In a good NEPA process, the result ironically is that many of the alternative courses of action are screened out during the process. The public usually urges the agency to focus energies on resolving issues if a preferred alternative has emerged that has broad appeal. In this situation, the document and written analysis of alternatives appropriately become a summary of what has been considered rather than a substantive analysis of courses of action. The alternatives analysis remains valuable to document accountability and to allow reconsideration of alternatives.

Impacts

The three types of impacts are direct, indirect, and cumulative. Each of these types of impacts has short- and long-term implications, which also need to be considered where the consequences are likely to be relevant. Three concepts in the regulations are worth special emphasis:

1. By defining "effect" and "impact" as synonymous, the NEPA regulations use the term "impact" to mean a consequence. In other words—and this point cannot be overemphasized—the definition of the term "effect" was not intended to define which effects are "environmental." The term "effect" must be read with the term "human environment" to understand which "environmental impacts" NEPA covers.
2. The regulations use the term "indirect" impacts, rather than "secondary" impacts, to convey the idea of a range or continuum of impacts, from immediate on-site effects to consequences that are deserving of consideration but are not "remote or speculative." Indirect impacts can occur off-site, such as downwind or downstream of a site, or on-site, such as cross-media impacts. Indirect impacts can also occur later in time, whether as a consequence of construction methods, during a project's operation, or after a facility's closure.

3. The regulations emphasize that the analysis be organized in whatever fashion will help decision makers and the public think about the impacts, discussing or focusing on the most important environmental impacts and choices (40 CFR §§ 1502.2 and 1502.16). There is no requirement to label an "impact" as direct, indirect, cumulative, short term, or long term. The NEPA regulations did not intend for any environmental impact study to be found defective on this basis.

MITIGATION CONCEPTS

Few words can compete with "mitigation" as a term that takes on a life of its own. Historically, the term had a positive connotation among fish, wildlife, and natural resource agencies, who struggled for decades to get legislatures, engineers, and public and private corporations to modify projects and expand monetary resources allocated to fish and wildlife conservation efforts. However, as government regulation and the awareness of widespread degradation of natural systems increased, mitigation gained a negative connotation.

On one side of the ledger, project proponents perceived mitigation measures as amenities which agencies or citizens sought that were unrelated to actual project impacts. They felt they were being blackmailed for project approvals. On the other side of the ledger, citizen groups perceived mitigation measures as tokens to development which were used by permitting agencies without really accounting for a project's impacts.

The NEPA regulations were drafted just as these polar perceptions were building. As a first important step in bringing a set of objective criteria to bear, the NEPA regulations introduced a widely accepted uniform definition of mitigation (40 CFR § 1508.20). Several features of this definition warrant attention, given the continued misconceptions about mitigation.

Mitigation includes "avoidance" of environmental harm, which is a basic tool for meeting NEPA's goals. Contrary to popular opinion, mitigation and avoidance are not separate or opposite terms. In fact, avoiding an impact is the first concept mentioned in the definition of mitigation. Although avoidance implies refraining from an action, avoidance can result in taking positive actions, often at lower monetary cost. For example, avoidance is the cornerstone of pollution prevention and source control, as well as an implicit element of sustainability.

Two elements of mitigation—minimizing impacts by limiting an action and rectifying impacts by restoring the affected environment—provide familiar tools. A fourth element of mitigation—reducing or eliminating an impact over time by preservation and maintenance operations during the life of an action—adds an important dimension relative to time, cost, uncertainty, and the effectiveness of mitigation measures. Decisions on proposals and the effectiveness of mitigation measures often involve uncertainty. Increasingly, mitigation measures require budgets for operation and maintenance activities such as monitoring and adaptive management, so that actual mitigation actions respond to actual environmental conditions rather than to assumptions or predictions. Although implied, some states, such as Washington, have expressly added "monitoring and taking appropriate corrective actions" as an element of the definition of mitigation.

Compensating for the impact by replacing or providing substitute resources or environments has been the most controversial element of mitigation, because it acknowledges that some impacts cannot be avoided and the affected environment cannot be rehabilitated. Since NEPA requires that significant adverse unavoidable impacts on long-term environmental productivity be disclosed, it makes sense to consider mitigation measures for these impacts. Unfortunately, of all of the elements of mitigation, compensation most easily lends itself to the twin abuses of regulatory "blackmail" and "bribery."

Compensatory mitigation has become especially controversial in the context of habitat destruction or filling of wetlands. Even where a project proponent would purchase and preserve another area that might otherwise be affected by development, concern remains that irreplaceable resources would be lost. A similar concern is that constructed wetlands or habitats may not prove successful or provide timely and sufficient functional values compared with the ecosystems being destroyed or replaced.

Consequently, the Environmental Protection Agency and the Army Corps of Engineers have adopted guidelines under Section 404(b) of the federal Clean Water Act that interpret the elements of mitigation defined by the NEPA regulations in a hierarchy, where compensatory mitigation is considered if avoidance, minimization, and restoration are not "practicable." Although this approach is consistent with the NEPA regulations, because of the critical environmental resource involved it would be a mistake to interpret the NEPA regulations as mandating a hierarchical approach in other contexts.

The NEPA regulations intentionally refrained from establishing a hierarchy of mitigation elements, given the wide diversity of proposed actions and types of impacts to which NEPA review applies. In practice, a serious application of NEPA policies will usually result in greater weight being given to non-compensatory mitigation approaches. Nonetheless, the NEPA regulations recognize that society will continue to change the face of the earth and that providing substitute resources or environments may be an appropriate way to mitigate certain environmental impacts.

A strict application of the hierarchy may actually defeat the overall environmental quality goals expressed by NEPA and other laws. For example, the greater the emphasis placed on watershed and ecosystem management or other areawide or regional planning efforts to sustain natural systems and human communities, the more appropriate that a higher priority be given to compensatory mitigation approaches. With good community-based planning and provisions for adaptive management and accountability, resources can be invested in preserving, restoring, enhancing, or increasing important habitat areas and functional values in an ecosystem, rather than piecemeal preservation of isolated or degraded remnants (assuming they do not have important functional values).

Another frequent area of confusion is whether mitigation measures are included within the proposal or are in addition to the proposal. The regulations expect that mitigation measures will typically be part of a proposal. In addition, reasonable mitigation measures that are not part of the proposed action must still be considered, as is apparent from the phrase "include appropriate mitigation measures not already included in the proposed action or alternatives" (40 CFR § 1502.14(f)).

Under the NEPA regulations, mitigation measures can be included at the outset in the description of the proposal, including the description of alternative courses of action. The NEPA regulations did not intend to penalize proponents for building mitigation measures into their proposals. On the contrary, the NEPA regulations are intended to encourage early or preliminary identification of potential adverse impacts and alternative approaches to a proposal to avoid or otherwise mitigate impacts (the following section in this chapter addresses "mitigated findings of no significant impact" or "mitigated FONSIs").

By definition, mitigation changes the environmental effects of a proposal. Mitigation is therefore proper to consider in deciding whether a proposal will have a significant environmental effect that requires preparation of detailed studies in an EIS (40 CFR § 1500.5(1)). It should not matter whether the mitigation was initially proposed or evolved in the EA or early planning process. In addition, if a reasonable range of mitigation measures is not already included in the description of the proposal and alternative courses of action, alternative or additional mitigation measures need to be identified through the impact assessment process (40 CFR § 1508.25(b)(3)). Most importantly, the NEPA regulations require mitigation measures to be considered in the evaluation and comparison of alternatives and in the final decision on a proposal, thus resulting in a public document which clearly states any mitigation commitments and monitoring that will be implemented (40 CFR § 1505.2(c) and 1505.3).

A persistent source of confusion about mitigation has been whether mitigation measures identified in NEPA documents are enforceable commitments. Are mitigation measures discussed in environmental impact analyses simply proposed for consideration, or have commitments been made to carry out the measures? The NEPA regulations embody three general rules to answer this question:

1. *Agency decision document*—NEPA documents are generally used to inform agency decisions on underlying governmental actions on a proposal. Since the final decision on mitigation measures usually occurs as part of the agency's decision on a proposal, the agency's NEPA Record of Decision or other decision document (such as a permit) on the proposal is generally the operative, enforceable document for identifying mitigation commitments, rather than the environmental studies. The agency's decision document can simply reference the NEPA document or relevant portions of it, such as an appendix listing the mitigation measures.

2. *Inclusion in proposal*—For many public and private proposals, however, the NEPA document is the only document that contains a relatively complete description of the proposed action. If the mitigation measures are already included in the description of a proposed action that is ultimately approved, the agency will have relied on this description in making a decision on the proposal, in contrast to alternative courses of action. Generally speaking, conditions listed in permits or other decision documents do not repeat the detailed description of a proposal, but rather address special provisions developed as a result of the agency and public review process. Any mitigation measures already included in the description of the proposed action were intended to be viewed as definite commitments, unless revised in the course of the environmental review and decision-making process. A substantial departure from implementing these elements would also open the door to supplemental environmental review, because the failure to carry out mitigation inherent in the proposal would represent new information and a substantial change in the action (40 CFR § 1502.9(c)).

3. *Plain language of NEPA document*—The NEPA regulations put unusual emphasis on writing clearly and in plain English. Generally, verbs such as "will" and

"would" represent mitigation commitments, while words such as "might," "could," and "should" represent mitigation measures that are under consideration but have not been adopted. As noted above, however, where a mitigation measure is not part of the description of the proposed action in an EA (or preferred alternative in a final EIS), one cannot assume the measure represents a commitment unless it is stated or referenced in the agency's final decision document or NEPA Record of Decision.

MITIGATED FONSIs AND THRESHOLD DETERMINATIONS

Use of Mitigated FONSIs

The NEPA regulations were written such that agencies were expected to: (1) design or revise proposed actions to incorporate mitigation measures based on initial EAs and any interagency or public review and (2) issue a finding of no significant impact (FONSI) if the proposed action would not have any significant environmental impacts, taking into account mitigation measures that will be implemented. The fact that a proposal could be designed or revised in the early planning process so that the proposal would not cause significant impacts reflects the profound success of NEPA, similar to today's emphasis on pollution prevention.

The NEPA regulations plainly require agencies to use a FONSI "when an action not otherwise (categorically) excluded will not have a significant effect on the human environment" (40 CFR 1508.13).

Given the premise behind the NEPA regulations that better decisions, not more paperwork, are what counts, improved guidance on how to use mitigated FONSIs and ensure public accountability would be valuable in furthering NEPA's goals and integrating the NEPA process with agency planning and permitting procedures.

The Intended and Changing Role of EAs

Because NEPA requires a "detailed statement" on proposals for major federal actions which significantly affect the quality of the human environment, the initial CEQ guidelines and subsequent NEPA regulations needed to invent a method for making the "threshold determination" of whether a proposal's impacts were likely to be significant enough to warrant preparation of a detailed statement (i.e., EIS).

The NEPA regulations provide a uniform framework for making this threshold determination, with substantial flexibility for the diverse activities of numerous federal agencies. Each agency is directed to adopt its own NEPA "implementing procedure" consistent with the NEPA regulations. Each agency's implementing procedure should identify agency actions that typically require EISs and those that do not ("categorical exclusions").

The remaining actions receive case-by-case review with an EA. Based on the impact analysis in an EA, an agency decides whether a proposal will have a "significant" environmental impact. If so, the agency proceeds to prepare an EIS focused on the significant impact or impacts, in order to assist the agency in making a decision on the proposal. If not, the agency issues a FONSI and proceeds to make a decision on the proposal. Public and interagency review is required in the EIS process and is often encouraged in the EA process (40 CFR §§ 1501.4(b) and 1506.6).

The NEPA regulations intend for every environmental review document to be properly scoped. EAs could range from a few pages to perhaps a few dozen pages if a proposal were designed or revised so that potentially significant impacts (identified in environmental studies supporting the EA) did not occur. EISs would likewise range from a few dozen pages if scoped to address one or two potentially significant impacts to a maximum of 150 pages for most proposals (and up to 300 pages for unusually complex proposals, including evaluation of alternative courses of action).

In practice, these intentions of the NEPA regulations have not been fulfilled. Instead, EIS preparation is often perceived and generally carried out as a multiyear study costing millions of dollars, which in turn has created strong incentives for agencies and applicants to avoid EISs. EAs have been prepared on many proposals that should otherwise have had focused EISs and public participation. Furthermore, because of the need for policy makers to develop policies, plans, and programs on a timely basis—whether to meet presidential, congressional, or judicial mandates or because of the limited tenure of any cabinet secretary or administration—the use of NEPA review in the development of non-project actions and agency strategic planning has been one of the major casualties.

At the same time, many EAs have grown in size to reduce the risk that the EAs and their accompanying FONSIs would be challenged or found inadequate. For many proposals, the "screening" role of the EA in making a threshold determination became a substitute for the EIS process. Rather than creating a continuum of environmental review with shorter, focused EA and EIS documents, the continuum for environmental documents on substantial proposals has been from large to larger documents. Agencies, tribes, non-governmental organizations, and members of the public have felt left out of the EA process, where public involvement may be omitted, and overwhelmed by the volume of paper when public involvement opportunities occur.

The NEPA regulations intend EAs to be used at any time in the NEPA process to assist agency planning and decision making (40 CFR § 1508.9(a)(2)). The uses can range from "thinking aloud" internally or with the public informally at the earliest stages of the planning process, to a conventional role in helping to make a threshold determination and to document the environmental review for proposals that do not have a significant impact, to use in analyzing or reporting monitoring or adaptive management results and the effectiveness of mitigation measures.

As the environmental impact assessment process has become more sophisticated, the EA can be the vital, flexible tool intended by the NEPA regulations. Accomplishing this goal will require that the various roles of the EA be expressly acknowledged by CEQ, that agency staff be retrained in the use of EAs, and that scoping and public and interagency review be used where appropriate, even if no EIS is involved.

EIS SIZE AND FORMAT

The NEPA regulations include a series of provisions intended to produce environmental review documents that focus on the most important environmental choices and that public and private decision makers and citizens would actually read. The provisions include scoping, format and length specifications, and other matters.

Scoping

The scoping process requires the EIS preparer to focus on the most important choices and consequences for environmental quality. This requirement is intended to force responsible officials to make preliminary decisions, to be tested by further agency and public review, regarding key issues and concerns.

Scoping can be misperceived as a specific early comment period and internal review, rather than an interactive thinking process with applicants, agencies, and the citizens to shape the scope and content of environmental analysis. Since the scope of an EIS continues to evolve in response to technical studies and public and agency consultation, the scoping process actually continues until the draft EIS is issued. The scoping process essentially recommences after the formal comment and consultation period ends with the draft EIS in that comments received must be responded to and the scope of the final EIS determined. Additional studies or analysis may be needed to prepare the final EIS, so that the thinking process of "scoping" is not concluded until the final EIS is issued.

When the scoping process is truly used as a thinking process—and when lead agency staff and applicants communicate with the public about their plans and intentions for the proposal, mitigation commitments, and the scope of any future environmental review and permitting—the process created by the NEPA regulations has proven remarkably successful in educating agencies and citizens and creating a constructive climate for identifying and discussing the key issues.

Format and Content

Since the main purpose of an EIS is to help decision makers in their choice about the course of action that will best further NEPA's policies (which includes coordination with other national policies), the NEPA regulations logically require: (1) a summary that highlights environmental choices, major conclusions, and areas of controversy and (2) the first major section in the EIS to be a comparative evaluation of the alternatives. In addition, EISs are required to state how the alternatives and decisions to be made will or will not achieve the substantive policies of Sections 101 of NEPA and other environmental laws (40 CFR § 1502.2(d)).

Many EISs do not yet comply with these basic requirements. For example, they treat the summary simply as an annotated table of contents and devote the first major section to describing the alternatives rather than to comparing their key impacts. Few EISs compare the alternatives with each other on the basis of NEPA's substantive goals, such as pollution prevention, sustainable development, or biological diversity.

The NEPA regulations intend to achieve several practical purposes by placing a concise comparative evaluation of alternatives at the beginning of the EIS. The reader gets the message early on that the EIS is about making choices.

A primary purpose of an EIS is to document that actual and appropriate consideration has been given to important environmental values in the decision process. Numerous sections of the NEPA regulations underscore the importance of focusing on the major issues and real choices facing decision makers and excluding less important matters from detailed study. Other provisions require that technical and background materials developed during the environmental review process be appended or referenced but not presented in the body of an EIS (40 CFR § 1502).

When the NEPA regulations require EISs to be "analytic rather than encyclopedic," the regulations are demanding that EIS writers synthesize extensive background information and use this information to evaluate the most significant aspects of how the proposal, including alternatives, will sustain or impair long-term environmental productivity, highlighting in comparative form the most important choices facing decision makers.

The synthesis and comparative evaluation are typically rushed at the end of the EIS preparation process. Some of the reasons include time pressures and perfunctory EIS preparation assigned to agency staff or consultants who are often not brought into the thinking processes of agency staff members actually developing or reviewing a proposal (who may be separate from the agency's environmental review staff). The result may be a standard executive summary and list of impacts, perhaps in comparative form; however, neither may serve the purposes set forth in the NEPA regulations (40 CFR §§ 1500.1, 1502.1, and 1502.2).

Length of EISs

The NEPA regulations require that "statements shall be concise, clear, and to the point, supported by evidence that the agency has made the necessary environmental analyses" (40 CFR § 1502.1). When Congress required a "detailed statement" in NEPA, legislators were familiar with committee reports prepared on major pieces of legislation that might run tens, not hundreds, of pages. A quarter century of judicial review under NEPA has demonstrated that EISs are not found inadequate because impact analysis is located in properly referenced and readily available technical reports or appendices.

A focused and brief EIS, as originally intended by the NEPA and its regulations, should be no longer than a detailed briefing memo to a cabinet secretary on a major policy design. At the same time, it is essential that agencies, members of the public, and judges be able to review a coherent, readable record of studies to support the comparative evaluation of significant issues in a short EIS. The EIS would need to be backed up by an annotated "user-friendly" guide to the numerous technical studies supporting the analysis, and these appendices would need to be easily available for review during comment periods.

Time Limits and Cooperating Agencies

The ability to set time limits for EIS preparation and the provision for cooperating agencies represent two important tools in the NEPA regulations that have not typically been used in practice (40 CFR §§ 1501.6 and 1501.7). These options are intended to be used in conjunction with scoping and other tools for reducing paperwork and delay listed in Sections 1500.4 and 1500.5 of the NEPA regulations.

Because these two provisions involve dedication of limited agency resources, lead agencies are reluctant to set time limits, and other agencies are reluctant to accept the responsibilities of cooperating agencies. Although agencies such as the Environmental Protection Agency and the Army Corps of Engineers have shown a willingness to participate, natural resource agencies whose involvement is often the most crucial, such as the Fish and Wildlife Service, have been reluctant. These provisions have worked successfully where several agencies have common interests or where substantial political pressure has been brought to ensure interagency coordination.

Overcoming Non-Compliance

Although the NEPA process continues to work effectively in many instances to open up agency review processes, the intent of the NEPA regulations to shrink EIS size and improve the format and content has had limited success. There are practical reasons for these shortcomings, and they provide important lessons. For example, agency staff responsible for NEPA compliance tend to be subject to the following limitations:

1. A system that penalizes failure more than rewarding success, thereby creating incentives to treat EIS adequacy, rather than usefulness, as the primary goal. This problem includes the production of documents on a predetermined schedule and budget that does not account for a dynamic scoping process, thus minimizing spirited public discussion and adhering to the tradition of basically copying the last similar EIS that was not found inadequate.
2. Use of the NEPA process as a paperwork exercise for decisions already made, thereby removing any incentive for the agency to do a thoughtful job of environmental review.
3. Lack of authority to make commitments for more senior decision makers, thereby giving inadequate direction or supervision to the consulting firms preparing EISs (many EISs are prepared by private consulting firms under the immediate direction of agency staff who are not the key decision makers).
4. Lack of knowledge of the NEPA regulations and their intent, thereby failing to use either the proper or the flexible tools provided by the regulations.
5. Lack of priority and resources for EIS preparation, which is often perceived in agencies and consulting firms as an unpleasant job, thereby ironically preventing responsible agency staff from putting in the time and effort needed to achieve a faster and better NEPA process.
6. Lack of explicit legal protection from CEQ (and support from EPA in its review of individual draft EISs) for taking risks to shorten EISs and carry out NEPA as intended by the NEPA regulations.

INTEGRATION WITH OTHER ENVIRONMENTAL LAWS AND PUBLIC PARTICIPATION

Over the past 25 years, the United States has created a substantial body of environmental law at the federal and local level. Many of these laws and their implementing regulations contain standards for the use or modification of the environment or require various environmental studies to be prepared for planning, permitting, or other decisions. Many have also required the preparation of plans for protecting or managing land and natural resources. Most require some degree of public involvement.

NEPA works well when environmental thinking and acting across the full range of environmental values occur as part of an agency's normal planning and decision process and its compliance with other environmental laws, including involving the public in its decision making. NEPA's role lies primarily in focusing on the gaps and overlaps amid this profusion of environmental plans and requirements, as discussed earlier, where it can fulfill a vital need to help achieve coordination.

The NEPA regulations emphasize and provide numerous incentives for integrating environmental review under NEPA with these other processes, starting from its basic policy directives (see, for example, 40 CFR §§ 1500.1, 1500.2, 1501.1, 1501.2, 1502.1, and 1502.2). The NEPA regulations also suggest many specific tools for achieving efficient integration, such as the use of scoping and tiering, combining or preparing environmental studies under NEPA and other laws concurrently, analyzing consistency with NEPA's policies and other laws together, combining documents under NEPA and other laws, and combining public participation under NEPA and other laws.

Integration through tiering has become especially important as federal, state, and local watershed and land management plans, transportation plans, and other areawide plans are prepared. When existing plans, regulations, rules, or laws provide environmental analysis and measures that avoid or otherwise mitigate the probable specific adverse environmental impacts of proposed actions, the NEPA regulations intend for these requirements to be integrated with, as opposed to duplicated by, subsequent environmental review under NEPA.

Although tiering (and the scoping of subsequent proposed actions) provides an important regulatory tool, it also enables project-level review to be more focused rather than eliminated. Proposed projects should continue to receive integrated environmental review in order to: (1) review and document consistency with adopted plans and regulations; (2) provide prompt and coordinated review by agencies, tribes, and the public on compliance with applicable environmental laws and plans, including mitigation for site-specific project impacts that have not been considered and addressed at the plan or regulation level; and (3) ensure accountability by government to applicants and the public for requiring and implementing mitigation measures.

RECORD OF DECISION AND ACCOUNTABILITY

The NEPA regulations require a Record of Decision when EISs are prepared (40 CFR § 1505.2). Since EISs are prepared on relatively few federal actions, this requirement has not resulted in integrating accountability for agency decisions with the vast majority of the environmental review documents prepared, except for agencies such as the Army Corps of Engineers, the Forest Service, or some agencies of the Department of Transportation, which have essentially combined their environmental impact assessment and permitting or grant programs.

More importantly, the NEPA regulations contain a key provision requiring agency accountability for the implementation of mitigation measures regardless of whether an

EIS has been prepared (40 CFR § 1505.3). As few agency implementing procedures have established more specific or standard protocols for implementing this provision, however, it may be time to revise the NEPA regulations or provide further guidance on compliance with this provision.

AN UNFINISHED AGENDA

The NEPA regulations have proven to be an unusually workable and durable set of federal rules. However, in conclusion, some of the unfinished agenda items or current issues related to the NEPA regulations include:

1. ***NEPA as more than a hurdle in the project approval process***—NEPA's niche in the authorization and permitting process for public and private projects is fairly well established, but there is substantial skepticism that NEPA can be reinvigorated to its intended broader role, at least in the near future. Although the courts have been blamed for many of the problems, they have in fact focused more on the quality than the quantity or format of the analysis. Any major change in how NEPA is used will require a dramatic retraining and reeducation effort, changing the perception of NEPA by senior officials, consultants, and the public, and greater legal support and protection in the NEPA regulations.
2. ***Use of NEPA early on for strategic planning***—NEPA analysis (often misunderstood to mean formal NEPA documents, such as EAs and EISs) generally occurs later than desirable or required. This is not likely to change without direction from senior agency officials, who are understandably reluctant to use NEPA because the standard EA/EIS process is not well designed for strategic planning or policy analyses. Although there are some federal models, such as the idea behind the legislative EIS, it is unlikely that sufficient consensus on regulatory changes to encourage early and creative use of environmental analysis under NEPA could be developed without demonstration or pilot projects mutually developed by key agencies and CEQ.
3. ***NEPA's role in emerging issues***—With the proliferation of environmental agencies, laws, and programs in the 25 years since NEPA's enactment, NEPA's comprehensive and balanced perspective and its coordination role could have been expected to serve a principal organizing role or focus for federal environmental activities. This is clearly the role anticipated both for NEPA and for CEQ by Executive Order 11514. Instead, agency turf has balkanized environmental and natural resources policy, law, and implementation. Although the NEPA regulations allow this role for ongoing domestic and global issues—such as pollution prevention, sustainability, biological diversity, environmental justice, ecosystem management, and so on—the question is whether different agency programs will continue to dominate and provide separate vehicles for addressing these subjects in the near future, or whether it is possible or desirable for the perception and practice of NEPA and the environmental impact assessment process to be changed in dramatic ways to meet these needs.

THE UNFINISHED BUSINESS OF NATIONAL ENVIRONMENTAL POLICY

6

R.N.L. Andrews

T he National Environmental Policy Act (NEPA), signed on New Year's Day 1970, marked the beginning of the "environmental era" in U.S. governance and policy. Twenty-five years later, its brief text remains unchanged by any significant amendment, and it has been imitated by over half the state governments, by over 80 other national governments, by regional economic institutions such as the European Union, and by international lending institutions such as the World Bank and Asian Development Bank. Its "impact statement" mechanism has also been widely emulated by advocates of other decision considerations; examples include "impact statements" for inflation, communities, economics, "regulatory flexibility" (small businesses), regulatory "takings," "family values," litigation, risks, and others.

In Chapter 3, Lynton Caldwell provides a detailed review of the law's history and intent and a knowledgeable perspective on its implementation to date. This chapter addresses two different points. The first is NEPA's significance as an administrative reform statute, a profoundly influential innovation in the processes by which administrative decisions are developed and made. The second is the unfinished business of creating a substantive national environmental policy for the United States, building on and going beyond the foundation laid in NEPA's Section 101.

CONTEXT

As Caldwell reminds us in Chapter 3, the authors of NEPA envisioned the law as a combination of three interdependent elements forming a coherent whole: (1) a substantive policy statement, applicable to all agencies of the federal government; (2) a series of "action-forcing provisions," most notably (but not exclusively) the requirement of "detailed statements" of environmental impacts and alternatives, to force implementation of the policy on an action-by-action basis; and (3) an organizational champion, the Council on Environmental Quality (CEQ), to oversee and report on the policy's implementation, to advise the president, and to lay the groundwork for new initiatives on the national agenda. Measured against this vision, Caldwell rightly laments the widespread preoccupation with the environmental impact statement (EIS) per se, the equally widespread inattention to the law's policy statement, and particularly the conversion of CEQ from an ongoing institutional force to an empty shell or to a personal staff of a particular president or vice president.

NEPA has an equally important history, however, as an administrative reform initiative, an innovative strategy to alter widespread and entrenched patterns of U.S. administrative decision making. One element of this initiative was the attempt to change all agencies' substantive responsibility without amending each one's authorizing statute one at a time. A second element, and the focus of what follows, was the attempt to compel implementation through the creation of new documentation requirements, which would formally open each major decision to review and challenge on environmental grounds by higher officials in the decision chain, by other agencies, by opponents outside government, and by the courts.

With or without a formal policy statement such as NEPA, a nation's actual national environmental policy is not merely what the government says its policy is, but the totality of the environmental consequences of its actions, some protecting and managing it, others promoting natural resource extraction and pollution, and still others rearranging and transforming it for human purposes. In the United States today, this total represents a historically uncoordinated patchwork of actions by many agencies, each authorized by separate statutes to pursue specific and sometimes conflicting missions affecting the environment. National environmental policy is not and cannot be made, therefore, by any one agency such as the Environmental Protection Agency (EPA), or even by a single Department of the Environment if such were created. It is made at least as much by the actions of the Departments of Agriculture, the Interior, Defense, Energy, Housing, and Transportation; by Justice Department decisions on environmental enforcement and prosecution priorities; and by others, such as State Department and U.S. Trade Representative decisions on foreign trade negotiations.

Much of this pattern originated with the agencies' roots in the Progressive philosophy of governance, introduced at the federal level by President Theodore Roosevelt at the turn of the century. The Progressive philosophy held that, among other things, many essential services from the natural environment can be provided more efficiently by government than by private entrepreneurs alone (for instance, transportation and water resource infrastructures, multiple-purpose management of water and forest resources, and others), to serve an overall goal of the general public interest; and that the functions of government should therefore be carried out by delegating substantial discretionary authority to administrative agencies staffed by non-political technical professionals rather than by detailed legislative micromanagement or by political patronage appointees (Pinchot, 1967; Hays, 1969).

Three important consequences resulted from the implementation of this philosophy. One was a proliferation of separate agencies, each authorized to pursue specific, technically defined, and often conflicting missions for the use of the environment and its resources. Examples included the Bureau of Reclamation (created 1902), the Forest Service (1905), the Public Health Service (1912), the National Park Service (1916), the Federal Power Commission (1920), the Tennessee Valley Authority (1933), the Grazing Service (1934), the Soil Conservation Service (1935), the Bureau of Land Management (1946), and the Atomic Energy Commission (1946). Other preexisting agencies were given additional but still narrowly defined missions: a leading example is the Army Corps of Engineers, whose mission was successively expanded from navigation and flood control to include municipal water supply, hydroelectric power, irrigation, water-based recreation, and other multiple uses of water.

Second, over time these agencies developed symbiotic alliances with particular client constituencies and congressional advocates who benefited from their missions, to ensure stable political support for their continuation and expansion. Even other federal and state agencies had little influence over these relationships. The water and highway agencies had close working relationships with their state counterparts, with their beneficiary constituencies, and with their political supporters in Congress, but other agencies, let alone other constituencies, had little or no influence or even advance knowledge of proposals that might affect their responsibilities.

Third, the Congress consistently undermined attempts to create an overall management capability within the executive branch to coordinate or integrate these agency mandates or even simply to resolve interagency conflicts. The most prominent example was the National Resources Planning Board, created by President Franklin Roosevelt under this and several other names but explicitly defunded by Congress in 1943. Virtually the sole exceptions were the creation of a Bureau of the Budget (1921, now Office of Management and Budget), a Council of Economic Advisors (1946), and the Executive Office of the President itself in 1946 (Graham, 1976).

Beginning not just with NEPA but as early as the 1940s and 1950s, this expansion of federal administrative discretion produced a growing array of opposition movements, academic critiques, and administrative reform initiatives. As early as 1954, a revitalized Sierra Club successfully challenged a federal water development proposal, Echo Park Dam, that would have backed water up into a protected national monument. By the late 1950s, scientists concerned about nuclear fallout were publicly confronting the discretionary power of the Atomic Energy Commission. Wilderness preservation groups in the 1950s challenged Forest Service logging practices and by 1964 secured legislation formally protecting wilderness areas from Forest Service discretion; and by the late 1960s, other groups were mobilizing to block federal projects of many kinds, particularly large-scale water development projects, interstate highway corridors through parks and urban neighborhoods, and federally licensed nuclear power plants (Sundquist, 1968; Richardson, 1973; Udall, 1994).

In the academic literature, a growing number of political scientists attacked the disparity between the Progressive ideal and the political reality of the agencies' behavior (Selznick, 1949; Maass, 1951; Foss, 1960; Morgan, 1965; McConnell, 1966). Others attacked the ideal itself, arguing on empirical grounds that political decisions tend to reflect not the interests of broad majorities but those of organized minorities with economic self-interests at stake (Olson, 1965), that administrative agencies tend to be "captured" by self-interested clients and congressional subcommittee members whose gains from their decisions are symbiotic to the agencies' needs for their political support and that agencies also tend to become advocates for their own organizational interests (Wildavsky, 1964), and that agencies become advocates for the individual and shared interests of their employees (Downs, 1957; Buchanan and Tullock, 1962). By the late 1960s, political theorists had developed a new consensus that the actions of government agencies did not demonstrably represent an overall "public interest" discovered and implemented by non-political expert administrators, as the Progressive philosophy had argued, but rather merely represented the political results of competing pressures and influences by organized interests both within and outside government—"interest group pluralism" (Lowi, 1969). In the pluralist view, the "overall public interest" therefore lay not in delegating discretionary authority to administrative elites, but in making them more accountable politically. The essential question was how best to do this.

One option was to radically narrow the fundamental principle of delegating discretionary authority to administrative agencies, by either requiring more explicit statutory standards for implementation or requiring statutory rather than administrative standard setting. Theodore Lowi advocated the former solution in an articulate critique written in 1969, which argued that "interest group liberalism" cannot plan, cannot achieve justice, and weakens democratic institutions by substituting informal bargaining for formal procedures. His "juridical democracy" proposed to invalidate all delegations of administrative discretion that were not accompanied by clear legislative standards for implementation (Lowi, 1969). The latter solution is reflected in several major environmental regulatory statutes, such as statutory air quality standards and statutory deadlines for EPA rule making. This solution is attractive to congressional staff and bureaucrat-bashers, but in practice it risks substituting even more rigidity (given the slowness and transaction costs of congressional action). It lodges power, in fact, not in the Congress as a whole but in self-interested subcommittee members and their staff, and it places on the Congress a set of demands for day-to-day technical decision making that that institution cannot effectively sustain (Andrews, 1993).

A second option was to continue delegating responsibility to administrators but compel them to justify their decisions more explicitly by science and economics (i.e., to articulate their definition of an "overall public interest" and its statutory basis and to defend the congruence of their decisions with it). Beginning in 1950, for instance, administrative guidance documents within the executive branch mandated benefit–cost analyses for all federal water development projects, based on language in the 1936 Flood Control Act, which limited federal water projects to those whose economic benefits exceeded their costs (U.S. Federal Interagency River Basin Committee, 1950; U.S. Bureau of the Budget, 1952; U.S. Senate, 1962; U.S. Water Resources Council, 1965). Unlike NEPA's environmental impact statements, however, these documents were mandated only by administrative guidelines and as such were enforceable only by presidential decisions and congressional appropriations and not by citizen challenges through the courts.[1]

Finally, a third option was to make administrative decision processes more transparently political, subject to judicially enforceable procedural requirements, and thus formally open not just to economic beneficiaries but to any affected interests that might organize themselves to participate. A series of laws and judicial precedents laid the foundation for this result. The Administrative Procedures Act of 1946 spelled out procedural standards for the Fifth Amendment's "due process" protections to constrain discretionary federal actions: burden of proof on the proponent of government action, notice and comment, public hearings, a reviewable record, substantial evidence, and judicial reversal of administrative actions that were judged arbitrary and capricious or beyond statutory authority (Administrative Conference of the United States, 1991). The Fish and Wildlife Coordination Act required the water resource development agencies to consult formally with the fish and wildlife conservation agencies, in order to minimize and mitigate impacts of their projects on fish and wildlife habitat (16 U.S.C. 661). The Freedom of Information Act required public disclosure of most government documents and decision rationales (excluding, however, most interagency communications, an exclusion that NEPA removed with respect to interagency comments on environmental impact statements [EISs]) (5 U.S.C. 552 et. seq).

Civil rights challenges to the licenses of segregationist radio stations in the 1960s produced broader changes in judicial doctrines of "standing to sue," allowing lawsuits on non-economic grounds. The result was the formation of numerous "public interest environmental law" organizations (Environmental Defense Fund, Natural Resources Defense Council, and Sierra Club Legal Defense Fund, among others) and a revolution—beginning in 1967 with *Storm King v. Federal Power Commission*—in the use of litigative tactics to challenge administrative decisions on environmental grounds. Several new environmental statutes even included provisions specifically permitting citizen suits to compel or challenge agencies' actions. These tactics were a radical departure from the strategies of more traditional conservation and preservation advocacy groups, which relied on lobbying and publicity rather than lawsuits or administrative reform challenges to influence Congress and the agencies. They represented an equally radical shift in American doctrines of governance, from ostensibly non-political administrative discretion to openly political administrative decision processes (Stewart, 1975).

NEPA AS ADMINISTRATIVE REFORM

NEPA was an important new contribution to these administrative reforms, enacted at a moment when political sentiment was both demanding a more activist role of government in protecting the environment and simultaneously attacking the agencies for promoting large-scale environmental transformation by construction projects. The "impact statement" device in particular was a distinctive innovation in administrative reform, even in comparison with the initial vision of its authors. The Senate bill had envisioned it simply as an additional "finding" by the responsible official concerning the anticipated environmental effects of the recommended action. Better actions, it assumed, would result from better ecological information documented within the normal decision process. In the Senate–House Conference version, however, new Senate language was inserted, redefining it as a "detailed statement" requiring explicit discussion of alternatives to the proposed action as well as their environmental impacts, mandating interagency consultation and review of the statements, and mandating public review and comment both of the statements and of the other agencies' comments on them (though exempting, at Senator Muskie's insistence, environmental protection regulatory actions from the requirement) (Andrews, 1976a).[2]

The effect of these changes was that the detailed EIS statement proved to be not a single action-forcing mechanism but rather the pivotal document of three such mechanisms: internal review, interagency comment, and public disclosure with consequent vulnerability to court challenge (Andrews, 1976b). Each had important effects. The first forced the consideration of new questions in project planning, required explicit consideration of environmentally preferable alternatives, led to hiring of environmental staff experts, and provided a new warning signal for potential controversies. The second forced coordination with all other agencies, federal, state, and local, whose missions might be impacted by a proposal. The third opened access to all potential stakeholders, rather than just client constituencies, accompanied by the threats of adverse publicity, political protest, and litigation. Valuable as the original proposed mechanism may have been, the second and third were more original and had far greater impacts. In effect, the EIS device combined the second and third strategies for increasing administrative accountability: documentation requirements and opening up the administrative decision process.

The administrative consequence of the EIS procedure was to open all federal agencies' actions to advance scrutiny, input, and a credible threat of costly litigation or other delays by anyone, from a major corporation or national environmental advocacy group to a state agency or local neighbors of a proposed site, who considered themselves stakeholders in the environmental outcome. It therefore gave each agency a far stronger incentive to involve all potential constituencies early in the process and to take their concerns into account in developing decision proposals. Regulations issued by the CEQ in 1978 formalized this incentive by mandating a "scoping" process, to involve public comment not just on the statement itself but in defining the scope of the assessment at the outset (range of impacts, alternatives, and other information to be developed and considered).

In this effect, whatever its other consequences, NEPA significantly altered the procedures and politics of U.S. administrative governance. In its first nine years, agencies prepared more than 11,000 impact statements; just over 1,000 of these were subjected to litigation, and the courts issued injunctions—normally halting the action or requiring changes (at least in the statement) before proceeding—against about 20% of those sued. Since 1989, agencies each year have prepared approximately 50,000 "environmental assessments" (preliminary documents used to determine whether or not to prepare formal impact statements) and 400 to 500 formal impact statements (Smythe, 1994). Given the procedural nature of the requirement, it is not possible to determine its full substantive effects definitively, but a substantial literature documents its influence in decisions to halt some major actions, to modify others, and not even to propose still others that might otherwise have been initiated (cf. Caldwell notes in Chapter 3). Today, it is almost difficult to remind oneself that prior to NEPA, federal agencies had essentially no responsibility to consider the full range of alternatives to their proposals or the consequences of their actions other than the implementation of their own mission and its cost, that they were largely free to define that mission in ways that suited powerful economic beneficiaries rather than the full range of stakeholders in the outcome, and that even other federal and state agencies often had no advance warning or input to decisions of other agencies that might seriously affect their responsibilities (Hufschmidt, 1974).

Finally, in a tribute to its effectiveness as an administrative device, the EIS has since been widely emulated not only by over half the states, many foreign nations, and inter-

national organizations and lending institutions, but also by advocates of other considerations: economic impact statements, inflation impact statements, regulatory impact assessments, risk assessments, community and housing impact statements, "regulatory
flexibility statements" (small business impacts), and others. The combined effect of
such requirements, of course, amounts to a considerable added burden of documentation
and justification, notwithstanding the values of thorough analysis and open decision
processes.

LIMITATIONS

In the ways in which it came to be administered in practice, however, the EIS requirement came to have important limitations as a tool of both national environmental policy
and administrative reform. First, most of the statements are produced by just a handful
of agencies (80% by just five agencies, the Forest Service, the Bureau of Land Management, the Department of Housing and Urban Development, the Army Corps of Engineers, and the Federal Highway Administration), and the overwhelming majority are
rubber-stamped without further challenge. Second, many are largely prepared by outside
consultants as paperwork requirements rather than as an integral part of the agency's own
thought process. The same agencies still make the decisions, the same congressional
committees oversee and fund them, and the same beneficiary constituencies still lobby
both the agencies and the committees for federal support.[3] Third, in practice, the primary
influence of the EIS is on controversial actions rather than on those that may be most
damaging to the environment. Not all controversial actions cause serious environmental
damage, though many do (some simply have the best-organized opponents), and conversely, the most serious environmental threats do not always attract effective opponents
(it is easier to mobilize opposition to site-specific actions than to broader and more
pervasive policies; cf. Olson, 1965).

A more fundamental limitation of the EIS—again, as administered rather than necessarily in principle—has been the rarity of its influence on truly major federal decisions
at the policy, programmatic, and legislative levels. By and large, the EIS requirement has
been applied to specific projects and management plans, but not to the broader policies,
legislative initiatives, or appropriation bills that underlie them, even though these too are
federal actions and create far more pervasive environmental impacts. "Project Independence," for example, a presidential policy initiative in response to the Arab oil embargo
of the early 1970s, called for widespread actions to accelerate exploitation of U.S. fossil
fuel resources; yet, while individual actions implementing this policy might require EISs,
the underlying policy was never subjected to one. Other examples include agricultural,
logging, and mining subsidies; environmental regulatory decisions (the one specific
exemption in NEPA); other energy policy initiatives; U.S. positions in trade negotiations;
and many other fundamental policies affecting the environment (see, for example, Faeth
et al., 1989; Repetto and Gilles, 1988; McKenzie et al., 1992). These too would benefit
from the systematic assessment and interagency and public input required by the EIS
process, but in practice most have not been subjected to it.

Finally, NEPA's EIS requirement is limited to proposed actions of the federal government. It does not address proposals that do not require federal action under existing

statutes, no matter how severely they may affect the environment; it neither authorizes nor compels federal agencies to propose additional actions to protect the environment; and it did not in any effective way force reconsideration of entrenched policy incentives that were already in effect.[4] It has little effect, therefore, on the cumulative effects of economic activity promoted by more fundamental patterns of public policy: combustion and energy use, agricultural production and land conversion, urban and suburban development and habitat destruction, coastal development and estuarine damage and other fragile ecosystems, and the impacts of trade policies. Cumulative loss of wildlife habitat, for example, was identified by a scientific committee of EPA's Science Advisory Board as one of the highest priority ecological risks facing the country and arguably, therefore, a central issue for national environmental policy, but NEPA has no influence on this issue except as it involves new action proposals on the federal lands (U.S. Environmental Protection Agency, 1990).

IMPLICATIONS

In effect, for environmental issues the EIS mechanism carries interest group pluralism to its most fully developed form, opening all administrative actions to what might be called "stakeholder democracy" (in contrast to elected representative governance, formal rule-based decision making, or the delegation of administrative discretion). NEPA is not the only instance of this shift. The introduction of negotiated decision making, in both siting and regulatory procedures, has similar implications (Fiorino, 1988).

Is this progress, regress, or merely, in some historically contingent way, incrementally better than what it replaced? It is arguably an improvement over the entrenched power of particular beneficiary constituencies wrapping their self-interests in the rhetoric of the "public interest." The old "iron triangles" are now more polycentric "issue networks," leaving administrative actions still heavily influenced by elites, but at least by elites representing a wider range of the interests and impacts involved (Heclo, 1978). However, it falls far short of coherent justification for what the long-term public interest really is in an environmental action proposal. Environmental advocacy groups, like business interests, can also be self-interested and shortsighted, especially in dealing with localized and site-specific proposals. It falls even farther short of philosopher John Rawls' seminal proposal that public policy decisions should be made as though behind a "veil of ignorance," in which we would decide as if we did not know how the results would affect us personally (male or female, rich or poor, black or white, living today or in the distant future) (Rawls, 1971).

Perhaps most fundamentally, the very approach to administrative reform that the EIS requirement exemplifies—the introduction of documentation requirements as an "action-forcing provision"—represents a trend that is both important and problematic. On the one hand, it greatly expands real access and accountability for those who seek to protect the environment, by providing a credible opportunity for challenge at the point of practical action. On the other hand, the cumulative results of this approach also include increased paperwork, stakeholder gridlock, and more external micromanagement of particular outcomes rather than correction of broad patterns of policy. By itself, this is not a national environmental policy: it is merely an important procedural weapon against specific proposals that are arguably at odds with such a policy.

The real task of defining and implementing a national environmental policy, in contrast, is hinted at in NEPA's policy statement, but still lies ahead. It is to this unfinished business that attention should now turn.

THE UNFINISHED BUSINESS OF NATIONAL ENVIRONMENTAL POLICY

What would a substantive national environmental policy include? NEPA itself provides a starting point: a declaration of policy to promote the general welfare, to maintain "productive harmony" between man and nature, and to fulfill the social, economic, and other requirements of present and future generations of Americans. It goes on to identify six implementing principles. Government agencies should strive to fulfill the responsibilities of each generation as trustee of the environment for succeeding generations; to assure for all Americans safe, healthful, productive, and aesthetically and culturally pleasing surroundings; to attain the widest range of beneficial uses of the environment without degradation, risk to health or safety, or other undesirable and unintended consequences; to preserve important historic, cultural, and natural aspects of our national heritage and maintain, where possible, an environment that supports diversity and variety of individual choice; to achieve a balance between population and resource use that will permit high standards of living and a wide sharing of life's amenities; and to enhance the quality of renewable resources and approach the maximum attainable recycling of depletable resources.

These principles by themselves, however, remain merely non-operational advice. They require unspecified trade-offs against other "essential considerations of national policy," and they contain no specific objectives, criteria, or benchmarks by which their achievement might be measured. The "action-forcing provisions" call for action-by-action consideration of these principles and for additional ecological research, but they too provide no clear substantive guidance.

Models for more operational statements of national environmental policy now exist. Several U.S. states, for instance, as well as several other countries, have now moved well beyond the U.S. federal government in this direction. Oregon, for instance, has defined a set of specific state "benchmarks"—operational objectives with specific criteria and deadlines for their achievement—for environmental as well as other state policy goals (Oregon Progress Board, 1991). North Carolina is conducting a similar process, incorporating explicit environmental benchmarks into a broader policy strategy for making the state more economically competitive. At least half a dozen states have now conducted formal "comparative risk assessments," using both technical experts and extensive public input to define the highest priority environmental hazards facing their states and to generate policy initiatives to reduce them (Minard and Jones, 1993).

An even stronger model is now available in the Netherlands, which recently produced explicit and detailed national environmental policies with operational targets for their achievement (Ministry of Housing, Physical Planning, and Environment, 1990; Bennett,

1991). The Dutch National Environmental Policy Plan is a 20-year strategic plan to be implemented jointly by the four primary environment-related ministries to achieve the essential elements of sustainable development. It states not only fundamental policy principles but also measurable objectives and benchmarks for simultaneously reducing emissions, using materials and energy more efficiently, and achieving high quality in both production processes and products in six basic sectors—agriculture, transport, industry, energy, building trades, and waste processing—with additional steps by research institutes, societal organizations, and consumers.

The fundamental difference between this national environmental policy and NEPA is that it sets measurable goals, not just general principles, grounded in a substantive vision of the environmental results it wishes to achieve, and it charges all agencies to take specific actions by explicit deadlines. It can be assumed that it too will face continuing political challenges and debate as the implementation deadlines approach, but the fact is that it has set such goals and directed its agencies to implement them. This is a major step beyond NEPA and is the real unfinished business that must be faced in the United States in order to build a real national environmental policy on the foundation NEPA has laid.

At the federal level, several recent initiatives offer steps toward a more explicit national environmental policy. One is the "sustainable development" agenda, which grew out of the 1987 report of the World Commission on Environment and Development (World Commission on Environment and Development, 1987) and the "Agenda 21" of the United Nations Conference on Environment and Development in 1992. President Clinton in 1993 appointed a President's Commission on Sustainable Development, which has so far produced additional discussion of policy principles for linking environmental protection, economic stability, equity, and empowerment but has not yet proposed specific objectives and progress measures.

A second initiative is a series of EPA actions by successive recent administrators to reassess and prioritize all its own programs on the basis of "comparative risk"; that is, to set policy priorities across EPA programs based on the best available judgments of which environmental problems are most serious. Subcommittees of EPA's Science Advisory Board, for instance, in 1990 identified a series of environmental hazards as producing the highest risks to human health and ecosystems: ambient air pollutants, worker exposure to chemicals, and pollution indoors and pollutants in drinking water (for health) and habitat alteration and destruction, species extinction and overall loss of biological diversity, stratospheric ozone depletion, and global climate change (for ecology and human welfare) (U.S. Environmental Protection Agency, 1987, 1990). The comparative risk assessment process does not by itself produce a national environmental policy—it does not include specific objectives or benchmarks for implementation, for instance, or essential guidance on trade-offs with other goals—but it does offer one clearly articulated set of substantive priorities as candidates for such a policy.[5]

A far more specific model is EPA's national environmental goals project, initiated in November 1993 (U.S. Environmental Protection Agency, 1994). This project's staff was charged to identify the specific environmental outcomes that EPA is seeking to achieve, to design goal-oriented strategies for achieving them, and to specify indicators for measuring progress toward them, based on broad public input as well as staff expertise. Once developed, it was to be used as a basis for goal-oriented budget and program priorities. Like the Oregon Benchmarks Study, this project sought to develop specific targets, benchmarks, and deadlines for achieving substantive environmental policy goals; for instance, "by the year xxx, at least yy percent of U.S. surface waters will fully meet state standards to protect aquatic life and human health," and "by the year 2000 we will reduce U.S. greenhouse gas emissions to 1990 levels." A draft five-year strategic plan issued in 1994 laid out the agency's long-range vision and guiding principles; a second edition was to be issued in 1995, incorporating the specific goals and a goal-based budget for fiscal year 1997. So far, this project has been strictly an EPA initiative and, importantly, lacks clear articulation of cost and other trade-offs, but it also provides a logical starting point for a broader, multiagency national environmental policy.

The key unfinished business of U.S. national environmental policy, in short, is to spell out at least the most fundamental substantive criteria for "conditions under which man and nature can exist in productive harmony" and to operationalize these in specific environmental results and benchmarks for their achievement, mandated to the agencies whose policies most directly affect them. It is time to get on with this task.

CONCLUSIONS

NEPA was significant both for its substantive statement of national environmental policy and as an administrative reform statute. In the name of broad environmental policy principles, the "action-forcing" EIS opened all agencies' actions both to interagency comment and to advance scrutiny, input, and a credible threat of challenge by anyone affected by the outcome. This innovation was both important and problematic. It greatly increased bureaucratic accountability for environmental consequences but also increased paperwork, stakeholder gridlock, and external micromanagement of particular outcomes rather than better policy. By itself, the EIS approach was not a national environmental policy but a procedural weapon against specific proposals that were at odds with such a policy.

The key unfinished business of U.S. national environmental policy is to spell out more explicit criteria for "conditions under which man and nature can exist in productive harmony" and to operationalize these in measurable benchmarks for all agencies whose policies affect them. Examples of such policies, while imperfect, now exist in the Netherlands, in some U.S. states, and in the EPA's national environmental goals project. The fundamental difference between these national environmental policies and NEPA is that they set operational goals and require measurable actions by all relevant agencies to achieve them. These models suggest key steps for implementing the vision NEPA articulated.

NOTES

1. It is somewhat ironic that environmental advocacy groups by and large were hostile not only to the agencies' self-interested distortions of benefit–cost analysis but to its use in principle, since it was itself an important administrative reform initiative aimed at challenging many of the same proposals that were politically motivated but economically as well as environmentally dubious. One probable explanation was the importance of other issues in which the two goals were not congruent; for instance, federal highway projects which were required by economic criteria to be

built on the least-cost corridor and alignment, which typically meant proposing them through parks and low-income neighborhoods. Several of the early NEPA lawsuits involved just such cases, such as the Overton Park case in Memphis.

2. One other change was made at the insistence of House conferees, changing Senate language that would have declared a "fundamental and inalienable right to a healthful environment" to a weaker statement that each person "should enjoy" such an environment, thus removing a possibility of litigation against the government to provide such an environment (Andrews, 1976a).

3. Note that a sizable majority of federal actions subject to the requirement are for approval of actions initiated outside the federal agency in the first place, such as permit and grant requests. The federal agency is ultimately responsible for the decision, and for consideration of its environmental impacts, but most of the project development documents—including but not limited to the environmental assessment underlying the EIS—are often prepared and submitted by the sponsors.

4. NEPA did require a one-time review by all agencies to identify any existing policies that prevented its implementation, but this elicited few substantive issues and in effect served only to foreclose subsequent legal claims that prior statutory missions prevented NEPA implementation.

5. EPA's use of an internal technical elite rather than a broader and more publicly accountable process for developing risk priorities has also been criticized (Hornstein, 1992), but this does not refute the need for a national environmental policy per se.

SELECTED REFERENCES

Administrative Conference of the United States. 1991. A Guide to Federal Agency Rulemaking, second edition. Washington, D.C.

Andrews, R. 1976a. *Environmental Policy and Administrative Change*. Lexington Books, Lexington, Massachusetts.

Andrews, R. 1976b. NEPA in Practice: Environmental Policy or Administrative Reform? *Environmental Law Reporter* 6:50001–50009.

Andrews, R. 1993. Long-Range Planning in Environmental and Health Regulatory Agencies. *Ecology Law Quarterly* 20(3):515–582.

Bennett, G. 1991. The History of the Dutch National Environmental Policy Plan. *Environment* 33(7):6–9, 31–33.

Buchanan, J. and G. Tullock. 1962. *The Calculus of Consent*. University of Michigan Press, Ann Arbor.

Downs, A. 1957. *An Economic Theory of Democracy*. Harper and Row, New York.

Faeth, P. et al. 1989. *Paying the Farm Bill: U.S. Agricultural Policy and the Transition to Sustainable Agriculture*. World Resources Institute, Washington, D.C.

Fiorino, D. 1988. Regulatory Negotiation as a Policy Process. *Public Administration Review* 46(July–August):764–772.

Foss, P. 1960. *Politics and Grass*. University of Washington Press, Seattle.

Graham, O. 1976. *Toward a Planned Society: From Roosevelt to Nixon*. Oxford University Press, New York.

Hays, S. 1969 [1959]. *Conservation and the Gospel of Efficiency*. Atheneum, New York.

Heclo, H. 1978. Issue Networks and the Executive Establishment. In *The New American Political System*. Anthony King, Ed. American Enterprise Institute, Washington, D.C., pp. 87–124.

Hornstein, D. 1992. Reclaiming Environmental Law: A Normative Critique of Comparative Risk Analysis. *Columbia Law Review* 92:562–633.

Hufschmidt, M. 1974. Environmental Statements and Water Resource Planning in North Carolina. Report No. 94. Water Resources Research Institute of the University of North Carolina, Raleigh.

Lowi, T. 1969. *The End of Liberalism*. W.W. Norton, New York.

Maass, A. 1951. *Muddy Waters: The Army Engineers and the Nation's Rivers*. Harvard University Press, Cambridge, Massachusetts.

McConnell, G. 1966. *Private Power and American Democracy*. Vintage Press, New York.

McKenzie, J. et al. 1992. *The Going Rate: What It Really Costs to Drive.* World Resources Institute, Washington, D.C.

Minard, R. and K. Jones with C. Paterson. 1993. *State Comparative Risk Projects: A Force for Change.* Northeast Center for Comparative Risk, South Royalton, Vermont.

Ministry of Housing, Physical Planning, and Environment. 1990. Highlights of the Dutch National Environmental Policy Plan. The Hague, The Netherlands.

Morgan, R. 1965. *Governing Soil Conservation: Thirty Years of the New Decentralization.* Johns Hopkins University Press, Baltimore.

Olson, M. 1965. *The Logic of Collective Action.* Harvard University Press, Cambridge, Massachusetts.

Oregon Progress Board. 1991. Oregon Benchmarks: Setting Measurable Standards for Progress. Report to the 1991 Oregon Legislature, Salem.

Pinchot, G. 1967 [1910]. *The Fight for Conservation.* University of Washington Press, Seattle.

Rawls, J. 1971. *A Theory of Justice.* Belknap Press of Harvard University Press, Cambridge, Massachusetts.

Repetto, R. and M. Gilles. 1988. *Public Policies and the Misuse of Forest Resources.* World Resources Institute, Washington, D.C.

Richardson, E. 1973. *Dams, Parks and Politics: Resource Development and Preservation in the Truman–Eisenhower Era.* University Press of Kentucky, Lexington.

Selznick, P. 1949. *TVA and the Grass Roots.* University of California Press, Berkeley.

Smythe, R. 1994. Renewing NEPA: NEPA Effectiveness Study. Potomac Resource Consultants, Chevy Chase, Maryland.

Stewart, R. 1975. The Reformation of American Administrative Law. *Harvard Law Review* 88:1667–1815.

Sundquist, J. 1968. *Politics and Policy; The Eisenhower, Kennedy and Johnson Years.* Brookings Institution, Washington, D.C.

Udall, S. 1994. *The Myths of August.* Pantheon, New York.

U.S. Bureau of the Budget. 1952. Budget Circular A-47, Washington, D.C.

U.S. Environmental Protection Agency. 1987. Unfinished Business. Office of Policy Analysis, Washington, D.C.

U.S. Environmental Protection Agency. 1990. Reducing Risk: Setting Priorities and Strategies for Environmental Protection. Report No. SAB-EC-90-021. Science Advisory Board, Washington, D.C.

U.S. Environmental Protection Agency. 1994. The New Generation of Environmental Protection. Draft. Washington, D.C.

U.S. Federal Interagency River Basin Committee. 1950. Subcommittee on Benefits and Costs. Proposed Practices for Economic Analysis of River Basin Projects ("Green Book"). Washington, D.C.

U.S. Senate. 1962. Policies, Standards, and Procedures in the Formulation, Evaluation and Review of Plans for Use and Development of Water and Related Land Resources. Senate Document 87-97. Washington, D.C.

U.S. Water Resources Council. 1965. Principles and Standards for Planning Water and Related Land Resources. Washington, D.C.

Wildavsky, A. 1964. *The Politics of the Budgetary Process.* Little, Brown, Boston.

World Commission on Environment and Development. 1987. *Our Common Future.* Oxford University Press, New York.

WHAT HAS NEPA WROUGHT ABROAD?

7

C. Wood

The National Environmental Policy Act (NEPA) has fathered not only a generation of "little NEPAs" within the United States but a burgeoning number of environmental impact assessment (EIA) systems all over the world. Some of these would be instantly acknowledged as NEPA progeny (for example, that in the Commonwealth of Australia), but U.S. EIA practitioners might have considerable difficulty in recognizing others (for example, that in New Zealand). On closer acquaintance, however, NEPA's parentage of all these EIA systems would be accepted without reservation. This chapter outlines the diffusion of EIA; the evolution of EIA in Canada, Australia and New Zealand, Europe, and the developing world; and analyzes the extent to which the essential elements of the NEPA process have been replicated or improved upon elsewhere.

EIA, as its fame has spread, has sometimes been seen as a panacea to environmental problems. It clearly is not, despite this belief in some developing countries. It is, however, necessary to establish the essential elements of NEPA and of the EIA process as it has been refined over the years. To simplify, these may be summarized as:

1. A statement of national environmental policy that anticipated the concept of sustainability
2. A central body or bodies responsible for EIA policy and system monitoring
3. A formal set of procedural EIA steps which includes the consideration of alternatives, screening, an environmental assessment, determining the coverage of the EIA (scoping), a draft environmental impact statement (EIS) usually prepared by the proponent, and a final EIS (but not impact monitoring) for most environmentally significant actions
4. Enforceability (through the courts)
5. Requirement of participation and consultation at several stages in the EIA process
6. Completion of the EIA process prior to the decision on the action being taken and formal consideration in it
7. Application to actions other than projects

DIFFUSION OF EIA

International attention was soon being directed to EIA as a result of the celebrated legal cases in the United States, which clarified NEPA's significance. The ramifications of NEPA were beginning to be accepted at a time of unprecedented interest in the environment, occasioned by the United Nations Conference on the Environment in Stockholm in 1972. The problems of burgeoning development, pollution, and destruction of the natural environment, which NEPA was intended to address, were perceived as universal. The rigorous project-by-project evaluation of significant impacts inherent in EIA was seized upon as a solution to many of these environmental problems by other jurisdictions, and elements of the U.S. EIA process were adopted by them. Most were, however, very cautious about importing NEPA-style litigation with EIA and made strenuous efforts to avoid doing so by integrating EIA within their national systems of government.

The methods of adoption varied; for example, cabinet resolutions, advisory procedures, regulations, and laws were employed. Probably the first overseas jurisdiction to declare an "extremely rudimentary environmental impact policy" (Fowler, 1982, p. 8) was the Australian state of New South Wales in January 1972. Canada, the Commonwealth of Australia, New Zealand, and France soon followed. While the first countries to adopt EIA were, like the United States, wealthy democracies, there was also considerable EIA activity in numerous Third World countries in the 1970s (Biswas and Agarwala, 1992). The diffusion of EIA has continued unabated.

Several international agencies have involved themselves with EIA. In 1974, the Organisation for Economic Co-operation and Development (OECD) recommended that member governments adopt EIA procedures and methods and, more recently, that they use EIA in the process of granting aid to developing countries (OECD, 1992). The United Nations Environment Programme (UNEP) has also made recommendations to member states regarding the establishment of EIA procedures and has established goals and principles for EIA. It subsequently issued guidance on EIA in developing countries (UNEP, 1988). Similarly (and somewhat belatedly), the World Bank ruled in 1989 that EIA should normally be undertaken by the borrower country under the bank's supervision and has prepared a sourcebook on EIA (World Bank, 1991).

This diffusion of EIA has resulted in a diverse vocabulary. In the Netherlands, EIA is known as MER (milieu-effectrapportage) and in Canada and the United Kingdom is known as environmental assessment. The EIS becomes an environmental statement in Britain; an environmental impact report under the original New Zealand provisions; and a consultative environmental review, a public environmental review, or an environmental review and management programme in Western Australia. The Commonwealth of Australia has both an EIS and a public environment report.

CANADA

It was inevitable that interest in NEPA should spill across the border from the United States to Canada. The Federal Environmental Assessment and Review Process (EARP) was established by a cabinet decision in December 1973. In 1984, these provisions for the environmental assessment of federal projects, programs, and activities were formalized in the Environmental Assessment and Review Process Guidelines Order (Government of Canada, 1984), which clarified the roles and responsibilities of the participants in the EARP procedures. The EARP guidelines were intended to be advisory, but following successful and highly publicized challenges in the courts by environmental groups in 1989, the 1984 Order-in-Council was held to be a law of general application.

EARP was administered by the Federal Environmental Assessment Review Office (FEARO), which has now been replaced by the Canadian Environmental Assessment Agency (CEA Agency). The CEA Agency is responsible for providing policy direction, procedural information, and periodic reports on environmental assessment (EA). It also provides the substantial secretariat for the reviews conducted by EA panels. These panels consist of three to seven independent members appointed by the Minister of the Environment for each referred proposal. The CEA Agency is also responsible for research on EA in Canada. Between 1984 and 1992, research was administered through a grant to the Canadian Environmental Assessment Research Council (CEARC).

The need for EARP reform had been widely recognized for some time, and the court cases emphasized the urgency for change and raised EA decision making to public prominence. Accordingly, the federal government introduced the Canadian Environmental Assessment Bill, which was given Royal Assent in June 1992 and proclaimed in force early in 1995.

The EA process under the Canadian Environmental Assessment Act (CEAA) bears many similarities to EARP but is much less discretionary. The 90-person, well-funded CEA Agency now has additional powers over the EA process. The CEAA system consists of two separate, sometimes successive procedures: the "self-directed assessment" and the "public review." Each of these procedures contains two assessment tracks, each with its own steps. The system allows for the vast majority of federally controlled projects to be dealt with as "screenings." A small number of projects are subject to "comprehensive study" and panel review and thus require an EIS. Notable positive features of the act are the provisions relating to cumulative environmental effects, the use of mediation, and follow-up provisions. Canada also has provisions for a participant funding program to help individuals and organizations to involve themselves in public reviews of projects (Wood, 1995).

The Canadian EA system delineated by CEAA fulfills many of the NEPA elements identified above. The main shortcomings are:

1. Lack of a statement of national environmental policy
2. Weakness of coverage (to federally controlled projects)
3. Marked distinction between likely effectiveness of screening and panel review procedures
4. Lack of centrality to decision making
5. Lack of a formal strategic EA requirement

On the other hand, while screening has been criticized (Gibson, 1992), EARP panel reviews have generally been seen as providing an excellent means of cooperatively identifying and mitigating the environmental effects of a handful of projects, partly as a result of intervenor funding.

How well CEAA works in practice will depend on the efforts and resourcefulness of the well-funded, 90-person CEA Agency and on the growing influence and expertise of environmental professionals within the responsible authorities and proponent organizations. Above all, however, as in the United States, the strength of the CEAA system depends upon the bedrock of public environmental concern and vigilance.

AUSTRALIA

By the early 1970s, it had become apparent that Australia's state-controlled land use planning systems, though stronger than those in the United States, lacked the power to prevent some of the worst excesses of development. The Commonwealth of Australia (Australia's federal government) recognized the need for stronger environmental control and looked with interest at the advantages of the U.S. federal EIA process. It announced an EIA policy in 1972 and the Environment Protection (Impact of Proposals) Act became law in 1974. Like NEPA, this act related only to federal activities (and not to those undertaken by state or local governments) and was independent of existing procedures. There was, however, quite deliberately far more discretion in the Australian Commonwealth system and, consequently, far less opportunity for resort to the courts than in the United States. All Australian states and territories have now passed legislation or set procedures in place to extend the scope of EIA to their own activities. Some, like Western Australia, have implemented EIA systems with significant features, such as impact monitoring (Wood and Bailey, 1994).

There have been various reviews of and amendments to the Commonwealth EIA system over its 21-year life (major reform is now imminent), and the EIA function of the Commonwealth has now been repositioned within a new Commonwealth Environment Protection Agency (EPA). The act now contains permissive powers for screening, for scoping, for the preparation of draft and final EISs, for consultation and participation, for assessment of the final EIS, for this assessment to be taken into account in decision making, for the provision of reasons for decisions, and for the holding of inquiries. There also exists a discretionary power to require monitoring of approved actions. EPA has a staff of about 30 to implement the requirements of the 1974 act, which applies to only a limited number of proposals in which the Commonwealth currently has a decision-making responsibility.

Rather like NEPA, the Impact of Proposals Act provides a legal framework that contains little procedural detail about the various stages of the EIA process. However, it does provide for the approval of administrative procedures. Accordingly, the Australian government issued the detailed Environment Protection (Impact of Proposals) Administrative Procedures, which were approved by the governor-general in 1975. They were extensively revised in 1987 (Commonwealth of Australia, 1987). The procedures set out the details of how the act is to be administered. Despite the number of reviews, there has been little fundamental change to the Commonwealth EIA system to date beyond the introduction of scoping and in 1987 the less rigorous and detailed "public environment report" procedure (Wood, 1995).

The Commonwealth of Australia EIA system contains most of the elements of NEPA. The principal shortcomings relate to:

1. Lack of a statement of national environmental policy
2. Weaknesses of screening and coverage

3. Effective lack of enforceability through the courts
4. Lack of centrality to decision making
5. Lack of practical application to actions other than projects

There have also been criticisms of duplication between the federal and state EIA systems, of delay, and of uncertainty (Australian and New Zealand Environment and Conservation Council, 1991).

The comprehensive public review of the Commonwealth EIA system mentioned above may well result in measures to resolve many of these shortcomings. However, the crucial measure—increasing the centrality of EIA to decision making—would require both public and political will and a strengthening of the Environment Protection (Impact of Proposals) Act.

NEW ZEALAND

New Zealand introduced its Mark I Environmental Protection and Enhancement Procedures, partially modeled on the Canadian EIA procedure, in 1974 by means of a cabinet minute. These evolved over the years, and in the latest version of the procedures (Ministry for the Environment, 1987), public agencies were required to undertake screening; agree on project-specific scoping guidelines with the Ministry for the Environment (MfE); consult with various statutory, local, and other authorities; publish an environmental impact report; submit it to a formal published "audit" by the Parliamentary Commissioner for the Environment (an "ombudsman" reporting not to the government but to Parliament); and agree to monitoring arrangements with MfE. This EIA process was subject to considerable public oversight but was largely discretionary and, in practice, related to only a limited number of public sector projects, virtually all of which were approved (Morgan, 1988).

Wells and Fookes (1988) summarized the need for reform to produce an EIA process which was "simple but effective, comprehensive but not complex, flexible yet consistent, authoritative yet accessible." At the same time, wide-ranging reviews of environmental administration and of local government resulted in complete reorganizations of both (Dixon, 1993). The Resource Management Act of 1991 (RMA), which swept away numerous previous acts, introduced EIA as a central element in a decision-making process designed to achieve the goal of sustainable management. This is EIA Mark II in New Zealand, and it is now, in principle at least, almost comprehensive and flexible in that it applies, at the appropriate level of detail, to all projects and, in addition, to policies and plans prepared under the RMA provisions.

The RMA makes broad provisions in relation to the EIA system and has devolved almost all responsibility for the administration of EIA from central to local government. The act provides the outline of the EIA process but leaves much detail to be provided by individual regional authorities in their regional policy statements and regional coastal plans and by territorial authorities in their district plans. In particular, the land use planning departments of the (generally poorly staffed) local authorities are responsible for dealing with proponents and making recommendations on the basis of the EIA.

The RMA contains provisions that effectively provide for a two-phase screening process and encourage scoping. It indicates the content requirements for an EIA report (which include alternatives), provides for public participation and consultation, and requires that the report be considered in the decision. In New Zealand, local authorities can commission an independent review of the EIA report at the developer's expense. The act also contains provisions relating to monitoring. In addition, RMA provides for public hearings into applications and for the call-in of requests for resource consents by the Minister for the Environment where issues of national significance are raised. There is a third-party right of appeal against local authority decisions, which are heard by a Planning Tribunal. Apart from the value of the precedents created by the tribunal's findings, the EIA system is also subject to scrutiny by the Parliamentary Commissioner for the Environment.

It is notable that RMA does not mention EIA by name, but that the procedures and aims of EIA suffuse both its policy and plan preparation provisions and its resource consent provisions (Dixon, 1993). In this sense, as in others, the highly sophisticated RMA makes a marked contribution to the advancement of sustainable development policy. It is, perhaps, unfortunate that the MfE employs only a very small number of central and regional office staff on EIA and that New Zealand should have relied quite so completely on local discretion in its Mark II EIA system. To leave local authorities with small professional staffs and little or no experience in EIA to evolve screening, scoping, review, and decision-making procedures individually seems courageous (Wood, 1995).

In comparison to NEPA, the New Zealand EIA system exhibits:

1. Absence of a strong central body responsible for EIA and system monitoring
2. Weaknesses in public participation
3. Practical lack of centrality of EIA to the decision

On the other hand, RMA provides for much greater coverage than NEPA and permits the nature of the EIA report to vary from a paragraph to a major tome.

Training and growing experience, further guidance, Planning Tribunal decisions, Parliamentary Commissioner interventions, the implementation of regional policy statements and plans and district plans, and perhaps the results of MfE "call-ins," will all undoubtedly help to realize the potential of New Zealand's innovative EIA system.

EUROPE

France implemented a formal EIA system in 1976. Ireland passed legislation that permitted, but did not require, EIA in 1976, and the West German cabinet approved an EIA procedure by minute in the same year. The Commission of the European Union first became interested in EIA in the early 1970s, like many other bodies, as a result of a concern to anticipate environmental problems and hence to prevent or mitigate them. The Commission of the European Communities (as it then was called) commissioned research investigations on EIA in 1975. These investigations found that many aspects of EIA procedure already existed within member states. As a consequence, it was suggested that the requirements of a European EIA system could be integrated into member state decision-making processes without the disruption or the litigation that characterized early American experience with NEPA. It was felt that project EIA should be the first stage of a European EIA system which would eventually encompass policies and plans once more than rudimentary experience of this type of assessment had been gained (Lee and Wood, 1978).

Following this research program, the commission issued its first preliminary draft directive in 1977. After more than 20 such drafts, not all of which were released, and substantial consultation (this is reliably reported to have been the most discussed European draft directive to date) (Sheate, 1994), the commission put forward a draft to the Council of Ministers in June 1980.

However, the Council of Ministers did not approve the draft directive. The British government was reluctant to accept the imposition of a mandatory system of EIA, at least in the form proposed. During subsequent negotiations between the commission and the British government, several of the more controversial aspects of the draft directive were deleted to meet the British position. In the course of the amendments, many types of industry were shifted from Annex 1, where their assessment would be compulsory, to Annex 2, where their assessment would be much more discretionary (Sheate, 1994). The British government withdrew its objections to the amended draft directive late in 1983, only for the Danish government to continue to express serious reservations about the undermining of the sovereign power of the Danish Parliament to approve development projects. A provision exempting projects approved by specific acts of national legislation (Wathern, 1988) paved the way for adoption of a much modified version of the draft directive in June 1985.

The net effect of these changes was the emasculation of the provisions in the earlier drafts of the directive, which had themselves been criticized by environmentalists as being overcautious and for not containing provisions for the commission to monitor and oversee the EIA system effectively. However, the directive in its adopted form provides a flexible framework of basic EIA principles to be implemented in each member state through national legislation, and there is nothing to prevent member states from instituting EIA systems which are more comprehensive and rigorous than the provisions put forward by the commission. Several countries, including Belgium, have considerably exceeded the requirements of some of the articles in the directive in their national EIA systems.

The directive places a general obligation on each member state to ensure that before consent is given, projects likely to have significant effects on the environment by virtue, *inter alia,* of their nature, size, or location are made subject to an assessment by using criteria and thresholds. This assessment may be integrated into existing project consent procedures or into other procedures, and most countries have adopted this approach. For example, Ireland has integrated EIA for the majority of projects into its land use planning system.

The compromises made in the gestation of the directive are very evident in its final "minimax" form. At its minimum, it requires that a limited list of projects be subjected to a limited form of EIA. At its maximum, it recommends that a much longer list of projects be subjected to a more universally recognized form of EIA. The commission no doubt hoped that practice in member states would prove to be well above the minimum required. More realistically, it may also have hoped that once the benefits of the flexible EIA system had become as apparent, as they have in the United States, it would become possible to strengthen it (Wood, 1995).

There is now some indication of how the European directive is being implemented in member states (Commission of the European Communities [CEC], 1993). By July 1991, all member states had incorporated some EIA provisions within their own legislation. However, seven years after it was required, transposition of the directive into national legislation is still not complete.

It was possible to observe considerable achievements in carrying into practice both the letter and the spirit of the directive, but these varied considerably between member states. The total number of projects subjected to EIA, and their composition, differed greatly between member states, even after differences in size and population had been taken into account. Although the directive is silent on scoping, several member states (including Germany) have made provision for scoping in their legislation. Access by the public to copies of EIA reports varied from the provision of complimentary copies, to purchase of copies and rights of reference, to instances where considerable persistence was necessary to consult even the non-technical summary. Generally, practice relating to participation and consultation varied from satisfactory in the northern liberal democracies like Denmark to unsatisfactory in the Mediterranean countries (many of which have emerged only relatively recently as democracies).

Despite the briefness of the implementation period examined, CEC (1993, p. 61) reported that:

> There is clear evidence that project modifications have and are taking place, due to the influence of the EIA process. However, there is also evidence that, as yet, its impact is not as widespread as intended and that modifications are mainly confined to those of a minor or non-radical nature...

CEC (1993, p. 63) cited this as evidence that the "planning, design and authorization of projects are beginning to be influenced by the EIA process and that environmental benefits are resulting."

Within the European Union, the Netherlands is generally acknowledged as having the most effective EIA system. Following numerous studies, the Netherlands published an official standpoint on EIA in 1979. It had already almost put its EIA system in place when the European directive on EIA was adopted (the EIA Act was passed in 1986) and has subsequently strengthened it. While some of the screening thresholds for projects are high in comparison to other European countries, the EIA system also applies to certain plans and programs. The Dutch system is notable for its emphasis on the treatment of alternatives, on scoping, and for the centrality of EIA to the decision on a project. It is also unique in the European Union in that it has a well-staffed and very influential EIA Commission and utilizes Canadian-style panels to scope and evaluate EIA reports (Wood, 1995). In comparison with NEPA, the Dutch EIA system only lacks a statement of national environmental policy. On the other hand, Dutch EIAs probably have more influence on decisions than EISs in the United States.

In marked contrast to the Netherlands, the EIA system in the United Kingdom was instituted as a direct response to the European directive. Despite government-financed studies dating from the mid-1970s and considerable non-statutory practice in EIA, it was not until 1988 that EIA was formally introduced. British regulations mainly (but by no means solely) relating to projects authorized under the town and country planning system mirror almost to the letter the provisions of the European directive (Department of the Environment, 1989). For most projects subject to EIA, the local planning authority is responsible for screening, consultation, participation, and decision making. There is no formal requirement for the consideration of alternatives, scoping, or monitoring, though this frequently takes place (Wood, 1995). In comparison with NEPA, the U.K. EIA system:

1. Lacks a statement of national environmental policy
2. Lacks a central body responsible for EIA
3. Lacks formal treatment of alternatives and scoping
4. Only formally permits participation at one stage in the EIA process
5. Lacks application to non-project actions

The U.K. EIA system (like the European directive) does, however, cover a much wider range of projects than NEPA.

Three years after the directive finally came into effect, it was apparent that EIA practice frequently left much to be desired (CEC, 1993). A number of measures were necessary before the full realization of the benefits obtainable from the implementation of the directive could be achieved. Commission proposals to initiate improvements in the treatment of alternatives, stronger screening, scoping, and better international consultation were put forward in 1994. Ironically, if they are enacted, these proposals would restore many of the provisions originally contained within the draft directive published in 1980.

With the demise of communism in Eastern Europe, there has been a rise in EIA. This is no coincidence; environmental degradation in many Eastern industrial areas has been marked and has increasingly engendered demands for amelioration. The countries of Eastern Europe have begun to put formalized EIA systems in place over the last few years. In some cases (e.g., Estonia), EIA has been introduced as part of a general law on environmental protection. In others (e.g., the Slovak Republic), a specific EIA law has been passed. In yet others (e.g., Romania), EIA has been introduced by means of ministerial decree. In most Eastern European countries, the EIA system has been modeled on the European EIA directive, but few have incorporated meaningful public participation. While some countries (e.g., Poland) utilize EIA Commissions to evaluate EIA reports, none requires scoping (European Bank for Reconstruction and Development, 1994) and most tend to focus on technical pollution control issues. This lack of meaningful public participation and concentration on technical issues is perhaps to be expected in countries only recently emerging from dictatorship.

DEVELOPING COUNTRIES

Just as there are significant differences in EIA systems in the developed world (where some countries have still not adopted EIA), so are there differences between EIA systems in developing countries. Thus, there are enormous variations between the situations in Latin America, Southeast Asia (where many countries have developed EIA systems), and

Africa (where many countries have not). As in Europe, however, the situation in different countries within continents varies considerably. Within Africa, for example, while the South African EIA system is sophisticated and EIA is becoming important in Zimbabwe, EIA is, as yet, unimportant in Somalia.

Despite these variations, it remains true that, on the whole, EIA in developing countries tends to be very different from EIA in the developed world. The most conspicuous difference relates to the fact that the first EIAs to be carried out were usually demanded by development assistance agencies on a project-by-project basis rather than as a response to a widespread indigenous demand for better environmental conditions.

There are exceptions, however, and the EIA requirements in, for example, Colombia (1974), Thailand (1975), and the Philippines (1977) predate those in many developed countries. Over the past decade, several developing countries have established their own formal legislative bases for EIA. Often, however, the necessary organization to enforce it is absent. EIA is therefore commonly a "top-down" requirement imposed by external agencies. While this may have been the case with the implementation of the European directive on EIA in certain countries, the "bottom-up" demand for environmental controls and the organizational capacity to implement them (which existed in many of the European Union countries) are often absent in the developing world.

This lack of demand is a consequence of the lack of political priority accorded to the environment in general, and EIA in particular, in many developing countries. While many officials in developing country environmental ministries, and others, may appreciate the relationship between rational management of the environment and long-term economic development (and thus be enthusiastic about EIA), most politicians do not. This lack of political will is allied both to existing systems, in which pressing environmental concerns (frequently fueled by severe environmental degradation) often cannot be effectively represented politically, and to widespread corruption.

Bisset (in Biswas and Agarwala, 1992, p. 217) has surmised that in developing countries:

> Most EIAs seem to have been a function of justifying a decision (usually to develop) which has been made and are concerned only with remedial measures. Rarely do they consider alternative courses of action at an early stage of the project planning cycle, in order to choose the most environmentally favorable.

While the importance of wealth in determining environmental awareness can hardly be exaggerated, there are examples of EIAs being undertaken successfully in many developing countries. These include EIAs in Brazil, China, Egypt, India, Indonesia, Malaysia, Pakistan, the Philippines, South Africa, and Thailand (Biswas and Agarwala, 1992).

The legal basis of EIA systems in many developing countries is weak, non-mandatory, or non-existent, and their coverage is patchy both in relation to the projects covered and especially in relation to the impacts assessed. Scoping, review, and public participation are frequently absent or embryonic in the developing world (Wood, 1995). Even in advanced countries like Hong Kong, which is still a British colony, there is no tradition of participation that EIA can link into.

Developing country EIA systems generally compare very unfavorably with the elements of NEPA. They often:

1. Lack a statement of national environmental policy
2. Lack a central body responsible for EIA
3. Lack procedural EIA process steps
4. Lack enforceability
5. Lack participation
6. Fail to exert real influence on decisions
7. Do not apply to non-project actions

As in the developed world, only widespread popular demand for environmental improvement will ensure that effective EIA systems are introduced in developing countries. The development assistance agencies have a major role to play here (see, for example, World Bank, 1991). Since the pace of change is so much greater in developing countries, it would be appropriate for a greater proportion of the world's EIA expertise (appropriately adapted) and resources to be devoted to the developing world if real progress toward sustainable development is to be made.

CONCLUSIONS

It is apparent from this brief review that many countries and jurisdictions have carefully considered the lessons of NEPA before adopting EIA. They have tried to make their EIA systems discretionary and to integrate them into existing decision-making procedures and into their peculiar national contexts, in order to avoid the litigation they perceive to be so prevalent in the United States. It is also quite clear that there is a marked relationship between the comprehensiveness and effectiveness of EIA systems and the tradition of environmental concern and participation (i.e., pluralist democracy) in the countries concerned.

As EIA has spread around the world, so has its nature been elaborated and clarified. There have been perhaps six main themes as EIA has evolved over the years, first in the United States and then elsewhere:

1. An early concern with the methodology of impact forecasting and decision making gave way first to an emphasis on administrative procedures for EIA and then, more recently, to a recognition of the crucial relationship of EIA to its broader decision-making and environmental management context.
2. A tendency to codification and away from discretion. This is evident, for example, in the enactment of federal Canadian EIA legislation after almost two decades of experience with administrative EIA procedures.
3. The refinement of EIA systems by the adoption of additional elements as experience has been gained. These include procedures for scoping (in, for example, New Zealand) and for monitoring the effects of implemented actions (for example, in Western Australia).
4. A concern to increase the quality of EIA by, for example, improving EIA reports, providing more opportunities for consultation and participation and increasing the weight given to EIA in decision making (as exemplified in the proposals to modify the European EIA directive).

5. A concern to increase the effectiveness of EIA in reducing environmental impacts and to ensure efficiency in terms of its costs in time, money, and manpower (as in the current Australian review of EIA).
6. A recognition that many variables are already resolved by the time the EIA of projects takes place and thus that some form of EIA of policies, plans, and programs is necessary (as, for example, in the Netherlands).

In a limited number of cases, other countries and jurisdictions have advanced beyond NEPA requirements. Examples include the use of EIA panels to increase centrality to decision making (as in Canada and the Netherlands) and impact monitoring (as in Western Australia). Generally, the experience of the United States in amending the NEPA process has been mirrored elsewhere. Attempts to omit the consideration of alternatives, scoping, the use of draft as well as final EIA reports, and meaningful public participation have generally proved unsustainable. As countries have adopted, modified, and refined their EIA systems, it is remarkable how much they have come to resemble the NEPA model, which has remained substantially unamended for over 15 years. That is testament in itself to what NEPA has wrought abroad.

SELECTED REFERENCES

Australian and New Zealand Environment and Conservation Council. 1991. A National Approach to Environmental Impact Assessment in Australia. ANZECC, Canberra.

Biswas, A.K. and S.B.C. Agarwala, Eds. 1992. *Environmental Impact Assessment for Developing Countries*. Butterworth-Heinemann, Oxford.

Commission of the European Communities (with the assistance of N. Lee and C.E. Jones). 1993. Report from the Commission of the Implementation of Directive 85/337/EEC and Annex for the United Kingdom. COM (93) 28, Volume 12, Brussels.

Commonwealth of Australia. 1987. Environment Protection (Impact of Proposals) Act 1974 Administration Procedures Order under Section 6 of the Act. 29 May 1987, AGPS, Canberra.

Department of the Environment. 1989. Environmental Assessment: A Guide to the Procedures. HMSO, London.

Dixon, J. 1993. The Integration of EIA and Planning in New Zealand: Changing Process and Practice. *Journal of Environmental Planning and Management* 36:239–251.

European Bank for Reconstruction and Development. 1994. Environmental Impact Assessment Legislation: Czech Republic, Estonia, Hungary, Latvia, Lithuania, Poland, Slovak Republic, Slovenia. Graham and Trotman, London.

Fowler, R.J. 1982. Environmental Impact Assessment, Planning and Pollution Measures in Australia. Department of Home Affairs and Environment, AGPS, Canberra.

Gibson, R.B. 1992. The New Canadian Environmental Assessment Act: Possible Responses to Its Main Deficiencies. *Journal of Environmental Law and Practice* 2:223–255.

Government of Canada. 1984. Environmental Assessment and Review Process Guidelines Order. *Canada Gazette* Part II 118(14):2794–2802.

Lee, N. and C.M. Wood. 1978. Environmental Impact Assessment of Projects in EEC Countries. *Journal of Environmental Management* 6:57–71.

Ministry for the Environment. 1987. Environmental Protection and Enhancement Procedures. MfE, Wellington.

Morgan, R.G. 1988. Reshaping Environmental Impact Assessment in New Zealand. *Environmental Impact Assessment Review* 8:293–306.

Organisation for Economic Co-operation and Development. 1992. Good Practices for Environmental Impact Assessment of Development Projects. Development Assistance Committee, OECD, Paris.

Sheate, W.R. 1994. *Making an Impact: A Guide to EIA Law and Policy*. Cameron May, London.

United Nations Environment Programme. 1988. Environmental Impact Assessment: Basic Procedures for Developing Countries. UNEP, Regional Office for Asia and the Pacific, Bangkok.

Wathern, P. 1988. *Environmental Impact Assessment: Theory and Practice*. Unwin Hyman, London.

Wells, C. and T. Fookes. 1988. Impact Assessment in Resource Management. Resource Management Law Reform Working Paper 20. Ministry for the Environment, Wellington.

Wood, C.M. 1995. *Environmental Impact Assessment: A Comparative Review*. Longman, Harlow, U.K.

Wood, C.M. and J. Bailey. 1994. Predominance and Independence in Environmental Impact Assessment: The Western Australia Model. *Environmental Impact Assessment Review* 14:37–59.

World Bank. 1991. *Environmental Assessment Sourcebook* (3 volumes). World Bank, Washington, D.C.

CURRENT TRENDS

CUMULATIVE EFFECTS AND OTHER ANALYTICAL CHALLENGES OF NEPA

8

L.W. Canter

The "technical heart" of the environmental impact assessment (EIA) process involves the prediction of changes (impacts) in selected features of the physical-chemical, biological, cultural, and socioeconomic environment which could occur as a result of a proposed action. The action could involve a proposed policy, plan, program, project, or permit. Direct, indirect, and cumulative impacts (changes) resulting from proposed actions should be addressed. Analytical approaches should be used in such impact predictions and subsequent comparisons of alternatives for accomplishing the identified need for the proposed action. Analytical approaches involve separating a whole into its parts and the use of scientifically based analysis as a method or process for impact predictions and comparative analyses.

Analytical approaches were implied in the National Environmental Policy Act (NEPA) adopted in 1970, in the Council on Environmental Quality (CEQ) guidelines of 1971 and 1973, and in the CEQ regulations of 1979. For example, in Section 102(b) of NEPA, the importance of methods usage by governmental agencies was noted as follows (NEPA, 1969):

> All agencies of the Federal Government shall...identify and develop methods and procedures, in consultation with the Council on Environmental Quality, which will ensure that presently unquantified environmental amenities and values may be given appropriate consideration in decision-making along with economic and technical considerations.

The scientific validity of such methods and related procedures was supported in Paragraph 1502.24 of the CEQ regulations as follows (CEQ, 1978):

> Agencies shall ensure the professional integrity, including scientific integrity, of the discussions and analyses in environmental impact statements. They shall

identify any methodologies used and shall make explicit reference by footnote
to the scientific and other sources relied upon for conclusions in the statement.
An agency may place discussion of methodology in an appendix.

While the need for analytical approaches in the EIA process has been clearly delineated, it should not be concluded that such approaches are simple and widely used. For
example, the range of impact concerns can encompass local, single-project issues to
programmatic studies of cumulative impacts of multiple projects over large geographical
areas. The following examples illustrate the range:

1. Prediction of the direct, indirect, and cumulative impacts resulting from the construction, operation, and subsequent decommissioning of a single project (e.g., a
   power plant or hazardous waste treatment facility) proposed for a specific location
2. Prediction of the direct, indirect, and cumulative impacts resulting from a multiyear
   resource extraction program (e.g., oil and gas developments or timber harvesting)
   over a wide geographical area which also contains other similar or unrelated
   resource extraction programs
3. Prediction of the direct, indirect, and cumulative impacts resulting from a sectoral
   plan (e.g., a regional transportation plan) in a large geographical region; this type
   of study leads to a programmatic environmental impact statement (programmatic
   EIS), which is referred to in Europe and elsewhere as a strategic environmental
   assessment

Key terms in the above examples include direct, indirect, and cumulative impacts.
Direct impacts (effects) are caused by the action and occur at the same time and place.
Indirect impacts are caused by the action and are later in time or farther removed in
distance but are still reasonably foreseeable; they may include growth-inducing effects
and other effects related to induced changes in the pattern of land use, population density
or growth rate, and related effects on air, water, and other natural systems, including
ecosystems (CEQ, 1978). Cumulative impacts refer to impacts on the environment which
result from the incremental impact of the action when added to other past, present, and
reasonably foreseeable future actions regardless of what agency (federal or non-federal)
or person undertakes such other actions. Cumulative impacts can result from individually
minor but collectively significant actions taking place over a period of time (CEQ, 1978).

Direct, indirect, and cumulative impacts are typically delineated in terms of environmental media or characteristics such as air quality, soil quality, surface and/or groundwater quantity and quality, noise, habitat changes, threatened or endangered plant or
animal species, historical and/or archaeological resources, visual quality, and socioeconomic changes in relation to physical infrastructure, educational systems, and utilities.
Examples of specific impacts that should be addressed include: (1) changes in air quality
in the vicinity of proposed power plants, industrial plants, waste incinerators, airports, or
highways; (2) changes in downstream terrestrial and aquatic habitats and land usage
patterns as a result of a proposed flood control or hydropower dam; and (3) changes in
local traffic and school system demands as a result of a decision to close or change the
mission of a military installation.

EXAMPLES OF ANALYTICAL METHODS

Numerous analytical methods (tools) have been utilized to meet the various activities required in the conduction of an environmental impact study, including impact identification, preparation of a description of the affected environment, impact prediction and assessment, and selection of the proposed action from a set of alternatives being evaluated to meet identified needs. The objectives of the various activities differ, as do the usable methods for accomplishing such activities. The term method as used herein refers to a structured scientific and/or policy-based approach for achieving one or more of the basic activities. Table 8.1 delineates 22 types of methods arrayed against seven typical activities in an impact study. An "X" in Table 8.1 denotes that the listed method type is or may be directly useful for accomplishing the specified activity. The absence of an X for any given type of method does not denote lack of usefulness for the activity; it merely suggests that it may be less useful for the activity. Detailed information on these types of methods is available elsewhere (Canter, 1996; Lohani and Halim, 1990).

Based on an inspection of Table 8.1, the following observations can be made:

1. Each listed type of method has potential usefulness in two to as many as six study activities.
2. Each listed study activity has 4 to as many as 19 listed method types that are potentially useful.
3. In a given impact study, several types of methods will probably be used even though the resultant EIS may not completely document their usage.
4. Each of the listed types of methods have advantages and limitations; these should be considered in selecting specific methods for usage in a given study.
5. While numerous types of methods have been developed, and additional ones are still being proposed and tested, there is no "universal" method that can be applied to all types of actions in all environmental settings and for all study activities. Accordingly, the most appropriate perspective is to consider methods as "tools" which can be selected and modified as appropriate to aid the EIA process.
6. Usage of methods does not ensure that all questions related to the impacts of a potential project or set of alternatives are addressed. Methods are not "cookbooks" in which a successful study is achieved by meeting the requirements of the utilized methods. Methods must be selected based on appropriate evaluation and professional judgment, and they must be used and the results interpreted with the continuous application of judgment relative to data inputs and analysis and value judgments. In fact, it should be noted that professional judgment pervades the entirety of Table 8.1.
7. Methods that are simpler in terms of data and personnel resources requirements and in technical complexity are probably more useful in the EIA process.

Table 8.1 encompasses methods for typical activities in an impact study. The critical activity from an analytical perspective is impact prediction. Accordingly, examples of selected types of methods for impact prediction, including analogs, indices, and qualitative and quantitative modeling, are presented in the next section.

TABLE 8.1 Synopsis of EIA Methods and Study Activities

Types of methods in EIA	Define issues (scoping)	Impact identification	Describe affected environment	Impact prediction	Impact assessment	Decision making	Communication of results
Analogs (look-alikes) (case studies)	X	X		X	X		
Checklists (simple, descriptive, questionnaire)	X	X	X				X
Decision-focused checklists (MCDM, MAUM, DA, scaling/rating/ranking, weighting)					X	X	X
Environmental cost–benefit analysis				X	X	X	
Expert opinion (professional judgment, Delphi, adaptive environmental assessment, simulation modeling)		X		X	X		
Expert systems (impact identification, prediction, assessment, decision making)	X	X	X	X	X	X	X
Indices or indicators	X	X	X	X	X		X
Laboratory testing and scale models		X		X			
Landscape evaluation			X	X	X		
Literature reviews		X		X	X		
Mass balance calculations (inventories)				X	X		X
Matrices (simple, stepped, cross-impact, scoring)	X	X		X	X	X	X
Monitoring (baseline)			X		X		
Monitoring (field studies of receptors near analogs)				X	X		
Networks (impact trees/chains, cause/effect or consequence diagrams)		X	X	X			

Method						
Overlay mapping via GIS			X	X	X	X
Photographs/photomontages (historical and current)			X	X		X
Qualitative modeling (conceptual)			X			
Quantitative modeling (media, ecosystem, visual, archaeological, socioeconomic, and simulation)		X	X			
Risk assessment (relative or quantitative and probabilistic)	X		X	X		
Scenario building			X		X	
Trend extrapolation		X	X			

Note: X denotes potential for direct usage of method for listed activity. MCDM = multicriteria decision making, MAUM = multiattribute utility measurement, DA = decision analysis, GIS = geographical information system.

IMPACT PREDICTION TECHNIQUES

The range of impact prediction techniques (methods) useful for the EIA process is broad and encompasses the use of analogs through sophisticated quantitative models; the range, which represents an expansion of certain types of methods listed in Table 8.1, is shown in Table 8.2. In a specific impact study, several prediction techniques may be required due to the impacts of concern, data availability or lack thereof, and the specificity of quantitative models.

Simple Techniques

Perhaps the simplest approach for impact prediction is to utilize analogs or comparisons to the experienced effects of existing similar projects or types of actions. This could be termed a "look-alike" approach in that information gathered from similar types of projects or actions, in hopefully similar environmental settings, could be utilized to qualitatively (descriptively) address the anticipated impacts of the proposed action. Professional judgment would be necessary in the transfer of such case study information for predicting specific impacts.

An inventory technique involves the compilation of environmental resources information for the defined study area through either the assemblage of existing data or the

TABLE 8.2   Impact Prediction Techniques Currently Used in the EIA Process

Simple techniques
- Analogs (case studies of similar actions)
- Inventory of resources in study area
- Checklists (simple, questionnaire, descriptive)
- Matrices (simple, stepped) or networks (impact trees, cause/effect or consequence diagrams)

Indices and experimental methods
- Environmental media indices (air, surface and/or groundwater quality or vulnerability, land or soil quality, noise)
- Habitat indices (Habitat Evaluation Procedures, Habitat Evaluation Systems) • or biological diversity indices
- Other indices (visual, quality of life)
- Experimental methods (laboratory, field, physical models)

Mathematical models
- Air quality dispersion
- Hydrologic processes
- Surface and groundwater quality and quantity
- Noise propagation
- Biological impact (Habitat Evaluation Procedures, Habitat Evaluation Systems, Wetland Evaluation Technique, population, nutrients, chemical cycling, energy system diagrams)
- Archaeological (predictive)
- Visual impact
- Socioeconomic (population, econometric, multiplier factors, health)

conduction of baseline monitoring, with the presumption then being that the particular resources in the existing environment, or portions thereof, will be lost or degraded in quality as a result of the proposed action. This can be used as a "worst-case" prediction, and for certain types of resources, it would be reasonable for usage in impact studies.

Often-used approaches for impact prediction involve checklists or interaction matrices. Checklists range from simple listings of anticipated impacts by project type, to questionnaires incorporating a series of detailed questions related to potential impacts and environmental resources, to descriptive checklists with information on impact calculations and interpretation. Interaction matrices include simple x–y matrices for identifying impacts and providing a basis for further evaluation in terms of categorization of impact magnitude and importance. Stepped or cross-impact matrices have also been developed for delineating secondary and tertiary consequences of proposed actions. Matrix modifications are referred to as networks (or impact trees or chains) or cause/effect or consequence diagrams; such modifications can also be utilized to trace the anticipated consequences of proposed actions. The key point relative to both checklist and matrix methods is that they yield qualitative results in terms of the predicted impacts; however, they can be useful initial tools when used in conjunction with environmental indices and/ or quantitative modeling.

Indices and Experimental Methods

An environmental index refers to a mathematical and/or descriptive summarization of information on a series of factors that can be used for purposes of classification of environmental quality and sensitivity and for predicting the impacts of a proposed action (Canter, 1996). The approach for impact prediction would be to quantify, or at least qualitatively describe, the change in the index as a result of the proposed action and to then consider the difference in the index from the with- and without-project (or other actions) conditions as one measure of impact. Indices are available for air quality, water quality, soil quality, noise, species diversity, the occurrence of cultural resources, visual quality, land usage compatibility, and quality of life (a socioeconomic index which can include a large number of specific factors) (Ott, 1978; Canter, 1996). One type of index that has received wide usage is based on habitat considerations and the utilization of Habitat Evaluation Procedures (HEP) or the Habitat Evaluation System (HES); these techniques are primarily based on the development of a numerical index to describe habitat quality and size for specific species or wildlife as a whole (U.S. Fish and Wildlife Service, 1980; U.S. Army Corps of Engineers, 1980).

Experimental methods range from conducting laboratory experiments, to developing coefficients for mathematical models, to determining the quality of leachate from dredged or solid waste materials, to conducting field experiments to measure changes in environmental features as a result of system perturbations. Physical models and laboratory simulations have been utilized to examine impacts related to hydrodynamic and/or ecological changes within microcosms of environmental settings. Experimental methods are primarily useful for predicting impacts on physical/chemical components and/or biological features of the environmental setting.

Mathematical Models

The most sophisticated approach for impact prediction involves the selection and use of quantitative models for predicting pollutant transport and fate and environmental cycling. In addition, models have been developed for ecosystem functions and system responses to man-induced perturbations. The purpose of the following brief review is not to describe the state-of-the-art of quantitative modeling but to provide some overview comments as to the availability of types of usable models.

Numerous models have been developed to address atmospheric dispersion from point, line, and area sources of air pollution (Turner, 1994; U.S. Environmental Protectional Agency, 1993). In addition, within recent years, models have been developed for long-range transport of pollution and for atmospheric reactions leading to photochemical smog formation or acid rain. Many air quality models are available in PC software; they represent a usable technology for many studies (Zanetti, 1990).

Hydrological models can be used to address rainfall–runoff relationships, surface and subsurface flows, and estuarine and coastal hydrodynamics (Anderson and Burt, 1985; James, 1993). Hydrological models can be considered in terms of black-box models, conceptual models, and deterministic models (Anderson and Burt, 1985). Black-box models depend upon establishing a statistical relationship between input and output variables. Conceptual models are typically based on a relatively small number of components, each of which is a simplified representation of one process element in the system being modeled. Deterministic models utilize physical theory; however, despite the simplifying assumptions necessary to solve the flow equations, they may have huge demands in terms of computational time and data requirements.

Surface and groundwater quality models are also plentiful, with major new developments within the last decade addressing solute transport in subsurface systems. Surface water quality and quantity models range from one-dimensional steady-state models to three-dimensional dynamic models that can be utilized for rivers, lakes, and estuarine systems (Henderson-Sellers, 1991; James, 1993; U.S. Army Corps of Engineers, 1987). Groundwater flow models have been recently modified to include subsurface processes such as adsorption and biological decomposition (Water Science and Technology Board, 1990).

Noise impact prediction models can be used for point, line, and area sources of noise generation (Magrab, 1975; World Health Organization, 1986). These models range in complexity from simple calculations involving the use of nomographs to sophisticated computer modeling for airport operations. The technology for noise impact prediction is well developed as a result of noise propagation research related to highways and airports. Noise models can be utilized to address continuous or discontinuous noise sources, including instantaneous noise generation related to construction-phase blasting.

Biological impact prediction models are often based on the use of habitat approaches. These index-based models include the HEP developed by the U.S. Fish and Wildlife Service (1980) and the HES and the Wetland Evaluation Technique (WET) developed by the U.S. Army Corps of Engineers (U.S. Army Corps of Engineers, 1980; Adamus et al., 1987). Prediction of impacts involves determination of the index under baseline as well as future with- and without-action conditions. Other biological impact models include species population models, species diversity indices, and biophysical models used for estimating chemical cycling and interchanges in terrestrial or aquatic ecosystems.

Energy system diagrams which account for energy flows within and between system components have been used in some impact studies. Ad hoc models may be needed to address particular impact concerns associated with a proposed action. Accordingly, the "building" of appropriate models for conservation and wildlife management, or enhancing an understanding of ecosystem responses to stresses, may be necessary. Information is available on the development of such models (Starfield and Bleloch, 1986; Armour and Williamson, 1988).

Predictive modeling is also possible for ascertaining the potential presence of historical or archaeological resources in geographical study areas (King, 1978). Such modeling is based upon evaluating a series of factors to indicate the likelihood of historical or archaeological resources being found; the factors are typically related to existing information, the likelihood for early occupations in the area, and other biophysical and sociological factors. This type of modeling is often used in the planning and conduction of site-specific archaeological field surveys.

Visual impact modeling approaches have been developed by several federal agencies, including the Forest Service, the Bureau of Land Management, the Soil Conservation Service, and the Army Corps of Engineers (Smardon et al., 1986). Visual impact models typically involve the evaluation of a series of factors, in some cases numerically and in other cases descriptively or by category, with the assemblage of the information into an overall visual quality or resources index for the study area. Videoimaging or simulation is also being used (Marlatt et al., 1993).

Impact prediction related to the socioeconomic environment is often based on the use of human population and econometric models (Canter et al., 1985). Population forecasting can range from simple projections of historical trends to the application of complicated cohort analysis models. Econometric models relate the population and economic characteristics of study areas so that interrelationships can be depicted between population changes and their consequences on economic features within given study areas. Other predictions for the socioeconomic environment, such as impacts on educational or transportation systems, can be addressed via multiplier factors applied to population changes. Health impact predictions may utilize descriptive (or conceptual) models, statistical models, matrices, or cause/effect diagrams (Turnbull, 1992).

Table 8.3 delineates substantive area examples of specific methods (techniques) that could be used for impact prediction within the EIA process. The techniques listed are not all mathematical models, nor do they represent a comprehensive delineation of all potential methods. Within each of the substantive areas typically addressed in an impact study, several techniques may be used for impact prediction. The techniques could be used for the direct, indirect, or cumulative impacts of a single project, or they could be used in impact studies related to programs, plans, or policies.

To illustrate in still more detail the availability of quantitative models, one item listed in Table 8.3 for the air environment is single to multiple source dispersion models. Table 8.4 delineates specific examples of such models as recommended by the U.S. Environmental Protection Agency (1993). These preferred models should be used for the sources, land use categories, and averaging times indicated; a brief description of each model listed is provided in Table 8.5 (U.S. Environmental Protectional Agency, 1993). The primary point of Table 8.4 is to demonstrate the increasingly greater detail which can be examined in conjunction with selecting analytical approaches for impact prediction. The

TABLE 8.3   Examples of Impact Prediction Techniques Organized by Substantive Areas

Air

1. Emission inventory
2. Urban area statistical models
3. Receptor monitoring
4. Box models
5. Single to multiple source dispersion models
6. Monitoring from analogs
7. Air quality indices

Surface water

1. Point and non-point waste loads
2. QUAL-IIE and many other quantitative models
3. Segment box models
4. Waste load allocations
5. Water quality indices
6. Statistical models for selected parameters
7. Water usage studies

Groundwater

1. Pollution source surveys
2. Soil and/or groundwater vulnerability indices
3. Pollution source indices
4. Leachate testing
5. Flow and solute transport models
6. Relative subsurface transport models

Noise

1. Individual source propagation models plus additive model
2. Statistical model of noise based on population
3. Noise impact indices

Biological

1. Chronic toxicity testing
2. Habitat-based methods
3. Species population models
4. Diversity indices
5. Indicators
6. Biological assessments
7. Ecologically based risk assessment

Historical/archaeological

1. Inventory of resources and effects
2. Predictive modeling
3. Prioritization of resources

Visual

1. Baseline inventory
2. Questionnaire checklist
3. Photographic or photomontage approach
4. Computer simulation modeling
5. Visual impact index methods

Socioeconomic

1. Demographic models
2. Econometric models
3. Descriptive checklists
4. Multiplier factors based on population or economic changes
5. Quality-of-life indices
6. Health-based risk assessment

models listed in Table 8.4 and the associated user's documentation are available from Computer Products, National Technical Information Service (NTIS), U.S. Department of Commerce, Springfield, Virginia.

Summary Observations on Impact Prediction

Impact prediction represents the technical or scientific heart, and the main analytical challenge, of the EIA process. There are numerous techniques that have been (or could be) used to systematically describe and/or quantify anticipated environmental changes from proposed actions. The available techniques require a range of input data, mathematical knowl-

TABLE 8.4   Preferred Models for Selected Applications in Simple Terrain (U.S. Environmental Protection Agency, 1993)

	Land use	Model[a]
Short term (i.e., 1–24 hours)		
Single source	Rural	CRSTER
	Urban	RAM
Multiple source	Rural/urban	MPTER or RAM
Complicated sources[b]	Rural/urban	ISCST2
Buoyant industrial line sources	Rural	BLP
Long term (i.e., monthly, seasonal, or annual)		
Single source	Rural	CRSTER
	Urban	RAM
Multiple source	Rural	MPTER
	Urban	CDM 2.0 or RAM[c]
Complicated sources[b]	Rural/urban	ISCLT2
Buoyant industrial line sources	Rural	BLP

[a] Several of these models contain options that allow them to be interchanged. For example, ISCST2 can be substituted for CRSTER and equivalent, if not identical, concentration estimates obtained. Similarly, for a point source application, MPTER with urban option can be substituted for RAM. Where a substitution is convenient to the user and equivalent estimates are assured, it may be made. The models as listed here reflect the applications for which they were originally intended.

[b] Complicated sources are those with special problems such as aerodynamic downwash, particle deposition, volume and area sources, etc.

[c] If only a few sources in an urban area are to be modeled, RAM should be used.

TABLE 8.5   Summary Information on Preferred Air Quality Dispersion Models Listed by the U.S. Environmental Protection Agency (1993)

Model	Description
CRSTER	CRSTER is a steady-state Gaussian dispersion model designed to calculate concentrations from point sources at a single location in either a rural or urban setting. Highest and second highest concentrations are calculated at each receptor for 1-hour, 3-hour, 24-hour, and annual averaging times. CRSTER may be used to model primary pollutants. Settling and deposition are not treated. Chemical transformations are treated using exponential decay. Half-life is input by the user. CRSTER is appropriate for the following applications: single point sources, rural or urban areas, transport distances less than 50 kilometers, and flat or rolling terrain (no terrain above stack height).

TABLE 8.5   Summary Information on Preferred Air Quality Dispersion Models Listed by the U.S. Environmental Protection Agency (1993) (continued)

Model	Description
RAM	RAM is a steady-state Gaussian plume model for estimating concentrations of relatively stable pollutants, for averaging times from an hour to a day, from point and area sources in a rural or urban setting. Level terrain is assumed. Calculations are performed for each hour. RAM may be used to model primary pollutants. Settling and deposition are not treated. Chemical transformations are treated using exponential decay. Half-life is input by the user. RAM is appropriate for the following applications: point and area sources, urban areas, flat terrain, transport distances less than 50 kilometers, and one-hour to one-year averaging times.
MPTER	The multiple-point Gaussian dispersion algorithm with terrain adjustment model is useful for estimating air quality concentrations of relatively non-reactive pollutants. Hourly estimates are made using the Gaussian steady-state model. Calculations are performed for 1- to 24-hour and annual average concentrations at each receptor and the highest through fifth highest concentrations at each receptor for each period. MPTER is appropriate for the following applications: point sources, rural or urban areas, flat or rolling terrain (no terrain above stack height), transport distances less than 50 kilometers, and one-hour to one-year averaging times.
ISC2	The industrial source complex model is a steady-state Gaussian plume model which can be used to assess pollutant concentrations from a wide variety of sources associated with an industrial source complex. This model can account for the following: settling and dry deposition of particles; downwash; area, line, and volume sources; plume rise as a function of downwind distance; separation of point sources; and limited terrain adjustment. It operates in both long-term and short-term modes. Chemical transformations are treated using exponential decay. The time constant is input by the user. ISC2 is appropriate for the following applications: industrial source complexes, rural or urban areas, flat or rolling terrain, transport distances less than 50 kilometers, one-hour to annual averaging times, and continuous toxic air emissions.
BLP	The buoyant line and point source model is a Gaussian plume dispersion model designed to handle unique modeling problems associated with aluminum reduction plants and other industrial sources where plume rise and downwash effects from stationary line sources are important. The output can include the total concentration, or, optionally, a source contribution analysis, and monthly and annual frequency distributions for 1-, 3-, and 24-hour average concentrations. The BLP model is appropriate for the following applications: aluminum reduction plants that contain buoyant, elevated line sources; rural areas; transport distances less than 50 kilometers; simple terrain; and one-hour to one-year averaging times.
CDM 2.0	The climatological dispersion model is a climatological steady-state Gaussian plume model for determining long-term (seasonal or annual) arithmetic average pollutant concentrations at any ground-level receptor in an urban area; CDM 2.0 may be used to model primary pollutants. Settling and deposition are not treated. Chemical transformations are treated using exponential decay. Half-life is input by the user. CDM 2.0 is appropriate for the following applications: point and area sources, urban areas, flat terrain, transport distances less than 50 kilometers, and long-term averages over one month to one year or longer.

edge on the part of users, and professional interpretation. Many of the quantitative models described earlier are available in PC software.

A challenge related to impact prediction is that, in a given study, decisions have to be made regarding the best available predictive technology in view of the location, size, and type of proposed project or other action, as well as the available budget and time requirements for the impact study. As a result, sophisticated quantitative models may not be utilized due to their need for extensive data input and model calibration. Accordingly, and as noted earlier, a range of analytical methods is typically drawn upon in the conduction of an impact study for a proposed action.

EXAMPLES OF ANALYTICAL TECHNIQUES USED FOR CUMULATIVE IMPACT PREDICTION

A frequently expressed analytical challenge in the EIA process is the purported lack of suitable techniques (models) for predicting cumulative impacts. However, this challenge may be misplaced in that many quantitative models/methods used for direct or indirect impacts can also be used to examine cumulative impacts. For example, the models/methods used for cumulative impact prediction in six U.S. Army Corps of Engineers projects are shown in Table 8.6, while Table 8.7 does the same for five U.S. Forest Service proposed actions (Cooper, 1995). All of the listed models/methods have also been used to address the direct impacts of single projects in specific locations.

DISCUSSION OF ANALYTICAL CHALLENGES

Table 8.8 delineates several analytical challenges relating to the prediction of direct, indirect, and cumulative impacts. Some challenges are scientifically or technically based, while others relate to decisions on the availability of study funding and required interpretation of study results. One of the greatest challenges involves identifying and selecting appropriate prediction techniques. As demonstrated earlier, there are many potential choices for a specific study; thus it is necessary to consider the type of project and associated impacts, the environmental setting, baseline data requirements, and professional skills and budgetary needs relating to the usage of the chosen prediction technique. Additional factors in the selection process may include the acceptability of the techniques by regulators, the validity of the scientific approach as recognized by substantive area professionals, time constraints, and the uncertainty related to the technique usage and results.

There are assumptions and limitations associated with various prediction techniques. For example, quantitative models can be used to address various components of the environmental system; however, such models are based upon simplifying assumptions related to the complexity of the included biophysical and/or socioeconomic components. Therefore, there is a need for considering environmental system complexity and related uncertainties in the appropriate interpretation of modeling results.

Another analytical challenge is associated with the calibration of quantitative models for usage within the specific setting of the proposed action. While calibration is not

TABLE 8.6 Examples of Cumulative Impact Prediction Methods Used in EISs by the U.S. Army Corps of Engineers (Cooper, 1995)

Trinity River and tributaries; Dallas/Fort Worth Metroplex; Dallas, Denton, and Tarrant counties, Texas (1986)—river channel and floodplain development	Several quantitative models were used, including: 1. QUAL-TX Model—The QUAL-TX model was used to quantify future water quality conditions of the river. The heart of the model is the Streeter-Phelps equation for the dissolved oxygen (DO) sag curve, which calculates DO based on biological oxygen demand and ammonia oxidation. The DO levels were predicted based on low flow conditions and stormwater runoff flows. 2. Habitat Evaluation Procedure—A cumulative impact analysis on wildlife was conducted using HEP. Habitat units for each alternative scenario were estimated based on three habitat types that were considered to have wildlife value. Baseline Habitat Suitability Indices (HSIs) were developed for each selected species. The HSI for each species, in each cover type, was then averaged to develop a composite HSI. 3. Earth Resources Data Analysis System (ERDAS) and Geographic Information System (GIS)—ERDAS consists of an integrated image-processing system. GIS was used to identify and classify various types of geographic data (type of vegetation and land use, soil type, slope, political boundaries, etc.) and record into an overall database. 4. HEC-1 Computer Program—The HEC-1 computer program, developed by the U.S. Army Corps of Engineers' Hydrologic Engineering Center at Davis, California, was used to simulate surface water runoff responses of the river basin (from precipitation) by representing the basin as an interconnected system of hydrologic and hydraulic components.
West bank of the Mississippi River in the vicinity of New Orleans, Louisiana (1986)—hurricane/flood protection	The HEP and the HES were both used to quantitatively predict habitat losses. The loss in habitat acres directly correlates to the cumulative loss of bottomland hardwoods, marsh, wooded swamp, and wetlands predicted for the proposed project. These methods are briefly described as follows: 1. Habitat Evaluation Procedure—The HEP was used to predict impacts on fish and wildlife resources. These impacts were determined by estimating the loss of habitat acres (i.e., bottomland hardwood, wooded swamp, marsh, and wetlands) in the project area. Habitat losses are measured in annual average habitat units (AAHUs). This analysis showed that implementation of the project would result in the loss of 1,990 AAHUs to seven evaluation species. 2. Habitat Evaluation System—The HES was also used to predict impacts on fish and wildlife resources. These impacts were determined by estimating the loss of habitat acres (i.e., bottomland hardwood, wooded swamp, marsh, and wetlands) in the project area. Habitat losses are measured in annualized habitat unit values (AHUVs). Unlike HEP, HES does not examine individual species, but instead evaluates general habitat characteristics that support fish and wildlife populations within an ecosystem.

Major rehabilitation effort, Mississippi River Locks and Dams 2-22, Illinois waterway from La Grange to Lockport locks and dams (1988)—navigation

A quantitative model called CONGEST was used in the study to predict impacts on the system's navigation traffic flow.

Amite River and tributaries, Comite River Basin, Louisiana, (1990)—flood control

Changes in historical land use were classified in the cumulative impact section of the EIS. Several quantitative models/methods were used to predict these cumulative changes, as follows:

1. Watershed Hydrologic Simulation (WAHS) Model—The WAHS model was used to simulate basin hydrology and predict watershed runoff.

2. Geographic Information Systems (GIS), Remote Sensing, and Overlay Mapping—GIS and overlay mapping techniques were used to construct maps of land cover in the study area to estimate land use changes. For example, these techniques were used to determine soil types in forested areas and predict flood potential if the forests were cleared. The WAHS model requires the use of spatially oriented data representing geomorphologic, climatologic, land use, soil, and stream-flow characteristics. This data has historically been difficult to obtain. However, the application of remote sensing and overlay mapping, in combination with GIS technology, greatly improved the flow of information and the collection of data.

Elk Creek Lake, Rogue River Basin, Oregon (1991)—dam/reservoir

Quantitative methods were described in the EIS to predict potential cumulative impacts on environmental resources, as follows:

1. WRE Model (Water Temperature)—The WRE model, developed by Water Resources Engineers, Inc., Walnut Creek, California, was used to simulate reservoir water temperatures.

2. WESTEX Model (Water Turbidity)—The WESTEX model, developed by the U.S. Army Corps of Engineers Waterways Experiment Station and the University of Texas, was used to simulate reservoir water turbidity.

3. CE-THERM (Reservoir Process)—The CE-THERM model was used to verify the reservoir processes in WESTEX.

4. QUAL II Model (River Flow/Process)—The QUAL II model was used to simulate the Rogue River to determine cumulative effects from all three dam projects.

5. Remote Sensing and Geographic Information Systems (GIS)—Remote sensing and GIS technology was used to forecast daily suspended sediment levels in tributaries of the Rogue and Applegate rivers, where observed data was unavailable, with the results used in the QUAL II model.

6. Habitat Evaluation Procedure—A cumulative impact analysis on wildlife was conducted using HEP.

7. HEC-5 Program—The HEC-5 computer program, developed in 1986 by the U.S. Army Corps of Engineers, Davis, California, was used to simulate flood control and conservation systems.

TABLE 8.6   Examples of Cumulative Impact Prediction Methods Used in EISs by the U.S. Army Corps of Engineers (Cooper, 1995) (continued)

Gulf Intracoastal Waterway (Section 216 Study), Sargent Beach, Matagorda County, Texas (1992)—erosion control for waterway	Several quantitative models/methods were used to forecast changes in the study area due to tropical storms and hurricanes. The EIS did not specifically link these models/methods to a cumulative impact study; however, the types of information they analyze are cumulative in nature. These models/methods are briefly described as follows: 1. HURISK Computer Model—The National Hurricane Center Risk Analysis Program (HURISK) was utilized to identify and access data on historical tropical storms and hurricanes that have passed within 75 nautical miles of the study area. 2. SLOSH Numerical Model—The National Oceanic and Atmospheric Administration Storm Surge Numerical Model (SLOSH) was utilized to simulate ocean surge levels in the study area, resulting from tropical storms and hurricanes. 3. COAST Program—A shoreline change analysis was performed using a zoom transfer scope from aerial photographs and using the COAST program to calculate areas and disturbances. Spatial variability in erosion rates was ascertained with this procedure. 4. SBEACH Response Model—The SBEACH response model was applied to simulate a beach profile based on cross-shore sand transportation caused by storm-generated winds and water levels.

TABLE 8.7 Examples of Cumulative Impact Prediction Methods Used in EISs by the U.S. Forest Service (Cooper, 1995)

Mt. Graham astrophysical area, Pinaleno Mountains, Coronado National Forest, Graham County, Arizona (1988)—land development	Cumulative impacts on the red squirrel population were assessed. Two quantitative methods used were: 1. Habitat Capability Model (HCM)—HCM was used to estimate the red squirrel population in the study area and predict reductions in population capability due to human actions. 2. POPDYN Model—POPDYN (a population dynamics model) was used to estimate the demographic response of a simulated red squirrel population over a 30-year period.
Ward timber sale, Gila National Forest, Catron County, New Mexico (1991)—timber sale	Quantitative models were used to describe cumulative impacts. The models identified in the final EIS are listed as follows: 1. RO3WILD Program—The RO3WILD computer model was used to simulate the combined effects of a number of habitat components on various wildlife species. The model provides a relative index to compare alternatives on how habitat capability is affected by changes in the habitat components. A habitat capability index was calculated for black bear, deer, elk, Albert's squirrel, red squirrel, and Merrian's turkey. 2. Watershed Analysis and Soil Report—The watershed analysis and soil report was utilized to ascertain cumulative effects on soil and water. Specific models were used in the analysis but not identified in the final EIS.
Jenkins timber sale, Payette National Forest, Adams County, Idaho (1993)—timber sale	Quantitative models were utilized to predict cumulative impacts. These models are listed as follows: 1. Simple Approach Smoke Estimation Model (SASEM)—SASEM, developed by the U.S. Bureau of Land Management, was used to calculate total suspended particulate concentrations (PM-10 equivalent), total particulates emitted (tons), and reductions in visual range due to smoke from controlled burns. 2. BOISED Sediment Model—BOISED was used to predict cumulative sediment yields from road construction and use, silvicultural activities, and fire and suppression tactics in small forest watersheds. 3. Equipment Clearout Area (ECA) Method—The ECA method was used to evaluate the existing condition of the subwatersheds. 4. Geographic Information Systems (GIS)—GIS was used in conducting an inventory of timberlands in the planning area. 5. Elk Habitat Effectiveness (EHE) Model—The study area contained 23 elk management units (EMUs). The EMUs are designed to follow geographical land textures and to include potential elk home ranges. EMUs are further broken down into issue reporting areas (IRAs). The Forest Plan established minimum EHE ratings for each IRA and EMU to indicate whether the elk habitat objective of providing a habitat capable of sustaining or increasing elk populations was being met. These ratings were calculated through the use of the West Central Idaho EHE model, which rates perfect elk habitat at 100%.

TABLE 8.7 Examples of Cumulative Impact Prediction Methods Used in EISs by the U.S. Forest Service (Cooper, 1995) (continued)

	6. MTVEST Investment Analysis Program—MTVEST was used to calculate the net present value of each alternative (economic value of project).
	7. Visual Quality Analysis—Visual quality objectives (VQOs) were assigned to the study area. The U.S. Forest Service Visual Management System was used to assign one of the several VQOs to each acre of land. These objectives can be used to describe how much change is acceptable in the existing landscape.
Snowmass ski area, White River National Forest, Aspen Ranger District, Snowmass Village, Pitkin County, Colorado (1993)—ski area development	Several quantitative models and methods were utilized to assess cumulative impacts. A few of these models are listed as follows:
	1. Box Model (Ventilated Valley Model)—This model was used to estimate ambient air concentrations of pollutants within the study area.
	2. COMPLEX I—COMPLEX I is an air transportation and dispersion model used to estimate potential effects on the Aspen non-attainment area and the Maroon Bells–Snowmass Wilderness.
	3. VISCREEN—VISCREEN is a visibility screening model employed to evaluate potential degradation of visibility.
	4. Universal Soil Loss Equation (USLE)—The USLE model was used to estimate changes in soil movement (erosion and sedimentation) to determine impacts on watershed resources.
	5. TRANSPLAN Model—A representative network, consisting of traffic analysis zones, was developed to assess the potential impacts to the project area's transportation system. Traffic impacts were forecasted through the year 2002 using the TRANSPLAN Model.
	6. T-Walk Water Resources Analysis—The T-Walk Water Resources Analysis was designed to determine if a specific land use activity had a degradative effect on a stream system.
Fox Ecosystem Restoration Project: Day and Dunning timber sales and other projects, Malheur National Forest, Grant County, Oregon (1994)—timber sales	One quantitative model was described in the EIS to predict cumulative impacts. This model, used to assess cumulative watershed risk from management activities, was the Forest Equivalent Roaded Area (ERA) Model. The ERA Model considers past, present, and proposed management activities to predict the cumulative watershed impacts from increased sedimentation, peak flows, and resulting changes in channel stability. Each management activity is assigned an index value based on the intensity of impacts and is then evaluated based on the percent of ground affected. The percentage is referred to as the ERA. All effects were compared to those generated by roads, which have the most pronounced effect on watershed function and health.

TABLE 8.8   Examples of Analytical Challenges

- Identification and selection of appropriate impact prediction techniques
- Consideration of assumptions, limitations, and uncertainties related to selected prediction techniques
- Calibration requirements related to selected quantitative models, including necessary baseline data
- Impact prediction and interpretation in the absence of adequate baseline data, including information needed for addressing cumulative impacts
- Delineation of appropriate temporal and spatial boundaries to address cumulative impacts
- Identification and selection of appropriate impact indicators
- Incorporation of a holistic perspective regarding impacts and their environmental system relationships
- Consideration of cumulative and synergistic impacts, along with possible transboundary impacts, in programmatic (strategic) impact studies
- Interpretation of predicted impacts based on institutional requirements, public values, and professional judgment

necessary for all models, it may be a fundamental requirement for some approaches. For example, calibration of groundwater flow and solute transport models may be required prior to their usage in an impact study. Accordingly, one of the limitations of model usage is that there may be insufficient site-specific baseline data to enable such calibration.

Site-specific baseline data are also needed to provide an appropriate basis for interpreting existing environmental quality and the predicted impacts of a proposed action. Limited or non-existent baseline data can increase uncertainty regarding the significance of the potential impacts of a proposed action. Also, when cumulative impact issues are being addressed, data will be required for past and present projects in the vicinity of the proposed action, along with information on reasonably foreseeable future projects in the area. Data gathering related to pertinent other projects often represents a considerable challenge in the EIA process.

There are many analytical challenges related to addressing cumulative impacts for single proposed actions. Such challenges begin with defining the temporal and spatial scales for use in the impact study. Cumulative environmental changes may occur over extended temporal and spatial scales (or boundaries) in comparison to direct or indirect effects of single projects. For example, the time scales may be much longer than normally utilized in planning and policy decisions. Spatial changes may transcend the boundaries of local project sites to include regional and even global scales. Changes over time and space can also accumulate and compound so that, in aggregate, the resultant effect exceeds the simple sum of previous changes (Spaling and Smit, 1993). Temporal and spatial crowding and other attributes can be used to delineate several types of cumulative impacts; these types, delineated as follows, also represent analytical challenges in the impact prediction process (Spaling and Smit, 1993):

1. Time crowding, characterized by frequent and repetitive environmental change, can cause the temporal capacity of an environmental medium to be exceeded.
2. Space crowding resulting from a high spatial density of environmental change that can alter a region's spatial pattern or processes.
3. Compounding or synergism may occur when two or more environmental changes contribute to another environmental change.
4. Time lags need to be considered when there are delays between exposure to a perturbation and response.
5. Space lags or extended boundaries can be associated with environmental changes appearing some distance from the source; for example, acid rain originating from several power plants in one area is frequently deposited at distant locations.
6. Thresholds may be exceeded and thus cause disruptions to environmental processes that fundamentally alter system behavior.

Because of the data requirements associated with many models or methods, an alternate tool for impact prediction might involve indicators of environmental quality. The concept would be to direct attention to a few selected factors in lieu of a comprehensive description of the setting and prediction of changes on multiple factors. Indicators refer to the use of single measurements of factors or biological species, with the assumption being that these measurements are "indicative" of the biophysical or socioeconomic system. Ecological indicators have been used for many decades (Hunsaker and Carpenter, 1990). Relative to pollution effects, an indicator organism is a species selected for its sensitivity or tolerance (more frequently sensitivity) to various kinds of pollution or its effects (e.g., metal pollution or oxygen depletion) (Chapman, 1992). Environmental indicators have also been suggested for monitoring the state of the environment in relation to sustainable development and associated environmental threats (Organization for Economic Co-operation and Development, 1991). The central challenge in using indicators is to appropriately select the pertinent indicators themselves.

Another analytical challenge in the EIA process is to overcome the narrow perspective often held by substantive area specialists, particularly with regard to interrelationships between environmental components and associated changes. The challenge is basically to utilize a holistic perspective in planning and conducting an impact study. This perspective is often absent in traditional academic programs that are related to the EIA process; examples of such programs include environmental engineering, environmental science, biology, geography, and regional and city planning.

As impact studies evolve in focus from single-project/direct impact concerns to programmatic or strategic impact studies encompassing multiple actions in large geographic areas, the analytical challenges become even more complicated. For example, among several items to be addressed in a strategic environmental assessment (SEA) for a policy, plan, or program, it has been noted that a discussion of cumulative and synergistic impacts should be included along with transboundary impacts (Economic Commission for Europe, 1992). In addition, methodologies utilized, availability of data, and uncertainties associated with their use should be described. SEAs may also need to be correlated with land use planning.

To illustrate the challenges related to SEAs, the topical outline for a SEA report for highway/transportation planning should include purpose and need; description of proposed actions, including the no action and other alternatives; description of existing environment of relevance to system planning; description of risk for significant effects of the proposed plan (relevant to system planning), including information on how environmental effects have been considered for alternatives (achievement of environmental goals); recommended mitigation principles; information on evaluation methods used; information on "scoping" or preceding policy formulation; and information on gaps in knowledge and important uncertainties (Organization for Economic Co-operation and Development, 1994). Impact predictions in SEAs for highway planning are usually based on a mixture of qualitative (descriptive) methods and quantitative methods involving factors that can be expressed numerically. Scaling, ranking, and monetary values have been used for evaluation of different options. Multicriteria analysis may include importance weights developed by pairwise comparisons of options. Whatever methods are used, it is important that they are described along with the effects (impacts) based on key indicators. Examples of indicators that could be used for SEAs in transportation planning include gases with greenhouse effects (expressed in CO_2 equivalents), oxides of nitrogen, consumption of primary energy, and total area of land required (Organization for Economic Co-operation and Development, 1994).

Coordination of highway/transportation planning with land use planning is one way to limit adverse environmental impacts, avoid conflicts, and achieve efficient and environmentally adapted transportation systems. Coordination is needed in both time and space; three approaches which could be used for such coordination are (1) integration of highway and land use planning in regions with conflicts; (2) conduction of land use planning parallel to highway/administration planning, for certain areas of land reserved for conservation purposes; and (3) highway zone planning in sensitive regions/areas, or for other specific reasons, when upgrading existing highways and surrounding areas (Organization for Economic Co-operation and Development, 1994).

As a final analytical challenge, it should be recognized that impact predictions developed via the use of various techniques must then be interpreted from several perspectives, including institutional requirements as represented by laws, regulations, and executive orders, while also giving due consideration to public values and professional judgment. While scientific principles and methods should be the fundamental basis for impact prediction, public policy and decision making based on value judgments are also integral to the EIA process.

CONCLUSIONS

The technical "heart" of the EIA process is related to the prediction of direct, indirect, and cumulative impacts of proposed actions. Numerous types of methods are available for usage throughout the various activities in an impact study. Impact prediction methods include simple techniques, indices and experimental methods, and mathematical models. Within any given impact category (for example, air quality impacts), there are several potentially pertinent impact prediction approaches, including sophisticated modeling. Examples of analytical challenges include the selection process for prediction techniques and/or impact indicators, model usage in the absence of adequate baseline data, and the delineation of temporal and spatial boundaries for cumulative impact considerations and for programmatic impact studies. Even though the challenges are great, it is important that the EIA process be based on technical approaches; accordingly, the application of scientific concepts is fundamental to effective project planning, impact analysis, and decision making. Finally, interpretation of predicted impacts should effectively blend both scientific and value judgments.

SELECTED REFERENCES

Adamus, P.R., E.J. Clairain, R.D. Smith, and R.E. Young. 1987. Wetland Evaluation Technique. Volume II: Methodology. U.S. Army Corps of Engineers, Waterways Experiment Station, Vicksburg, Mississippi.

Anderson, M.G. and T.P. Burt. 1985. Modelling Strategies. In *Hydrological Forecasting*. M.G. Anderson and T.P. Burt, Eds. John Wiley and Sons, New York, pp. 1–13.

Armour, C.L. and S.C. Williamson. 1988. Guidance for Modeling Causes and Effects in Environmental Problem Solving. Biological—89(4). National Ecology Research Center, U.S. Fish and Wildlife Service, Ft. Collins, Colorado.

Canter, L.W. 1996. *Environmental Impact Assessment*, second edition. McGraw-Hill, New York.

Canter, L.W., S.F. Atkinson, and F.L. Leistritz. 1985. *Impact of Growth*. Lewis Publishers, Chelsea, Michigan.

Chapman, D., Ed. 1992. *Water Quality Assessments*. Chapman and Hall, London, pp. 183–198.

Cooper, T.A. 1995. Cumulative Impact Assessment Practice in the United States. MES thesis. University of Oklahoma, Norman, pp. 136–168.

Council on Environmental Quality. 1978. National Environmental Policy Act—Regulations. *Federal Register* (November 29) 43(230):55978–56007.

Economic Commission for Europe. 1992. Application of Environmental Impact Assessment Principles to Policies, Plans, and Programmes. ECE/ENVWA/27. United Nations, New York, pp. 7–8.

Henderson-Sellers, B. 1991. *Water Quality Modeling, Vol. IV: Decision Support Techniques for Lakes and Reservoirs*. CRC Press, Boca Raton, Florida.

Hunsaker, C.T. and D.E. Carpenter. 1990. Environmental Monitoring and Assessment Program—Ecological Indicators. EPA/600/3-90/060. U.S. Environmental Protection Agency, Research Triangle Park, North Carolina.

James, A., Ed. 1993. *An Introduction to Water Quality Modeling*. John Wiley and Sons, West Sussex, England.

King, T.F. 1978. The Archaeological Survey: Methods and Uses. Heritage Conservation and Recreation Service. U.S. Department of the Interior, Washington, D.C.

Lohani, B.N. and N. Halim. 1990. Environmental Impact Identification and Prediction: Methodologies and Resource Requirements. Background Papers for Course on Environmental Impact Assessment of Hydropower and Irrigation Projects, August 13–31. International Center for Water Resources Management and Training (CEFIGRE), Bangkok, Thailand, pp. 152–182.

Magrab, E.B. 1975. *Environmental Noise Control*. John Wiley and Sons, New York.

Marlatt, R.M., T.A. Hale, and R.G. Sullivan. 1993. Video Simulation as Part of Army Environmental Decision-Making: Observations from Camp Shelby, Mississippi. *Environmental Impact Assessment Review* 13(2):75–88.

National Environmental Policy Act. 1969. Public Law 91-190. U.S. Congress, Washington, D.C.

Organization for Economic Co-operation and Development. 1991. *Environmental Indicators*. Paris, pp. 8–10.

Organization for Economic Co-operation and Development. 1994. *Environmental Impact Assessment of Roads*. Paris, pp. 34–43.

Ott, W.R. 1978. *Environmental Indices: Theory and Practice*. Ann Arbor Science Publishers, Ann Arbor, Michigan.

Smardon, R.C., J.F. Palmer, and J.P. Felleman. 1986. *Foundations for Visual Project Analysis*. John Wiley and Sons, New York.

Spaling, H. and B. Smit. 1993. Cumulative Environmental Change: Conceptual Frameworks, Evaluation Approaches, and Institutional Perspectives. *Environmental Management* 17(5):587–600.

Starfield, A.M. and A.L. Bleloch. 1986. *Building Models for Conservation and Wildlife Management*. MacMillan, New York.

Turnbull, R.G., Ed. 1992. *Environmental and Health Impact Assessment of Development Projects*. Elsevier Science Publishers, London.

Turner, D.B. 1994. *Workbook of Atmospheric Dispersion Estimates,* second edition. Lewis Publishers, Boca Raton, Florida.

U.S. Army Corps of Engineers. 1980. A Habitat Evaluation System for Water Resources Planning. Lower Mississippi Valley Division. Vicksburg, Mississippi.

U.S. Army Corps of Engineers. 1987. Water Quality Models Used by the Corps of Engineers. Information Exchange Bulletin, Vol. E-87-1. Waterways Experiment Station. Vicksburg, Mississippi.

U.S. Environmental Protection Agency. 1993. Guideline on Air Quality Models (Revised). EPA-450/2-78-027R. 40 Code of Federal Regulations, Chapter 1, Part 51, Appendix W, pp. 962–969, 1003–1012.

U.S. Fish and Wildlife Service. 1980. Habitat Evaluation Procedures (HEP). ESM 102. Washington, D.C.

Water Science and Technology Board. 1990. *Groundwater Models—Scientific and Regulatory Applications*. National Academy Press, Washington, D.C.

World Health Organization. 1986. Assessment of Noise Impact on the Urban Environment. Environmental Health Series No. 9. Regional Office for Europe, Copenhagen.

Zanetti, P. 1990. *Air Pollution Modeling—Theories, Computational Methods, and Available Software*. Van Nostrand Reinhold, New York.

CAN NEPA PREVENT "ECOLOGICAL TRAIN WRECKS"?

9

N.B. Dennis

A recent issue of *NAEP* (National Association of Environmental Professionals) *News* (Winter 1994) featured an article by Kathleen McGinty, chair of the Council on Environmental Quality (CEQ), in which she introduced two examples of the Clinton administration's "new generation of environmental protection: EPA's Common Sense Initiative, a multimedia, sector-specific approach to pollution regulation, and Ecosystem Management, the (new) paradigm for managing the nation's natural resources." Both were characterized as revolutionary but grounded in common sense. Ecologists have known for decades that what we do with one resource affects the others, but federal agency operations, McGinty said, have failed to account for such interactions: agencies have operated independently, often in the same area but under different rules. "Often the results were catastrophic—ecological and economic train wrecks, such as conflict over timber cutting in the Pacific Northwest or the collapse of fisheries on the East Coast."

An earlier article in the *San Francisco Chronicle* had reported Interior Secretary Bruce Babbitt as stating that to avert "national train wrecks," the Clinton administration planned to shift federal policy away from a single-species approach to one that "looked at entire ecosystems" (as quoted in Stevens, 1993). Later, in reference to the developing impasse over federal listing of the California gnatcatcher as "threatened," Babbitt was quoted as seeking to make the California process a national model for avoiding the type of "environmental train wrecks" that have occurred in the Everglades and the Pacific Northwest (as quoted in Whalen, 1994). Secretary Babbitt's communications director stated: "Rather than a collision point occurring year after year over individual endangered species, we need to plan ahead and look down the road" (McClurg, 1993). A press release issued by the Department of Interior in 1994 stated that conservation agreements (to be developed by five federal agencies and state fish and wildlife agencies for selected sensitive, candidate, and proposed species and groups of species, habitats, and ecosystems) "will be of particular value for those species that require an inter-forest, inter-regional, and/or ecosystem approach to effectively conserve" their habitats, while at the same time avoiding future "economic train wrecks" (as quoted in Mueller, 1995).

In several different contexts, the train wreck metaphor signals major conflicts in the environmental process. This chapter picks up Secretary Babbitt's now-familiar metaphor (with variations) and shifts the focus by asking whether the National Environmental Policy Act (NEPA) can prevent ecological train wrecks. The implication of the question is that NEPA as law and procedure may be an appropriate mechanism to prevent major environmental conflicts—collisions or "national train wrecks"—of the kind alluded to by both McGinty and Babbitt, notwithstanding the fact that such ecological train wrecks may have been prompted by other environmental laws, notably the Endangered Species Act (ESA) or Section 404 of the Clean Water Act (hereafter Section 404). Or the collision course may have originated in a pre-NEPA era and, through lack of scientific knowledge, political coordination, regulatory action, and/or funds, led to such cumulative phenomena as the "collapse of fisheries on the East Coast" (McGinty, 1994).

NEPA is substantively and procedurally unlike either the ESA or Section 404, but the laws are necessarily linked, since NEPA review is involved—with some exceptions—in all major and thousands of minor federal actions, including ESA and Section 404 permit actions. The question remains: Can NEPA prevent major collisions (including those caused by actions regulated under ESA or Section 404), intervene constructively and minimize the damage, or at least restore the victims? A simple answer would be "no—not by itself" or "yes—but it depends." Certainly the answer is not straightforward. At the outset, implementation of NEPA varies widely among federal agencies, from highly integrated (in planning processes) to minimally compliant. Further questions lie just below the surface: Has NEPA in actual practice prevented ecological collisions? (Successes are always more difficult to document than failures. How many hundreds of train wrecks have been averted by effective NEPA analyses?) To what extent has NEPA itself been the proximate cause of ecological train wrecks? Do we recognize in NEPA a potential for environmental problem solving that is not being fully realized?

This chapter addresses the central question by examining several ESA conflicts (two of which are known to have prompted the "train wreck" metaphor), NEPA's role in these and other major conflicts, and NEPA's opportunities and limitations in preventing ecological train wrecks. Although the emphasis is on the ecological term in the pair of terms used by both Babbitt and McGinty ("ecological and economic train wrecks"), the economic term is essential to understanding the cause of train wrecks. The commentary is informal, based on the author's observations during 25 years of participation in environmental impact assessment (EIA), predominantly in California and western states, beginning with the enactment of both NEPA and the California Environmental Quality Act (CEQA) in 1970. The NEPA experience throughout most of this period has entailed working directly or indirectly with 16 federal agencies, including federal land, natural resource, and water management agencies, regulators, and/or joint project sponsors through federal funding. Because many experiences have involved preparation of joint NEPA and CEQA analyses, a California perspective is inescapable.

WHAT IS AN "ECOLOGICAL TRAIN WRECK"?
THE MEANING OF THE METAPHOR

"Train wreck" as a metaphor for ecological conflict suggests a collision course—or courses—of action; a complete breakdown, "derailment," the grinding to a halt (gridlock; logjam) of a working institutional system—perhaps one that already was suboptimal but at least was operational. It suggests the possibility of human error, limited vision, and failure to predict accurately what lies ahead or to "read the landscape," resulting in fatalities, losses, and other costs, in a real and symbolic sense.

It is an imperfect metaphor to apply to the majority of environmental conflicts in that it suggests a linear event; most real train wrecks occur on single tracks, they involve two trains at most, and the technical causes for the collision, including human error, can be pinpointed or readily inferred. In contrast, most environmental conflicts are non-linear, characterized by multiple "tracks" and multiple "trains" (multiple stakeholders, resources, agency mandates and programs, spatial and temporal scales, approaches, objectives, and values). The causes of ecological collisions are often obscure, accumulating over time and becoming evident only when collision is imminent or when all trains are stalled; countless environmental problems may fall below the level of perceived significance, or low-priority problems may be causing chronic degradation long before they become measurable, much less susceptible to federal action. Nor does the metaphor reveal differences in the assessment of damage; for example, the fatalities and costs in an ecological train wreck could involve either "natural" (plants, animals) or human inhabitants of an ecosystem, or both, depending on the outcome and the "stakes" and perspectives of those affected. The values assigned to the fatalities and environmental costs would have to extend beyond utility and familiar forms of market quantification. Environmental activists would assess damages in terms of loss of intrinsic biodiversity values and future options, land developers would assess damages in the currency of land costs and costs associated with unpredictability and delay, and public officials would equate losses with tax revenues and jobs.

McGinty (1994) cited two examples. As a category, the first might be called "cumulative resource depletion or degradation," exemplified by the collapse of fisheries on the east coast (Ludwig et al., 1993); further examples could include the decline of native salmon fisheries in waters of California and the Pacific Northwest or the cumulative loss of wetlands through agricultural conversion in many parts of the United States (Office of Technology Assessment, 1984; Dennis and Marcus, 1984). The second category frequently follows from the first and might be called "endangered elements of biodiversity," that is, train wrecks stemming from the listing of species as threatened or endangered under the ESA, exemplified by the conflict between logging interests and the northern spotted owl habitat preservation interests in late successional and old-growth forest in the Pacific Northwest (to simplify a complex set of issues). A third kind of ecological collision—familiar to most NEPA practitioners—would be the "major controversial project," exemplified by the $1.3 billion hydroelectric Kemano Completion Project in British Columbia. The project was recently terminated as a consequence of predictions of impacts to salmon fisheries, after many years of planning, environmental analysis, engineering, and partial construction (Howard, 1995). There are many examples of this type. Finally, a fourth type, "the catastrophic accident," most closely fits the metaphor, exemplified by the July 14, 1991 spill of 19,000 gallons of metam sodium (a solid, water-soluble organic toxin used as a soil fumigant) from a derailed, overturned railcar into the upper Sacramento River above Shasta Dam, the primary source of federally managed water supply in California. The last example was literally an ecological train wreck.

A hypothetical role for NEPA can be related to any of these four types of ecological train wrecks. Although the first three examples may share common ecological issues, they differ in spatial and temporal distribution patterns; in institutional, regulatory, and political contexts; and therefore in their susceptibilities to NEPA review. NEPA has practical limitations that are well known: the causes of impacts might fall short of the definition or threshold of a "federal action," they might occur on private land and elude federal jurisdiction altogether, or the cause of impact and cleanup remedies might be covered largely by regulations or processes functionally equivalent to NEPA (or CEQA), as in the case of the Sacramento River metam sodium spill. The etiology of an accidental event such as this spill is sufficiently distinct from the other types to warrant dropping it from the present discussion. Even where applicable, NEPA might not be available in an appropriate or timely manner to prevent a "collision," due to complex and diffuse origins, such as represented by overexploitation of fishery stocks coupled with physical changes to watersheds and incremental inputs of pollutants into large systems like Chesapeake Bay or the San Francisco–San Joaquin Bay/Delta Estuary (Bay-Delta). The growing evidence of degradation might be under extensive scientific scrutiny but escape all but local, incremental project-level impact analysis for years before cumulative impacts became susceptible to regional programmatic attention under NEPA. By that time, certain species might have reached dangerously low population levels, warranting listing under the ESA—the sure sign of a train wreck in process.

THE ENDANGERED SPECIES ACT, ECOLOGICAL TRAIN WRECKS, AND NEPA

Tensions among differing values are the principal underlying causes of environmental conflicts, or ecological train wrecks (Caldwell, 1993). Perhaps more than any other federal environmental statute, the ESA highlights the tension between economic development and conservation (Bonnett and Zimmerman, 1991). Because the metaphor was prompted by events ensuing from the listing of species under the ESA, and because evolving interpretations and applications of the ESA now frequently drive considerations of biodiversity and ecosystems in NEPA analyses, a brief review of general circumstances of the ESA and four illustrative cases provide insight into Babbitt's use of the metaphor. The purpose is not to analyze the effectiveness of the ESA per se, but to sort out NEPA's relationship to the ESA.

The enactment of the ESA in 1973 was actually the third congressional attempt to engage the federal government in protecting species from extinction. After previous weak attempts in 1966 (passage of the Endangered Species Preservation Act) and 1969 revisions to better protect both species and habitat, the substantially new 1973 ESA represented the legislature's best effort to keep up with rapidly developing scientific knowledge of biological diversity and the recognition of widespread species extinctions (O'Connell, 1992). It also followed the passage of NEPA, which had set the stage for more expansive consideration of "ecological information" in many subsequent environmental statutes, as well as in federal decision making in general.

The basic logic of the ESA was to protect single species: the act was intended to provide a much-needed ultimate safety net for those species facing extinction. The provision in Section 2(b) of the ESA for protecting imperiled species and "the ecosystems upon which (they) depend" and for designating critical habitat went fairly far, for its time, toward protecting biodiversity beyond the single-species level. Since that time, however, scientific recognition that a species-based approach to biodiversity conservation is seriously limited has outstripped the ability and/or willingness of the political process to expand statutory protection to include larger "units" of biodiversity, such as whole ecosystems (O'Connell, 1992), although ESA procedure is attempting to move in that direction. The act has been amended several times since 1973, but economic interests have pressured successfully against any broadening of statutory authority. An amendment added in 1982 (Section 10(a), discussed below) that was intended primarily to reconcile the economic concerns of private (i.e., non-federal) landowners with habitat conservation has also had mixed success in widening the scope of protection to include private lands.

The debate continues over whether biodiversity is best protected through focus on ecosystems or through focus on species and whether the ESA can adequately protect biodiversity by either measure (Rholf, 1991; O'Connell, 1992). Some would say that this is a false dichotomy: both single-species management and ecosystem management are part of a continuum of steps necessary to protect biodiversity (Wilcove, 1994). Most would admit, however, that the ESA as currently written and interpreted by the courts cannot be counted on to protect ecosystems or even protect all deserving single species. Further debate over congressional reauthorization of the ESA continues into 1997. The Supreme Court reviewed and upheld the definition of "harm" in Section 9 of the act, which had been narrowly construed to exclude habitat modification or degradation (*Sweet Home Chapter of Communities v. Babbitt*). However, the outcome of the reauthorization debate will have serious implications for future protection of habitats (and potentially ecosystems) of endangered species. Debate also continues concerning ESA's impacts on local economies and its ability to reconcile the conflicting goals of ecological and economic sustainability.

These debates inevitably spill over into how ecological analyses are conducted under NEPA and, conversely, how NEPA review of ESA permit actions is conducted. The NEPA process has become a primary vehicle for public intervention into how the ESA is carried out by agencies in their other planning activities. It is acknowledged that NEPA analyses are most often statute driven or regulation driven (CEQ, 1993). Among the various environmental statutes that address aspects of the nation's biodiversity (for example, Marine Mammal Act, Wilderness Act, Migratory Bird Treaty Act, Bald Eagle and Golden Eagle Protection Act, Clean Water Act, etc.), the ESA is still the most powerful and, therefore, has become a focal point in NEPA analyses for consideration of biodiversity. Used as a surrogate for broader habitat issues and an "umbrella" covering less protected species, the presence of a threatened or endangered species within a project's zone of impact offers the potentially most enforceable opportunity (excepting Section 404) to include in a NEPA analysis discussion of biodiversity, minimally at a species/population level and preferably at a habitat or even ecosystem level.

At the same time, a narrow reading of both NEPA and ESA obligations offers the project sponsor and federal agency (if different from the sponsor) the opportunity to confine mitigation commitments to only fully protected species, leaving open to discretion such questions as which other species (candidates for listing? other species at risk?) and habitats should be considered "significant" losses of biodiversity if impacted and therefore deserving of mitigation. The majority of federal agencies and/or project sponsors are reluctant to enter into voluntary mitigation commitments for impacts that might be relegated to a less-than-significant status.

Mission Blue Butterfly and San Bruno Mountain (California) Habitat Conservation Plan

The 1982 ESA amendment added Section 10(a) to allow non-federal landowners or developers to obtain a permit for limited "incidental take" of an endangered species after first preparing a habitat conservation plan (HCP). No means existed under the ESA for a private party to negotiate incidental take, such as through consultation between federal agencies and the U.S. Fish and Wildlife Service (FWS), as prescribed in Section 7 of the act. Lindell Marsh, a visionary land use lawyer in Southern California, successfully proposed the "HCP process" to Congress, in his words, "marking the beginning of a major paradigm shift in national policy for conserving biological diversity" (Marsh, 1994). The specific case involved proposed residential development of 3,000 acres on the lower slopes of San Bruno Mountain, a regionally visible landmark to airline passengers departing San Francisco International Airport. The initial focus of federal attention was the mission blue butterfly (*Icaricia icarioides missionenis*), listed as endangered in 1976. As a result of the listing, plans for development had been stalled through the mid to late 1970s.

The new Section 10(a) was not accompanied by any guidance as to how the HCP process should be implemented, but Marsh believed that the only way to reconcile the ideas and concerns of multiple parties was to move away from traditional regulatory "command and control" toward a collaborative approach, based on two policy objectives: (1) biodiversity should be conserved (the term "biodiversity" actually had not yet entered the environmental lexicon) and (2) the right to own property is a basic freedom. Carrying out the San Bruno Mountain HCP required "building a model" for future HCPs. An outside facilitator was engaged to achieve constructive communication among affected parties, and the *underlying logic of NEPA* was applied as follows: the affected constituencies considered alternatives that transcended artificial governance boundaries; they thoroughly "scoped" the issues; and, through technical analysis and identification of impacts, they were able to narrow alternatives to a preferred set of actions (Marsh, 1994). Fifty-one species with varying degrees of "official" protection were included in the studies and management agreements of the HCP, at a cost of $1.5 million (Marsh, 1994).

This brief summary does not capture the extensive conflicts, controversies, and necessary commitment of individuals that accompanied the lengthy process; nor does it sound like a real "ecological train wreck." In fact, it proved to be a historic experiment in trying to prevent future train wrecks, moving as it did away from project-by-project review, fragmented ineffective mitigation, and adversarial, quasi-judicial decision making (Marsh, 1994), still too often a characteristic of both EIA and ESA processes. The EIA process, in this instance a joint CEQA/NEPA document, used a programmatic approach that encompassed the habitat enhancement and management actions detailed in the HCP to protect a large complement of species and laid out conditions for phased urban development allowed by the plan. The direct application of EIA, in itself, did not prevent an incipient train wreck; however, application of the underlying logic of NEPA was instrumental in defining the analytic paradigm and the public elements of a preventive strategy for San Bruno Mountain that has worked to the satisfaction of most, if not all (Sigg, 1993).

Because of the fundamental paradigm shift, the HCP procedure was slow to catch on (Marsh, 1994). By 1990, only 5 HCPs had been completed; by late 1994, 30 HCPs, mostly for single species, had been approved and 130 were in process, many of them expanded to encompass multiple species. This would appear to have become a well-established and accepted procedure for preventing many potential train wrecks. However, the HCP process has a number of serious limitations in its capacity to protect animals and plants and reconcile land use conflicts: the process tends to be reactive, triggered only when a proposed development is likely to cause harm; it continues to be applied primarily on a project-by-project basis; and it does not work well for small parcels with limited opportunity to separate development from areas reserved for habitat enhancement and protection (Ebbin, 1994). Accompanied by NEPA analysis, the ESA Section 10(a) process has not assuaged the tension that exists between environmental and developer interests. Environmentalists have been actively involved in developing HCPs, but they also maintain a skeptical close watch, using the companion NEPA/CEQA public review as one opportunity for intervention and legal challenge as necessary: "Citizens should be aware that the HCP/incidental taking permit process is not a panacea, and in fact can be fraught with many problems, including reliance on inadequate scientific data, inadequate monitoring and enforcement, failure to provide for species recovery, and use of HCPs in lieu of recovery plans or formal designation of critical habitat" (Mueller, 1994). Developers, in turn, have said in effect: "Show me one landowner who has ever come out happy by being open with the government about this issue. We're not fools."

Northern Spotted Owl and Old-Growth Forests of the Pacific Northwest

If the mission blue butterfly created controversy in the San Francisco Bay region, the listing in 1990 of the northern spotted owl (*Strix occidentalis occidentalis*) as being threatened with extinction touched off a veritable train wreck that had been in process throughout the 1980s as old-growth forest stands continued to be logged. The northern spotted owl–timber resource debacle, one of the most volatile environmental issues in recent memory, was, therefore, an appropriate locus for Babbitt's metaphor. The controversy over the logging of old-growth forests throughout the Pacific Northwest goes far beyond the immediate ESA protection of the owl and other species, which have been viewed by environmentalists as a symbol of the struggle to preserve Earth's dwindling biological resources represented by ancient forests, and, conversely, by the timber industry and local economies dependent on that industry as an "irrational barrier to economic development" and harbinger of regional economic doom (Bonnett and Zimmerman, 1991).

At a more practical level, the listing embroiled three federal land management agencies (the Forest Service [FS], the Bureau of Land Management [BLM], and the National Park Service [NPS]); state resource agencies in Washington, Oregon, and California; and private forested-land owners in the immediate questions of how to protect the owl, how much habitat to protect, and how to set acceptable limits for harvesting late successional and old-growth forests. It also engaged salmon fishers, Native Americans, mill workers, local small business owners, environmentalists, scientists, and timber executives (Johnson, 1993)—traditional combatants over increasingly limited and functionally interdependent resources.

For many years prior to the first petition for listing of the northern spotted owl by "Green World" in 1987, the federal agencies had had duties to protect the owl under the National Forest Management Act (NFMA) and the Migratory Bird Treaty Act and to evaluate dwindling owl habitat in NEPA analyses. The areas set aside by forest plans for owl habitat were smaller, however, than the areas calculated by biologists as necessary for maintenance of viable populations (Bonnett and Zimmerman, 1991). Since the listing of the northern spotted owl, much of the controversy has centered on this core problem: how to support with scientific data the delineation of appropriate habitat conservation areas (HCAs); no standards or guidelines accompany the ESA to direct the application of biological data to the design of reserves or reserve systems for imperiled species (Murphy and Noon, 1992).[1]

The long-running battle in the Pacific Northwest survived two presidential administrations without resolution or satisfactory approach, until President Clinton and Vice President Gore met with the combatants in April 1993. The issues went far beyond the spotted owl and old-growth forest; they began with sometimes unrecognized differences in how people viewed the environment and natural resources (e.g., utilitarian versus ecological valuations, acceptable levels of ecological and economic risk, and the inevitable differences in the meaning of "sustainable" strategies and "environmentally sound" development) (Johnson, 1993). The April 1993 conference and the studies and products that followed had import for the future of the ESA, forest management, ecological and economic sustainability, and potentially for the practice of NEPA. A series of ecosystem management assessments were conducted by interdisciplinary teams that considered from economic and social as well as ecological perspectives how alternative conservation strategies might affect hundreds of species (Forest Ecosystem Management Assessment Team, 1993; Franklin, 1994). The President's Forest Plan for a Sustainable Economy and Sustainable Development for the Pacific Northwest, released in July 1993, placed a limit on annual timber harvest, created a system of old-growth reserves, and proposed federal funding for a five-year program for economic revitalization.

The debate is not over, and the answers to broader issues are still evolving, among them (Freedman, 1994, 1995; Noss, 1994; Holling, 1978, 1993): How can concepts such as the health of ecosystems and species viability be linked with the economic and social well-being of people? How can short-term economic goals be reconciled with long-term protection and sustainability of ecosystems? How can NEPA address these complex issues and relate more effectively with the NFMA forest planning process as well as with other natural resource laws? Can NEPA "fit" with the kind of adaptive management paradigm required for dynamic planning?

In the strategy to resolve this ecological and economic train wreck in the Pacific Northwest, NEPA is just one of many steps (Freedman, 1995). At a minimum, NEPA provides a framework for identifying and comparing the consequences of alternatives (U.S.D.A. Forest Service, 1994). It also affords a primary opportunity for broad public participation and legal challenge, although it has been found that the NEPA process is of greater value to environmental litigants in providing access to information that is useful in preparing non-NEPA lawsuits (Taylor, 1984). The formulation of alternatives for management of old-growth and late successional forests has not been without challenge. In 1995, "Option 9" was the latest in a long series of alternative plans developed by the FS, BLM, and FWS to protect habitat for the northern spotted owl; it appeared to be the most acceptable version of the Clinton administration's forestry plan for federal lands in the Pacific Northwest (Sierra Club, 1995). Option 9 was regarded as a setback by environmentalists because of the allowable levels of timber harvest in old-growth forests on which it is premised; however, it also served as a means of stabilizing the conflict between "enviros" and "timber beasts" (Sierra Club, 1995). Among other provisions, Option 9 designated 660,000 acres in northwestern California as "adaptive management areas," areas designated for experimental logging and watershed restoration projects (see also Swanson and Franklin, 1992). Alternative plans such as Option 9, indeed the FS's legal authority to plan on an ecosystem basis, have also been challenged by the timber industry. The court rejected industry arguments against ecosystem planning, pointing out that planning on an ecosystem basis may be the only way to meet legal requirements (Sierra Club, 1995).

The Pacific Northwest is emblematic and a forewarning of future ecological and economic train wrecks, perhaps on a smaller scale. Many rural areas that adjoin and are economically dependent on federal public lands, especially forested lands, are experiencing economic shock from radical shifts in forest management philosophy away from traditional multiple-resource management toward ecosystem management (Kusel, 1994). Because the new objectives of ecosystem management are not fully defined, much less fully operative, the question arises: Is NEPA flexible enough to document and analyze these shifts as they are occurring, that is, *is NEPA an adaptable statute and procedure?* Furthermore, in contexts where "government" is deeply distrusted, NEPA is perceived less as an opportunity for community participation than as another symptom of "top-down policy" expected from government. The most vital strategies that have emerged for perhaps avoiding future train wrecks in the rural communities of the Pacific Northwest and in other forest-dependent communities are not related to either formal participation procedures or the expected legal challenges by national environmental interests. Rather, they represent "bottom-up" initiatives, developed by local residents who, with their own and the communities' future welfare in mind, acknowledge the need to find creative ways to reconcile the goals of economic vitality and environmental stewardship (Johnson, 1993; Kusel, 1994). In these environments, NEPA faces multiple challenges, among them to be adaptive to changing methods of resource management and to identify and merge "bottom-up" public initiatives with the federal government's "top-down" policies and participative strategies.

California Gnatcatcher and the Natural Communities Conservation Planning Process (NCCP)

A third case of incipient collision was referred to by Babbitt as a "national model" for avoiding environmental train wrecks. This "model" planning process can be viewed as an effective approach to overcoming the single-species constraints and the procedural gauntlet of the ESA through regional collaboration and planning. It also reveals that EIA practice (in this case CEQA) is typically flawed by project-specific "tunnel vision": in retrospect, the transformation of "coastal sage scrub" to urban development in five southern California counties, and consequent reduction of habitat for dependent species, occurred incrementally and was documented in numerous CEQA environmental impact reports (EIR is the environmental impact statement [EIS] analogue in California). Under this project-specific (or at best county-specific) scrutiny, the cumulative loss to urban development of 85% of a habitat that had occupied 2.5 million acres was not thoroughly appreciated until the early 1980s.

Coastal sage scrub habitat is distributed discontinuously over an area of about 6,000 square miles in the western, coastal portions of five counties. It is non-descript in superficial appearances, but species rich. A doctoral candidate studied and identified a subspecies of California gnatcatcher (*Polioptila californica californica*) that inhabits a range extending from Los Angeles County to Baja, California, and includes some of the most valuable real estate in the world (Mann and Plummer, 1995). Projecting that the habitat would be gone or irreparably fragmented in 20 years as a result of intensive development, the Natural Resources Defense Council assisted the research in requesting FWS for listing on an emergency basis in 1990 (Mann and Plummer, 1995). FWS did not announce its intention to list the gnatcatcher until 1991. By that time, 30 more species were potentially listable and another 30 were under consideration; a total of 96 were "in trouble" (Mann and Plummer, 1995). The California gnatcatcher was listed as threatened in 1993, with special provisions (ESA Section 4(d)): (1) that no HCP would be required if property owners and affected municipalities agreed to a regional planning process created by the state of California in 1991—the NCCP, which could serve in place of the HCP process, and (2) that an allowable "take" of 5% would be permitted while studies were underway (Clark, 1995).[2]

The California governor's and legislature's express purpose in authorizing the broad regional planning framework of the NCCP in 1991 was to "get ahead of the curve of single-species listing and the state's projected population growth—32 million people at present, projected to reach 41 million by the year 2010." If effective, the NCCP process might even obviate the need for future new listings of species sharing habitat with an already listed species (Mantell, 1994). The practical purpose was to form collaborative working relationships among resource agency staff, landowners, local governments, conservationists, and others to undertake regional multispecies, community, or ecosystem planning efforts—anticipatory rather than reactive, voluntary, in advance of or in conjunction with state and federal single-species listings programs, and with responsibility for land use controls and incentives residing in the hands of local government and landowners. Although the broad authority of the NCCP process was authorized only on a pilot program basis for the 300,000 to 400,000 remaining acres of coastal sage scrub habitat in southern California, it could be applied to other regions of the state.

In a manner that has generally eluded NEPA and CEQA analyses, the NCCP process—and to a degree the HCP process where applied regionally—has brought together the many interests and institutions necessary for regional collaborative planning. However, the "jury is still out" as to the ability of NCCP to resolve debates over the real-world effectiveness of reserves, corridors, and other linking mechanisms designed to preserve this remnant piece of California biodiversity (Silver, 1994). "Although the southern California habitat planning experiment has the potential to provide concrete regional models for reconciling the competing demands of biodiversity conservation and economic development, without rigorous incorporation of scientific principles into the program the promise of a national model will be lost" (Notthoff, 1994).

A recent status report finds this much heralded voluntary planning program "in danger of falling into a state of disarray" (Mueller, 1995): a Scientific Review Panel has been disbanded; state financial contributions for land acquisition, an important part of implementation, have not been forthcoming; local development projects have been approved without heeding recommended constraints to protect habitat; and there is continued uncertainty as to whether the NCCP process is supposed to be used in lieu of listing species—absent continued listings, there is little regulatory incentive for developers and local governments to participate in the program (Mueller, 1995). No clear role for NEPA or CEQA appears in this now tenuous planning implementation "model," but it appears that what was touted as a state-initiated planning program has become a de facto federal program (Mueller, 1995). An ecological train wreck is still possible.

Other Agreements Designed to Avert Train Wrecks:
San Francisco–San Joaquin Bay/Delta Estuary Agreement

A number of joint policies and multiagency agreements during 1994 represent attempts by the two agencies that share responsibility for the ESA—the Departments of Interior (FWS) and Commerce (National Marine Fisheries Service [NMFS])—in conjunction with other federal agencies, to accomplish multiple objectives: shore up and clarify ESA procedures and scientific standards; ensure that ESA's ecosystem-based goals are integrated with other environmental laws and agency responsibilities, including NEPA, the Clean Water Act, and others, and that various cooperative approaches, such as public/private partnerships, are used; and inform and involve state agencies in all aspects of ESA actions (Mueller, 1995).

The FWS–NMFS joint policies have been applied with constructive effect to another example of the kind of ecological and economic train wreck cited by Babbitt and McGinty—viz., the decades-long conflict over water supply versus fish and wildlife in the California Bay-Delta Estuary. Other metaphors have been used: "water wars," "relentless water battles," "California's most intractable water problem," and so on. Two-thirds of California's water runoff moves through the Bay-Delta Estuary, two-thirds of California's salmon swim through the Bay-Delta each year, and the region helps sustain the environmental and economic health of the entire state (Wheeler, in California Executive Council on Biological Diversity, 1995). The municipal, industrial, and agricultural users of the state and federal water supplies that commingle in the delta extend the full length of the state. Vast physical changes to the contributing watersheds and extensive "replumbing" of both federal and state water delivery systems that are "wheeled" through the delta, along with pollutant inputs from thousands of point and non-point sources, have changed the fundamental character of the estuary. Federal and state efforts to produce water quality standards to protect both water supply and beneficial habitat uses have continued unsuccessfully for more than a decade. It took the legal impediment of listing two fish species as endangered and threatened—winter-run chinook salmon and delta smelt, respectively—to achieve some agreements.

On December 15, 1994, representatives of the state and federal governments and urban, agricultural, and environmental interests ("CalFed") agreed to a framework plan to protect the endangered and threatened fishery resources in the Bay-Delta Estuary (U.S. Department of Interior et al., 1994; Mueller, 1995; California Executive Council on Biological Diversity [California Biodiversity Council], 1995). This is only one of many contributing studies and agreements that have scrutinized the Delta while species' populations were obviously dropping to dangerous levels. Among others, a U.S. Bureau of Reclamation (BOR) programmatic EIS is currently reviewing the impacts of the federal water supply, allocation, and delivery system for the Central Valley Project in California, which necessarily includes impacts on the Bay-Delta Estuary. But this is only one piece of a solution. What is perhaps unique about the Bay-Delta Estuary agreement is that instead of focusing, as have most past efforts, on water quality standards, it takes a fundamental ecosystem approach (theoretically), putting to an end the uncertainty of fragmented, piecemeal management. The role of NEPA/CEQA is relegated to an add-on discussion of the agreement: "the water rights phase, scheduled to begin in July 1995, also requires an EIR to comply with CEQA" (California Biodiversity Council, 1995). (As of December 1995, the terms of the Bay-Delta Estuary agreement were being challenged by congressional representatives from California, prompted by the state's agricultural interests.)

The "California Experiment" in regional biodiversity planning includes more than the NCCP, the array of single-species and regional multispecies HCPs in process, and the Bay-Delta Estuary agreement. Other agreements among state and federal agencies, local governments, and environmental interests are being designed to anticipate and minimize or avoid future collisions between important components of the state's biodiversity and the growing population (Wheeler, 1995; Mantell, 1994). In these collaborative efforts, the ESA, not NEPA, is the "driver," notwithstanding the fact that the policy language to support such efforts is central in NEPA, whereas it is incidental in ESA. Nor is CEQA, since its inception a more powerful impact assessment tool than NEPA on non-federal lands in California, leading the way, although both NEPA and CEQA undoubtedly are responsible for the "underlying logic" and articulation of broad environmental policy that have made such collaboration possible.

MAJOR CONTROVERSIAL PROJECTS AS ECOLOGICAL TRAIN WRECKS

Neither Babbitt nor McGinty cited such an example, but a major controversial project is probably the most common type of case warranting the epithet "train wreck" and the one in which NEPA's role typically is most clearly defined. One of the earliest collision cases in NEPA memory was the proposed reconstruction of the West Side Highway in lower Manhattan, jointly sponsored by the state of New York and the city of New York in the early 1970s. The Westway Project was promoted as an innovative urban design that would prove to be a mechanism for revitalizing Manhattan's West Side and stimulating jobs. Project opponents pursued an evolving strategy. They first challenged the adequacy of the 1974 draft EIS, mobilizing their opposition around a range of issues such as the ability of the project to meet its primary objective of improved transportation. Opponents subsequently contested the final EIS's claim that the "interpier area," an extended reach of old piers along the eastern (Manhattan) Hudson River shoreline that was targeted for major landfill for the project, was incapable of supporting significant aquatic life. After prodding by the U.S. Environmental Protection Agency, the Westway Project conducted a 13-month study which revealed that this area of the Hudson River supported 22 species of fish. The demise of the Westway Project (sporadic reincarnations aside) may have been attributed to delay; however, the scientific studies indicated the extent of likely environmental impacts on the aquatic ecosystem and thereby dealt the final death blow (Ozawa, 1991). (The study of fisheries in the Hudson River also was instrumental in, among other factors, preventing further development of power plants in the Hudson River Valley [Ozawa, 1991].)

Several points can be made about this early NEPA case that beg the question as to whether NEPA *causes* ecological train wrecks (i.e., invites controversy, long and costly delays in the decision process, and potential demise of a project) or *prevents* them (i.e., prevents the occurrence of an ecologically "bad" project). As in most past and contemporary collision cases, the provisions of NEPA were being carried out as an "overlay" to other more substantive statutes. In that instance, the U.S. Army Corps of Engineers (Corps) was the federal lead agency, with responsibilities under both the Rivers and Harbors Act of 1899 (Section 10) and the Federal Water Pollution Control Act Amendments (Clean Water Act, Section 404) to regulate the placement of fill in the Hudson River. Under the impetus of challenge in the courts, the Corps' implementation of Section 404 and EPA's development of guidelines under Section 404(b)(1) were evolving throughout the 1970s. The key to opposition, delay, and eventual demise of the project, however, resided largely in NEPA's procedural provision for access by the public and other agencies and the opportunity for legal challenge, giving the appearance that NEPA per se had the substantive effect of "killing" the project.

At the same time, the extended scientific studies that disclosed the rich aquatic environment of the Hudson River interpier area and predicted environmental damage to fisheries were probably pivotal in the decision to abandon the project—that is, to prevent an ecological train wreck—although the scientific argument also may have served as a convenient surrogate for other points of opposition. Whether the demise of the project represented an "excellent action" by the Corps and other agencies as encouraged in CEQ regulations (§ 1500.1(c)), or the project's failure to meet substantive provisions of Section 404, or the successful legal tactics of opposition would have to rest with the parties at interest.

NEPA'S OPPORTUNITIES AND LIMITATIONS IN PREVENTING TRAIN WRECKS

The cases discussed above suggest that NEPA, or one of its state EIA analogues, plays a role in virtually every incipient train wreck, but as an available mechanism to prevent such events it does not appear to be "front and center." This is somewhat surprising in view of NEPA's wide applicability and imitation. Certainly NEPA set the stage in 1970 for consideration of ecological information in the environmental statutes that followed; it provided the "underlying logic" for a widely imitated analytic and statutory paradigm; it opened the public's door into governmental decision making and profoundly changed agency behavior with respect to the environment; and it has increased the relevance and improved the quality of science-based decisions, largely forced by the growing influence of internal and external technical specialists (Taylor, 1984). But in the development of solutions to the most volatile train wrecks, NEPA (EIA) has not been in the vanguard. This may indicate that NEPA has intrinsic limitations, that it is not being properly implemented or fully exploited as public policy, or that it inevitably functions in accordance with varied circumstances. NEPA's apparent limitations should be examined, since they may suggest ways to rethink and more accurately define a constructive role in preventing train wrecks.

Policy Limitations

The first reason for questioning NEPA's potential substantive effect in preventing ecological collisions resides in a close reading of its statutory language. If ambiguity is a limitation, then flexibility—an alternative way of viewing the same language—may be an opportunity that few other environmental statutes can enjoy. The Supreme Court has confirmed that NEPA itself does not mandate particular results but simply prescribes necessary process and prohibits uninformed decisions. It cannot prohibit unwise agency action or prevent agencies from deciding that other values outweigh the environmental costs (*Robertson v. Methow Valley Citizens Council* [1989]). NEPA's primary importance lies in its role as an environmental overlay on the statutory responsibilities of all federal agencies. Where existing statutory coverage exists for resources of concern, ecological damage (theoretically) can be kept under control, with NEPA providing some assurance and public access to decisions (Mandelker, 1984).

An ecological perspective and apparent ecological priority can be inferred from a selective reading of NEPA's policy language in Sections 101, 102, and 204 (e.g., "prevent damage to the environment and biosphere"; "enrich the understanding of the ecological systems and natural resources important to the Nation"; "preserve important [historic, cultural and] natural aspects of our national heritage"; "maintain an environment which supports diversity [biodiversity]"; "utilize a systematic, interdisciplinary approach which will insure the integrated use of the natural and social sciences"; "initiate and utilize ecological information in the planning and development of resource-oriented projects"; [CEQ shall] "conduct investigations...relating to ecological systems"; and "document...changes in the natural environment, including the plant and animal systems").

Implied are ecological value concepts that are linked to and reinforced by science, but human utility is also present and integral: "attain the widest range of beneficial uses of the environment without degradation..."; "fulfill social, economic, and other requirements of present and future generations..."; and "achieve a balance between population and resource use...." These latter statements of policy are open to a wide interpretive spectrum.

There is a danger in extracting the ecologically oriented statements out of the overall policy context and drawing the inference that an agency's "excellent action" should necessarily be one that best protects, restores, and enhances the (ecological) environment (CEQ regulations § 1500.1(c)). This assurance is unwarranted for a number of reasons, for the most part thoroughly discussed in the voluminous body of literature debating NEPA's substantive versus procedural effect. Taylor (1984) refers to NEPA as a "balancing act, not a statute with specific environmental standards." Sagoff (1987) identifies the fundamental dichotomy in NEPA's policy goals: the goals are explicitly ethical, reflecting social virtues such as intergenerational justice, respect for nature, and reverence for life; they also reveal the importance of economic interests, acknowledging the possibility that these interests may conflict with attempts to protect the environment. He characterizes three differing interpretations of NEPA substantive policy paraphrased as follows:

1. A *moral* reading gives environmental values priority over economic and commercial interests; economic growth is a means, an instrumental goal, while environmental quality is an end in itself, founded in the ecological principles articulated by Aldo Leopold and essential to the quality of existence. In fact, the existence of environmental problems stems from a legacy of economic and technological premises, pursued in the absence of ecological knowledge. The apparently benign environmental intent of NEPA's policy language is diluted, however, by "weasel words," such as "practicable" and "fullest extent possible."

2. A *market* point of view sees NEPA as a call to agencies to allocate resources more efficiently and prevent wasteful exploitation. NEPA neither bestows moral priority to environmental values nor suggests that environmental values should "trump" economic interests, but rather calls for weighing these values equitably along with other wants and preferences. Environmental protection under this interpretation is founded in the utilitarian conservation movement epitomized by Gifford Pinchot: the central benefit of the use of the earth is for the good of man.

3. A *mitigation* reading of NEPA policy relieves some but not all of the tension: it is not necessary to choose between economic growth and environmental protection. Scientific analysis and technology, if applied appropriately as mitigation, can minimize or even eliminate conflict between economic development and environmental protection in specific contexts. NEPA policy thus suggests that it is possible to preserve the environment and at the same time sustain a high standard of living. In this view, NEPA is seen as a means to avoid rather than confront the hard choices that sustain an enforceable environmental policy as found in more substantive statutes such as the ESA (Sagoff, 1987).

A fourth, *pragmatic,* interpretation of NEPA may come closer to explaining the courts' deference to the predominantly procedural role that NEPA plays in the activities of most federal agencies. "Congress did not (intend to) strike a balance between economic growth and environmental protection, but rather achieved what it intended: a new, complex political process, effectively used to improve the social and environmental sensitivity of government decision-makers" (Sagoff, 1987).

This procedural interpretation was generally affirmed in a survey of California local municipalities that are responsible for implementing CEQA (NEPA's analogue) for all discretionary public and private projects. Asked whether CEQA protects rare plants, one experienced official replied: "CEQA cannot and is not intended to 'protect' endangered species. Rather, the CEQA process is really an informational process; as such it is effective in providing the public with notice of a threat to the environment. The combination of mitigation (and monitoring) requirements and the requirement that decision makers make findings related to…alternatives and mitigation measures in public are probably the most protection CEQA can offer. *Real protection should be provided in other state and federal laws*" (emphasis added) (Dennis, 1994).[3] A similar question can be asked: "Can NEPA protect biodiversity?" and a qualified response given: "NEPA is an appropriate legal mechanism through which to ensure that conservation of biological diversity is *addressed* in federal decisions" (Henderson et al., 1993).

Those who criticize the courts for failing to uphold the "substantive intent" of NEPA—viz., that it is the policy of the federal government to use all practicable means to create and maintain conditions under which man and nature can exist in productive harmony and fulfill the social, economic, and other requirements of present and future generations of Americans—fail to appreciate how much dissonance must be heard in the process of determining just what constitutes the real substance of "productive harmony" between ecological and economic objectives. Don Erman observed during an ecosystem management conference (University of California, Davis, 1994) that the "old goal" of forestry management was efficiency—to maximize production of goods from resources for human use. The "new (ecosystem management) goal" is confused, not defined, but generally reflects the need to protect both ecosystems and species and to gain a better understanding of "sufficiency." The essential connection and psychic dissonance (evident in sessions of this conference) lie between economic possibility and ecological necessity; how much is needed to maintain ecosystems? Furthermore, what is good science, and what can science do to resolve the dissonance? (Erman, 1994).

NEPA Is Only One Paradigm

A second limitation to the expectation that NEPA can prevent ecological train wrecks is a question more of NEPA's proper "fit" than functional limitation. NEPA is one (but only one) paradigm for "managing" natural resources. Practitioners tend to ascribe to the NEPA—and EIA—process the possibility of almost limitless shapes as an analytic, planning, and decision-making framework (Lawrence, 1994); "impact assessment can be whatever you make it" (Livingston, 1981, in Meredith, 1992). At a minimum, NEPA analyses and procedures can be designed for review of federal policies, plans, and programs, as well as projects. This breadth of application has produced many variants, demonstrating, for example, the wide utility of programmatic EIA documents.

This boundless faith of EIA practitioners in the versatility of the process is evident in periodicals, conferences, and local debates focusing on the fine points of EIA analysis. But as a problem-solving paradigm, "EIA is only one of many forms of environmental intervention" (Lawrence, 1994). It is humbling, therefore, to meet with colleagues in applied ecological sciences who are actively engaged in natural resource management and who share almost every interest—except NEPA consciousness. A recent conference illustrates this point.

Some 400 natural resource planners, scientists, managers, environmental advocates, and officials attended a conference entitled "Ecosystem Management: Designing with Nature" (University of California, Davis, 1994). They represented diverse federal agencies—FS, BOR, Natural Resource Conservation Service, BLM, NPS, FWS, Corps of Engineers, and others. Also in attendance were representatives of California state agencies, conservation organizations, local officials, and citizens, including speaker Gary Snyder, a well-known poet long identified with the biocentric Deep Ecology environmental movement and with bioregional initiatives such as those that have emerged in California and the Pacific Northwest (Johnson, 1993; Kusel, 1994).

Numerous presentations addressed two dual questions: What is ecosystem management, and how are agencies charged with implementing President Clinton's ecosystem directive going to manage their land and water resources as ecosystems? A larger political and social question emerged: What is the appropriate governance of ecosystems? A corollary also emerged: What should be the roles of the federal government, state government, and local communities—and ordinary people—in ecosystem management? These questions are raised in varying degree by all of the ESA cases above. Issues such as those cited by McGinty (1994) were also discussed: the (admitted) failure by mission-oriented, multiple-resource federal agencies to account for interactions among resources or to cooperate with other agencies in their management.

Conspicuously absent from discussion, except for brief mention, "NEPA" was seen by only one speaker as a significant player in the management of ecosystems (Freedman, 1994), although it was evident on questioning that virtually any major action by a federal agency to make the concept of ecosystem management operational would undergo NEPA review and analysis. Other statutes and the processes and conflicts that flow from them appeared to be of greater immediate relevance to these resource managers—notably basic public land management statutes, such as NFMA and the Federal Land Planning and Management Act, as well as numerous other environmental statutes enacted in the past 25 years. One agency official said: "NEPA has altered agency process, but the ESA, because of its mistaken emphasis on single species, has been a more powerful force driving ecosystem and biodiversity management" (Muller, 1994). Presentations and panel discussions indicated that public land managers are attempting to move away from traditional multiple-use management, integrating both ecosystem management and environmental impact analysis (the "underlying logic of NEPA") directly into other planning activities (i.e., integrating the prediction of consequences into the traditional rational comprehensive planning model) (Coggins, 1990; Dickerson and Montgomery, 1993).

It appears that NEPA's relative position in the panoply of environmental mandates and programs directed toward conserving biological diversity through both species and ecosystem management depends in part on one's perspective and often on one's professional preoccupations; in recent literature on ecosystem management and the closely related concept of biodiversity in ecological applications, NEPA is rarely mentioned in discussions of science in relation to federal environmental policy and programs (Swanson and Franklin, 1992; Kessler et al., 1992; Franklin, 1993; Tracy and Brussard, 1994; Irwin and Wigley, 1993; Wilcove, 1993; Naiman et al., 1993; and others). The same is true of conservation biology (Noss, 1994; Rholf, 1991; O'Connell, 1992; Brussard et al., 1992; Grumbine, 1994). Both forums, of course, are designed primarily for scientists, not for public policy specialists or EIA practitioners.

Conversely, one finds in periodicals and publications focused on environmental management and EIA, in particular, a strong, if implied, argument that NEPA can—and should—be the key player in assuring that biodiversity is analyzed using the now familiar "systematic interdisciplinary approach" and that NEPA documents should be influential in agencies' substantive decisions and allocation of resources (Southerland, 1992; Henderson et al., 1993; Hirsch, 1993; Bruns et al., 1993; CEQ, 1993; and others).

NEPA and Sustainability

A third apparent limitation to NEPA's capacity to prevent ecological train wrecks may in fact represent opportunity that is frequently overlooked (or avoided). Just below the surface of the conflicts that characterize ecological and economic train wrecks are dual questions involving resource limits and exploitation: What are sustainable limits to use of resources, and what levels of use are nonsustainable (i.e., constitute overexploitation)? Without ever using the term "sustainability," NEPA lays out basic policy and some of the substantive requirements for its consideration but rarely confronts the issues directly:

> Section 101(b): "...fulfill the responsibilities of each generation as trustee of the environment for succeeding generations..." and "achieve a balance between population and resource use..."

> Section 102(C): "include...a detailed statement on...(iv) the relationship between local short-term uses of man's environment and the maintenance and enhancement of long-term productivity, and (v) any irreversible and irretrievable commitment of resources which would be involved in the proposed action should it be implemented..."

Practitioners of NEPA have made substantial strides in expanding the scope and rigor of examination of the ecological aspects of sustainability through improved consideration of biodiversity (Hirsch, 1993; CEQ, 1993; Office of Technology Assessment, 1987), cumulative impact analyses (Hunsaker, 1993; Williamson, 1993), direct attempts to define sustainability and apply useful biophysical measurements (Goodland, 1994; Carpenter, 1990), and methods to effectively incorporate the principle of sustainability into EIA (Gibson, 1993). Cumulative impact analyses lack practical utility, however, unless they are linked to permissible limits of resource use and ecological and social impact (Rees, 1988). It is questionable whether NEPA in itself can promote the opportunities to rigorously examine the complex questions involved in ecological sustainability. Scientific information, even if it were perfect, is only one input to the decision-making process (Caldwell, 1993); the implied social and economic objectives cannot be addressed solely through the application of science. Decisions concerning sustainable limits presuppose deliberate planning at a variety of spatial scales and a political commitment to the imposition of ecological limits—carrying capacity—on growth. NEPA EISs can assemble empirical physical, biological, social, and economic data; assist in constructing future scenarios by involving the appropriate interests; analyze the cumulative consequences (risks and opportunities) of scenarios; and present the results of analysis to decision makers and the public. However, NEPA has structural limitations in its ability to conduct the kinds of research that are needed (e.g., long-term studies of species' populations and community dynamics and experimental manipulations of natural and modified ecosystems) (Committee for the National Institute for the Environment, 1994).

"The focus of EIA is on the state of the environment and the natural resource base and how they have been affected by the practices of the local population, rather than on trying to understand the constraints under which people operate and how such constraints may influence their behavior" (Gow, 1992).

Agency Implementation of NEPA

A final limitation concerns the inconsistent implementation of NEPA. As with other limitations, the flip side of limitation is the opportunity for "improvement." One of the first lessons a practitioner of NEPA learns is that there are almost as many NEPAs as there are federal agencies. Adopted procedures may share the basic canon of the NEPA statute and CEQ regulations, but they are separated and rendered idiosyncratic by individual mission, authorization, and statutory responsibilities; the nature and distribution of managed resources; sources and level of funding; and by administrative design. The mission, mandates, and technical interests of the Federal Aviation Administration, for example, are different from those of the Corps, EPA, or FWS, although their mandates and NEPA responsibilities must be reconciled where airports, wetlands, and endangered species coincide, a not infrequent condition. The General Services Administration manages a variety of federal properties and projects in both urban and undeveloped contexts; the military services manage large blocks of public land with sensitive ecological resources while carrying out a national security mission.

A corresponding variety in NEPA implementing procedures reveals differences and deficiencies, especially in extent and specificity of emphasis on scientific standards, content, and methodology. Investigators have agreed that "the purpose of environmental impact assessment has never been to produce the best science for its own sake, nor to make politics more like science" (Malik and Bartlett, 1993; Caldwell, 1993). Good science is essential in the implementation of NEPA, but EIA is essentially a political process (Bartlett, 1986, in Malik and Bartlett, 1993). Although scientific rigor may not be consistently practiced in the EIA process, many of the same agencies that implement NEPA are otherwise engaged in rigorous science within other organizational sectors and in connection with specific programs. Science is not necessarily lacking from agencies' deliberations and actions; it is simply not always reflected in environmental assessments (EAs) and EISs.

In 25 years, however, the objectives of scientific analysis in NEPA documents have become more clearly formulated and analysis more focused on relevant issues, and analytic techniques have become more sophisticated. In EIA documents of the 1970s, scientific "impact analysis" was more likely to consist of vast descriptive catalogues of species. The ecological issues now so prevalent in the literature of applied ecology and conservation biology—biodiversity, ecosystem management, and sustainability—were recognized at that time but had not been articulated as such or been applied to environmental analysis.

Furthermore, the basic intent of NEPA—viz., shifting the ethic and practices of federal agencies to take environmental factors into consideration along with traditional economic and technical factors—has generally been accomplished. The shift in mentality has had fundamental impacts on the manner in which agencies carry out the required NEPA process: (1) there is less chance to make a major environmental mistake (i.e., cause a train wreck by approving a "bad" project), (2) the EA or EIS now serves more as a focal point for ensuring that a project is consistent with environmental regulations and other mandates, and (3) agencies are dealing with increasingly complex issues in EISs (e.g., biodiversity, global climate change, cumulative impacts [and sustainability]) (Dickerson and Montgomery, 1993).

NEPA AS "PARTNER" IN PREVENTING ECOLOGICAL TRAIN WRECKS

In this period of emphasis on "biodiversity, ecosystem management, and sustainability reformation," NEPA's role is still evolving, driven by the pressures of more substantive laws and by rigorous public scrutiny that is its hallmark. Public land managers clearly see the need for science, adaptive management, and public outreach in their plans and programs, but they do not necessarily view NEPA as the primary mechanism for planning and allocating resources. NEPA is regarded by some as limited in its procedural flexibility to reflect or integrate with adaptive approaches to resource management; the lack of provision for monitoring and feedback alone renders it non-adaptive (Noss, 1994). On the other hand, comprehensive reviews reveal that biodiversity, a basic issue in ecological train wrecks, is being considered in more responsible NEPA analyses (CEQ, 1993; Hirsch, 1993; Henderson et al., 1993).

Agencies are required to integrate the requirements of other more substantive laws and consult with the agencies that administer them, ensure scientific research and integrity, integrate the NEPA process early with planning (and design and resource management) functions "to head off potential conflicts" (§ 1501.2), and consult with participants from state and local governments and publics. NEPA serves to coordinate consideration of the substantive requirements of other environmental statutes that are limited in scope but more powerful as substantive laws in their ability to enforce protection of components of biodiversity (CEQ, 1993). Furthermore, in its requirement to consider a range of ecosystem "health" factors, as well as specific species, proper application of NEPA may be able to reduce conflicts over resource allocation now burdening the ESA (CEQ, 1993).

Federal resource agencies are also entering into collaborative federal–state–local interagency agreements, such as the California Biodiversity Agreement, Sierra Nevada Ecosystem Project, and San Francisco Bay-Delta Estuary agreement, and numerous multiagency multiple-species HCPs, such as the NCCP, designed to plan for appropriate development and long-term protection of the coastal sage scrub habitat of the California gnatcatcher (Sprague, 1994; Wheeler, 1995; Grumbine, 1994; Johnson, 1993; Erman, 1994; Ebbin, 1994; Marsh, 1994; Mantell, 1994). None of these collaborations supersedes the requirement for NEPA (or CEQA) procedural review, but they suggest that EIA is playing a *role* but not necessarily leading the strategic effort.

It is fully recognized that NEPA provides one of the most accessible means of legal challenge to agency planning processes that are mandated by other laws. For example, a recent settlement with the Sierra National Forest in California concerning alleged violations of NEPA in relation to grazing management contained terms requiring NEPA analyses for all of 30 grazing allotments and a grazing amendment to the Forest's Land

and Resource Management Plan (*California Trout et al. v. U.S. Forest Service et al.* [1994]). The settlement "will, for the first time, provide an opportunity for the scientific community, conservation groups, and all interested parties to participate in grazing management decisions affecting the Sierra National Forest" (Roberson, 1995).

Therefore, NEPA can be viewed as a very broad "umbrella" that can encompass ("disclose") the contributions of many other analytic and planning paradigms, as envisioned partially in CEQ regulations § 1502.25, and most important, that can afford opportunity for meaningful public engagement. But in any view, NEPA is only one "step along the way" in a much larger, evolving adaptive management paradigm ("assess-plan-implement-monitor-evaluate-adjust plan-etc.") directed toward the goal of reconciling resource protection and diverse societal needs (Freedman, 1995).

In view of both its opportunities and limitations, NEPA may be better construed as an important and unique—but not singular in effect—member of a complex "partnership" of statutes and other directives; agencies; both governmental and non-governmental organizations, programs, and initiatives; scientists who are both internal and external to the EIA process; and ordinary people. All of these players are essential if future ecological and economic train wrecks are to be prevented. The partnership is stabilized by a few prominent and established components and procedures, but the membership otherwise is patchy, sometimes redundant or overlapping, inconsistently implemented, diverse in scale and tactics, not smooth or predictable, but somehow effective in varying degree and generally moving in a forward direction.

NOTES

1. Abundant literature is available for those wishing to revisit the legal, scientific, and rural economic issues (Bonnett and Zimmerman, 1991; Murphy and Noon, 1992; Johnson, 1993; U.S.D.A. Forest Service, 1994; among many others).

2. Listing of the California gnatcatcher was vacated by the court in 1994 due to the non-availability of certain statistical data supporting the taxonomy and range of the bird and subsequently reinstated temporarily, pending court review (Clark, 1995).

3. Although CEQA is modeled after NEPA, the policy language, supported in the courts, is designed to strongly encourage the adoption of the environmentally favorable course of action and to require adoption of the least damaging alternative(s) and mitigations to lessen significant effect or find that these (alternative and mitigations) are infeasible, supported by substantial evidence in the record. This requirement distinguishes CEQA's substantive effect from NEPA's primary procedural effect.

SELECTED REFERENCES

Bonnett, M. and K. Zimmerman. 1991. Politics and Preservation: The Endangered Species Act and the Northern Spotted Owl. *Ecology Law Quarterly* 18(1):105–171.

Bruns, D.A. et al. 1993. An Ecosystem Approach to Ecological Characterization in the NEPA Process. In *Environmental Analysis: The NEPA Experience*. S.G. Hildebrand and J. Cannon, Eds. Lewis Publishers, Boca Raton, Florida.

Brussard, P., D. Murphy, and R. Noss. 1992. Strategy and Tactics for Conserving Biological Diversity in the United States (editorial). *Conservation Biology* 6(2):157–159.

Caldwell, L.K. 1993. Achieving the NEPA Intent: New Directions in Politics, Science, and Law. In

Environmental Analysis: The NEPA Experience. S.G. Hildebrand and J. Cannon, Eds. Lewis Publishers, Boca Raton, Florida.

California Executive Council on Biological Diversity. 1995. New Bay-Delta Standards May Yield Truce. *California Biodiversity News* 2(2):6–7, 10 (c/o The Resources Agency, Sacramento, California).

Carpenter, R. 1990. Biophysical Measurement of Sustainable Development. *The Environmental Professional* 12:356–359.

Clark, J. 1995. NCCP Gains Ground in Southern California's Gnatcatcher Habitat. *California Biodiversity News* 2(2):1, 4–5.

Coggins, G.C. 1990. *Public Natural Resources Law.* Clark Boardman Callaghan, New York.

Committee for the National Institute for the Environment. 1994. A Proposal to Create a National Institute for the Environment, Appendix A—Environmental Research Needs: Nineteen Case Examples. *The Environmental Professional* 16(2):146–164.

Council on Environmental Quality. 1993. Incorporating Biodiversity Considerations into Environmental Impact Analysis Under the National Environmental Quality Act. CEQ, Executive Office of the President, Washington, D.C.

Dennis, N. 1994. Does CEQA Protect Rare Plants? *Fremontia* 22(1):3–13 (California Native Plant Society, Sacramento, California).

Dennis, N. and L. Marcus. 1984. Status and Trends of California Wetlands. Prepared for California Assembly Natural Resources Committee. Joint Publications Office, State Capitol, Sacramento, California.

Dickerson W., and J. Montgomery. 1993. Substantive Scientific and Technical Guidance for NEPA Analysis: Pitfalls in the Real World. *The Environmental Professional* 15(1):7–11.

Ebbin, M. 1994. Preserving Biodiversity: Looking at the Big Picture. *National Wetlands Newsletter* 16(5):5–6, 13.

Erman, D. 1994. The Role of Science in Ecosystem Management. Presentation at Conference: Ecosystem Management: Designing with Nature. University of California–Davis, Sacramento, October 25–27.

Forest Ecosystem Management Assessment Team (FEMAT). 1993. Forest Ecosystem Management: An Ecological, Economic, and Social Assessment. USDA Forest Service Pacific Northwest Region, Portland, Oregon.

Franklin, J. 1993. Preserving Biodiversity: Species, Ecosystems, or Landscapes? *Ecological Applications* 3:202–205.

Franklin, J. 1994. Preserving Biodiversity: Species in Landscapes—Response to Letters to Editor. *Ecological Applications* 4(2):208–209.

Freedman, L. 1994. Examples of Ecosystem Approaches to Planning. Presentation at Conference: Ecosystem Management: Designing with Nature. University of California–Davis, Sacramento, October 25–27.

Freedman, L. (Assistant Director for Natural Resources, U.S. Office of Forestry and Economic Development, Portland, Oregon). 1995. Personal communication.

Gibson, R.B. 1993. Environmental Assessment Design: Lessons from the Canadian Experience. *The Environmental Professional* 15(1):12–24.

Goodland, R. 1994. Towards a Definition of Environmental Sustainability. *The Environmental Professional* 16(3):193.

Gow, D.D. 1992. Poverty and Natural Resources: Principles for Environmental Management and Sustainable Development. *Environmental Impact Assessment Review* 12(1/2):49–65.

Grumbine, R.E. 1994. What Is Ecosystem Management? *Conservation Biology* 8(1):27–38.

Henderson, S., R.F. Noss, and P. Ross, 1993. Can NEPA Protect Biodiversity? In *Environmental Analysis: The NEPA Experience.* S.G. Hildebrand and J.B. Cannon, Eds. Lewis Publishers, Boca Raton, Florida.

Hildebrand, S.G. and J.B. Cannon, Eds. 1993. *Environmental Analysis: The NEPA Experience.* Lewis Publishers, Boca Raton, Florida.

Hirsch, A. 1993. Improving Consideration of Biodiversity in NEPA Assessments. *The Environmental Professional* 15(1):103–115.

Holling, C.S., Ed. 1978. *Adaptive Environmental Assessment and Management.* John Wiley and Sons, New York.

Holling, C.S. 1993. Investing in Research for Sustainability (Forum response to Ludwig 1993). *Ecological Applications* 3(4):552–555.

Howard, C. 1995. British Columbia Kills Dam that Threatened Salmon. *San Francisco Chronicle* January 27, C4.

Hunsaker, C. 1993. Ecosystem Assessment Methods for Cumulative Effects at Regional and Global Scales (1993). In *Environmental Analysis: The NEPA Experience.* S.G. Hildebrand, and J.B. Cannon, Eds. Lewis Publishers, Boca Raton, Florida.

Irwin, L.L. and T.B. Wigley. 1993. Toward an Experimental Basis for Protecting Forest Wildlife. *Ecological Applications* 3(2):213–217.

Johnson, K. 1993. Reconciling Rural Communities and Resource Conservation. *Environment* 35(9):16–20, 27–33.

Kessler, W.B. et al. 1992. New Perspectives for Sustainable Natural Resources Management. *Ecological Applications* 2(3):221–225.

Kusel, J. 1994. Working from the Bottom Up: Grassroots, Community, and Bureaucracy. Presentation at Conference: Ecosystem Management: Designing with Nature. University of California–Davis, Sacramento, October 25–27.

Lawrence, D.P. 1994. Designing and Adapting the EIA Planning Process. *The Environmental Professional* 16:2–21.

Livingston, J. 1981. Environmental Impact Assessment—It's Whatever You Make of It. *Probe Post* November:12–14.

Ludwig, D., R. Hilborn, and C. Walters. 1993. Uncertainty, Resource Exploitation, and Conservation: Lessons from History. *Ecological Applications* 3(4):547–549; reprinted from *Science* 260(17):36.

Malik, M. and R.V. Bartlett. 1993. Formal Guidance for the Use of Science in EIA: Analysis of Agency Procedures for Implementing NEPA. *The Environmental Professional* 15:34–45.

Mandelker, D. 1984. *NEPA Law and Litigation.* Clark Boardman Callaghan, New York.

Mann, C. and M.L. Plummer. 1995. California vs. Gnatcatcher. *Audubon.* January/February 38–48:100–194.

Mantell, M. 1994. The California Experiment. *National Wetlands Newsletter* 16(5):9–10, 18.

Marsh, L. 1994. A Paradigm for Biodiversity Conservation. *National Wetlands Newsletter* 16(5):7–8, 18.

McClurg, S. 1993. Biodiversity and the Endangered Species Act. *Western Water* September/October (Water Education Foundation, Sacramento, California).

McGinty, K.A. 1994. Looking Ahead to the Next 25 Years: The Clinton Administration's Approach to Environmental Policy. *NAEP News* 19:5/6.

Meredith, T. 1992. Environmental Impact Assessment, Cultural Diversity, and Sustainable Rural Development. *Environmental Impact Assessment Review* 12(1/2):125–138.

Mueller, T.L. 1994. Guide to the Federal and California Endangered Species Laws. Planning and Conservation League Foundation, Sacramento, California.

Mueller, T.L. 1995. Guide to the Federal and California Endangered Species Laws, Supplement. Planning and Conservation League Foundation, Sacramento, California.

Muller, K. 1994. Perspectives on Ecosystem Management. Presentation at Conference: Ecosystem Management: Designing with Nature. University of California–Davis, Sacramento, October 25–27.

Murphy, D. and B.R. Noon. 1992. Integrating Scientific Methods with Habitat Conservation Planning: Reserve Design for Northern Spotted Owls. *Ecological Applications* 2(1):3–17.

Naiman, R.J., H. Decamps, and M. Pollock. 1993. The Role of Riparian Corridors in Maintaining Regional Biodiversity. *Ecological Applications* 3(2):209–212.

Noss, R. 1994. Perspective on Ecosystem Management. Presentation at Conference: Ecosystem Management: Designing with Nature. University of California–Davis, Sacramento, October 25–27.

Notthoff, A. 1994. Opinions on NCCP: Keeping Science in the Driver's Seat. *National Wetlands Newsletter* 16(5):11–12.

O'Connell, M. 1992. Response to: "Six Biological Reasons Why the Endangered Species Act Doesn't Work and What to Do About It." *Conservation Biology* 6(1):140–143.

Office of Technology Assessment. 1984. Wetlands: Their Use and Regulation. OTA-O-206. U.S. Government Printing Office, Washington, D.C.

Office of Technology Assessment. 1987. Technologies to Maintain Biological Diversity (1987). U.S. Government Printing Office, Washington, D.C.

Ozawa, C.P. 1991. *Recasting Science: Consensual Procedures in Public Policy Making.* Westview Press, Boulder, Colorado.

Rees, W. 1988. A Role for Environmental Assessment in Achieving Sustainable Development. *Environmental Impact Assessment Review* 8:273–291.

Rholf, D.J. 1991. Six Biological Reasons Why the Endangered Species Act Doesn't Work—and What to Do About It. *Conservation Biology* 5:273–282.

Roberson, E. 1995. Land Management Analyst's Report. *Bulletin of the California Native Plant Society* 25(1):6; personal communication.

Sagoff, M. 1987. NEPA: Ethics, Economics, and Science in Environmental Law. *Law of Environmental Protection,* Vol. 2. S.M. Novick, Ed. Clark Boardman Callaghan, New York.

Sierra Club. 1995. Ruling Upholds Forest Option 9 (adapted from Mark Lawler, in *Cascade Chapter National Forests Committee Newsletter,* and Ryan Henson, in *Wilderness Record). Sierra Club Yodeler* 58:2.

Sigg, J. 1993. Habitat Conservation on San Bruno Mountain: It Isn't Working. *Fremontia* 21(4):11–14 (California Native Plant Society).

Silver, D. 1994. Opinions on NCCP: In the Land of Many Promises. *National Wetlands Newsletter* 16(5):12–13.

Southerland, M.T. 1992. Consideration of Terrestrial Environments in the Review of Environmental Impact Statements. *The Environmental Professional* 14:1–9.

Sprague, G.L. 1994. The Role of Science in Ecosystem Management, Presentation at Conference: Ecosystem Management: Designing with Nature. University of California–Davis, Sacramento, October 25–27.

Stevens, W.K. 1993. Babbitt to Stress Habitat Protection. *San Francisco Chronicle,* February 17, p. A3.

Swanson, F.J. and J.F. Franklin. 1992. New Forestry Principles From Ecosystem Analysis of Pacific Northwest Forests. *Ecological Applications* 2(3):262–274.

Taylor, S. 1984. *Making Bureaucracies Think: The Environmental Impact Statement Strategy of Administrative Reform.* Stanford University Press, Stanford, California.

Tracy, C.R. and P.F. Brussard. 1994. Preserving Biodiversity: Species in the Landscape—Letter to the Editor. *Ecological Applications* 4(2):205–207.

University of California, Davis. 1994. Conference on Ecosystem Management: Designing with Nature. University of California–Davis, Sacramento, October 25–27.

U.S.D.A. Forest Service. 1994. Final Supplemental Environmental Impact Statement on Management of Habitat for Late Successional and Old-Growth Forest Related to Species within the Range of the Northern Spotted Owl, April 13, 1994, and Record of Decision.

U.S. Department of Interior et al. 1994. Principles for Agreement on Bay-Delta Standards Between the State of California and the Federal Government, December 15.

Whalen, J. 1994. Planning for the Future of Development. *National Wetlands Newsletter* 16(5) 14–15.

Wheeler, D.P. 1995. From the Chair (of California Executive Council on Biological Diversity). *California Biodiversity News* 2(2):1.

Wilcove, D. 1993. Getting Ahead of the Extinction Curve. *Ecological Applications* 3(2):218–220.

Wilcove, D. 1994. Preserving Biodiversity: Species in Landscapes—Letter to the Editor. *Ecological Applications* 4(2):207–208.

Williamson, S.C. 1993. Cumulative Impact Assessment and Management Planning: Lessons Learned to Date. In *Environmental Analysis: The NEPA Experience.* S.G. Hildebrand, and J.B. Cannon, Eds. Lewis Publishers, Boca Raton, Florida.

THE CASE FOR CONTINUOUS MONITORING AND ADAPTIVE MANAGEMENT UNDER NEPA

10

R.A. Carpenter

The environmental assessment (EA)/environmental impact statement (EIS) process of the National Environmental Policy Act (NEPA) is a procedural, one-time, rather rapid determination of environmental impacts from major federal actions before they are taken. The documentation is to be concise and yet cover alternatives to the proposed action, including no action. Impacts are predicted, and mitigation measures to reduce or avoid unacceptable adverse consequences are recommended. The action may then proceed with due consideration of this additional information along with other relevant factors.

The realities of uncertainty inherent in environmental sciences, however, mean that the actual course of the project or activity, and its impacts, are usually far different. Technological perturbations interact with natural variations and produce often surprising ecological responses. A preferred way of dealing with uncertainties is emerging—to conduct the project in an adaptive manner, continuously modifying management practices as necessary in order to achieve the productive objectives while continuing to protect the environment.

NEPA and Council on Environmental Quality (CEQ) regulations provide for *continual* monitoring and assessment. The policy is "...to create and *maintain* conditions under which man and nature can exist in productive harmony..." (Section 101(a) of NEPA). Section 2 of the Purpose of NEPA includes "to enrich the *understanding* of the ecological systems...." Section 102(2)(A) directs all agencies to "utilize a systematic...approach," and Section 102(2)(B) calls for "methods...which will insure that presently unquantified environmental amenities and values may be given appropriate consideration...." It is the famous Section 102(2)(C) that sets the requirement for what is usually a one-time EIS, which is to include "the relationship between local short-term uses of man's environment and the *maintenance* and enhancement of long-term productivity...." The CEQ is to define and *analyze* changes in the environment and interpret their causes (Section 204(6)) (emphasis added throughout).

Monitoring for compliance with an EIS is explicitly covered in the CEQ regulations (CEQ, 1992) § 1505.2(c) ("a monitoring and enforcement program shall be adopted and summarized where applicable for any mitigation") and § 1505.3 ("agencies may provide for monitoring to assure that their decisions are carried out and should do so in important cases").

Monitoring is necessary for many more purposes than just auditing for compliance. The success of mitigation measures that are installed must be evaluated. Monitoring must be able to detect changes due to human activities against a background of natural variation. Adaptive environmental management usually requires an early alert for rapid response to adverse changes. Predictive models used in the EIS must be validated and modified if they are not reflecting reality. Cumulative effects from other activities are to be summed up, and this is a strong argument for monitoring. Thus, a continuous assessment, and not just the predecision EA/EIS, is indeed intended and mandated by NEPA and will be essential to meet the expectations of adaptive environmental management. This is an important new stage in the evolution of the act as its implementation proceeds.

UNCERTAINTIES UNRECOGNIZED IN 1967–70

Prediction is the essence of the process that produces EAs and EISs. In its most elementary conception, the objective of NEPA Section 102 was simply to force bureaucrats to look beyond their primary mission in planning projects. They were to forecast plausible adverse changes in the natural environment from their actions. Two future environments are to be predicted—one with the proposed action, and one without—because the environment is not static in any event. No particular precision or scope of the prediction was specified; giving environmental concerns proper weight in the decision-making process was revolutionary enough.

Environmental quality aspects were scattered 25 years ago in a few existing statutes, including laws for air and water pollution control, pesticides, soil conservation, and land management. Human health protection standards are set with a margin of safety to allow for uncertainties in exposure, toxicity, and individual response. A "tolerable soil erosion rate" may be established by considering variations in soil depth and soil-building processes. Allowable harvests from forests and fisheries recognize uncertainties in stock replacement. Environmental impact assessment (EIA), in cases with these established standards, should predict whether the standards would be met and what changes or mitigation measures would be necessary to meet them. Risk assessment is one means of dealing explicitly with uncertainty, and many environmental standards are promulgated with some notion of an acceptable risk or margin of safety, although the level varies widely (over several orders of magnitude) among the different health protection regulations.

In contrast to the many specific pollution abatement and environmental quality protection laws, some passed before NEPA and most since then, the "environment" in

NEPA is a broad holistic concept and not a collection of narrow cause–effect inter-actions. After World War II, there was a flurry of concern about the adequacy of natural resources, but the congressional emphasis of the 1960s was on environmental quality (Kidd, 1992). Human health effects of pollutants, while complex, were beginning to be relatively well understood and quantified. *Silent Spring,* Mississippi River fish kills, and DDT-damaged pelicans were recent events not yet elucidated. The novel purpose, then, of NEPA concerns not only human health and welfare but ecological systems, the biosphere, and all renewable natural resources (see NEPA Purpose, Section 2 [42 U.S.C. § 4321]). The state of the sciences at this grand scope and scale was, and is, characterized by large, significant, and varied uncertainties that severely limit and frustrate prediction.

STATE OF ECOLOGY AT THE TIME OF DEVELOPMENT AND PASSAGE OF NEPA

A Joint House–Senate Colloquium to discuss a National Policy for the Environment was held on July 17, 1968. This unusual event took the form of a joint hearing before the Senate Committee on Interior and Insular Affairs (Senator Henry Jackson, D-Washington, Chairman) and the House Committee on Science and Astronautics (Representative George Miller, D-California, Chairman). It was also in an unusual place—the hearing room of the Joint Committee on Atomic Energy, exactly in the middle of the Capitol building below the dome, strategically located so as to avoid members of either body having to go to the other's quarters.

It is fair to say that the testimony that day comprised the views of most of the leading environmental scientists from government, academia, non-government conservation organizations, and even business interests. Most of the discussion supported the emerging perception that human activities were having important and lasting detrimental effects on nature and that industrial expansion plus high consumption could overwhelm the resilience and assimilative capacity of the environment. Environmental impact was seen as a function of technology, affluence, and population—the $I = P \times A \times T$ model familiar today. Another theme had simultaneously been introduced in the Congress, that of technology assessment, in which all of the unanticipated consequences (not just environmental) of innovation would be delineated. Some observers expected that this concept would subsume EIA, and the CEQ guidelines do incorporate technology assessment in programmatic assessments (§ 1502.4(c)(3)). Instead, the more comprehensive Technology Assessment Act was passed in 1972.

But there were a few warnings of another type. A submission from the Ecological Society of America noted that "…the problem area that beckons ecology in the future, the area that we know the least about and that represents a quantum jump, is the ecosystem.…If ecologists succeed in attacking the ecosystem in a way that yields testable hypotheses and predictive information, the theories so generated are certain to bear directly on these national 'practical' problems [pollution, resource management].…When a theory of ecosystems emerges, it will be one of the major synthesizing ideas in science, perhaps rivaled only by the theory of evolution and natural selection in this respect" (U.S. Congress, 1968). Dr. David Gates, then director of the Missouri Botanical Garden, said,

"Modern science has not unraveled the intricate, complex interactions and underlying mechanisms of most ecosystems. The attempts to do so have been pitifully few and analytically weak. The number of ecologists available for such work are tragically scarce." Electronic computers had not yet been employed in manipulating mathematical models of ecosystem structure and function.

With these scientific inadequacies clearly in front of them, the Congress proceeded, in NEPA, to declare the purpose "to enrich the understanding of ecological systems and natural resources important to the Nation...." All agencies shall "...[prepare] a detailed statement by the responsible official on...the environmental impact of the proposed action..." (Section 102(2)(C)) and "...initiate and utilize ecological information in the planning and development of resource-oriented projects..." (Section 102(2)(G)). The CEQ shall "...conduct investigations, studies, surveys, research, and analyses relating to environmental quality..." (Section 204(5)).

Thus, NEPA is seen to have been strongly based on a scientific capability that did not yet exist, but which, with the mandated development of ecology, presumably would become available. In 1976, a paper entitled "The Scientific Basis of NEPA—Is It Adequate?" was presented at a congressionally sponsored Workshop on the National Environmental Policy Act (R.A. Carpenter, 1976). The paper noted that "in the first six years of the Act, a profound and unanticipated change in bureaucratic procedures had been wrought by the EIS procedural function, and the *Calvert Cliffs* decision (ordering federal agencies to trade off environmental impact against economic and social factors in a 'finely tuned and systematic balancing analysis'). In contrast to this bureaucratic development, the scientific basis of NEPA had been obscured and neglected." In 1974, an ad hoc CEQ Committee on Ecological Research found that ecological efforts were scattered throughout the government with little coordination or definition of priorities. "Without a federal focus, response to problems which require ecological information or capability will continue to be fragmented, costly, redundant, and reflexive rather than strategic, efficient, and contributory to national goals and productivity" (CEQ, 1974).

It is only fair to note that some observers did not agree then, and probably would not now, that the quality of scientific content was at least as important as procedure in making NEPA effective. Their argument was that NEPA established social and other human factors as equally important to a full treatment of impact and a fully balanced decision on a pending action. They objected to the "heavy orientation toward scientific aspects of environment and slight concern for the human dimensions of policies" (U.S. Congress, 1976). Obviously, there is no National Social Policy Act or Social Impact Statement, and so the NEPA/EIS has become a vehicle of opportunity for a variety of social activist programs over the years. It could be argued that such broad coverage, weighing in all human considerations, leads to vague and inconclusive decisions within the NEPA procedure.

The EA/EIS is a decision document, not a scientific research report. The review of EISs by the U.S. Environmental Protection Agency (EPA) is mostly for scope and not for data or model quality. The great proportion of NEPA procedures are at the EA level rather than the full EIS. The predictions in an EA are made more quickly, on less data, so that their accuracy is presumably lower. The mix of substance and procedure will continue to be debated, but as NEPA issues become increasingly controversial, better science is needed (Dickerson and Montgomery, 1993).

THE CONTINUED EVOLUTION OF NEPA

While the opinions of those who downplay the role of science in NEPA should be considered, a recent review of the literature supports the position that the classical and traditional EIA of the NEPA process deals with changes in the biogeophysical natural system that manifest themselves as impacts on human health, welfare, and the condition of ecosystems. EIA has been, and is being, enriched and extended, however, in several directions which are, for the most part, helpful if the basic biogeophysical assessment is properly completed. This is evidence for the fundamental soundness of the act and its ability to serve current and future national goals.

Additional Types of Impact Analyses

Several important analyses related to environmental impact have been identified. For example, extended benefit–cost analysis and economic valuation bring the externalities (impacts that are identified and quantified by EIA) onto the accounting ledger sheet for addition to, or more likely subtraction from, the obvious and direct economic benefits of the project, in the common denominator of money. Unless impacts are expressed in monetary terms, they may be disregarded, or inadequately weighed in decisions about the project. The trend is to move beyond the mere incorporation by reference, as is required in CEQ regulations § 1502.23.

Cumulative effects analysis (CEA) is a special effort mandated by NEPA and expressed in the CEQ regulations. For example, 40 CFR § 1502.16 calls for discussion of direct and indirect effects and their significance. Effects are further defined in § 1508.8. In setting the scope of EISs, § 1508.25 specifies connected actions, cumulative actions, and impacts that may be cumulative. Significance, according to § 1508.27, increases if the action is related to other actions with individually insignificant but cumulative significant impacts. Terming an action temporary, or breaking it into small components, does not decrease significance. Cumulative impact is defined in 40 CFR § 1508.7 as resulting from adding incremental impacts of other past, present, or reasonably foreseeable future actions. Several stressors may impact concurrently and/or individually minor impacts may build up over a period of time. These additive effects may be somewhat removed in space or time from the direct immediate impacts, so that skill is necessary in setting the correct boundaries of the assessment or else the task becomes unwieldy. CEA is not a separate analysis but simply a reminder that projects do not occur in isolation and that the holistic environment integrates, or even magnifies, what may seem to be independent consequences of different development activities.

CEA has a different, usually additional, scope compared with the ordinary EA/EIS focus on direct impacts, single perturbation, simple cause–effect relationship, short time frame, and individual site. CEA changes the viewpoint of the analyst from the effects of an action to the affected value or site. Each impacted environmental resource value or site will have a different set of potential stressors and thus a different scope, depending on impact origin, stressor characteristics, or exposure pathways. Each project or action interacts with others in a variety of ways. The current condition and vulnerability of the impacted environment determine, to a large extent, the importance of additional impacts.

Social impact assessment focuses on how environmental changes affect organizations, institutions, and the behavior of various individuals and groups. But the CEQ regulations (§ 1508.14) note that "...economic or social effects are not intended by themselves to require preparation of an environmental impact statement." The quantification of these effects is less well developed than in the natural sciences, but some useful information can be presented.

Environmental risk assessment (ERA) deals explicitly with uncertainty by presenting probability distributions of the frequency of occurrence of adverse impacts and the range of the damage. Likelihood and severity are expressed probabilistically rather than by single values (e.g., the mean). For example, infrequent but potentially highly damaging spills of a toxic chemical need to be studied probabilistically, not merely as "what if" questions.

Risks to human health from environmentally transmitted toxics are expressed in terms of individual exposure dose and potency. Risks to the integrity of ecosystems use the condition of discrete sites as the assessment end point, in a sense equivalent to the individual person in human health ERA. The stress/response relationship for ecosystems is much less quantitative.

NEPA recognizes risk in Section 101(b)(3): "...that the nation may attain the widest range of beneficial uses of the environment without degradation, risk to health or safety, or other undesirable and unintended consequences...." In the CEQ regulations, "significantly" is defined in terms of intensity: "This refers to the severity of impact" (§ 1508.27 (b)) and "the degree to which the possible effects on the human environment are highly uncertain or involve unique or unknown risks" (§ 1508.27(b)(5)). The latter would seem to infer that uncertainty increases the intensity and, therefore, the significance of an impact (i.e., the absence of evidence is not evidence of absence). However, uncertainty alone does not increase significance, because much about the environment is uncertain. The severity of an impact is important too. In discussing incomplete or unavailable information, the regulations explain that "...'reasonably foreseeable' includes impacts which have catastrophic consequences, even if their probability of occurrence is low, provided that the analysis of the impacts is supported by credible scientific evidence, is not based on pure conjecture, and is within the rule of reason" (§ 1502.22(b)).

Comparative risk assessment (CRA) analyzes several different hazards or sources of harm to the same individual, or valuable ecosystem site, in terms of relative risk. Although uncertainties may cloud calculated absolute values of risk, when assumptions remain constant, relative differences in risks are significant and can assist in setting priorities among alternative environmental programs so as to get the most risk reduction per unit expenditure. CRA can lead to risk-based strategic planning, as it has in the EPA, since all governments have more demands for environmental programs than can be funded.

Life cycle assessment (LCA) has to do with the environmental impacts of products from their inception to final disposal. For example, a cloth diaper can be compared with a disposable diaper in terms of total environmental impacts of each. Waste minimization is a powerful means of reducing pollution and LCA can identify some opportunities.

Finally, environmental justice (EJ) deals, for example, with the equity of locating waste treatment facilities in poverty-depressed areas and how the costs of environmental protection are distributed within society. Executive Order 12898 of February 11, 1994 added an analysis of EJ to the EIS required under the NEPA (White House, 1994).

Higher Levels of Decision Making

Another dimension of evolution for NEPA has to do with levels of policy and planning. In 1970, the EIS was an "action-forcing" requirement linked to individual projects. EIA has been adapted and adopted around the world with this same project focus. It is, however, widely accepted that project-focused EISs are not adequate for all levels of decision making. Some needed extensions are being investigated, including generic EISs, programmatic EISs, regional master planning, development strategies, and environmental considerations in national budgets.

Generic EISs cover the common impacts of similar projects that are unlikely to vary with location. For example, building power lines across the landscape will generate impacts, but they are about the same wherever the line is located. Therefore, the EIS for any particular line may draw upon a generalized impact analysis. As experience has grown, the efficiency of a generic assessment has increased its use beyond the limited suggestion in § 1502.4(c)(2) of the CEQ regulations.

Programmatic EISs address the impacts of large-scale repetitive projects, such as strip mining of coal in a region of generally homogeneous terrain. An overall assessment may suffice for many individual project localities. Sectoral EISs highlight the impacts of development in an industrial sector by comparing different technologies that may eventually be chosen. For example, if the initiating project is a highway, the sectoral approach would assess alternative transportation modes to accomplish the same goal, such as light rail transit. The CEQ regulations § 1500.4(i) note "using program, policy, or plan environmental impact statements and tiering from statements of broad scope to those of narrower scope...."

Regional master planning is the most attractive level for managing the environment. Here, an entire river basin, watershed, air quality district, managed ecosystem, coastal zone, or island is analyzed at one time for probable environmental impacts of all kinds of economic development. Current and future pollution controls are estimated. Vulnerable and valuable natural areas are marked for conservation. Industrial parks are sited in appropriate areas where wastes and infrastructure can be concentrated for the most cost-effective management. It is interesting that this logical approach is employed more frequently in some developing countries than in the United States with its long-held antipathy toward "government plans." The CEQ regulations touch on this concept in § 1502.4(c)(1).

Development strategies require environmental assessments because they select technologies and set priorities and timetables for large financial investments. For example, whether or not to exploit some natural endowment of mineral resources may have great environmental consequences that should be assessed at the outset. The strategy of dependence on large hydropower projects around the world has shown the usefulness of comprehensive assessment, including the effects of displacing many persons from the reservoir zone.

The concept of sustainable development can only be realized and implemented through an extension of EIA to allow judgment as to whether a current management strategy or practice is or is not sustainable and whether or not some proposed new strategy or practice will be sustainable. There are mixed views on the practicality of reducing to practice this attractive concept. Peter Berle (1995), chairman of the board of the National Audubon Society, warns that "the complexity and red tape surrounding environmental impact statements is such that requiring sustainability-impact statements would drive everyone crazy. But we can take some immediate steps. Eliminating subsidies that encourage unsustainability is an obvious strategy. We could begin by developing government purchasing guidelines that favor the use of sustainably produced products."

There are numerous difficulties in the quantitative biophysical measurement of sustainability (R.A. Carpenter, 1990, 1994). It is true that NEPA does not describe the kind of environment that was to be the goal of national policy, and values were recognized as changeable over time, but the general strong acceptance of sustainability as a constraint on economic growth will likely result in the eventual inclusion of an assessment of sustainability as one of the criteria for a complete NEPA procedure.

National budgets should have specific reference to environmental protection expenditures and to environmental degradation costs. The availability of full environmental cost accounting is growing and is based on the same quantitative biogeophysical indicators and measurements as are generated in the basic EIA. So-called "green report cards" are being considered by the Organization for Economic Co-operation and Development and by the World Bank, for noting the environmental management performance of various countries.

Continuous Assessment

The evolution of NEPA considered in detail in this chapter is in the time dimension. This extension is well recognized in international development assistance. For example, when training foreign practitioners in EIA, an English letter acronym can be used as a mnemonic for the essential features of successful assessment: e stands for Early (begin EIA as soon as the project is conceived), i stands for Integrated (combine EIA with economic and engineering studies), and a stands for Always (continue to provide management with environmental information throughout the life of the project) (R.A. Carpenter, 1995).

The old sequence of "predict impacts and mitigate" is seen to fail because of scientific uncertainties. The new paradigm is "predict and mitigate as best you can, expect surprises, monitor, adapt." The supplemental statements of § 1502.9 to the snapshot, one-time EA/EIS are not the continuous assessment needed to meet the NEPA goal of "maintaining productive harmony." Table 10.1 shows the sequence of monitoring and assessment to advise management throughout the entire life of a project activity. Although scientific research is not the purpose of the NEPA EA/EIS, treating the project as an experiment involves hypothesis testing with "informative" manipulation at time and spatial scales usually much larger than could be arranged for research, which would, therefore, be extremely valuable to scientific progress.

WHY PREDICTIONS ARE INADEQUATE

Science is the activity of understanding the regularities of the universe and revealing the simple laws that produce them. Prediction to guide human actions is also a primary goal of science, but uncertainties interfere by causing what actually occurs to differ from what was expected. Scientific truth is inherently uncertain. The scientific method constructs

TABLE 10.1   Adaptive Environmental Management: The Project as an Experiment

	• Project conception
	• Environmental baseline, "before"
⇓	• Prediction—EIA
	• Mitigation, prevention of unacceptable adverse consequences
	• Implementation of project
T	• Monitoring "during and after" for:
I	Mitigation compliance and effectiveness audit
M	Evaluate predictive methods/models
E	Improved design of other similar projects
	Scientific purposes
	Public information
	Surprise, unexpected consequences
⇓	• Adaptation and correction of project activities
	• Continued monitoring

hypotheses that are then rejected (falsified) or conditionally accepted on the basis of existing evidence from experiments or empirical observations. An accepted hypothesis may always be rejected in the future if additional information is seen to falsify it. Within this truth-seeking methodology, information is characterized by kinds and degrees of doubt, changeability, and availability.

The CEQ regulations seem to cover, in part, the problem of inadequate predictive capability in § 1502.22: "If the information relevant to reasonably foreseeable significant adverse impacts cannot be obtained because the overall costs of obtaining it are exorbitant or the means to obtain it are not known, the agency shall include within the environmental impact statement: (1) a statement that such information is incomplete or unavailable; (2) a statement of the relevance of the incomplete or unavailable information to evaluating reasonably foreseeable significant adverse impacts on the human environment; (3) a summary of existing credible scientific evidence which is relevant to evaluating the reasonably foreseeable significant adverse impacts on the human environment; and (4) the agency's evaluation of such impacts based upon theoretical approaches or research methods generally accepted in the scientific community."

Surprise

Uncertainties may be organized into three groups on the basis of opportunities for them to be reduced. The first category includes uncertainties that cannot be eliminated but whose magnitude and relative importance can be estimated. Surprise is a manifestation of uncertainty which, by definition, cannot be predicted. These include the so-called unknowable responses or true surprises that stem from the self-organizing, ever-changing character of ecosystems and their response to perturbations that are unprecedented (at least in the current ecosystems). For example, surprising consequences in ecosystem behavior are likely as a result of rapid climate change. Another source of surprises are the rare stochastic events, such as major earthquakes and large volcanic eruptions. Multiple causes and non-linear responses are also sources of unknowable outcomes. Totally unanticipated rapid and adverse changes in ecosystems may arise from apparently unrelated policy or social events. Very long-term effects sometimes become evident only long after the original cause, and explanation may be confounded.

A more familiar source of uncertainty is natural variation. Any "signal" that a change in condition is due to human action is often hidden in the "noise" of natural fluctuation in the value measured (just as static obscures a radio message). Stochasticity is the variation in response of an ecosystem due to random, uncontrolled factors such as weather and not due to the stressor being studied. Uncertainties have relative importance depending on their size. If stochasticity is large, then reduced error in the knowledge base cannot help much, and predictive power remains limited. Scientific research cannot decrease natural variability. "Nature is highly variable, and observations at any point in time and space are only snapshots of a dynamic system....Survey and monitoring results must be used as probabilistic statements and not as certainties" (Marr et al., 1987).

Another example of surprise is the potential for what are called "chemical time bombs." Long-lasting chemicals, such as heavy metals and refractory organic compounds, may not be toxic or bioavailable in the chemical combination or form in which they first are introduced into the biosphere. They are ignored in conventional ecotoxicology and thus are not mitigated as a result of the preparation of an EIS. However, accumulating in soils, sediments and groundwater, they can undergo transformations due to changes in land use, climate, acidification, redox potential, and cation exchange capacity. The responses of biota to these pollutants are time delayed and non-linear.

Lack of Understanding

The second category is uncertainties arising from lack of ecological understanding and explanatory principles upon which dependable predictive models can be constructed. Reduction of these uncertainties is possible through ecological research, but that is inherently difficult and long term. Control and replication of experiments, the essentials of the scientific method, may be practically impossible. Non-linear temporal and spatial scaling makes transferring results of research and monitoring difficult. Even the formulation of appropriate testable hypotheses is a barrier to ecological research. Ethical arguments arise about the subtle shifts of the burden of proof between exploiter and conservator, depending on how the hypothesis is stated and how the experiment is designed.

Ecological research has not emphasized large area investigations, and that scale (regions such as the American Midwest agricultural heartland, large marine ecosystems, or the boreal forests) is most important in monitoring and predicting impacts. The few studies that have been conducted of ecoregions or biomes reveal some of the sources of natural variation.

Concurrently, new research shows that combining large-scale experiments with long-term and comparative studies may obviate the necessity to tackle each ecosystem stress problem as if it were unique. "The challenge is not to eliminate uncertainty, for that is impossible, but to assign priorities to the tractable uncertainties and reduce them as rapidly as possible through targeted research" (S.R. Carpenter et al., 1994). Improved understanding may be on the way, but ecologists are cautioning against raising false expectations.

Bias

The category of uncertainty that can most readily be reduced has to do with data quality. Decision makers should be involved in data quality management to express the decision error rate that is acceptable to them (i.e., the probability of making an incorrect decision based on data that inaccurately estimate the true state of nature). Better monitoring program design can make data collection more efficient and cost effective. Bias is a source of uncertainty due to measurement and sampling errors of the parameters in a model (e.g., field instruments, laboratory analyses, sample collection, and population variability). These may be reduced at some cost. More use can be made of prior similar studies and existing information.

There are also institutional aspects to data quality, such as budget disruptions and policy changes, that prevent time series from accumulating, but all of these quality aspects are amenable to standardization and control. More important is what to measure.

The NEPA Record in Dealing with Uncertainty

A recent wide-ranging review of official department and agency procedures for implementing NEPA found only 1 of 27 agencies met the following criteria of scientific quality: "Do agency procedures require the discussion of risks, uncertainties, or gaps in knowledge? Do they provide any specific guidance regarding concepts or methods for addressing uncertainty or risk?" (Malik and Bartlett, 1993). Additionally, Culhane et al. (1987) analyzed EIS predictions and found that two-thirds of the statements made only qualitative projections. Only one-third of the forecasts were accurate with hindsight.

The NEPA process is not scientific research, mainly because of the time pressure, and the same standards should not be applied to both. "At the same time, however, federal agencies increasingly have to address areas of greater technical uncertainty, where the scientific content of documents will be more important. This poses new and significant problems for the NEPA process" (Dickerson and Montgomery, 1993).

ADAPTIVE ECOSYSTEM MANAGEMENT

This, then, is today's state-of-the-science as summarized by Walters and Holling (1990):

> [I]n no place can we claim to predict with certainty either the ecological effects of the activities, or the efficacy of most measures aimed at regulating or enhancing them. Every major change in harvesting rates and management practices is in fact a perturbation experiment with highly uncertain outcome, no matter how skillful the management agency is in marshaling evidence and arguments in support of the change.

They go on to explain:

> Almost by definition, the impacts will be the consequence of disturbances that are unlike any the natural system has yet experienced....the post-project system

is a new system, and its nature cannot be deduced simply by looking at the original one. If the project planning and development sequence fundamentally incorporates adaptive assessment throughout all of its stages, then the ecological response of both the old and the new systems will be studied...assessment merges into environmental management....Environmental assessment should be an ongoing investigation into, not a one-time prediction of, impacts.

It is remarkable that the preferred way to deal with uncertainty in environmental management was promulgated in the mid-1970s by the ecologists working with C.S. Holling at the University of British Columbia (and later at the International Institute for Applied Systems Analysis near Vienna). That their method, adaptive environmental management (AEM), has not been widely implemented is more of a comment on institutional failures and the stubbornness of conventional economics than the merit of the idea. AEM is not so much a confrontation, or embrace of uncertainty, as it is a wise capitulation to the inevitable. In other words, mankind cannot know precisely what it is doing, so surprise should be expected; ecosystems are not static, but continually change, and this is the source of their resilience; avoid irreversibilities; and design projects with built-in continuous assessment and remedial mechanisms.

The U.S. National Research Council (1986) has noted the connection of AEM to monitoring. "Viewing a project or action as an experiment can aid in designing a program to monitor effects. Such monitoring can have two major advantages: the detection of unexpected effects can be used as a basis for altering procedures, and the monitoring information can be used in the planning or design of similar projects or actions." (See also Table 10.1.)

Kai Lee, in the recent book *Compass and Gyroscope,* observes that "the adaptive approach is needed if scientific uncertainty is not to thwart socially timely action" (Lee, 1993). But he goes on to agree that data are sparse and inexact, theory is limited, and surprise is unexceptional. Furthermore, AEM must cross jurisdictional and political boundaries and cover time scales longer than terms of elective office or budget and business cycles.

Managers usually arrange for measurements that relate directly to their primary goal. Holling has studied a variety of managed ecosystems that failed or were unsustainable (Holling, 1995). He reports a sequence of events common to each of the systems studied. The management goal was always to reduce variability (for economic advantage) of some target parameter, such as cattle grazing, stocking density, fish population, or occurrence of fire or insects in forestry. In each case, control was achieved as measured by the target variable. Natural capital increased and was stored, but slowly the total system changed to become more homogeneous, brittle, and less resilient—an accident ready to happen. At the same time, management, having succeeded in its primary purpose, switched its concentration to improved efficiency in shifting cattle among paddocks, hatching fish, fighting fires, and spraying insects. Measures of the status and trends of conditions in the whole ecosystem were too difficult or too expensive.

The stabilized managed systems were attractive to investors and were further developed. These economic/social/ecological systems became increasingly vulnerable to drought in pastures, inbreeding in fish hatcheries, and contiguous forests that spread insect outbreaks and fires. Also, the other goods and services from the now simplified ecosystems declined. Ultimately, each system could not sustain production of the target commodity, and the rigidified management and investment made reorganization and remediation more difficult. Measurements that might have guided adaptive management were not available. It is interesting to see how this analysis of ecosystem management is parallel to the conclusions of Alvin Toffler about the now rejected principles of the latter stages of the industrial revolution. He identifies standardization, specialization, synchronization, concentration, maximization, and centralization as leading to large rigid organizations that became inefficient and are now being replaced (Toffler, 1980).

There has been a substantial shift in ecological theory since 1970, and it has not meant improvement in predictive capability. In fact, the prognosis may have worsened. In these examples, the old hypothesis of a stable nature fails to match reality. Holling proposes a discontinuous change hypothesis instead. Four ecosystem functions interact at different rates and times. Exploitation dominates at first and slowly yields to conservation at the climax stage. Then creative destruction, such as fire or pest outbreak, moves the system rapidly through a renewal stage using the readily available nutrients and back to exploitation (Holling, 1986). Knowing where the ecosystem is in this cycle allows adaptive management.

AEM is active learning (i.e., learning by doing). While there are non-technical impediments to learning, such as loss of institutional memory, and inherent ecological problems of replication and control, learning is the most rational procedural response to uncertainty (Hilborn, 1992). The rate of learning is reflected in the reduction of the standard deviation of the prediction error. This has been demonstrated in the manipulation of whole lake ecosystems. "As experimentation creates greater variance in the forcing variable, results are increasingly informative about responses of the total biomass. Manipulation is a very effective way of improving the capability to predict ecosystem change in experimental systems" (S.R. Carpenter et al., 1994). For learning to occur, well-designed data collection systems must be in place as the development begins, and the data must be relevant and statistically reliable. Munn (1994) suggests some general indicators of ecosystem integrity and sustainability: primary productivity, efficiency of nutrient recycling, species diversity, population fluctuations, pest prevalence, and spatial patchiness.

The White House has created an Interagency Ecosystem Management Task Force of 12 assistant secretaries and announced the principle of using monitoring, assessment, and the best science available in meeting a policy goal of ecosystem management (Joy, 1995). The U.S. Forest Service is developing adaptive management procedures (Kaufmann et al., 1994). "These features are important in keeping ecosystem management aligned with the best knowledge available while coping with information gaps. The treatment of management activities as experiments is critical because it provides an avenue to test unproven concepts believed intuitively to be correct, and it provides focus for monitoring the results of these activities." The Department of the Interior's Bureau of Land Management has also published its plans to adopt this approach (Bureau of Land Management, 1994), along with the Park Service and the Fish and Wildlife Service, the other principal land management agencies. In contrast, the EPA's "culture" of protecting human health has, so far, limited its consideration of ecosystems (U.S. EPA, 1994).

The Problem of the "Project"

AEM runs counter to the "project" character of decision making under NEPA as well as in the private sector. The money for development comes from tax revenues and private investment capital, largely in project-sized amounts. The EA/EIS procedure is instigated by each particular federal action.

It is obvious that sustainable management of ecosystems and protection of environmental quality (as goals of NEPA) must be planned and implemented on a biome or regional scale, far larger than most projects or individual actions. Although EIA is being successfully moved to higher levels of the decision hierarchy (program, sectoral, and regional master planning), it is difficult to overcome the bias (and tyranny) of the project. Even when environmental damages are quantified and monetized for internalization into the economic analysis, it is on a project basis. Continuous assessment and adaptive management can be the bridge between the immediate EA/EIS emphasis and the long-term policy objectives of NEPA.

The "project" is also a cause of resistance to AEM, which is, candidly, an experiment. Economic and financial analyses assume that projects will be carried forward as planned, even though contingencies for other (non-environmental, conventional) uncertainties (e.g., labor troubles and market fluctuations) are recognized. Large investments have their own irreversible character. The mid-course corrections envisioned by AEM may well require radical departures from original project objectives. The specter of actually stopping, abandoning, or deconstructing a project is implicit to some stakeholders when the idea of AEM is broached. Financiers are just unable to compute an investment that is forthrightly labeled an experiment.

AEM will have to be sold to financial decision makers; it is not reasonable that they will easily accept what appears to be a blind-faith underwriting of ecological research. A reasonable approach is to work with their own retrospective evaluations to show that the continuing lack of scientific knowledge and statistically reliable monitoring data is a hazard to even the environmentally benign projects. There are always times in the operational course of a project when changes can be made relatively easily, and these opportunities could well lead to increased profit, longer life, and enhanced reputation of all concerned. Responsiveness to more accurate and timely biophysical information is also needed to judge the cost effectiveness of mitigation measures mandated by environmental regulations and to check predictive models of the project. The benefit–cost ratio of improvement in ecological understanding and monitoring should be substantially greater than one.

The second selling point is to gain support for regional environmental master planning, particularly in major watersheds, estuaries, and coastal areas. Contributions to study these natural systems from all development interests could be coordinated and organized by the local government. Ecologically sensitive areas could be identified; research begun on the major ecosystems; cumulative effects of past, current, and future development analyzed; and estimates of carrying capacity established. Long-term ecological research sites are an example of what is needed. While real-time assessment for mid-course corrections cannot be conducted as scientific research, it can draw upon the results.

CONTINUOUS ASSESSMENT UNDER NEPA

Monitoring has some fundamental problems in being adequate for these tasks. It is not competitively attractive to scientists in contrast with other career advancement opportunities in research. Budget commitments to long-term monitoring are unpopular with administrators. The optimum cost-effective level of monitoring is difficult to establish at the outset. Practical scientific problems include overcoming natural variation, choosing meaningful indicators of environmental conditions, data gathering in the field and under extreme conditions, sampling and analytical errors, and correct statistical design.

Canter reviews monitoring in the United States and a number of other countries. He finds NEPA and the CEQ regulations lacking in specific requirements other than for the implementation of mitigation measures (Canter, 1993).

The post-audit is required by permitting agencies and would be one source of information on the results of uncertainties. It is, however, embroiled in fears of self-incrimination by industry. The very continued assessment by managers that would help them to improve prediction can also bring a notice of violation of standards. If the audit is done by an independent group, the necessary data may be considered proprietary and cannot be made available without revealing trade secrets.

Audits of one federal agency by another agency, or outside contractor, encounter similar barriers to access to needed information. In federal agencies, there is a natural reluctance to second guess their predictions just for scientific curiosity when there is no legal pressure to monitor the actual impacts of their projects and when a thorough audit would be expensive. Culhane concludes that "...we will never be able to improve our impact prediction methods unless we test them against the reality of actual post-project impacts." He then urges agency acceptance of post-EIS audits on the logic of "...some combination of an effectiveness-oriented managerial style, conflict-averse risk management, and a systems-analytic scientific mindset" (Culhane, 1993).

THE COUNCIL ON ENVIRONMENTAL QUALITY SHOULD TAKE THE LEAD

The CEQ should assume leadership in getting continuous assessment accomplished to the extent necessary. (The CEQ regulations already cover monitoring for compliance with mitigative measures recommended in EAs and EISs). The authority under NEPA Section 204(5) and (6) should be sufficient; this authority is "(5) to conduct investigations, studies, surveys, research, and analyses relating to [ecological systems and] environmental quality; (6) to document and define changes in the natural environment, including the plant and animal systems, and to accumulate necessary data and other information for a continuing analysis of these changes or trends and an interpretation of their underlying causes...." The function, insofar as it pertains to ecological systems (see brackets), was transferred to the EPA when it was established on December 2, 1970 by executive order in Reorganization Plan No. 3 (President of the United States, 1970). That agency, however, because of its justifiable preoccupation with human health and setting and enforcing pollution regulations, has never been able to achieve the required expertise or level of effort in ecological research. The National Science Foundation has operated a productive program of basic research in ecology and related disciplines, but it is, properly, academic and not focused on ongoing management problems.

Several complementary approaches are available to the CEQ:

1. Take full advantage of data generated in monitoring for compliance, and extract the information for AEM to the extent possible. Encourage agencies to broaden this monitoring, where marginal costs may be low, to be of greater value for AEM. Devise regulations for environmental "audits" associated with permits and other official supervision of mitigation measures so that they do not discourage the collection and use of information for AEM.

2. Provide leadership in arranging retrospective analyses of representative actions where predictive models have been important. Monitoring to evaluate the accuracy of predictive methods is essential for their improvement. Much of the same data would be useful for AEM.

3. Specify in the CEQ regulations that AEM and relevant monitoring be built into all federal agency "programs" and "plans" that warrant an EIS. As contrasted with individual projects, these more comprehensive long-term actions anticipate subsequent revisions and would benefit from AEM.

4. Despite the economy of dual-purpose monitoring as suggested in the above, specially designed programs of measurement for each technological perturbation and each ecosystem site will be most cost effective. Therefore, CEQ should select certain projects for additional AEM monitoring and negotiate with project proponents to bear the costs, if only as an insurance premium. Where there is no willingness to undertake the AEM approach, and no legal means to require it, CEQ funding could be justified for a limited number of demonstration programs.

5. Select certain valuable and vulnerable sites for environmental master planning, including baseline and continued monitoring to make AEM more easily implemented there. This is beginning to occur in some watersheds under regional, multistate, and EPA sponsorship.

6. Document some of the few ongoing applications of AEM in CEQ annual reports. For example, the implementation of the Pacific Northwest National Forest management plan will require AEM, in principle at least (James, 1994).

7. Enlist the environmental science community in establishing the most useful biogeophysical measurements for assessing and monitoring the functional condition of ecosystems (Cairns and Niederlehner, 1993). The work of the EPA Environmental Monitoring and Assessment Program should be immediately applicable to this purpose.

NEPA has proved to be robust and capable of evolving as changes occur in American priorities for the natural environment and in ecological science understanding. A mandate for the continual assessment that is now perceived as necessary to sustain "productive harmony" can indeed be found in NEPA.

SUMMARY

Getting concerns about the environment on the decision-making table before federal actions are taken is the recognized business of NEPA, but keeping them there is just as important. It is increasingly recognized that human interventions into natural systems seldom proceed as originally planned. Scientific uncertainties prevent environmental impacts from being reliably or precisely predicted. Thus, the style of management must provide for monitoring to guide mid-course corrections in adapting to inevitable surprises. The one-time preapproval EA/EIS procedure remains essential but is not sufficient to assure the goal of NEPA "to...maintain conditions under which man and nature can exist in productive harmony..." (NEPA, 1969). This chapter has explored the dichotomy between long-term policy and project initiation action under NEPA, the extent to which NEPA encourages continuous assessment for timely feedback to managers, and the practical difficulties involved in doing so.

It is concluded that the CEQ is authorized and capable to foster and implement continuous assessment (beyond the routine monitoring for compliance with mitigation measures) for a recommended strategy of adaptive environmental management.

ACKNOWLEDGMENT

The author wishes to thank J. Watson for helpful suggestions and for searching references to monitoring and management in the CEQ regulations.

SELECTED REFERENCES

Berle, P. 1995. Building for a Sustainable Future. *Audubon* January–February:6.

Bureau of Land Management. 1994. Ecosystem Management in the Bureau of Land Management: From Concept to Commitment. BLM/SC/GI-94/005+1736. U.S. Department of the Interior, Washington, D.C.

Cairns, J. and B.R. Niederlehner. 1993. Ecological Function and Resilience: Neglected Criteria for Environmental Impact Assessment and Ecological Risk Analysis. *The Environmental Professional* 15:116–124.

Canter, L. 1993. The Role of Environmental Monitoring in Responsible Project Management. *The Environmental Professional* 15:76–87.

Carpenter, R.A. 1976. The Scientific Basis of NEPA—Is It Adequate? *Environmental Law Reporter* 6 ELR:50014.

Carpenter, R.A. 1990. Biophysical Measurement of Sustainable Development. *The Environmental Professional* 12:356–9.

Carpenter, R.A. 1994. Can We Measure Sustainability? *Ecology International Bulletin* 21:27–36.

Carpenter, R.A. 1995. Environmental Risk Assessment. In *Environmental and Social Impact Assessment*. F. Vanclay and D. Bronstein, Eds. John Wiley, Chichester, England.

Carpenter, R.A. and J.E. Maragos, Eds. 1989. How to Assess Environmental Impacts on Tropical Islands and Coastal Areas. Training Manual for South Pacific Regional Environment Programme (SPREP). Environment and Policy Institute, East-West Center, Honolulu.

Carpenter, S.R. et al. 1994. Complexity, Cascades, and Compensation in Ecosystems. In *Biodiversity: Its Complexity and Role*. M. Yasuno and M.M. Watanabe, Eds. Global Environmental Forum, Tokyo.

Council on Environmental Quality. 1974. The Role of Ecology in the Federal Government. CER, CEQ, and Federal Council for Science and Technology, U.S. Government Printing Office, Washington, D.C.

Council on Environmental Quality. 1992. Regulations for Implementing the Procedural Provisions of the National Environmental Policy Act. 40 CFR Parts 1500–1508.

Culhane, P. 1993. Post-EIS Environmental Auditing: A First Step to Making Rational Environmental Assessment a Reality. *The Environmental Professional* 15:66–75.

Culhane, P., H. Friesma, and J. Beecher. 1987. *Forecasts and Environmental Decisionmaking: The Content and Predictive Accuracy of Environmental Impact Statements.* Westview Press, Boulder, Colorado.

Dickerson, W. and J. Montgomery. 1993. Substantive Scientific and Technical Guidance for NEPA Analysis: Pitfalls in the Real World. *The Environmental Professional* 15:7–11.

Hilborn, R. 1992. Can Fisheries Agencies Learn from Experience? *Fisheries* 17(4):6–14.

Holling, C.S. 1986. The Resilience of Terrestrial Ecosystems: Local Surprises and Global Change. In *Sustainable Development of the Biosphere.* W.C. Clark and R.E. Munn, Eds. Cambridge University Press, Cambridge, England.

Holling, C.S. 1995. Measurements for a Sustainable Biosphere. In *The Definition and Measurement of Sustainability: The Biophysical Foundations.* M. Munasinghe and W. Shearer, Eds. Joint publication of the United Nations University and The World Bank, Washington, D.C.

James, F. 1994. Joint ESA/AIBS Review of President Clinton's Plan for the Management of Forests in the Pacific Northwest. *Bulletin of the Ecological Society of America* 75(2):69–75.

Joy, C. (U.S. General Accounting Office) 1995. NEPA in Land Use Planning and Ecosystem Management. Remarks delivered at the DOE/CEQ NEPA 25th Anniversary Conference, Tyson's Corner, Virginia, March 21–22.

Kaufmann, M.R. et al. 1994. An Ecological Basis for Ecosystem Management. GTR RM-246. Rocky Mountain Forest and Range Experiment Station, Fort Collins, Colorado.

Kidd, C.V. 1992. The Evolution of Sustainability. *Journal of Agricultural and Environmental Ethics* pp. 3–26.

Lee, K.N. 1993. *Compass and Gyroscope.* Island Press, Washington, D.C.

Malik, M. and R. Bartlett. 1993. Formal Guidance for the Use of Science in EIA: Analysis of Agency Procedures for Implementing NEPA. *The Environmental Professional* 15:34–45.

Marr, B., W. Mitter, R. Palmer, and R. Carpenter, 1987. Cost-Effective Data Acquisition: Guidelines for Surveying and Monitoring Watersheds. East-West Center, Honolulu.

Munn, R. 1994. Monitoring for Ecosystem Integrity. In *Ecological Integrity and the Management of Ecosystems.* S. Woodley, J. Kay, and G. Francis, Eds. St. Lucie Press, Delray Beach, Florida.

NEPA. 1969. The National Environmental Policy Act of 1969, as amended (Public Law 91-190, 42 U.S.C. 4321–4347).

President of the United States. 1970. Reorganization Plan No. 3 of 1970, 35 F.R. 15623. The White House, Washington, D.C.

Toffler, A. 1980. *The Third Wave.* Morrow, New York.

U.S. Congress. 1968. Joint House–Senate Colloquium to Discuss a National Policy for the Environment on July 17, 1968. Hearings Doc. #8. U.S. Government Printing Office, Washington, D.C., p. 157.

U.S. Congress. 1976. Workshop on the National Environmental Policy Act. Serial No. 94-E. U.S. Government Printing Office, Washington, D.C.

U.S. Environmental Protection Agency. 1994. Managing Ecological Risks at EPA: Issues and Recommendations for Progress. EPA/600/R-94/183. U.S. EPA, Washington, D.C.

U.S. National Research Council. 1986. *Ecological Knowledge and Environmental Problem-Solving.* National Academy Press, Washington, D.C.

Walters, C. 1986. *Adaptive Management of Renewable Resources.* MacMillan, New York.

Walters, C. and C.S. Holling. 1990. Large-Scale Management Experiments and Learning by Doing. *Ecology* 71:2060–2068.

White House, 1994. Executive Order 12898, Federal Actions to Address Environmental Justice in Minority Populations and Low-Income Populations. Executive Office of the President, Washington, D.C.

HIGHLIGHTS OF NEPA IN THE COURTS

11

W.M. Cohen and M.D. Miller

Since the National Environmental Policy Act (NEPA) was first enacted, it has generated much litigation. There have been thousands of reported NEPA decisions from the courts. NEPA's importance and strength emanate to a large extent from the approach the courts have taken to construing the statute and its application. The purpose of this chapter is to review some of the more significant judicial rulings on NEPA issues.

CALVERT CLIFFS—PROCEDURAL STRENGTH

The significance of the ruling in *Calvert Cliffs v. Atomic Energy Commission,* 449 F.2d 1109 (D.C. Cir. 1971), lies not so much in the precise application of NEPA as ruled upon by the court, but in the breadth, scope, and tone of the court's language at a time when NEPA was in its infancy. "The sweep of NEPA is extraordinarily broad, compelling consideration of any and all types of environmental impact of federal action" (*Id.* at 1122). This opinion begins with the definition of the court's role in interpreting NEPA. "Our duty, in short, is to see that important legislative purposes, heralded in the halls of Congress, are not lost or misdirected in the vast hallways of the federal bureaucracy" (*Id.* at 1111).

Under the facts of the case, the Atomic Energy Commission (AEC) adopted rules to incorporate environmental considerations into its decision-making process. The petitioners argued that the rules adopted did not meet the standards set forth in NEPA. The court agreed with the petitioners. The AEC was under an obligation "to consider environmental issues just as they consider other matters within their mandate." Indeed, Judge J. Skelly Wright wrote that: "[The Commission's] responsibility is not simply to sit back, like an umpire, and resolve adversary contentions at the hearing stage. Rather, it must itself take the initiative of considering environmental values at every distinctive and comprehensive stage of the process beyond the staff's evaluation and recommendation" (*Id*. at 1119).

The court found that the AEC's rules limited full consideration of environmental issues. The following rules were at issue in the case. The AEC did not require consideration of environmental issues by the independent hearing board unless they were raised by outside parties or staff members. Environmental concerns could not be raised if the hearing was noticed prior to March 4, 1971, even though NEPA was already in effect at that time. The hearing board was prohibited from undertaking its own environmental review if another responsible agency had already concluded that its environmental standards were met. If, prior to NEPA's passage, a construction permit had been issued, but not an operating permit, environmental issues did not need to be considered in deciding whether to issue an operating license.

The court addressed the petitioners' contentions by clarifying certain terms found within NEPA. The term "accompany the proposal" in 42 U.S.C. 4332(C) (last sentence) is interpreted as a requirement that environmental factors be considered throughout the entire agency review process and not merely that some environmental assessment "accompany" the papers throughout the process.

The purpose of the "detailed statement" is to aid in the agency's own decision-making process and to advise other interested agencies and the public of the environmental consequences of the planned action.

The court found that the procedural provisions in NEPA Section 102 are much more rigid than the general substantive policy in Section 101. One of the most important aspects of NEPA is its requirement that all federal agencies consider environmental issues. The court interprets "fullest extent possible" as providing the mandate that the procedural requirements are not discretionary but must be carried out. If the procedure used to reach a decision does not include consideration of environmental factors, it is the responsibility of the court to reverse.

Therefore, NEPA mandates a case-by-case balancing judgment on the part of federal agencies; in each case, the particular economic and technical benefits of an action must be weighed against the environmental costs. Certification by one agency that its own environmental standards are satisfied does not mean that another agency's balancing act will result in the same outcome.

NRDC V. MORTON—ALTERNATIVES

The Council on Environmental Quality (CEQ) regulations and commentators have referred to the consideration of alternatives as the heart of the environmental impact statement (EIS). The courts have applied a rule of reason saying that the agency preparing an EIS need not consider every conceivable alternative. It must consider a reasonable range of viable alternatives. One of the early and important NEPA cases to address alternatives was *NRDC v. Morton*, 458 F.2d 827 (D.C. Cir. 1972).

In *NRDC v. Morton*, Secretary of Interior Morton proposed an oil and gas lease off the coast of Louisiana. Prior to the opening of bids, conservation groups brought suit to enjoin the sale. The agency prepared an EIS to accompany the sale, but the plaintiffs contended that the EIS did not adequately consider alternatives. Specifically, plaintiffs argued that energy needs could be met by federal action eliminating oil import quotas. The secretary did not consider the environmental consequences of the alternative because it involved "complex factors and concepts, including national security, which [were] beyond the scope of [the] statement."

The case set forth many parameters for the scope of alternatives to be considered in an EIS. An agency must look at "reasonable" alternatives, but this is not limited to measures which the agency itself can adopt. When the proposed action is an integral part of a coordinated plan to deal with a broad problem, the range of alternatives that must be evaluated is broadened. While the Department of the Interior did not have authority to undertake certain alternatives, such actions are within the purview of Congress and the president. The EIS is not only for the agency but also for the guidance of others and must provide them with the environmental effects of both the proposal and the alternatives for their consideration.

The discussion of alternatives need not be exhaustive; see *Vermont Yankee*, 435 U.S. 519, 551–3 (1978). The discussion must provide information sufficient to permit a reasoned choice of alternatives so far as environmental aspects are concerned, including alternatives not within the scope of authority of the responsible agency. *NRDC v. Morton* also counsels that it is inappropriate to disregard alternatives merely because they do not offer a complete solution to the problem.* However, see *Wildlife Fed. v. York*, 761 F.2d 1044, 1048 (5th Cir. 1985), and *Resources Ltd. v. Robertson*, 8 F.3d at 1401–2 (9th Cir. 1993), which suggest that a reasonable range of alternatives does not extend to those that do not serve the objectives of the agency action.

NRDC v. Morton holds that the mere fact that an alternative requires legislative implementation does not automatically establish it is as beyond the domain of what is required for discussion, particularly since NEPA was intended to provide a basis for consideration and choice by the decision makers in the legislative as well as the executive branch. But see *N.Y.C. v. DOT*, 715 F.2d at 743 (2d Cir. 1983) ("Statutory objectives provide a sensible compromise between unduly narrow objectives…and hopelessly broad societal objectives that would unduly expand the relevant range of alternatives"). Nevertheless, "the smaller the impact, the less extensive a search for alternatives" need be (*River Road Alliance v. Corps of Engineers*, 764 F. 2d 445, 452 [7th Cir. 1985]; see also *Olmstead Citizens for a Better Community v. U.S.*, 793 F.2d 201, 208–9 [8th Cir. 1986] and *Idaho Conservation League v. Mumma*, 956 F.2d 508, 520 [9th Cir. 1992]).

METHOW VALLEY AND *CABINET MOUNTAINS*—MITIGATION

The use of mitigation in the NEPA process is very much in vogue these days. CEQ has indicated that currently agencies prepare about 50,000 environmental assessments (EAs)

---

* With regard to the time for preparing an EIS, the Supreme Court made it clear that as a matter of law an EIS is required only just prior to the final agency decision. The moment at which an agency must have a final EIS ready "is the time at which it makes a recommendation or report on a *proposal* for federal action." *Aberdeen & Rockfish R. Co. v. SCRAP*, 422 U.S. 289, 320 (1975). See also *Kleppe v. Sierra Club*, 427 U.S. 390, 405–406, fns. 15 and 20 (1976). CEQ, through regulations and guidance, has urged even earlier preparation of EISs.

and 500 EISs per year. Many of the EAs conclude that there will not be a significant impact on the human environment because of the introduction of mitigation which holds the impact to the environment below the threshold of significance. Accordingly, the agency does not prepare an EIS and issues a finding of no significant impact (FONSI). Two important cases considering mitigation are *Robertson v. Methow Valley Citizens Council,* 490 U.S. 332 (1988), and *Cabinet Mountains v. Peterson,* 685 F.2d 678 (D.C. Cir. 1982).

In *Methow Valley,* the U.S. Forest Service issued a special-use permit authorizing Methow Recreation, Inc. to construct a ski resort at Sandy Butte in the North Cascade Mountains in the state of Washington. Methow Valley Citizens Council challenged the decision, claiming that NEPA required the Forest Service to include a detailed mitigation plan in the EIS. The Supreme Court held that this was not required.

In order to issue a special-use permit, the Forest Service must examine the general environmental and financial feasibility of a proposed project. Since the issuance of a special-use permit is a major federal action, the Forest Service must then prepare an EIS. If the permit is issued, the permittee must prepare a master plan for development, construction, and operation. An additional environmental analysis must then be conducted before construction may begin.

In its EIS, the Forest Service addressed the possible adverse effects on wildlife and air quality and discussed possible mitigation measures, but did not present a fully developed mitigation plan. The lower courts held that this failure to develop an actual plan violated NEPA's "hard look" requirement. The Supreme Court, however, stated that there is a "fundamental difference between a requirement that mitigation be discussed in sufficient detail to ensure that environmental consequences have been fairly evaluated and a substantive requirement that a complete mitigation plan be actually formulated and adopted."

The Court is not stating that mitigation is unimportant. In fact, the Court discusses in depth both the origin and the application of the mitigation requirement. The requirement that an EIS identify and evaluate possible mitigation measures arose from both the language of NEPA and from CEQ regulations. The CEQ regulations mandate discussion of possible mitigation measures when defining the scope of the EIS, addressing alternatives and consequences of the proposed action, and explaining the ultimate agency decision. In *Methow Valley,* the mitigation measures are within state and local, not federal, jurisdiction. If a fully developed mitigation plan were required, the federal agency could not act until the state and local agencies determined which mitigation actions were necessary.

However, where mitigation becomes the basis for an agency decision not to prepare an EIS, the mitigation plan must be complete. In that way, mitigation becomes the rationale for the agency's finding of no significant impact.

In *Cabinet Mountains Wilderness,* the Forest Service approved a mineral exploration project in the Cabinet Mountains Wilderness Area in Montana after conducting an EA and issuing a decision notice and FONSI. The decision was challenged on the grounds that the Forest Service violated NEPA by not preparing an EIS. Both the district and circuit courts held that no EIS was required because the Forest Service included mitigation measures to address all the environmental concerns.

This wilderness area is one of the few that support the endangered grizzly bear. After preparing an EA, sending it out for comment, and holding five public meetings, the Forest Service concluded that the exploration project could adversely affect the grizzly bear. Pursuant to the Endangered Species Act, the Forest Service consulted with the Fish and Wildlife Service (FWS). The FWS proposed an alternative that would not adversely affect the grizzly. This proposal was incorporated into the final EA and the FONSI was issued.

In upholding the Forest Service's decision not to prepare an EIS, the Court noted that an EIS is only required for major federal actions "significantly affecting the quality of the human environment." An EIS is not required if the agency takes a "hard look" at the problem, identifies relevant areas of environmental concern, makes a convincing case that impact is insignificant, or, if there is a significant impact, convincingly establishes that changes in the project sufficiently reduce it to a minimum. In sum, mitigation measures may be considered when deciding whether to prepare an EIS. By incorporating the FWS mitigation measures into its final proposal, the Forest Service compensated for the adverse effects of the original proposal and no longer needed to prepare an EIS.

FRITIOFSON AND THOMAS—CUMULATIVE IMPACTS

Courts have required that agencies consider impacts of the proposal they are examining along with those of other activities when cumulative impacts are reasonably foreseeable. The task is a difficult one for the agencies, and the courts have applied a standard of judicial review deferential to the agencies. Two important rulings on cumulative impacts from two different courts in the same year are *Fritiofson v. Alexander,* 772 F.2d 1225 (5th Cir. 1985), and *Thomas v. Peterson,* 753 F.2d (9th Cir. 1985).

In *Fritiofson,* the U.S. Army Corps of Engineers (Corps) issued a permit to a developer to dredge canals on West Galveston Island, Texas. Environmental groups and neighboring landowners filed suit to compel the Corps to prepare an EIS. The district court held that no dredging could take place until an EIS was prepared. The developer appealed on the grounds that the EA prepared prior to the issuance of the permit was adequate. The court of appeals held that the Corps did not adequately consider cumulative impacts. However, the court reversed the district court's order that an EIS be prepared on the ground that, until the cumulative impacts are adequately analyzed, it is premature to decide whether an EIS must be prepared.

The court drew a distinction between cumulative impacts which a NEPA analysis, in that case an EA, must examine and the scope of cumulative actions which an EIS must include. However, all NEPA analyses, including EAs, must examine the impacts of "past, present, and reasonably foreseeable future actions." (See also 40 CFR 1508.7.) Thus, the obligation to examine cumulative impacts in EISs and EAs is broader than the obligation to include cumulative actions within the scope of an EIS.

However, the court counseled that "we do not mean to suggest that the consideration of cumulative impacts at the threshold stage [in an EA] will necessarily involve extensive study or analysis of the impacts of other actions." Specifically, the court interpreted the CEQ regulations concerning cumulative impact analysis to require that the agency preparing an EA identify the area in which impacts will be felt; other impacts that are expected in that area, including those from past, present, and reasonably foreseeable actions; and the overall impact if all the actions were to occur.

In *Thomas,* plaintiffs challenged the Forest Service's approval of a timber road in the Nez Perce National Forest. The Forest Service prepared separate EAs for the timber road and the corresponding timber sales. In its timber road EA, the Forest Service failed to consider the impacts of the proposed timber sales the road was designed to facilitate. The court held that the Forest Service was required to prepare an EIS which considers the combined impacts of the timber road and timber sales.

The court reached this conclusion by analyzing the CEQ regulations requiring connected actions to be considered in the same EIS and the need to consider cumulative impacts. The timber road and sale are connected actions because but for the timber sales the road would not be built and the timber sales cannot go forward without the road.

The road and sales will also have cumulatively significant impacts. The Fish and Wildlife Service was concerned that the increased sediment deposits in the Salmon River from the road and sales would harm the river's salmon and steelhead trout and that the critical habitat for the endangered gray wolf would be affected. According to the court, these concerns raised substantial questions as to whether the road and sales will have cumulative effects on the environment and, on that basis, an EIS should have been prepared.

PANE—SOCIOECONOMIC IMPACTS

Under the CEQ regulations and several judicial rulings, the EIS requirement is triggered by significant physical impacts to the environment. Where an EIS is being prepared, it must also consider socioeconomic impacts. However, socioeconomic impacts are not what drive the decision to prepare an EIS. The definition of "human environment" emerging from the case law is restated at § 1508.14 of the CEQ regulations:

> [E]conomic or social effects are not intended by themselves to require preparation of an environmental impact statement. When an environmental impact statement is prepared and economic or social and natural or physical environmental effects are interrelated, then the environmental impact statement will discuss all of these effects on the human environment.

An important ruling from the Supreme Court arose out of the Three Mile Island disaster and resulted in a decision concerning socioeconomic impacts (*Metropolitan Edison v. People Against Nuclear Energy* [PANE], 460 U.S. 766 [1983]). Metropolitan Edison planned to resume operation of the reactor which was not operating at the time of the accident. Plaintiffs contended that the Nuclear Regulatory Commission failed to comply with NEPA when it authorized resumption of the operation of the unaffected reactor at Three Mile Island without considering the psychological harm to the community living near Three Mile Island and to their friends and relatives caused by the fear of another accident.

The court held that psychological harm from the risk of an accident was too far removed from the scope of physical harm contemplated by NEPA. NEPA does not require an agency to consider every possible environmental effect of an action, but only those with impact upon the physical environment. An analysis of the relationship between the effect and the change in the physical environment caused by the action determines whether the effect must be considered. This is essentially the tort concept of proximate cause. Mental stress from mere "risk" of an accident does not meet this threshold test. The Court's concern is that "if contentions of psychological health damage caused by risk were cognizable under NEPA, agencies would…be obligated to expend considerable resources developing psychiatric expertise that is not otherwise relevant to their congressionally mandated functions." While *PANE* excludes psychological impacts from the scope of NEPA, it also endorses cases excluding other socioeconomic impacts such as "the risk of crime from the operation of a jail or other public facility" (*Id.* at 776; see also *Missouri Coalition for the Environment v. Corps of Engineers*, 866 F.2d 1025, 1033 [8th Cir. 1989], and *Glass Packaging Institute v. Regan*, 737 F.2d 1083, 1092 [D.C. Cir. 1984]).

VERMONT YANKEE—PARTICIPATION IN THE ADMINISTRATIVE PROCESS

The courts have viewed the NEPA process as an aspect of administrative law and have applied administrative law principles which evolved from litigation under the Administrative Procedures Act. The standard of judicial review in such situations is deferential to the agency and includes an expectation that those who would challenge an agency decision would participate in the agency's administrative proceedings.

The Supreme Court has made this clear in *Vermont Yankee v. NRDC*, 435 U.S. 519 (1978). The Nuclear Regulatory Commission (NRC) issued licenses for the construction of two nuclear reactors in Michigan. After the initial application was filed, several environmental groups intervened, under the name Saginaw, to contest the application on environmental grounds. The licensing board denied their discovery requests and then held a hearing to provide information for the draft EIS. After the EIS was issued, Saginaw submitted additional contentions. The EIS was subsequently revised and issued in final form. The licensing board then held further hearings in which Saginaw failed to participate. Despite the lack of participation, the board continued to consider those issues for which Saginaw had presented evidence or participated in cross-examination. The board granted the construction license and its issuance was affirmed by the appeal board. At the time of the appeal, the CEQ issued EIS regulations and mentioned, for the first time, the necessity of considering energy conservation as an alternative, but exempted any EISs filed prior to January 28, 1974. This ruling confirmed the existence of confusion surrounding whether the statutory scheme compelled the consideration of energy conservation. However, in the interim, the AEC, in another case, ruled that this confusion did not mean that conservation should not be considered. In light of this ruling, Saginaw moved for a reopening of the proceedings and a clarification of this NRC ruling. The NRC refused on the grounds that energy conservation was not reasonably available and that Saginaw failed to follow even the most minimal procedural requirements.

The issue of the NRC's duty to consider energy conservation and the role the intervenors should have played was ultimately considered by the Supreme Court. The Court held that the notion of alternatives is "bounded by some notion of feasibility." The need for boundaries is explained by noting that "[t]ime and resources are simply too limited to hold that an impact statement fails because the agency failed to ferret out every possible alternative, regardless of how uncommon or unknown that alternative may have been at the time the project was approved."

The Court assessed the reasonableness of the NRC's consideration of alternatives based on the "information then available to it" (*Id.* at 553). The Court acknowledges that "NEPA places upon an agency the obligation to consider every significant aspect of the environmental impact of a proposed action" (*Id.* at 553). However, the Court holds that "it is incumbent upon intervenors who wish to participate to structure their participation so that it is meaningful, so that it alerts the agency to the intervenors' position and contentions. This is especially true when the intervenors are requesting the agency to embark upon an exploration of uncharted territory, as was the question of energy conservation in the late 1960's and early 1970's."

FOET—NEW TECHNOLOGY

NEPA case law makes clear that the statute extends to research and new technology. This point is illustrated by a ruling concerning biotechnology development. In *Foundation on Economic Trends (FOET) v. Heckler,* 756 F. 2d 143 (D.C. Cir. 1985), the National Institutes of Health (NIH) approved the deliberate release of genetically engineered organisms containing recombinant DNA. The court affirmed a ruling of the district court enjoining the release until a more in-depth environmental analysis was conducted.

Following a brief history of the congressional, judicial, and regulatory interpretations of NEPA, Judge J. Skelly Wright highlights the emphasis Congress placed upon NEPA's applicability to new technologies. "New and expanding technological advances" are enumerated in the statute as actions which may affect the environment. The legislative history makes it clear that Congress was concerned with the environmental effects of new technologies and intended the NEPA to apply in full force. The court concludes the background by stating that: "NEPA thus stands as landmark legislation, requiring federal agencies to consider the environmental effects of major federal actions, empowering the public to scrutinize this consideration, and revealing a special concern about the environmental effects of new technology" (*Id.* at 147).

The NIH promulgated standards prohibiting the deliberate release of organisms containing recombinant DNA in 1976 and then revised the standards in 1978, giving the director the power to approve deliberate releases. An EIS only accompanied the 1976 standards. The EIS did not specifically address the release of these organisms because of the ban, but it did note that if these organisms were released, they could cause environmental problems.

In 1983, the NIH director approved the experiment at issue. The University of California at Berkeley planned to apply bacteria-containing recombinant DNA to potatoes, tomatoes, and beans to increase the frost resistance of these crops. In approving the experiment, the NIH claimed that it considered environmental consequences in a document that was equivalent to an EA. The court found, however, that the few statements addressing the environmental impact of dispersion of these organisms failed to reach the level required for an agency to decide not to prepare an EIS. The conclusory statements of "no impact" were not sufficient to satisfy the NIH's duty under NEPA.

Judge Wright compared this case to *Calvert Cliffs* and reemphasized the broad interpretation of NEPA first articulated there. "This case poses a no less formidable challenge: to ensure that the bold words and vigorous spirit of NEPA are not similarly lost or misdirected in the brisk frontiers of science" (*Id.* at 145).

PUBLIC SERVICE CO. AND *ZABEL*—AFFIRMATIVE USE OF NEPA

Since NEPA's enactment, there have been only a few judicial rulings where federal agencies have used NEPA affirmatively as a basis for their actions. Two of the more significant decisions are *Public Service Co. v. Nuclear Regulatory Commission,* 528 F.2d 77 (1st Cir. 1978), and *Zabel v. Tabb,* 430 F.2d 199 (5th Cir. 1970).

In *Public Service Co. v. Nuclear Regulatory Commission,* the Public Service Company of New Hampshire (PSCO) challenged the NRC's order to reroute transmission lines from the Seabrook Nuclear Power Plant. The order was issued to minimize environmental harm. The original routes would have placed transmission lines through the Pow Wow River cedar swamp, affecting the relatively scarce Atlantic white cedar, the flights of migratory waterfowl, and low-impact recreational activities, and around the Packer Bog, resulting in the cutting of Atlantic white cedar.

The PSCO argued that the NRC did not have the authority to order changes to transmission routes. Even if it had the authority, the orders could not be based on NEPA requirements. The court found that the NRC had the authority to order changes to transmission routes and that under NEPA the NRC not only had the authority but had an obligation to minimize adverse environmental effects. But see *Methow Valley,* 490 U.S. at 350. The court reiterates that NEPA "imposes a duty upon federal agencies to act so as to effectuate the purposes of the statute to the fullest possible degree."

In *Zabel v. Tabb,* Zabel and Russell, owners of land next to and under Boca Ciega Bay in Pinellas County, Florida, brought suit to compel the Army Corps of Engineers to issue a permit to allow the dredging and filling of 11 acres of the bay so that they could construct a trailer park. The Corps denied the permit on the grounds that there would be harmful effects on fish and wildlife resources in the bay. The district court held that the Corps had no power to consider environmental effects of the action, but could only consider whether or not the action interfered with navigation. The court of appeals held that not only was the Corps allowed to consider the environmental effects but under NEPA was required to consider the effects and could deny a project based on such adverse environmental impacts.

With regard to the issue of whether NEPA expands an agency's jurisdiction, it should be noted that the CEQ regulations provide that the lead agency shall "condition funding of actions on mitigation" and shall include "appropriate conditions in grants, permits or other approvals" (§ 1505.3). Accordingly, the regulations appear to assume that NEPA provides additional jurisdictional authority.

Of course, these two decisions must be read in light of the more recent ruling in *Robertson v. Methow Valley Citizens Council,* 490 U.S. 332, 350, 353 (1989): "NEPA itself does not mandate particular results, but simply prescribes the necessary process...

[I]t would be inconsistent with NEPA's reliance on procedural mechanisms—as opposed to substantive, result-based standards—to demand the presence of a fully developed plan that will mitigate the environmental harm before an agency can act."

GREENPEACE AND *MASSEY*—DOES NEPA APPLY OUTSIDE OF THE UNITED STATES?

Since NEPA's enactment, the courts have tended to avoid a broad ruling on whether the statute applies generally to the impacts of governmental activities outside of the United States. In part to resolve some of the confusion in this area, the government promulgated Executive Order 12114 (Environmental Effects Abroad of Major Federal Actions), 3 CFR 356 (1980). This executive order did not extend NEPA itself, but extended the purposes of NEPA under specific circumstances to impacts of federal actions outside the United States. Two recent rulings in this murky area of extraterritoriality are *Greenpeace v. Stone,* 748 F. Supp. 749 (D. Hawaii 1990), appeal dismissed for mootness, 924 F.2d 175 (9th Cir. 1991), and *Environmental Defense Fund v. Massey,* 986 F.2d 528 (D.C. Cir. 1993).

In *Greenpeace v. Stone,* plaintiffs sought to enjoin the transport of nerve gas through the Federal Republic of Germany (FRG) to Johnston Atoll in the central Pacific on the grounds that the U.S. Army had not complied with NEPA. Under agreements entered into by Presidents Reagan and Bush, and pursuant to congressional mandate, the Department of the Army undertook a joint plan with the West German Army to remove chemical weapons from their storage site in the FRG and to transport them to Johnston Atoll, a U.S. territory in the Pacific Ocean, for incineration. The Army prepared EISs pursuant to NEPA on construction and operation of the incinerator on Johnston Atoll and an EA pursuant to Executive Order No. 12114 on the environmental impacts of the ocean shipment of the munitions from an FRG port to Johnston Atoll. No environmental analysis, under either NEPA or the executive order, was prepared on the movement of the munitions within the FRG.

Plaintiffs filed suit against the Department of the Army to enjoin movement of the munitions from the FRG to Johnston Atoll on the grounds that NEPA required a comprehensive EIS covering all aspects of the transportation and disposal of the FRG stockpile. The court held that NEPA did not apply to the transport within the FRG.

The court read NEPA to stand for the proposition that Congress "intended to encourage federal agencies to consider the global impact of domestic actions and may have intended under certain circumstances for NEPA to apply extraterritorially." However, the court also stated that action under NEPA "should be taken 'consistent with the foreign policy of the United States.'" It concluded that applying NEPA requirements to the transport within the FRG would infringe upon the jurisdiction of the FRG, noting the FRG's agreement and cooperation with the United States and its defeat of challenges of the action in its own courts. The court also found that the transoceanic transport was a necessary consequence of the stockpile removal and implicated the same foreign policy considerations.

In *Environmental Defense Fund v. Massey,* plaintiffs challenged the National Science Foundation (NSF) plans to incinerate waste at McMurdo Station in Antarctica, arguing that NEPA applies extraterritorially and, thus, that the NSF should have prepared an EIS. The Supreme Court had recently held that a civil rights statute did not apply extraterritorially on the premise that statutes are not to be applied abroad, absent expressed congressional intent. However, in this case, the appellate court held that the presumption was not relevant because NEPA applies to federal decisions and all decision making involving federal actions abroad presumably occurs in the United States. In addition, the impacts of this particular action would be felt in Antarctica, which does not have a sovereign and over which the United States asserts significant legislative control. It thus reasoned that there is no potential for clashes with another sovereign and made it clear that it was not deciding whether NEPA would apply to actions involving a foreign sovereign. In a more recent decision, *NEPA Coalition of Japan v. Aspin,* 837 F. Supp. 467 (D.D.C. 1993), the Court read the *Massey* decision as limited to Antarctica and declined to apply the statute to the Navy's operation of bases in Japan pursuant to treaty.

SPOTTED OWL DECISION—ECOSYSTEM ANALYSIS AND MITIGATION

The controversy over the northern spotted owl and old-growth federal forests of the Pacific Northwest has continued since the 1970s. Court injunctions severely restricted new timber sale programs on federal forests in northern spotted owl habitat. In 1993, President Clinton convened the Forest Conference in Oregon to address the human and environmental needs served by the federal forests of the Pacific Northwest and northern California. The president directed his cabinet to craft balanced, comprehensive, and long-term policy for the management of over 24 million acres of public land. The proposal of the Departments of the Interior and Agriculture was analyzed in a draft EIS that received over 100,000 public comments during a three-month public comment period. The final EIS was made available to the public in February 1994. It took an ecosystem analysis approach.

On appeal, plaintiffs in *Seattle Audubon Society v. Lyons,* 871 F. Supp. 1291 (W.D. Wash. 1994) challenged the forest management plan adopted by the secretaries of Agriculture and Interior for the management of federal lands in Washington, Oregon, and northern California that are within the geographic range of the northern spotted owl. Among other things, plaintiffs claimed that the defendants failed to follow the requirements of NEPA.

The court addressed in great detail federal defendants' compliance with NEPA. It held that the EIS satisfied the requirements of NEPA.

This was the first time a court passed judgment on the legality of federal agencies taking an ecosystem approach to management. The court went beyond upholding the agency's approach to management. After reviewing NEPA and the other statutory requirements the agencies were obliged to meet (e.g., Endangered Species Act, National Forest Management Act), the court concluded: "Given the current condition of the forests, there is no way the agencies could comply with the environmental laws without planning on an ecosystem basis." The opinion notes that "courts have repeatedly encouraged the Forest Service, the BLM [Bureau of Land Management], and FWS to turn from disparate strategies for managing...forests to a cooperative approach."

Second, the court determined that the agencies considered an appropriate range of alternatives, including a "no action" alternative, as required by NEPA. The court noted that the ten alternatives analyzed in depth encompassed a variety of measures and strategies, as well as an 18-fold difference among probable timber outputs. Thus, it held that the range of alternatives examined in this broad EIS permitted a reasoned choice, as required by NEPA.

Third, the court stated that the plan adequately analyzed the effects of the Forest Plan on the northern spotted owl and on various aquatic species. It noted that the EIS responded sufficiently to opposing scientific opinion and took the requisite "hard look" at the relevant data. However, the court made clear that careful monitoring will be needed to assure the legality of the plan. Indeed, it stated that "[i]f the plan as implemented is to remain lawful, the monitoring, watershed analysis, and mitigating steps called for by the ROD [record of decision] will have to be faithfully carried out, and adjustments made if necessary."

Finally, the court found that the EIS dealt adequately with incomplete information, cumulative impacts, commitment of resources, mitigation measures and monitoring, other environmental factors, economic issues, and the alleged deprivation of public comment on changes to the final EIS. Throughout its findings on these issues, the court emphasized the importance of monitoring as "central to the plan's validity." Indeed, it noted that if for any reason the monitoring was not done, the plan would have to be reconsidered. The court noted:

> Careful monitoring will be needed to assure that the plan, as implemented, maintains owl viability. New information may require that timber sales be ended or curtailed. But on the present record, the FSEIS adequately discloses the risks and confronts the criticisms as required by NEPA.

In summary, in no other judicial ruling on NEPA compliance has monitoring become so critical. Here, it plays an important role in both assessing the changing situation and in looking at new information and research as they become available.

CONCLUSION

NEPA is the most versatile and well known of the modern environmental laws passed by Congress. This brief analysis reflects the important role the courts have played in making NEPA the strong and vital law that it is.

THE CEQ NEPA EFFECTIVENESS STUDY: LEARNING FROM OUR PAST AND SHAPING OUR FUTURE

12

H. Welles

For over 25 years, the National Environmental Policy Act (NEPA) has been the nation's most eloquent declaration of environmental policy. It has provided policy and goals for the protection, maintenance, and enhancement of the environment and a process for implementing these goals within federal agencies. It also established the Council on Environmental Quality (CEQ) within the Executive Office of the President to provide a leadership role in information gathering and reporting, program review, and policy development, all for the purpose of integrating concern for environmental quality into federal decision making.

Numerous other countries, multilateral and bilateral development institutions, and nearly half the states within the United States have emulated NEPA in their laws and policies. The primary tool at the focus of this change is known in NEPA as the "detailed statement," more widely recognized nationally as the environmental impact statement (EIS) and internationally as the environmental impact assessment (EIA). The process of preparing the detailed statement is the predominant vehicle for evaluating proposed federal actions with respect to their significance in affecting environmental quality. It is praised on the one hand for improving the environmental management of federal projects. On the other hand, it is viewed as an inefficient process, triggered too late, taking too long, and costing too much, relative to the environmental benefits achieved. Few dispute, however, that the NEPA process has changed federal agency approaches to environmental decision making. The challenge is in determining in which ways and to what extent.

The purpose of this chapter is to shed some light on NEPA's evolution and perceptions of its effectiveness and efficiency, information needs, and recommendations for improvement.[1] To address these issues, CEQ engaged a broad spectrum of people involved with and/or affected by NEPA. As illustrated in Figure 12.1, this includes the

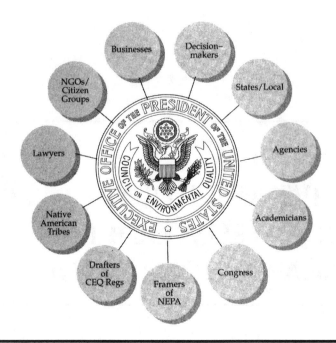

FIGURE 12.1   NEPA effectiveness study partners.

original framers of the NEPA legislation, the drafters of the CEQ regulations, Native American tribes, lawyers involved in NEPA litigation, environmental non-governmental organizations (NGOs), citizen groups, businesses seeking federal licenses and permits, government decision makers, state and local governments, NEPA practitioners inside and outside of government, academicians who have written and spoken about NEPA, and congressional staff. CEQ sought input via meetings, workshops, conferences, personal interviews, papers, and surveys. The nature of CEQ's analysis, with a few exceptions, yields primarily qualitative information. Quantitative indicators of NEPA have not been systematically collected. Of course, political considerations per se are outside the scope of this study, although they may be paramount in some cases.

Over the years, several important evaluations of the NEPA EIS process have been conducted (Andrews, 1975; CEQ, 1976; Environmental Law Institute, 1981; Center for Advanced Studies in Science, Technology and Public Policy, 1982; Blaug, 1993). Among the major challenges of these reviews have been (1) identifying appropriate indicators to measure effectiveness and efficiency, (2) obtaining sufficient data on these indicators, and (3) separating the impacts of NEPA from other environmental and planning policies and regulations. Although there have been numerous books, papers and conferences since the passage of NEPA, these issues remain unresolved. In 1994, considering the current efforts in the United States to streamline federal government, with 25 years of accumulated EIS experience to evaluate, and with an international review of country EIS policies in process, the time was ripe for CEQ to undertake a comprehensive review of the effectiveness and efficiency of NEPA within the limitations of the available information (CEQ, 1994i).

TABLE 12.1 Examples of NEPA Successes

1. Increases public involvement in decision making
2. Creates a standard framework for decision making
3. Fosters better coordination of federal projects
4. Improves understanding of ecosystems
5. Creates more environmentally sound federal actions

Commencing in the spring of 1994, CEQ began reaching out to a cross-section of NEPA stakeholders to identify (1) the major strengths of NEPA (i.e., what it has accomplished over the last 25 years), (2) the limitations and gaps within the process that hinder effective and efficient outcomes, (3) the key problems warranting immediate attention, and (4) solutions to tackle the shortcomings in the NEPA process. This national study focused on the effectiveness of the "detailed statement" process and not NEPA's other mandates, such as the provision of advice to the president, the annual report, and general policy development. It concentrated specifically on the EIS and environmental assessment (EA) processes called for generally in Sections 102(2)(C) and 102(2)(E) of the act and more specifically in the CEQ regulations.

Despite the limitations inherent in research of this nature, the results of this study confirm CEQ's fundamental premise that assessing the environmental effects of federal proposals, as required by NEPA, is a powerful and effective decision-making tool. Study participants identified a number of areas and cases in which NEPA is working well by fostering the integration of environmental protection into activities that promote economic growth. Several of these are listed in Table 12.1 and will be discussed in other sections of this chapter. On the other hand, the study also confirmed that the process needs improvement and its efficiency enhanced. Priority areas identified as needing additional work are summarized in Table 12.2. These issues are not in conflict with the areas identified in Table 12.1; rather, they largely reflect the need to more widely replicate identified successful techniques to more effectively achieve the overall goal of NEPA.

The issues listed in Tables 12.1 and 12.2 are not new; they have been raised in previous studies and analyses. What is new, however, is:

1. A clear identification of trends (litigation is decreasing, many more EAs are prepared relative to EISs, and the use of mitigated EAs is on the rise)

TABLE 12.2 NEPA Issues Needing Attention

1. Better integration of environmental and socioeconomic analyses
2. Earlier start on analysis
3. More targeted monitoring programs
4. Improved collection of necessary baseline data
5. More rigorous analysis of data
6. Better communication among and inclusion of stakeholders

2. A consensus about significant NEPA successes
3. A consensus about areas that need work

Based on the feedback from the research, CEQ is developing a more proactive approach to make the NEPA process more effective and efficient. In particular, CEQ found the lack of record keeping and monitoring associated with the NEPA process problematic. Without baseline data collection, determinations of if and how federal activities change the environment cannot be made. Without in-process project monitoring, mitigation for initially unidentified impacts cannot be accomplished. Without post-project auditing, the accuracy of original EA/EIS predictions cannot be determined. The analysis of information generated at all these stages tells the story of NEPA's effectiveness. To date, only piecemeal data sets exist. Given the tight resources facing every agency today, much additional monitoring is unlikely. However, more efficient data collection and analysis should be feasible.

CURRENT POLICY PERSPECTIVE

In the United States over the last 25 years, more than 26,000 EISs and, because no reporting is required, an unknown but much larger number of EAs have been prepared on actions ranging from missile production, to road construction, to forest plans, to hydroelectric facilities (see CEQ annual reports on environmental quality). The promulgation of guidelines and regulations, development of case law, and years of public and private sector experience with EIS implementation in a climate of constant change have all contributed to significant improvements to (1) the process, (2) the development of environmental science and assessment methods, and (3) the environment, at least in some cases.

NEPA has been praised for preventing many actions with potentially severe adverse environmental impacts from taking place. It is also praised for causing modifications to proposed actions to reduce or avoid such impacts. Advocates claim that NEPA fosters public involvement in the planning and decision-making processes of U.S. federal agencies. It certainly has increased public access to information about agency planning activities. Nearly 100 federal agencies have designated officials with NEPA responsibilities, revolutionizing consideration by government agencies of the environmental effects of their proposed projects and programs. Nearly half the states have developed their own localized NEPA laws (CEQ, 1994a,f,i,j,k, 1995a).

On the other hand, coupled with these praises are criticisms of the process. Individuals adversely affected argue that the EIS process produces too little improvement for the amount of dollars and human resources currently expended and that it inconsistently addresses their concerns. Others, who appreciate NEPA's mandate, still criticize the process as too narrowly interpreted and not capable of achieving NEPA's intended goals and suggest that perhaps other evolving considerations such as sustainable development and ecosystem management can provide more dynamic, substantive, and sophisticated approaches to protecting the environment. However, these concepts are not inconsistent with NEPA and could be integrated into the existing NEPA framework rather than creating an entirely new system. Still others claim that the preoccupation with the preparation of NEPA documents and fears of related litigation have actually undermined agencies' powers, responsibilities, and initiatives and may have lessened environmental improvements and innovations which could have accrued under environmental protection regulations and citizen involvement (CEQ, 1994a,i, 1995a,c; Fairfax, 1978).

Congress enacted NEPA to enable environmental quality to compete on an equal footing with other important policies. However, NEPA is not an action-forcing statute. The courts have restricted its application and agencies are not required to choose the environmentally preferred alternative. Section 102(2)(B) of the act only requires "that presently unquantified environmental amenities and values may be given appropriate consideration in decision making along with economic and technical considerations." Experience with NEPA demonstrates that environmental quality frequently suffers a competitive disadvantage, particularly due to the lack of commitments and procedures to ensure "appropriate consideration." One of the greatest challenges is placing a value on certain environmental impacts in a way that is comparable with other impacts or vice versa (Bausch, 1991; CEQ, 1994a, 1995d). For example, calculating the construction budget of a road is much simpler than calculating the quantitative and qualitative impact of that road on flora and fauna.

STUDY METHODOLOGY

Through informal discussions with representatives of several sectors of society concerned with the NEPA process, CEQ confirmed that a study of the effectiveness and efficiency of NEPA was of great interest and that such an evaluation would likely help to improve the process itself and contribute to current efforts to streamline government. Thus, CEQ began the study in 1994 with two informal conferences to assist with initial issue identification: one on March 28, with about 80 federal environmental officials, and one on May 19, comprising environmental professionals representing the environmental community, other public interest organizations, and businesses and consulting firms involved in the preparation or review of NEPA documents. Simultaneously, a review of the published professional literature on NEPA and EIA was made (CEQ, 1994i). By June 1994, an initial list of key strengths and limitations of NEPA was developed, based on the opinions and advice of more than 100 environmental professionals and the literature review. Those contacted included federal agency NEPA officials, leaders of environmental and other public interest organizations, representatives of businesses affected by NEPA, consulting firms engaged in the conduct of environmental studies pursuant to NEPA, and environmental law professors and lawyers in private practice.

Based on this input, CEQ then launched a more extensive effort to (1) validate and/ or adjust, as necessary, the preliminary list of NEPA strengths and limitations; (2) explore ways to improve the effectiveness and efficiency of the process; and (3) identify case studies where NEPA has caused positive or negative experiences.

Figure 12.1 illustrates the 11 key partnership clusters. For example, CEQ requested Dr. Lynton Caldwell (Bentley Professor of Political Science Emeritus and Professor of Public and Environmental Affairs at Indiana University, and one of the original authors of NEPA) to write a paper, with input from the other framers of NEPA, on how well the original intent of NEPA has been achieved. CEQ asked Ken Weiner (currently an attorney with Preston, Gates, and Ellis of Washington State, former attorney at CEQ and one of the authors of the NEPA regulations) to work with the other authors of the CEQ NEPA regulations to review the effectiveness and efficiency of the regulations and to develop suggestions for improvement. Several meetings and workshops were conducted with federal, state, and local government officials; congressional staff; and NGOs. Surveys were conducted of Indian tribe representatives, businesses, citizens, NEPA litigators, and academia.

Although one of CEQ's goals in this study was to highlight NEPA's strengths, more emphasis and energy have been placed on identifying the key limitations to the effectiveness and efficiency of NEPA's implementation. The four criteria for identifying priority areas are (1) consensus among the majority of stakeholders that the issue was significant, (2) realistic solutions exist to address the problem, (3) CEQ has the authority to address the problem, and (4) there is potential for cost-effective improvement.

DEFINITION OF EFFECTIVENESS AND EFFICIENCY

The effectiveness and efficiency of environmental impact analysis of U.S. federal projects, plans, programs, and policies can only be understood in the context of NEPA in its entirety. The "detailed statement" is a tool to realize the national environmental policy goals specified by the act. An agency's NEPA implementation has no "beginning" or "end." NEPA is a policy statement that environmental values will be integrated into all agency activities. The EIS helps an agency achieve that goal, but preparation of "good" EISs does not equate to "effective" NEPA implementation. Better decisions should flow from the analysis. Section 1500.1(c) of the CEQ regulations states: "Ultimately, of course, it is not better documents but better decisions that count. NEPA's purpose is not to generate paperwork—even excellent paperwork—but to foster excellent action. The NEPA process is intended to help public officials make decisions that are based on understanding of environmental consequences, and take actions that protect, restore, and enhance the environment."

For the purposes of the study described herein, effectiveness is defined as the protection and/or enhancement of the environment through the development and use of high-quality interdisciplinary information and analysis in planning and decision-making processes. This information should be developed with input from multidisciplinary experts and the public for use in decision making, thus helping agencies to consider environmental values in planning and implementation. Efficiency is defined as the preparation of EAs and EISs in the least amount of time, money, and paperwork, without sacrificing quality and risking harm to the environment or the economy. Although perhaps seemingly contradictory, both effectiveness and efficiency can be achieved if the NEPA process is properly managed.

THE ROLES OF THE COURTS AND THE CEQ REGULATIONS

Two major factors have largely driven the way in which NEPA is interpreted and implemented: decisions of the courts and CEQ guidance and regulations (CEQ, 1994d, 1995d).

Initially after NEPA's passage, litigation and court decisions determined the direction of NEPA. One of the first cases, *Calvert Cliffs v. Atomic Energy Commission,* 449 F.2d 1109 (D.C. Cir. 1971), set the tone for all subsequent NEPA cases. In this case, petitioners argued that the rules the Atomic Energy Commission (AEC) adopted to incorporate environmental considerations into its decision-making process did not meet the standards set forth in NEPA. The court agreed with the petitioners and found that the AEC's rules lacked full consideration of environmental issues, even though an EIS was performed. The court made several important points regarding NEPA and federal agency compliance with respect to the substantive and procedural aspects of NEPA. The substantive policy in Section 101 of NEPA was considered flexible: "It leaves room for a responsible exercise of discretion and may not require particular substantive results in particular problematic instances." However, the procedural provisions in Section 102 were not deemed as flexible. They are designed to ensure that all federal agencies do in fact exercise the substantive discretion given them. NEPA's procedural requirements "must be complied with to the fullest extent, unless there is a clear conflict of statutory authority." The AEC's interpretation of NEPA was deemed inadequate by the court. It ruled that it is not enough that environmental data and evaluation merely "accompany" an application through the review process. NEPA requires that an agency—to the fullest extent possible—consider alternatives to its actions that would reduce environmental damage. Several determinations were made to force the AEC to consider environmental issues just as it considers other matters within its mandates.

Unlike the courts, CEQ guidelines and the regulations lend credence to both the procedural and substantive provisions of NEPA. Charles Warren, former chairman of the CEQ, stated in a preamble to the regulations that the EIS "has tended to become an end in itself, rather than a means to making better decisions...[and has] often failed to establish the link between what is learned through the NEPA process and how the information can contribute to decisions which further national environmental policies and goals" (43 Federal Register 230, 1978, p. 55978). Thus the NEPA regulations "are designed to gear means to ends—to ensure that the action-forcing procedures of Section 102(2) of NEPA are used by agencies to fulfill the requirements of the Congressional mandated policy set out in Section 101 of the Act" (43 Federal Register 230, 1978, p. 55980; Boggs, 1993). Without the support of the courts endorsing substantive goals of NEPA, however, the ability to force agencies to select environmentally preferred alternatives has been limited.[2] This debate over procedure and substance is important and warrants greater attention by Congress, the administration, and the courts themselves.

THREE SIGNIFICANT TRENDS IN NEPA'S IMPLEMENTATION

CEQ's research reveals three major trends. First, NEPA litigation has dropped significantly, from a high of 189 cases in 1974 to 81 in 1992. Although the number of cases has fluctuated from year to year, the number has consistently been below 100 since 1984 (CEQ, 1974–93.) The most frequent defendants have been the Departments of Interior, Transportation, and Agriculture and the Environmental Protection Agency (EPA) (CEQ, 1993). Second, many more EAs are prepared today than EISs—approximately 50,000 EAs to 500 EISs annually (the number for EISs includes draft, final, and supplemental

EISs). In 1989, 10,000 to 20,000 EAs were estimated to be prepared annually compared to approximately 400 EISs.[3] This is significant because EISs require a much more rigorous review of potential environmental impacts and greater public involvement than EAs. The intent of an EA is to determine whether or not there is a finding of no significant impact (FONSI); if significant impacts are expected to occur, the EIS process is triggered. Third, agency actions triggering NEPA have increasingly incorporated mitigation in order that the agency might utilize a categorical exclusion, or issue a FONSI, thereby obviating the need for an EIS—or even an EA (Blaug, 1993; CEQ, 1993).[4] EAs with such built-in mitigation measures are often referred to as "mitigated FONSIs."

NEPA'S SUCCESSES

Even with weak enforcement of its "substantive" goals, NEPA has been successful in many ways. First, as outlined in Table 12.1, it provides an avenue for public information, education, and involvement in the planning and decision-making processes for many federal actions. Prior to NEPA, the public had no means to engage in the debate about socioeconomic and environmental costs and benefits, nor did they have recourse to challenge the federal government if they felt a proposed project or program did not balance environmental protection with economic development. Second, NEPA creates a standard framework for integrating environmental considerations into the planning and decision-making processes. Before the issuance of guidance and regulations by CEQ as a result of NEPA, the integration of environmental values into decision making did not occur on any consistent basis. Third, NEPA mandates an interdisciplinary approach to impact assessment which fosters early and open information exchange among professionals (from multiple disciplines). Fourth, this coordination often triggers the collection and analysis of pertinent ecological, social, and economic information, for use in improving federal decisions. Prior to NEPA, the collection of and access to such information was less consistent or non-existent. Fifth, proposed activities with blatant adverse environmental impacts (often discovered in the NEPA process) are now commonly modified or abandoned early on.

Overall, the feedback obtained via CEQ's research indicates that because of NEPA, decision makers are more informed and make better decisions which can save money and lessen harm to the environment in the long run and that these benefits usually outweigh the costs and delays associated with the process (CEQ, 1994a,b,f, 1995a).

ISSUES NEEDING IMPROVEMENT

Table 12.2 summarizes a list of issues where NEPA requires improvement based upon project participant consensus. These limitations are not in conflict with the list of NEPA strengths; rather, they are reflective of the fact that the process needs modification to more effectively achieve the overall goal of NEPA. The majority of this section explores these limitations in greater depth and lists other limitations on which there was less emphasis—all organized primarily around input received from federal, state, and local government officials; academics; NGOs; citizens; businesses; and Native American tribes.

Inside the Agencies—Planning and Decision Making

Timing

The greatest hindrance to effective implementation of NEPA by agencies is when, and how, the NEPA process is triggered (see Table 12.2). In general, agency and private sector planning processes begin much earlier than the NEPA process. Frequently, alternatives and strategic choices are foreclosed by the time an environmental impact analysis is commenced, thus limiting the potential contribution of other agencies, states, tribes, and the public in the planning and decision-making process and foregoing an opportunity to assess the cumulative impacts of proposals. Almost all study participants support the need to apply NEPA earlier in agency planning, and even at the policy and program levels, in order for it to play a vital role as a tool in ecosystem management and sustainable development. They believe this would enhance the attainment of environmental quality objectives on a broader, more cost-effective scale.

In order to initiate NEPA earlier, study participants proposed several ideas. One of the most prevalent suggestions was for CEQ to provide clearer guidance on what is meant by and how to implement strategic-level environmental impact analysis. The term "strategic" may take on different meanings, depending on the context in which it is used. For example, in Europe, a strategic EIS is an EIS of a program rather than a project-level EIS, whereas in the United States, the term "strategic" has been used to refer to the concept of conducting EAs and EISs earlier in agency planning prior to program design—an example being an EIS prepared on a national energy strategy. Some agencies already conduct programmatic EAs/EISs, but the "strategic" (pre-programmatic) EA/EIS concept is embryonic. However, results of this study indicate that, at minimum, CEQ should reiterate that the CEQ regulations require environmental impact analysis of policies, plans, and programs. Development of a publication by CEQ describing NEPA as a tool for strategic decision making and providing case studies of effective applications would be most helpful (CEQ, 1994c,g,i, 1995a).

Documentation and Analysis

Agencies tend to examine identified project-level environmental effects in near-microscopic detail, which may explain their reluctance to apply NEPA to policies and programs. Fear of litigation is commonly cited as the driving force to prepare overly detailed and lengthy EISs. Often the lengthiness of EISs is attributed to descriptive material rather than a more focused analysis, which would be more useful to decision makers. The reluctance to prepare EISs for programs and policies reflects the fear that microscopic detail will be expected but not possible. This is driven by the concern that material contained in program statements may be challenged even though it may be revisited in documents prepared for specific projects that are spawned by those programs. Moreover, the need for finality must somehow be balanced with the need to consider changed circumstances. Agencies should be encouraged to treat weaknesses in program documents (whether caused by changed circumstance or simply the passage of time) in subsequent project-oriented documents. Quite frequently, a project proposal generated from such a programmatic EIS only requires an EA rather than an EIS to make up for any limitations of the programmatic EIS. Distribution of examples of successful less-detailed environmental analyses of programs and policies would improve agency understanding of the potential effectiveness of such analyses (Bausch, 1991; CEQ, 1994b,c,f,g,i).

Agencies are often on tight time schedules due to pressure for efficient fulfillment of missions, assurance that funds will be dispersed, and scrutiny from Congress and political constituents. According to many federal agency NEPA liaisons, the EIS process is still frequently viewed as merely a compliance requirement rather than a tool to aid better decision making. Sometimes agencies try to cut the process short, stopping with an EA rather than conducting a more in-depth analysis via an EIS. If an EA with mitigation will reduce impacts below a level of significance while otherwise complying with NEPA, decision makers often select that route. However, mitigated EAs can entail less rigorous scientific analysis, little or no public involvement, and consideration of fewer alternatives, all of which are at the very core of NEPA's strengths. Moreover, because of insufficient analysis of coherent ecosystems, EAs do not always reflect the potential cumulative effects of a proposal (CEQ, 1994g, 1995a).

These observations emphasize the need for an in-depth study to determine the number and scope of FONSIs and "mitigated FONSIs" prepared by federal agencies. No such data currently exist. Comparisons should be made between mitigated FONSIs and EISs in quality, length, and cost. Interestingly, the true costs of EISs are only roughly estimated, while the costs of EAs are less well known and certainly not routinely documented. When asked, NEPA liaisons commonly state that their agency EISs cost less than 1% of total project costs. This is the same figure quoted in a 1976 CEQ analysis of six years experience by 70 federal agencies (CEQ, 1976). Blaug's 1993 survey found the mean preparation costs of non-mitigated EA FONSIs to be $1,240 and the mean preparation cost of mitigated EA FONSIs to be $31,192. The Department of Energy (DOE) recently found a very broad range in the cost of EAs and EISs (i.e., EAs ranging from $5,000 to $500,000 and EISs ranging from $200,000 to $50 million). DOE determined that the costs by and large are directly related to the complexity and controversy of the project. Clearly, an EA associated with the transport and disposal of high-level uranium waste will cost more than an EA for determining grazing allotments (DOE, 1995).

Since the costs of EAs and EISs are of growing concern to government and business, better tracking and record-keeping mechanisms should be instituted. Similarly, the benefits of NEPA should be tracked and calculated. Analyses should also be conducted on costs associated with litigation, including the cost of delay. Any benefits resulting from litigation should also be accounted for in qualitative and/or quantitative terms.

Application of EAs

Almost across the board, CEQ was encouraged to provide more guidance on the preparation and use of EAs, including increasing public involvement, more rigorous analysis of data, and a broader consideration of alternatives. This cannot be accomplished effectively without greater in-depth knowledge of the current application of EAs. However, potential improvements already evident could be reinforced through workshops and conferences. In particular, CEQ could formally accept "mitigated FONSIs" as worthwhile under specified circumstances and issue guidance on their use, including provision of mechanisms for public comment.

Baseline Data Collection, Monitoring, and Mitigation

The old paradigm for effective environmental management was "predict, mitigate, and implement." A new paradigm has emerged: "predict, mitigate, monitor, and adapt." The two latest threads, monitor and adapt, reflect the need to monitor the accuracy of predictions and allow for flexibility in the process to build in mid-course corrections. Without monitoring, demonstrating the value of EAs or EISs is extraordinarily difficult. Monitoring has been inconsistent, and it is unknown how frequently mitigation measures are implemented and the extent to which monitoring actually triggers adaptive management. Over the years, increasing attention has been directed toward applying the NEPA process to the environmental management of a project over its life cycle, but this has not been instituted in a systematic manner. The best opportunities for positive on-site environmental management occur during the construction, operation, and post-operational phases of the proposed project. The CEQ/Canter (1995a) report indicates that these activities can incorporate monitoring conducted for a variety of purposes, including implementation and evaluation of mitigation measures identified during the EIA process, project-operational decisions to minimize detrimental environmental impacts and enhance ecosystem management, and periodic conduction of environmental audits from the perspective of regulatory compliance and/or documentation of experienced impacts.

Many analyses are severally hampered by a lack of quality environmental baseline data upon which a scientific or thorough analysis of alternative effects can be based. Without baseline data, an accurate assessment of a project's impact on the environment is severely hindered. The lack of baseline data collection results largely from the lack of government institution support. There is no systematic approach to data acquisition or management specifically to address environmental impact analysis (Carpenter, 1976).

The recommendations derived from the study reported herein include: (1) increase permit-related monitoring; (2) develop a technical manual on how to plan and implement post-project monitoring, including reporting considerations and the use of monitoring results in project-operational decision making; (3) develop guidance on mitigation planning and implementation, including examples of successful measures; and (4) issuance of an executive order stipulating that mitigation and mitigation reporting are requirements (CEQ, 1994b,c,f,g, 1995a).

Monitoring will help in evaluating the effectiveness and efficiency of projects. Information generated could be integrated into qualitative and/or quantitative analyses indicating the costs and benefits of the project. NEPA does not mandate a cost–benefit analysis, nor does it require extensive analysis of beneficial effects. However, Georgia and Maryland's mini-NEPAs require agencies to consider an action's adverse and beneficial effects, while Connecticut, Georgia, Montana, and Wisconsin require an explicit cost–benefit analysis (Landis et al., 1995). It is well known that certain facets of value cannot be conveyed in quantitative terms, thus posing limits to cost–benefit analysis (Dixon et al., 1994). Nonetheless, if presented in association with relevant qualitative analyses, it provides another important piece of information to the decision maker. It also helps to address the concerns of NEPA critics who claim the EIS process does more harm than good. Thus, the EA/EIS process is intended to complement the traditional engineering, socioeconomic, and financial and economic analyses and to provide practical information to decision makers.

Several recommendations were provided regarding the need for a reiteration of CEQ regulations stating that "a monitoring and enforcement program shall be adopted and summarized where applicable for any mitigation measure" (1505.2(c)). This appears to be of particular relevance to mitigated EAs because they are based on much less information and analysis than are EISs. It was also suggested that CEQ prepare guidance for agencies on how to develop plans for implementing a monitoring program within the NEPA context (CEQ, 1994g). Such guidance could incorporate a process for including monitoring costs in project budgets and encouraging training of procurement officers on how to integrate NEPA into contractual agreements.

Another monitoring issue to address at a different level is whether or not agency procedures are keeping pace with the ever-more complex framework within which the NEPA process should be applied (i.e., ecosystem management, cumulative analyses, etc.) (CEQ, 1994g, 1995a). Many agencies have failed to update their NEPA procedures published in the early 1980s (Bausch, 1991). Federal agency officials should consult with CEQ not just during crises or in the context of formal agency proceedings, but early and informally in any program effort where questions concerning approaches to environmental quality issues are presented. CEQ is empowered to assist federal agencies and departments in appraising the effectiveness of existing and proposed facilities, programs, policies, and activities in coordinating efforts within the federal government to protect and improve environmental quality. It is the responsibility of individual departments and agencies to actively seek the assistance of CEQ, since it lacks the resources to monitor all federal government programs and activities (Bausch, 1991). At a minimum, CEQ should be involved early in the review of any proposed changes to agency NEPA procedures. The current challenge is how to make periodic updating more urgent and in the self-interest of federal agencies generally.

Expertise

One other important need identified by almost every cluster is the improvement of agencies' NEPA expertise. It was suggested that CEQ, in coordination with federal agencies, develop a "Needs Assessment of NEPA Training." Three areas of training needs have been deemed important by most of the NEPA liaisons: (1) continued training on both procedural and methodological aspects of the EIA process for new personnel or those needing updates on new techniques, (2) special training in addressing interaction with Indian tribes and other minority or special interest communities, and (3) awareness training for senior agency decision makers.

Agencies Strategically Working Together

Each federal agency is responsible for managing the NEPA process with respect to its own policies, programs, and projects. Due to the nature of many federal activities, more than one agency may be involved in the development of a NEPA document—either more than one agency is directly involved with the action, or it has responsibility by law to cooperate on the EIS. As stated in CEQ's "Forty Most Asked Questions" (1981), "After a lead agency has been designated (Sec. 1501.5), that agency has the responsibility to solicit cooperation from other federal agencies that have jurisdiction by law or special expertise on any environmental issue that should be addressed in the EIS being prepared." Similarly, when appropriate, input from relevant state and local agencies and Indian tribes should also be sought. Allocation of each entity's responsibilities should be clarified, at the latest, during the scoping process (CEQ, 1994c,g).

Coordination is required when more than one agency is planning a project or program affecting the ecosystem or when the expertise and/or approval of one agency is needed for the completion of another agency's project. When two or more agencies are implementing projects in the same ecosystem, cumulative environmental impacts can result. NEPA liaisons have indicated that other agencies do coordinate on a limited basis, but that in general such coordination is difficult to achieve. Coordination and collaboration are more frequent when each agency has a vested interest in the project or overall plans (CEQ, 1994g,i).

Simultaneously, agencies such as the U.S. Fish and Wildlife Service (FWS) are responsible for reviewing other agency draft EISs with respect to threatened and endangered species issues. The FWS, the Army Corps of Engineers, and the Advisory Council for Historic Preservation were highlighted as needing to improve their assistance to agencies in the development and assessment of all reasonable alternatives and to do so in a more timely manner. For example, the FWS needs to work with the other agencies to find some efficient mechanism to ensure that review of alternatives occurs, instead of just consideration of the preferred alternative. At a minimum, FWS input should be obtained informally early in the development of alternatives. This would help to surface unforeseen problems that could cause delays later in the process (CEQ, 1994f,g).

A number of other recommendations evolved from participant input, including having CEQ: (1) establish lead agency authority to require cooperation from other federal agencies and (2) promote joint lead agency status for preparation of environmental impact analyses. Also recommended was for CEQ to develop a NEPA computer network to promote communication and coordination among federal agencies along with state and local governments, Indian tribes, and the public sector. CEQ has initiated such a network, NEPANET, in conjunction with the Department of Defense. Similarly, CEQ is developing a Cumulative Effects Handbook that also addresses issues of agency coordination. Additionally, there is wide support from agency NEPA liaisons that CEQ continue to conduct NEPA liaison meetings at least twice a year.

The Public Shaping Government Decisions

One of the undisputed strengths of NEPA, and the EIS process specifically, is that it provides the principal avenue for public information and consequent involvement in the planning and decision-making processes of the federal government. It was the intent of the framers of the act and the drafters of the regulations to open the NEPA process to public scrutiny and informed input (NEPA Title I, Section 101 and 40 CFR 1500.1 and 1500.2.)

For the purposes of this chapter, the public is defined as any entity outside the federal government structure including (1) NGOs, citizens, and state and local agencies; (2) businesses; and (3) academicians. To obtain public input during the study reported herein,

CEQ conducted a citizen survey, held meetings with NGOs in Washington, D.C. as well as in several states, and conducted a business survey and a survey of academicians. In addition, CEQ sponsored a study focusing on NEPA and the cultural environment.

NGOs and Citizens

The majority of participants thought that the success of NEPA was opening the decision-making process for public input and that this NEPA process has improved the effectiveness of project design with respect to minimizing impacts on the environment. On the other hand, they pointed out that openness, affirmative action, and responsiveness to public involvement and input still vary considerably from agency to agency (CEQ, 1994a,b,f,i).

In general, these groups view the NEPA process as largely a one-way communication track, and they are not satisfied that their input is being used effectively. They claim the agencies give insufficient emphasis to communication and education efforts needed to achieve informed public participation early in the NEPA process. Consequently, litigation or the threat of litigation is often used by individuals and citizens groups for resolving environmental conflicts. From a positive perspective, alternative dispute resolution techniques, along with the development of more objective and user-friendly documents, might help reduce litigation (CEQ, 1994a,b,f,i).[5]

Also strongly endorsed was the initiation of an education and information process throughout agencies to reinforce public involvement as a substantive two-way communication process. Agencies need to find better, more creative outreach modes in addition to Federal Register notifications; examples include using existing citizen and/or NGO networks as part of the notification process, placing notices in main sections of newspapers, conducting news conferences, and using computer networks where appropriate. The process works most effectively when agencies highlight major project characteristics and potential major issues before public meetings are held and when they determine if special informational programs are required to prepare citizens to participate in the meetings. Well-conducted scoping processes can reduce controversy, encourage information exchange, and serve to focus the subsequent analysis of issues and alternatives (CEQ, 1994a,f).

NGOs and citizens stated that one of the largest problems related to the effectiveness of NEPA is the timing of public involvement in the process. The public is frequently poorly informed about, and hence not sufficiently involved in, the preparation and review of EAs, as contrasted with EISs. This is not to say that every EA requires the same level of public scrutiny. It was recommended that CEQ develop guidance to agencies to notify the public that they are preparing an EA. Depending on the level of response agencies generate by notices, they should determine whether additional public outreach for that particular proposed activity is warranted. It was also suggested that CEQ develop a publication of case studies and techniques for citizen involvement in environmental effects monitoring (CEQ, 1994a,f).

When considering the public as a whole, including government, an issue of concern to CEQ is the quality of the cultural environment. In addition to the fact that NEPA requires that agencies consider effects on the cultural environment, there are practical policy reasons for doing so. The cultural environment and the natural environment are inextricably linked; one cannot exist without impacts on the other. According to the CEQ/King and Rafuse (1994h) report, "The cultural environment—comprising the socio-cultural institutions of our communities, our lifeways, and the physical places and things that reflect our communities' heritage—is the environment in which most people live most of the time. It is the quintessential human environment, whose degradation erodes the quality of our very society. For this reason alone it deserves careful consideration in agency planning." In other words, we need to consider the impacts of federal actions on both our cultural environment (e.g., historic buildings and areas, archaeological sites, and sacred places such as burial grounds) and natural environment.

Several specific recommendations are included in the CEQ/King and Rafuse (1994h) report. In summary, it concluded that CEQ now has a rare opportunity to improve the way the cultural environment is addressed in NEPA analyses. The Guidelines and Principles for Social Impact Assessment (National Oceanic and Atmospheric Administration, 1994) has just been issued. The Advisory Council on Historic Preservation is revising its regulations, with a specific charge to improve coordination with NEPA requirements. Executive Order 12898 concerning environmental justice has been issued, underscoring the need to better identify and understand the communities on which federal actions may have impacts. Finally, the European Community, Canada, Australia, and the World Bank are all engaged in initiatives to better address aspects of the cultural environment. Accordingly, carefully crafted guidance from CEQ could have significant worldwide impact on the way the cultural environment is considered in government planning.

Businesses

CEQ sent a questionnaire to a variety of businesses that had been involved in NEPA compliance within the past few years (CEQ, 1995e). The purpose of the questionnaire was to obtain the views of business managers concerning the perceived benefits to the company of NEPA, how compliance with the NEPA process had affected their business decision making in terms of incorporating environmental considerations into investment analyses, whether in their view the NEPA process involves a reasonable amount of time and expenditure of money for the environmental benefits obtained, and what recommendations they would offer for improving NEPA's effectiveness and efficiency as applied to the private sector. The following discussion is an overview of the survey's major findings.

Private sector activities affected by NEPA can be divided into several categories: (1) regulated industries (e.g., energy; genetically engineered plants and animals; foods, drugs, and cosmetics; railroads, etc.); (2) private uses of federal lands (e.g., oil, gas, minerals, timber, etc.); (3) other permits (e.g., filling of wetlands and obstruction of navigable rivers, point source discharges into waterways, ocean mineral exploration, etc.); and (4) financing. For industries that are highly regulated, the NEPA process typically becomes intertwined with permitting, and it often is difficult to separate NEPA from other regulations.

It is important to recognize that private entities generally make decisions in a manner very different from the process imposed upon public agencies. Moreover, agencies may request proprietary information, even though confidentiality can be requested. These factors can create friction and frustration among business managers when private activities are forced into the public process and put under the public microscope. Such situations can arise with respect to governmental regulation other than NEPA and may have affected how survey participants responded to the CEQ questionnaire. A logical further step would be to distinguish between regulations associated with NEPA and other laws to determine which are of most concern.

The NEPA process may constitute the first broad-based public exposure of a company's proposal to undertake a particular project. Even when a company is in a highly regulated industry, there may be limited involvement of citizens and other government agencies in many of its regulatory proceedings. Almost all of the respondents in the heavily regulated electric power industry believe that NEPA, at least in theory, provides a useful framework for integrating environmental considerations into private decision making. However, other companies felt that existing regulations already provide sufficient environmental protection and that preparation of an EA or EIS simply causes delays. They expressed the opinion that both they and state and local governments have become more environmentally sensitive, and, as a consequence, federal supervision may be overdone in some cases.

Company reactions were mixed and fell into the following categories:

- The NEPA process has provided useful input into project designs.
- NEPA results in duplication of state environmental regulations, but at the same time it can provide a rational framework for environmental studies.
- There should be more balancing of NEPA costs with actual environmental benefits.
- NEPA is no longer necessary.
- The expense of NEPA compliance may be reasonable, but the time required generally is not.

In general, the private sector would prefer more flexibility in the process, more trade-off analysis between costs and benefits, more deference to state environmental regulators, and a more efficient and less time-consuming process. CEQ is currently evaluating specific recommendations provided by respondents through the survey (CEQ, 1995e).

Academicians

As part of this overall study, CEQ conducted a survey of academicians by asking them to identify and prioritize NEPA strengths and issues that need to be improved relative to NEPA and the NEPA process. The 31 survey participants represented 12 different disciplines from 21 states; the majority of the participants have over 20 years of professional experience in teaching, research, and/or practice related to the NEPA process.

The academician survey focused primarily on the manner in which agencies implemented and administered the NEPA process. The academic cluster survey results support the contention that NEPA is accomplishing its fundamental goal—requiring agencies to include environmental considerations in project planning and decision making along with the more traditional engineering (or technical) analyses and economic evaluations. The four strengths of NEPA considered to be of greatest importance to the academic respondents were (1) NEPA encourages agencies and decision makers to acknowledge potential environmental consequences to the public, opening up the process; (2) NEPA and subsequent CEQ regulations encourage agencies and decision makers to think about environmental consequences before resources are committed; (3) the CEQ regulations have created a standard framework for including environmental considerations as a tool in decision making; and (4) NEPA and the CEQ regulations encourage agencies and decision makers to obtain information on potential environmental impacts (CEQ, 1995a).

The survey participants also prioritized issues of concern which need improvement in the NEPA process. The five most important issues include: (1) the need for post-EIS follow-up in terms of monitoring, implementation of mitigation measures, ecosystem management, and environmental auditing; (2) the need for methodological approaches for addressing cumulative impacts and attention to reducing institutional barriers related to the proper analysis of cumulative impacts; (3) the need for training of federal personnel involved in implementing the requirements of NEPA; (4) the need for early consideration of the EIA process in project planning and decision making; and (5) the need for the integrated consideration of biophysical and social/economic sciences, along with risk assessment, in the EIA process. Each of these five issues is the subject of specific recommendations in the final report covering the need for preparation of relevant guidance by CEQ, appropriate modifications of the CEQ NEPA regulations, and follow-up training (CEQ, 1995a).

Agencies Engaging the States, Local, and Tribal Governments

In the 1970s, many states confirmed their support of the NEPA EIS concept by passing similar or even more stringent state laws and policies. In fact, 17 states, Puerto Rico, and the District of Columbia have passed statutes or declared gubernatorial executive orders based on NEPA. California, Washington, and New York are known as the more progressive states with respect to their EIS processes. Other states have relied on different models to develop environmental impact review procedures for public and private activities, such as the American Land Institute's Model Development Regulations (Landis et al., 1995). In many cases, the state environmental policy acts are construed more broadly and applied more stringently than NEPA.

Like the states, Indian tribes are subject to federal environmental protection requirements. Since Indian lands are held in trust by the federal government, they are often classified the same as federal lands for regulatory purposes. The applicability of NEPA is triggered whenever a tribe proposes major federal activities on its own land. Tribes find themselves in the position of having to comply with federal requirements, as do federal and state governments, but with far fewer financial and technical resources (CEQ, 1994e).

A major focus of the CEQ study reported herein was to learn of state and tribal perspectives regarding their interaction with the federal government with respect to NEPA; another emphasis was on what lessons the federal government might learn from state EIS processes. As part of this effort, EPA conducted a questionnaire survey of all states to address these issues. CEQ focused on New York, Washington, and California with respect to mini-NEPA and NEPA coordination and lessons learned. CEQ, EPA, and the North Carolina Department of Environment, Health, and Natural Resources held a southern states conference in North Carolina on November 16–17, 1994 to address state–federal interaction with respect to EISs. CEQ also sponsored a study to investigate the effectiveness of the state delegation process (CEQ, 1994k). Lastly, CEQ sponsored the Natural Resources Department of the Tulalip Tribe, in Washington State, to conduct a survey of Native Americans from various geographic regions within the United States, national and regional tribal resource organizations, and academics and professionals who work with tribes in their management of natural resources.

States and Local Government

One of the common themes raised by states was the minimal time allowed for state review of federally proposed actions. Better channels of communication are needed to ensure that documents reach the state reviewers in a timely manner. In the survey conducted by EPA, 67% of the respondents claimed not to learn about federal proposals early enough to effectively participate in the federal decision-making process (CEQ, 1994j). Several recommendations were proposed to address this problem: (1) federal agencies should provide forewarning of forthcoming proposals through monthly meetings with relevant state agencies, memos, or via the new NEPANET; (2) federal agencies should send the documents directly to state agencies rather than to federal clearinghouses, and the clearinghouses should be used to verify that all relevant state agencies receive copies; (3) if possible, federal agencies should convey to the state agencies which sections of the documents warrant the most attention; (4) if a coordinated state response is needed, where appropriate, states should informally convey their initial issues to federal agencies to speed up the process of communication; and (5) state agencies can speed up the review process by dividing the document (e.g., one agency reviews water issues while another addresses biodiversity, etc.) (CEQ, 1994b,f,j).

Similarly, both state and federal agencies need to communicate better regarding forthcoming projects in order to reduce delays and conflicts late in policy, program, and project review cycles. Lead agencies should notify other agencies of forthcoming projects at the time they receive their planning authority. Federal and state agencies commonly involved in federal and state EIS review processes should establish regular informal meetings or telephone conferences to discuss forthcoming and currently proposed activities. Participants at the North Carolina Conference encouraged the use of such forums to improve communication between state and federal stakeholders. They also suggested that CEQ develop case studies showing benefits of early state and federal coordination in planning. Teleconferencing and NEPANET are other mechanisms that should speed up the communication process. There is a clear need to develop a list of key NEPA-related offices at the federal, state, and local government levels in order to improve communication channels. This should be widely distributed via hardcopy and/or via NEPANET (CEQ, 1994b,f,j).

One state indicated that its own Environmental Policy Act allows a state or local agency to adopt a federal NEPA document to meet its own state mini-NEPA. However, the reverse rarely occurs whereby federal agencies adopt state mini-NEPA documents in lieu of a federal NEPA document. Moreover, many states have strict environmental or regulatory processes which may not permit efficient coordination with federal NEPA and other regulatory efforts. Occasionally this results in the preparation of repetitive or overlapping documents for the same project. This emphasizes the need to adopt a cooperative approach between development of state and federal environmental impact documents (CEQ, 1994j).

The states also noted that when they cannot resolve a conflict with a federal agency over an EIS, their only recourse is litigation, which is costly and time consuming. They would like to see an administrative hearing process developed or state governors allowed to refer their concerns to CEQ, similar to the federal agency referral process (CEQ, 1994b,c,f,j).

The Tribes

The summary of the Tulalip survey states that tribal respondents assessing the effectiveness of NEPA for protecting tribal resources find participation in the process a worthwhile but arduous endeavor with hard-won results. Their experience in the NEPA process has been hindered due to limited financial and staff resources coupled with the failure of agencies to invite and empower tribes to participate effectively (CEQ, 1994e).

Despite process problems, the respondents envisioned continued participation in NEPA matters and made a number of recommendations that would enhance their ability to participate. The key recommendations include:

1. Fostering a better government-to-government relationship with agencies
2. Providing culturally relevant NEPA training for tribes
3. Ensuring firm tribal funding to maintain staff dedicated to NEPA matters
4. Assuring consistent NEPA implementation between agencies
5. Broadening the definition of cultural resources and providing a mechanism to keep cultural information confidential where "sensitive"
6. Providing agencies with training in tribal governance and cultural resource matters
7. Providing training and funding for the Bureau of Indian Affairs so that it can more effectively carry out NEPA functions
8. Modifying and elevating the role of EPA so that it reviews NEPA decisions
9. Encouraging EPA to assist tribes in developing and participating more effectively in environmental programs in general

Most of these recommendations could be accomplished through better and earlier involvement of tribes in the process by agencies (CEQ, 1994e).

CONCLUSIONS

The results of this study, while less than comprehensive given limited CEQ staff and resources, portray the important achievements of NEPA and emphasize shortcomings in the process which need improvement. Also of significance, the results highlight the marked gaps in information which limit the ability to adequately assess the effectiveness and efficiency of NEPA. Without information about the number of EAs prepared, the costs of EISs and EAs, monitoring data to determine the degree of effectiveness of mitigation, and information from project, program, and policy audits, it is impossible to measure effectively successes or failures of NEPA. A major finding of this study is how seldom systematic data collection occurs and, therefore, how little factual information exists to substantiate many perceived successes and limitations of NEPA.

This is not to belittle, however, the research and analysis reflected in the myriad articles and books written about NEPA or the valued input received from this study's numerous participants. Nor is this deemed to imply that perceived impacts of NEPA are invalid. However, if the true impacts of NEPA are to be delineated, greater emphasis must be given to systematic tracking and evaluating inputs and outputs of the process through improved record keeping, monitoring, and auditing.

NOTES

1. The views represented in this chapter are those of the project participants and do not necessarily represent those of the CEQ.
2. It appears, however, that agencies increasingly select the environmentally preferred alternative, or at least do not select the worst alternative in terms of negative impacts on the environment. However, this is not an empirically known fact and one that warrants analysis.
3. An exact estimate of EAs prepared is difficult to obtain due to the lack of a central reporting requirement as exists with the EISs, which are all sent to EPA. The most recent figures are based on a CEQ survey conducted in 1992 (Blaug, 1993).
4. A specific analysis has not been conducted in order to document this statement. CEQ draws this conclusion based upon feedback from agency NEPA liaisons and EPA's Office of Federal Activities, which reviews all EISs and some EAs and categorical exclusions (CEs).
5. For more information on alternative dispute resolution, see Chapter 17 by Bingham and Langstaff.

SELECTED REFERENCES

Andrews, R.N.L. 1976. NEPA in Practice: Environmental Policy or Administrative Reform? In Congressional Research Service, Implementing NEPA's Substantive Goals: A Symposium.

Bausch, C. 1991. NEPA Integration: Effective, Efficient Environmental Compliance in the 1990s. CEQ Workshop Proceedings. Fairfax, Virginia, March 13–15.

Blaug, E. 1993. Use of the Environmental Assessment by Federal Agencies in NEPA Implementation. *The Environmental Professional* 15:57-65.

Boggs, J.B. 1993. Procedural vs. Substantive in NEPA Law: Cutting the Gordian Knot. *The Environmental Professional* 15:25–33.

Calvert Cliffs' Coordinating Committee v. Atomic Energy Commission, 1972. 449 F.2d 1109, 1 ELR 20346 (D.C. Cir. 1971), cert. denied, 404 U.S. 942.

Carpenter, R.A. 1976. The Scientific Basis of NEPA—Is It Adequate? *Environmental Law Reporter* 6 ELR:50014.

Center for Advanced Studies in Science, Technology and Public Policy. 1982. A Study of Ways to Improve the Scientific Content and Methodology of Environmental Impact Analysis. Final Report to the National Science Foundation on Grant PRA-79-10014. School of Public and Environmental Affairs, Indiana University, Bloomington.

Council on Environmental Quality. 1974. Environmental Quality. Annual Report of the Council on Environmental Quality. Washington, D.C.

Council on Environmental Quality. 1976. Environmental Impact Statements: An Analysis of Six Years' Experience by Seventy Federal Agencies. Washington, D.C.

Council on Environmental Quality. 1977–78. Environmental Quality. Annual Report of the Council on Environmental Quality. Washington, D.C.

Council on Environmental Quality. 1981. Forty Most Asked Questions Concerning CEQ's National Environmental Policy Act Regulations. Washington, D.C.

Council on Environmental Quality. 1992. Environmental Quality. Annual Report of the Council on Environmental Quality. Washington, D.C.

Council on Environmental Quality. 1993. Environmental Quality: The Twenty-Fourth Annual Report of the Council on Environmental Quality. Washington, D.C.

Council on Environmental Quality. 1994a. A Survey of Citizen Activists. Submitted by B. Kemp (Labat-Anderson). Washington, D.C.

Council on Environmental Quality. 1994b. CEQ Minutes: State/Federal Conference on National Environmental Policy Act Coordination Issues. North Carolina Department of Environment, Health and Natural Resources, and EPA, Durham, North Carolina, November 16–17.

Council on Environment Quality. 1994c. Effectiveness and Efficiency. Submitted by K. Weiner. Washington, D.C.

Council on Environmental Quality. 1994d. EIA Effectiveness Study Legal Issues. Submitted by D. Bear (Center for Marine Conservation). Washington, D.C.

Council on Environmental Quality. 1994e. Indian Tribes Assess the Effectiveness of the National Environmental Policy Act. Submitted by K. Ordon (The Tulalip Tribes of Washington). Washington, D.C.

Council on Environmental Quality. 1994f. Meeting Minutes with States (California, New York, and Washington). October–November. Washington, D.C.

Council on Environmental Quality. 1994g. Meeting Notes for the NEPA Liaison Conference. Prepared for CEQ. November 15. Washington, D.C.

Council on Environmental Quality. 1994h. NEPA and the Cultural Environment: An Assessment and Recommendations. Submitted by T.F. King and E. Rafuse. (CEHP, Inc.). Washington, D.C.

Council on Environmental Quality. 1994i. Renewing NEPA: NEPA Effectiveness Study Report, Phase I. Submitted by R.B. Smythe (Potomac Resource Consultants). Washington, D.C.

Council on Environmental Quality. 1994j. State–Federal Coordination Survey Summary. Submitted to CEQ and EPA Office of Federal Activities by S. Moore. Washington, D.C.

Council on Environmental Quality. 1994k. The Delegation of National Environmental Policy Act (NEPA) Responsibilities to State and Local Agencies. Memorandum by J. Mostyn (Labat-Anderson). Washington, D.C.

Council on Environmental Quality. 1995a. Academic Cluster Survey for NEPA Effectiveness Study. Submitted by L.W. Canter (University of Oklahoma). Washington, D.C.

Council on Environmental Quality. 1995b. Highlights of NEPA in the Courts. Submitted by W.M. Cohen and M.C. Miller (Department of Justice). Washington, D.C.

Council on Environmental Quality. 1995c. Identifying NEPA Effectiveness Issues. Submitted by S. Ruffin and A. Winston (Enercorp Federal Services Corporation). Washington, D.C.

Council on Environmental Quality. 1995d. Implementing NEPA: A Non-Technical Political Task. Submitted by L.K. Caldwell (University of Indiana). Washington, D.C.

Council on Environmental Quality. 1995e. NEPA Effectiveness/ Efficiency Study—Business Cluster. Prepared by J. Pershing (CEQ). Washington, D.C.

Department of Energy. June 1995. Congressional testimony.

Dixon, J.A., S.L. Fallon, R.A. Carpenter, and P.B. Sherman. 1994. *Economic Analysis of Environmental Impacts*. Earthscan Publications, London.

Environmental Law Institute. 1981. NEPA in Action: Environmental Offices in Nineteen Federal Agencies. Washington, D.C.

Executive Order 12898. 1994. Federal Actions to Address Environmental Justice in Minority Populations and Low-Income Populations. Washington, D.C.

Fairfax, S.K. 1978. A Disaster in the Environmental Movement. *Science* 199:734–748.

Landis, J., R. Olshansky, R. Pendall, and W. Huang. 1995. Fixing CEQA: Options and Opportunities for Reforming the California Environmental Quality Act. California Policy Seminar, Berkeley.

National Oceanic and Atmospheric Administration. 1994. Guidelines and Principles for Social Impact Assessment. Prepared by the Interorganizational Committee on Guidelines and Principles for Social Impact Assessment. National Marine Fisheries Service, U.S. Department of Commerce, Washington, D.C.

NEPA. 1969. The National Environmental Policy Act of 1969 as amended (Public Law 91-190, 42 U.S.C. 4321–4347).

U.S. Congress. 1995. Senate Subcommittee on Oversight and Investigations of the Senate Committee on Energy and Natural Resources. Oversight Hearing into the Application of the National Environmental Policy Act. Testimony Prepared by Robert Nordhaus, U.S. Department of Energy. 104th Congress, First Session, June 7.

INCREASING THE EFFICIENCY AND EFFECTIVENESS OF NEPA THROUGH THE USE OF TECHNOLOGY

13

R. Webster

The National Environmental Policy Act (NEPA) is the cornerstone environmental statute in the United States, providing the mechanism through which the general public participates in environmentally significant decisions made by the federal government. Public access to this decision-making process exposes the trade-offs associated with federal decisions: balancing technological feasibility, economic viability, and environmental costs. The value of the NEPA process is currently undergoing evaluation after 25 years of NEPA experience (EIA Centre, 1994). While the use of NEPA as a true decision-making tool is becoming more common, some criticism is directed at seeming inefficiencies in the process. Right or wrong, there is the impression that much of the NEPA process is expensive, time consuming, and often arrives too late to affect real decision making. While much of this criticism is unfairly focused upon NEPA (rather than overall project management), the issue of efficiency and effectiveness is one worth visiting.

The quality of a NEPA analysis is adversely affected by a lack of resources (economic and human) and time. While these are not unique to the environmental portion of a project's decision process (applying to technological feasibility and economic justifications as well), the environmental component of the equation has inherent attributes that magnify the effects of these constraints on the quality of the analysis and on its subsequent value to the decision maker. The similarities in the overall process are illustrated in Figure 13.1, which depicts the decision-making process afforded to military decision makers (U.S. Army War College, 1992–93).

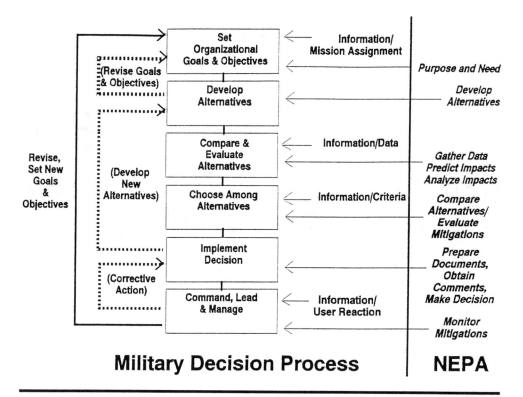

Military Decision Process | **NEPA**

FIGURE 13.1 The military decision-making process parallels NEPA (U.S. Army War College, 1992–93).

The basic decision-making paradigm shown in Figure 13.1 has been used for centuries, and the NEPA process elements (in the right-hand column) reflect and complement the general paradigm. NEPA practitioners will recognize the similarities to the NEPA process, which is identical to this time-honored blueprint for military decision making. The decision support system is sound, and modifications to the system can only reduce its ability to support sound decisions. Since the elimination of steps in the process will only lead to less acceptable, poorly informed decisions, the efficiency challenge lies in bringing efficiency to the decision support process by both expending less resources in the analysis and becoming more timely in the presentation of factors affecting decision making.

The composition and nature of the process are the same: identify the need, establish the alternatives, weigh the advantages and disadvantages, and then make and implement the decision. This constitutes the NEPA paradigm, except for the inclusion of the specific requirement for public involvement (input) to the process and the complexities brought to the environmental challenge by inherent characteristics, statutes, regulations, or guidance.

The major difference in the two approaches is the element of public participation. Assuming that public participation is required in federal decision making (and will not

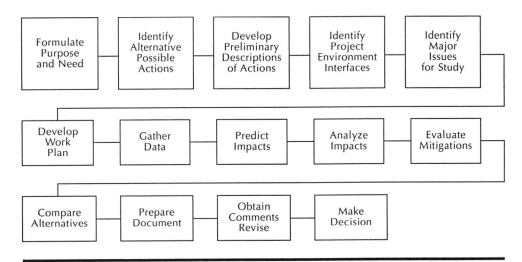

FIGURE 13.2   Major EIS tasks.

be eliminated), the only viable opportunities to increase efficiency lie in the performance of the steps involved.

The detailed steps associated with the NEPA process "life cycle" are shown in Figure 13.2. It is through these steps that the decision paradigm (illustrated in Figure 13.1) is implemented in the environmental context. While the major steps in the NEPA process are the same as any rational decision-support process, any efforts to simplify or improve the steps (identified in Figure 13.2) are hampered by inherent characteristics, statutes, regulations, and guidance which are unique to NEPA. Examples include:

1. *NEPA analysis starts late*—Pragmatically, environmental analysis starts long after technological and economic issues have been analyzed and a "reasonably foreseeable" action has been established. Experienced NEPA practitioners will recall waiting for the "purpose and need" of the project and the "description of proposed actions and alternatives," which often result from an analysis of technological and economic viability. Thus, planning for a project is often already well underway before the NEPA process is initiated.

2. *Time frames become inflexible*—The environmental analysis has regulatory minimum time frames for the process, which all too often become project management's optimistic "critical path," with adherence to these milestones used as a measure of performance. These optimistic timelines often take precedence over the quality of the analysis in the ranking of project priorities.

3. *Analysis and data requirements are complex*—Once the need for a multidisciplinary approach is established, the resultant analyses may require considerable work (data acquisition and analysis) in order to address all the required and necessary disciplines. For example, a comprehensive environmental analysis must address such issues as soils, geology, biology, cultural resources (historic and archaeological), sociology, economics, infrastructure (utilities, buildings, etc.), noise, water quality, air quality, hazardous/toxic materials, traffic, geography,

aesthetics, land use, air space, and myriad other (possibly site-specific) issues. Each may require only a small amount of data and analysis, but the total aggregate investment of the organization can still be quite high, and the coordination of individual efforts and focused presentation of results can be very difficult.

4. *New and necessary concepts in environmental analysis are evolving*—As an example, the incorporation of "biodiversity" concepts into ecosystem analysis is essential for the long-term sustainability of natural resources. Articulated approaches to achieve this goal illustrate the need for more regional and broader data to address NEPA analysis requirements (Council on Environmental Quality, 1993). A better treatment of "cumulative" impacts is also being required in the environmental impact assessment process, addressing incremental environmental destruction by projects which, while individually insignificant, can represent a major issue if considered "as a whole" (McCold and Holman, 1995). An adequate "aggregate" analysis of the proposed action and those actions that are "reasonably foreseeable" can add considerably to the complexity of analysis. Finally, the recent release of an executive order and subsequent executive office memoranda requires additional analysis to determine not only the extent of the impacts but also the nature or composition of those populations affected by the impacts and the spatial distribution of those effects (Office of the President, 1994).

5. *Data to drive analyses are difficult to obtain*—Baseline data for a given project are seldom readily available, yet numerous agencies and institutions are constantly acquiring and storing data. Information (the synthesis of data) is constantly created, but it is often difficult to locate and its integrity must be verified. Access to numerous federal databases has only recently become available in a practical sense, as a result of better communications and the advent of technologies such as CD-ROM. These data sources include the U.S. Geological Survey, Environmental Protection Agency, National Oceanic and Atmospheric Administration, and Soil Conservation Service. While other efforts at the creation of national databases appear very promising, the content of all these data collection efforts must be identified, characterized, standardized, and made efficiently available to the NEPA community (U.S. Department of Defense, 1992; Jenkens, 1988).

6. *Significance haunts the practitioner*—Nothing is so painful as the "so what" response to a presentation of model results. Significance is based on context and intensity, and within each technical discipline, different criteria can apply (historical perspective, violation of standards, etc.). Over 25 years, there should have been some evolved standard interpretive aids for determination of significance.

TECHNOLOGICAL OPPORTUNITIES

Technological trends give rise to a considerable hope for addressing many of the above issues. The technological era has certainly contributed to the current environmental condition, and the NEPA community should (perhaps ironically) exploit the benefits of this era while illuminating the environmental costs of the era and attempting to lessen the negative effects associated with future legacies.

As a result of the NEPA paradigm's congruence with that associated with a sound decision-making process, common efficiencies can be afforded through the use of technology (word processing, spreadsheets, and graphics) which constitutes common business automation in the modern world. The advantages of these common tools are well established, and outside of the need for better and more widespread use, they will not be further addressed herein.

There are some areas of current technological growth which appear to be especially exciting and worthwhile to the NEPA analyst. Each technological trend can potentially have unique impacts upon the question of NEPA efficiency and effectiveness. Each can affect different elements of the NEPA process life cycle, and integration of these technologies, and the resultant "symbiosis," appears promising.

Some "global" trends (affecting all technological applications) will significantly affect the growth and application of computer technology in the near future (five years). The increased speed and reduced cost of computer chips will eventually place the current "workstation" level of technology easily into the "niche" that the personal computer occupies today. The further development and increased application of multiuser, multitasking computers will be assured as analysts strive to fully utilize the computer power which they will readily have at their disposal. Parallel processing concepts (and accompanying improvements in software engineering) will almost assuredly place the power of recent supercomputers on desktops in a few (five to ten) years. As all of this occurs, many heretofore practical limits to analysis will disappear. Visualization and detailed modeling will be readily available. The analyst will be able to evaluate and visualize successive alternatives and approaches much faster and more efficiently. "Turnaround" (to use terminology of a bygone era) between the analysis of successive scenarios will be minimal, placing the burden of productivity squarely on the human portion of the interaction.

Beyond the global (or overall) technology trends, specific (and immediate) potential technological areas of interest include the use of Geographic Information Systems, imagery (satellite and aircraft), and the Internet (and related tools). Other technologies are emerging but can easily become separate discussions. These three tools, separately and integrated, can address many of the current "root causes" of the NEPA efficiency/effectiveness issue, directly stimulating increased peer interaction, better utilization of existing baseline data, and extension of the scale of environmental analysis (important in cumulative effects analysis and ecosystem management).

Geographic Information Systems

Geographic Information Systems (GISs) have the potential to truly revolutionize the NEPA analysis process, particularly for those organizations practicing land resource management. Most traditional environmental phenomena are "spatially based"; they occur over some areal expanse. Much of the historical difficulty in explaining or illustrating potential environmental impacts has been due to attempts to present information in a tabular or verbal format when, in the words of someone famous, "a picture speaks a thousand words." Many times, this same picture conveys different things to different reviewers, and the use of GIS technology to summarize and present conclusions is very effective. Traditionally, geographers have produced maps, but the dynamics of a fully functional GIS allow the analyst to expand beyond map production, producing more alternatives and combinations of alternatives than would evolve using simple mapping skills. Using the wealth of the database and the GIS analysis tools, the analyst can visualize the impacts and then share the final "vision" with the decision maker and the public.

The geographic location of proposed projects is often the result of separate detailed site-selection studies. Once candidate sites are selected, environmental impact analysis often commences. A GIS allows the analyst to "invert" this process and allow the technology to identify candidate sites using the GIS database to combine numerous decision or selection criteria and display results. This process is the epitome of multiobjective decision making: criteria can be added or dropped, measures of acceptance for the criteria can be strengthened or relaxed, and optimum or alternative sites (from an environmental viewpoint) can be identified. This can, on many occasions, also reduce overall project costs, since the cost of mitigating impacts can be significant and may not be present at an alternate site. This approach to alternative selection is perhaps best conceptually illustrated in the pioneering work of Ian McHarg, and it seems appealing (under NEPA) to use natural, environmental conditions to select and evaluate alternatives to a proposed action (McHarg, 1969). The limitation of McHarg's approach (a favorite in the 1970s) was the large labor component required to produce analyses. The subsequent proliferation of PCs and the recent emergence of practical GISs have significantly enhanced the viability of his conceptual approach (Atkinson et al., 1995).

The provision of adequate, trained personnel (and accompanying organizational support) has often led to the phenomenal growth in the use of the GIS in day-to-day organizational activities. One such application is shown in Figure 13.3. The organizational decision ("to GIS or not to GIS") is a case-specific decision; no standard "rules of thumb" apply. Organizations with fixed geographic locations (Department of Defense

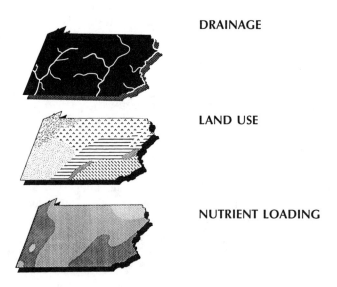

DRAINAGE

LAND USE

NUTRIENT LOADING

FIGURE 13.3   Sample application of GIS to environmental concerns.

installation, U.S. Park Service, U.S. Forest Service, etc.) have an advantage. High numbers of projects or numerous proposed activities also imply a utilization rate that would positively affect the return on investment (ROI). Some applications will benefit mainly from satellite imagery (relatively inexpensive), while others will require lower altitude imagery (potentially expensive), and an appreciation of such trade-offs is important and significant to those facing investment decisions (Smart Maps, 1995). These and other elements have to be evaluated and understood by the organizational management before an informed decision on GIS can be made.

Potential benefits of GIS implementation include both efficiency (when the GIS is used to reduce the costs of a task that without GIS would have to be handled using some other method) and effectiveness (when the GIS is used to perform some task that either could not or would not be done without GIS) (U.S. Geological Survey, undated).

In instances where the knowledgeable commitment to a GIS has truly been made, the payback (ROI) can be significant. In the best of conditions, the GIS has led to the creation of a spatially based "corporate database," receiving contribution and use by all elements of the larger organization (not just the environmental elements). In such cases, these other (non-environmental) organizational elements find themselves utilizing environmental data in their day-to-day decision making, another "significant feather in an ideal NEPA cap."

In a pure NEPA application, the corporate database allows for very efficient NEPA analysis and makes the situation much easier to address within the "critical time path" of a given project. Less elapsed time is required to acquire project-specific data and preposition the NEPA analyst to better participate in the decision-making process. In such cases, the analyst is prepared to contribute much earlier in the process and (through the wealth of the prepositioned database and analysis capabilities of a GIS) can often become more of a perceived asset to the organization and be recognized as such.

Imagery

Imagery, from aircraft or satellites, is an underutilized technical resource, although it is readily available. When supplemented by a GIS, this source of information can often allow an analyst to "see" things better than from any other perspective (the "forest and tree" analogy applies here). Through both simple visual interpretive techniques (Way, 1991) and computer enhancement and analysis (Milazzo, 1983), archaeological treasures have been located (GRASS, 1991), environmental monitoring (for cumulative effects) has been established (Tulalip Tribes, 1993; Washington Department of Natural Resources, 1994; U.S. Forest Service, 1994), and environmental disturbance has been measured. The use of such imagery can potentially reduce the costs of environmental field work, although "ground truth" information will always be required. Recent discussions (following the reduction in world tension) have stimulated the potential release of detailed imagery, which has up to now been in the exclusive hands of intelligence and security agencies of the U.S. government. If these sources are released for environmental use, the increase in available detail will certainly make imagery even more valuable for impact analysis.

The use of higher resolution imagery is particularly important to the environmental analyst. As the broader concepts of ecosystem management and regional environmental management become more accepted, a greater reliance on remote sensing will evolve, using expensive, original field data collection for necessary "ground truth" (Westervelt et al., 1995). Costs and efficiency will dictate a more general approach than the traditional exclusive reliance on field work, and the release of the high-resolution imagery of governmental agencies will significantly advance the utility of this approach. The use of such an approach, coupled with emerging national database efforts, will broaden the scale of biological studies and monitoring which are essential for cumulative effects analysis, sustainability studies, and ecosystem management.

Internet

The Internet, at its basis, is an extension of common E-mail (Krol, 1992). Significantly, however, it represents an opportunity for the analyst to expand the "virtual workplace" to worldwide status, allowing for the needed, unlimited linkage with peers. Through the Internet, it is entirely possible that "virtual office mates" may never actually meet but may enjoy a long, productive working relationship. The efficiency of this electronic linkage will lead to the sharing of dialog and information in pursuit of mutual benefit (productivity, learning, etc.). Extensions of the Internet concept, accompanied by the addition of faster data transmission rates, will include the transfer or sharing of entire databases between individuals and organizations, potentially addressing an often major impediment to meeting a critical NEPA analysis timeline (lack of easily available environmental baseline data). A GIS linked to a family of compatible, fully functional Internet databases is a desirable potential tool.

MOSAIC and other similar tools (designed to interface with the Internet) hold considerable promise for stimulating peer interaction (Phaffenberger, 1994). Access to the capabilities of other individuals, organizations, and institutions will become even more commonplace as such "user-friendly" tools are developed. The ability to search for assistance, evaluate the candidate sources, and initiate communication, all within the same interactive computer session, make acceptance of such tools inevitable.

Current Council on Environmental Quality (CEQ) efforts to establish NEPANET promote this concept. While preliminary development (for a variety of pragmatic reasons) may initially dictate the use of other non-Internet approaches, the overall target implementation on the Internet (with an interface such as MOSAIC) should be a CEQ goal. Growth in the use of the Internet will inevitably lead to turmoil brought on by the effects of both free market forces and the desire for equity (both economic and social). If the Internet survives this period, it clearly represents the future, at least for those who hope to survive (and flourish in) the expanding information revolution.

The implications of the Internet are also potentially fruitful relative to stimulating public interaction and participation. Certainly, interest groups will become proficient in the use of this tool, and, hopefully, more individuals will view the Internet as a means of reinforcing the exercise of their rights in an open, democratic process. The emancipation of individuals (from reliance on written communications and subsequent time requirements) is a major positive attribute of electronic communications. If the Internet becomes a common component of NEPA practice, more people will inevitably participate.

As practitioners begin to "surf the Internet," the computer becomes a valuable information source, no longer merely processing paper and performing calculations. The "Management in the 1990s" program, directed by the Sloan School at the Massachusetts Institute of Technology, illustrated that the major value of successful computer implementation was through improved communications and information technology (Massachusetts Institute of Technology, undated). As an aid to communication and information gathering, it can be a valuable asset in the constant search to maintain technical currency within a given discipline. It is conceptually and technologically possible to program (teach) a PC to search through databases and literature and identify items of interest to the analyst, allowing the analyst (master) to review the night's work over the first cup of coffee in the morning. This is only a minor extension of the concept of a lens (focusing on the outside world) to interface with the literature and the work of one's peers (Malone et al., 1986; Loi et al., 1988). Perhaps that time has come, although an original view of a "paperless society" may not be here (yet) (Lancaster, 1978).

Other Technologies

Other technologies in addition to GIS, imagery, and the Internet can also affect the practice of NEPA analysis. The use of video imaging to convey impacts has been very valuable in the creation of public trust and involvement, when coupled with appropriate interaction. The current inventory of environmental impact statements accumulated over the last quarter century, represents a wealth of information that could be used if automated access were provided with appropriate key wording and indexing technology. Technologists must force the issue of data standards and transfer protocols if the true peer interchange of data is to occur. The current development of "bibliometrics" holds considerable promise for attaining some degree of sustained technical currency. Risk assessment methodologies will assuredly change the content and orientation of environmental impact analysis. The quest for new approaches (technology insertion) should be continuous, thus increasing the productivity of the NEPA analyst and the value of NEPA analysis in support of decision making. In order to limit the scope of this discussion, these are not examined at this time. The three major areas addressed previously can be viewed as "enabling technologies" that will incorporate others and provide overall mechanisms for technological growth.

The Sloan School effort did identify and analyze one essential ingredient necessary for (or common in) successful utilization of computer information technology and subsequent increases in ROI. Organizations must be prepared to alter their means of doing business. In every case where automation was unaccompanied by such change, productivity did not increase, and the technology investments of the organization did not realize expectant returns. In addition, the analysis identified the value of "strategic alliances" as a means to reduce duplication among compatible organizations and foster joint success. This change in philosophy allowed for the joint survival of interrelated organizations instead of the all too familiar "us or them" paradigm. The potential implications of the MIT work for NEPA practitioners are that:

1. Technology should be embraced in the constant pursuit of increased efficiency, effectiveness, and productivity.
2. Organizations should expect changes in their operational paradigm if these benefits are to be achieved.
3. The main value of technology implementation may lie in communications and alliance building within the NEPA process.

TOOL BUILDING AND THE FUTURE

NEPA has been in effect for 25 years. In its formative years, discussions necessarily started with terminology and definitions ("irreplaceable and irretrievable commitments of resources," "significance of impacts," and "reasonably foreseeable") and the interpretation of other statutory language which is still discussed today and sufficiently vague to ensure continued discussion into the future. During the last 25 years, however, much has been learned about pragmatic environmental impact analysis; examples include standardized or systematic approaches, the location or acquisition of data, selection of models, interpretation of results, and other steps and decisions which lead to a final environmental document. These processes are often duplicated time and time again (by new people for new projects), and model and data selection and implementation still often consume considerable project time. While some attempts at a comprehensive, systematic means of increasing efficiency and effectiveness are being made (Dickerson et al., undated), focused technology development is still inviting.

About the time of NEPA's passage, the software industry (through USENET and other often UNIX-oriented software entities) was initiating and developing the concept of software "tool building." Conceptually, this approach allowed the software producer (programmer) to develop "tools" for specific use in the work environment. These discrete pieces of software code could then be linked (through the concept of "pipes" and "filters") using the attributes of a given piece of software without requiring a new development effort every time it was used. In fact, in a UNIX environment, numerous processes could simultaneously use this code (tool) in myriad simple applications, although only one copy might actually exist. Hence, each programmer started with a unique toolbox. Some of these "tools" were shared among programmers and eventually became corporate (organizational) "workbenches." (Two resultant pilot efforts in this regard were the Writer's Workbench and the Analyst's Workbench). The desirable attributes of the specific tools were the basis for their widespread use and eventual incorporation as organizational standards.

In NEPA analysis, there are numerous models available (Canter, 1993), and academia constantly produces new and better models for most disciplines. However, in 25 years of practical application, much has been learned about various models and applications of these specific tools. Some have worked well, while others have not. Some are simple and expedient, while others are complex, cumbersome, and slow. Some are driven by readily available data, while others require original data acquisition or sampling. Some are suited to NEPA, while others are not. Some, if modified, would be better suited to NEPA.

In each of the steps in an impact study, technical exploitation can certainly create savings in time. In almost all cases, the use of the Internet (or other electronic media) is a sure mechanism for speeding up the NEPA process. However, if extensive peer utilization and exchange were encouraged/fostered, NEPA practitioners could more readily benefit from the "strategic alliance" concept referenced in the Sloan School publications and better benefit from the technology as a result of "organizational change."

Baseline data could be identified, obtained, evaluated, and used more readily through the application of technology. While careful evaluation would still be required to ensure against misuse and guard against the "garbage-in, garbage-out" pitfall, certainly these technological trends will increase access to available data.

The ability to deal with cumulative impacts and issues associated with the sustainability of biodiversity will require new and different scales of analysis. As a result, these new technologies will be both inviting and essential. The use of these technologies is already widespread, and their exploitation is inevitable, particularly given the advancing trends in computer and communications technology.

The synthesis of experience and technology could considerably improve the efficiency of the NEPA process. Taking the appropriate steps from Figure 13.2, some potential gains from technological applications can be identified, as shown in Table 13.1. Major additional gains, however, will accrue through greater peer support and alliance and through the integration of these individual tools.

Integration of a number of tools into a workbench (NEPA Analyst's Workbench) would seem feasible in the near future. The depth of the workbench might be considerably inconsistent in content between disciplines, and numerous unique issues would be part of each discipline. The use of such a workbench would certainly never be mandatory, thus allowing the selection of alternate tools. However, a good deal of effort (in the analysis and selection of tools and data) could be eliminated, thus strengthening the response and reputation of NEPA analysis as a timely part of agency decision making.

TABLE 13.1   Application of New Technology in the NEPA Process

Step	*Application*	*Improvements*
Identify project/environment interfaces	Internet	Time
Identify major issues for study	Internet	Time
Develop work plan	Internet	Time
Gather data	Internet, imagery	Time, baseline data
Predict impacts	GIS, imagery	Time, biodiversity
Analyze impacts	GIS, imagery	Time, cumulative impacts, biodiversity
Evaluate mitigation	GIS, imagery	Time, cumulative impacts, biodiversity
Compare alternatives	GIS	Time, cumulative impacts, biodiversity
Prepare document	GIS	Time
Obtain comments/revise	Internet	Time

Once models, data, or other tools are identified, specific tools could be made available (or access could be provided) through the workbench. The workbench could be based on a PC, workstation, or the Internet (or a combination). If designed and promoted by the current practitioners of NEPA analysis, the workbench approach could serve to provide standards in the NEPA "industry," promote consistency in the approach to NEPA analysis, and promote more harmony, productivity, and cooperation among peers.

SUMMARY

There is currently an ongoing debate about the efficiency and effectiveness of NEPA. This debate stems from commonly held perceptions that (1) NEPA requires extensive resources, (2) the time and costs are inappropriate, and (3) NEPA seldom affects actual decision making. While the actual decision-making process specified by NEPA is often a well-founded and well-accepted process, the perceived and actual productivity and effectiveness of the NEPA analysis must change if the process is to survive. The issue of efficiency and effectiveness is not uniquely applied to NEPA; areas of business and professional endeavor are (of necessity) becoming better at delivering a product in the interest of survival, and NEPA analysis is not exempt from these same contemporary pressures. The incorporation and use of new technology are often the answer in business applications, and several technologies hold considerable promise for NEPA application. These technologies (GIS, imagery, the Internet, and their use in combination) can go far toward addressing pragmatic NEPA issues (time, baseline data, cumulative impacts, biodiversity, determination of significance, etc.). In addition, the NEPA professional stands to gain even more from the integrated use of these technologies across the life cycle of the NEPA process.

SELECTED REFERENCES

Atkinson, S.F., F.A. Schoolmaster, D.I. Lyons, and J.M. Coffey. 1995. A Geographic Information Approach to Sanitary Landfill Siting Procedures: A Case Study. *The Environmental Professional* 17(1):20–26.

Canter, L.W. 1993. Environmental Impact Quantification Manual for USAREUR. Report to Battelle Research Triangle Park Office, Research Triangle Park, North Carolina.

Council on Environmental Quality. 1993. Incorporating Biodiversity Considerations into Environmental Impact Analysis Under the National Environmental Policy Act. Washington, D.C.

Dickerson, J.A., V.R. Tolbert, A.A. Richmond, and M.S. Salk. Undated. Techniques and Guidelines for Streamlining NEPA: Four Ideas, Nine Tools. NEPA Symposium, Session 6D.

EIA Centre. 1994. *EIA Newsletter 9*. Department of Planning and Landscape, University of Manchester, Manchester, England, p. 2.

GRASS. 1991. GRASS GIS Critical to Army's Land Management Program—Fort Benjamin Harrison Finds Artifacts from Ancient Composite. *GIS World* 4:6–9.

Jenkens, R.E. Jr. 1988. Information Management for Conservation of Biodiversity. In *Biodiversity*. E.O. Wilson, Ed. Academy Press, Washington, D.C., pp. 231–239.

Krol, E. 1992. *The Whole Internet User's Guide and Catalog*. O'Reilly and Associates. Sebastopol, California.

Lancaster, F.W. 1978. *Toward Paperless Information Systems*. Academic Press, New York.

Loi, K., T. Malone, and K. Yu. 1988. Objective Lens: A "Spreadsheet" for Cooperative Work. MIT No. 89-071. Massachusetts Institute of Technology, Cambridge.

Malone, T.W., K. Grant, F. Turbok, S.A. Brobst, and M.D. Cohen. 1986. Intelligent Information Sharing Systems. MIT No. 86-025. Massachusetts Institute of Technology, Cambridge.

Massachusetts Institute of Technology. Undated. Management in the 1990's—Research Program Mission Statement. Sloan School of Management, Cambridge.

McCold, L. and J. Holman. 1995. Cumulative Impacts in Environmental Assessment: How Well Are They Considered? *The Environmental Professional* 17(1):2–8.

McHarg, I. 1969. *Design with Nature*. Doubleday and Company, Garden City, New York.

Milazzo, V.A. 1983. Specifications for Updating USGS Land Use and Land Cover Maps. Open File Report 83-116. U.S. Geological Survey, Washington, D.C.

Office of the President. Executive Order 12898. 1994. Federal Actions to Address Environmental Justice in Minority Populations and Low-Income Populations, and Executive Office Memorandum dated February 11. Washington, D.C.

Phaffenberger, B. 1994. *MOSAIC Users Guide*. MIS Press, New York.

Smart Maps. 1995. Smart Maps: Forestry's Newest Frontier. *American Forests*, p. 20.

Tulalip Tribes. 1993. Portage Creek Non-Point Pollution Assessment. Seattle, Washington.

U.S. Army War College. 1992–93. Army Command, Leadership, and Management: Theory and Practice. Carlisle Barracks, Pennsylvania, pp. 7-2–7-7.

U.S. Department of Defense. 1992. Legacy Resource Management Program. Report to Congress. Office of the Deputy Assistant Secretary of Defense for the Environment, Washington, D.C.

U.S. Forest Service. 1994. The General Guide to Pilot Watershed Analysis. Washington, D.C.

U.S. Geological Survey. Undated. GIS Benefit Study. Prepared for U.S. Army Construction Engineering Research Laboratory, Champaign, Illinois.

Washington Department of Natural Resources. 1994. Washington Watershed Analysis Guide, Version 3. Olympia, Washington.

Way, W.D. 1991. Terrain Analysis. *Military Operations Series*. Gordon Press, New York.

Westervelt, J., X. Wu, and S. Ribanszky. 1995. Correlating Satellite Imagery and Ground Truth Data with a Back-Propagation Neural Network. U.S. Army Construction Engineering Research Laboratory, Champaign, Illinois.

PUTTING PEOPLE IN THE ENVIRONMENT: PRINCIPLES FOR SOCIAL IMPACT ASSESSMENT

Interorganizational Committee on Guidelines and Principles for Social Impact Assessment*

I n a recent article in the *Atlantic Monthly* entitled "The Age of Social Transformation," management expert Peter Drucker called for the preparation of environmental impact statements (EISs) to examine the impacts of federal action on the nation's competitive position brought on by technological change. With a continuing current focus on the role of the federal government in providing for quality of life through fewer environmental regulations, it would be more reasonable to understand the social consequences of our actions by providing better guidance for social impact analysis using the EIS process already in place. The impact of major federal actions on the human environment was a key component of the National Environmental Policy Act (NEPA) and required that these considerations be addressed in EISs. At times during the last 25 years, decision makers and bureaucrats have assumed that humans existed separate and apart from the natural environment. This misconception has led to a lack of recognition of how human communities respond, adapt, or even become extinct based on significant federal

---

* This chapter represents the work of the Interorganizational Committee on Guidelines and Principles for Social Impact Assessment. The members of the committee were Rabel J. Burdge and Gary Williams, Rural Sociological Society; Lynn Llewellyn, American Psychological Association; Kurt Finsterbusch and William R. Freudenburg, American Sociological Association; Richard Stoffle, American Anthropological Association and Society for Applied Anthropology; James Thompson and C.P. Wolf, International Association for Impact Assessment; and Peter Fricke, Robert Gramling, Arnold Holden, and John S. Patterson as members-at-large. The materials assembled in this chapter do not in any way reflect the views or the official position of the agencies, educational institutions, and professional organizations listed.

---

actions affecting the environment. Human communities pose a special analytical problem in that they want to be a part of planning for federal actions.

Social and economic impact assessment has gone through a "boom and bust" cycle similar to the cycles of the western "boomtowns" during the energy development period of the 1970s. Social scientists were hired by federal resource management agencies during this period but were let go when the boom ended. The departure of these social scientists from agency positions meant neither practitioners nor proponents for social impact analysis were present within agencies. Without strong guidance for social impact analysis in the regulations implementing the procedural provisions of NEPA, the practice of social impact assessment (SIA) suffered.

SIA AND THE NATIONAL ENVIRONMENTAL POLICY ACT

Passage of NEPA of 1969, particularly the requirement for EISs (further clarified in 40 CFR Parts 1500–1508, Regulations for Implementing the Procedural Provisions of the National Environmental Policy Act, 1986), clearly underscored the importance of the human environment and opened the door for consideration of social as well as environmental impacts of federally funded projects in the United States. NEPA seeks to have agencies "utilize a systematic, interdisciplinary approach which will insure the integrated use of the natural and social sciences and the environmental design arts in planning and in decision making which may have an impact on man's environment; identify and develop methods and procedures…which will insure that presently unquantified environmental amenities and values may be given appropriate consideration in decision-making along with economic and technical considerations." The regulations also point out that the "human environment" is to be "interpreted comprehensively" to include "the natural and physical environment and the relationship of people with that environment" (40 CFR 1508.14). Agencies need to assess not only so-called "direct" effects but also "aesthetic, historic, cultural, economic, social or health" effects, "whether direct, indirect, or cumulative" (40 CFR 1508.8).

Since the passage of NEPA, a host of regulations have included social and human concerns in the decision-making process—sometimes through public involvement programs. For example, the Comprehensive Environmental Response, Compensation, and Liability Act of 1980, known as the Superfund Act, and the Superfund Amendments and Reauthorization Act of 1986 call for working with affected publics through community relations plans and assessing community and state acceptance of Superfund plans affecting local populations. Superfund actions are not necessarily considered under NEPA; therefore, it is imperative that social impacts of Superfund actions be part of the community's right to know.

The United States is not alone in its attempt to understand social impacts before making decisions. For example, the World Bank included sociological components in its 1984 operational manual on project design and implementation. More recent guidance published in the World Bank's *Environmental Assessment Sourcebook: Policies Procedures, and Cross-Sectoral Issues* (1991) includes chapters on social and cultural issues and institutional aspects of expanding environmental reviews. The sourcebook also includes a chapter on involving diverse publics in project design and implementation. The

U.S. Agency for International Development also has recognized the importance of social impacts of its projects and requires a social soundness factors analysis to accompany project proposals.

Despite these direct and related activities, there are five major barriers to the practice of SIA within the context of EISs as prepared in the United States:

1. People are not viewed as part of the natural environment, and, therefore, technical areas (disciplines) are not integrated in EISs. This leads to a situation where social and economic impacts are not connected to the other environmental responses, and the other environmental impacts are not interpreted in terms of their special meaning to important subcategories of the population (e.g., farmers and Native Americans).
2. There are no regulations or guidelines for social or economic impact assessment that are required for all federal agencies.
3. As in the case of EISs, a poorly conducted SIA reproduces itself (i.e., there is a tendency for people to put the same material in the current EIS that they put in the last EIS, whether or not it was appropriate).
4. Although scoping may be extensive, the public role in defining the "range of alternatives" considered in the EIS is often minimal (thus affecting the inclusion of social impacts).
5. The social (and political) variables considered in the decision-making process are often not the ones included in the SIA.

To address these problems, the Interorganizational Committee, comprised of academics and practitioners as well as representation from professional organizations, was formed in 1988. The purpose of the committee was to develop guidelines and principles for SIA to assist agencies and agency managers to overcome some of the inadequate administration and application of the SIA process. A set of guidelines and principles was developed to assist agencies and private interests in fulfilling their statutory obligations under NEPA and related authorities. Application of these guidelines and principles by trained social scientists will help in identifying potential impacts on people, communities, and society before decisions subject to the NEPA process are made.

STEPS IN THE SOCIAL IMPACT ASSESSMENT PROCESS

The Interorganizational Committee suggests that a SIA should contain the ten steps outlined in Figure 14.1. These steps are logically sequential but often overlap in practice. This sequence is patterned after the environmental impact assessment (EIA) steps as listed in the Council on Environmental Quality (CEQ) regulations (1986).

Step 1: Public Involvement

This step involves the development of an effective public involvement plan to involve all potentially affected publics. This requires identifying and working with all potentially affected groups, starting at the very beginning of planning for the proposed action. Groups affected by proposed actions include those who live nearby; those who will hear,

```
Step 1:  Public Involvement
              ↓
Step 2:  Identification of Alternatives
              ↓
Step 3:  Baseline Conditions
              ↓
Step 4:  Scoping
              ↓
Step 5:  Projection of Estimated Effects
              ↓
Step 6:  Predicting Responses to Impacts
              ↓
Step 7:  Indirect and Cumulative Impacts
              ↓
Step 8:  Changes in Alternatives
              ↓
Step 9:  Mitigation
              ↓
Step 10:  Monitoring
```

FIGURE 14.1   Steps in the social impact assessment process.

smell, or see a development; those who are forced to relocate because of a project; and those who have interest in a new project or policy change but may not live in proximity. Others affected include those who might normally use the land on which the project is located (such as farmers who have to plow around a transmission line). Still others include those affected by the influx of seasonal residents, who may have to pay higher prices for food or rent or pay higher taxes to cover the cost of expanded community services.

Once identified, representatives from each group should be systematically interviewed to determine potential areas of concern/impact and ways each representative might be involved in the planning decision process. Public meetings by themselves are inadequate for collecting information about public perceptions. Survey data can be used to define the potentially affected population. In this first step, the pieces are put in place for a public involvement program which will last throughout the EIA and SIA processes.

Step 2: Identification of Alternatives

This step involves describing the proposed action or policy change and reasonable alternatives. The proposed action is described in enough detail to begin to identify the data requirements needed from the project proponent to frame the SIA. At a minimum, this includes:

1. Locations
2. Land requirements
3. Needs for ancillary facilities (roads, transmission lines, and sewer and water lines)
4. Construction schedule
5. Size of the work force (construction and operation, by year or month)
6. Facility size and shape
7. Need for a local work force
8. Institutional resources

A list of SIA variables may be found in the Interorganizational Committee Report (1994, 1995) and used as a guide for obtaining data from policy or project proponents. Sometimes the description of the proposed alternatives may not include all the information needed for an SIA. Another problem is the provision of summary numbers when disaggregated numbers are needed. For example, the social assessor may be given numbers for the total peak work force of a construction project when information is needed on local, in-migrating, and non-local commuting workers for each phase of construction.

Step 3: Baseline Conditions

This step involves describing the relevant human environment/area of influence and baseline conditions. The baseline conditions are the existing conditions and past trends associated with the human environment in which the proposed activity is to take place. This is called the baseline study. For construction projects, a geographical area is identified along with the distribution of special populations at risk, but for programs, policies, or technology assessments, the relevant human environment may be a more dispersed collection of interested and affected publics, interest groups, organizations, and institutions. The generic set of dimensions for investigation listed below would include the following aspects of the human environment for construction projects and geographically located programs and policies (the SIA variables cited by the Interorganizational Committee, 1994, require similar information):

1. Relationships with the biophysical environment, including ecological setting; aspects of the environment seen as resources or problems; areas having economic, recreational, aesthetic, or symbolic significance to specific people; residential arrangements and living patterns, including relationships among communities and social organizations; attitudes toward environmental features; and patterns of resource use
2. Historical background, including initial settlement and subsequent shifts in population; developmental events and eras, including experience with boom–bust effects, as well as a discussion of broader employment trends; past or ongoing community controversies, particularly those involving technology or the environment; and other experiences likely to affect the level or distribution of the impacts on local receptivity to the proposed action
3. Political and social resources, including the distribution of power and authority, the capacities of relevant systems or institutions (e.g., the school system), friendship networks and patterns of cleavage or cooperation among potentially affected groups, levels of residential stability, distributions of sociodemographic charac-

teristics such as age and ethnicity, presence of distinctive or potentially vulnerable groups (e.g., low income), and linkages among geopolitical units (federal, state, county, local, and interlocal)

4. Culture, attitudes, and social-psychological conditions, including attitudes toward the proposed action, trust in political and social institutions, perceptions of risks, relevant psychological coping and adjustment capacity, cultural cognition of society and environment, assessed quality of life, and important values that may be relevant to or affected by the proposed action

5. Population characteristics, including the demographics of relevant groups (including all significant stakeholders and sensitive populations and groups); major economic activities; future prospects; the labor markets and available work force; unemployment and underemployment; population and expected changes; availability of housing, infrastructure, and services; size and age structure of households; and seasonal migration patterns

The level of effort that is devoted to the description of the human environment should be commensurate with the size, cost, and degree of expected impacts of the proposed action. At a minimum, the existing literature on comparable or analogous events, knowledgeable experts, and readily available documents, such as government reports, should be consulted. On-site investigations and the use of previous field studies and surveys are recommended, as are rapid appraisals and mini-surveys.

Step 4: Scoping

After obtaining a technical understanding of the proposal, identify the full range of probable social impacts that will be addressed based on discussion or interviews with members of all potentially affected publics and through the EIS public scoping process. The social impact assessor selects the important SIA variables for further assessment and deletes from further consideration those variables deemed unimportant. Consideration needs to be devoted both to the impacts perceived by the proponent agency and to those perceived by affected groups and communities. The principal methods to be used by experts and interdisciplinary teams are reviews of the existing social science literature, public scoping, public surveys, and public participation techniques. It is important for the views of affected people to be taken into consideration. Ideally, all affected people or groups contribute to the selection of the variables assessed through either a participatory process or by review and comment on the decisions made by responsible officials and the interdisciplinary team. Early scoping is encouraged and can take place before Step 3.

Relevant criteria for selecting significant impacts comparable to those spelled out in the CEQ regulations (40 CFR 1508.27) include the following:

1. Probability of the event occurring
2. Number of people, including indigenous populations, that will be affected
3. Duration of impacts (long term vs. short term)
4. Value of benefits and costs to impacted groups (intensity of impacts)
5. Extent that the impact is reversible or can be mitigated
6. Likelihood of causing subsequent impacts

7. Relevance to present and future policy decisions
8. Uncertainty over possible effects
9. Presence or absence of controversy over the issue

Step 5: Projection of Estimated Effects

This step involves investigating the probable impacts of the proposed actions. The probable social impacts will be formulated in terms of predicted conditions without the actions (baseline projection), predicted conditions with the actions, and predicted impacts that can be interpreted as the differences between the future with and without the proposed actions. The empirical procedure is based on a SIA model developed by the Interorganizational Committee (1994, 1995).

Investigation of the probable impacts involves five major sources of information: (1) data from project proponents; (2) records of previous experience with similar actions as represented in reference literature as well as other EISs; (3) census and vital statistics; (4) documents and secondary sources; and (5) field research, including informant interviews, hearings, group meetings, and surveys of the general population. The investigation of the social impacts identified during field interviews and scoping is the most important component.

Methods of projecting the future lie at the heart of social assessment, and much of the process of analysis is tied up in this endeavor. In spite of the long lists of methods available, most fall into the following categories:

1. Comparative method
2. Straight-line trend projections (taking an existing trend and simply projecting the same rate of change into the future)
3. Population multiplier methods (each specified increase in population implies designated multiples of some other variable, e.g., jobs and housing units)
4. Scenarios such as (a) logical imaginations based on construction of hypothetical futures through a process of mentally modeling the assumptions about the variables in question and (b) fitted empirical similar past cases used to analyze the present case, with experts adjusting the scenario by taking into account the unique characteristics of the present case
5. Expert testimony (experts can be asked to present scenarios and assess their implications)
6. Computer modeling (involving the mathematical formulation of premises and a process of quantitative weighing of variables)
7. Calculation of futures foregone (a number of methods have been formulated to determine what options would be given up irrevocably as a result of a plan or project, e.g., river recreation and agricultural land use after the building of a dam)

The record of previous experience is very important to the estimation of future impacts. It is largely contained in case reports and studies and the experience of experts. Variations in the patterns of impacts and responses in these cases also should be registered. Expert knowledge is used to enlarge this knowledge base and to judge how the study case is likely to deviate from the typical patterns. The documents and secondary sources provide information on existing conditions, plans, reported attitudes, and opinions and contribute to the case record. The field research involves interviews with persons who have different interests at stake, different perspectives, and different kinds of expertise. Wherever feasible, it should also involve a search through a wide range of documentation that is often available (in forms that range from official statistics and the minutes of meetings to the patterns of coverage and letters to the editors).

The opinions of various individuals and groups toward the proposed change should also be part of the record. Surveys are valuable to assess public opinion properly, because spokespersons for groups do not always represent the views of the rank and file. Statements at public meetings and by spokespersons should not be used as projections, but as possible impacts to be evaluated through other means.

Step 6: Predicting Responses to Impacts

This step involves determining the significance of the identified social impacts. This difficult assessment task is often avoided, but the responses of affected publics (parties) frequently will identify significant subsequent impacts. After direct impacts have been estimated, the assessor must next estimate how the affected people will respond in terms of attitude and actions. Their attitudes before implementation predict their attitudes afterwards, though data increasingly show that fears are often overblown and that expected (often promised) benefits fail to meet expectations. This literature should be consulted.

The actions of affected groups are to be estimated using comparable cases and interviews with affected people about what they expect to do. So much depends on whether local leadership arises (and the objectives and strategies of these leaders) that this assessment step often is highly uncertain, but at least policy makers will be notified of potential problems and unexpected results. This step is also important because adaption and responses of affected parties can have consequences of their own, whether for the agency that proposes an action (as when political protest stalls a proposal) or for the affected communities, whether in the short or long term.

Step 7: Indirect and Cumulative Impacts

This step addresses subsequent impacts and cumulative impacts. Indirect impacts are those caused by the direct impacts; they often occur later than the direct impact or farther away. Cumulative impacts are those impacts that result from the incremental impacts of an action added to other past, present, and reasonably foreseeable future actions, regardless of which agency or person undertakes them (see 40 CFR 1508.7). A community's residential and retail growth and pressures on government services following the siting of a major project are examples of indirect and cumulative impacts. While they are more difficult to estimate precisely than direct impacts, it is very important that indirect and cumulative impacts be clearly identified in the SIA.

Step 8: Changes in Alternatives

This step involves recommending new or changed alternatives and estimating or projecting their consequences. Each new alternative or recommended change should be assessed separately. The methods used in Step 5 (estimation) apply here, but usually on a more modest scale. More innovative alternatives and changes probably should be presented in an experimental structure. Expert judgment and scenarios are helpful in developing project and policy alterations. The number of iterations here will depend upon time, funding, and the magnitude of the project or policy changes.

Step 9: Mitigation

This step involves the development of a mitigation plan. A social impact assessment not only forecasts impacts but should identify means to mitigate adverse impacts. Mitigation includes avoiding the impact by modifying or not taking an action; minimizing, rectifying, or reducing the impacts through the design or operation of the project or policy; or compensating for the impact by providing substitute facilities, resources, or opportunities (see 40 CFR 1508.20). Ideally, mitigation measures are built into the selected alternative, but it is appropriate to identify mitigation measures even if they are not immediately adopted or if they would be the responsibility of another person or government unit.

By articulating the impacts that will occur and making efforts to avoid or minimize the adverse consequences or compensating the residents or the community for the losses, benefits may be enhanced and avoidable conflicts can be managed or minimized.

Step 10: Monitoring

This step involves the development of a monitoring program that is capable of identifying deviations from the proposed action and any important unanticipated impacts. A monitoring plan should be developed to track project and program development and compare real impacts with projected ones. It should spell out (to the degree possible) the nature and extent of additional steps that should take place when unanticipated impacts or impacts larger than the projections occur.

Monitoring programs are particularly necessary for projects and programs that lack detailed information or that have high variability or uncertainty. It is important to recognize, in advance, the potential for surprises that may lie completely outside the range of options considered by the SIA. If monitoring procedures cannot be adequately implemented, then mitigation agreements should acknowledge the uncertainty faced in implementing the decision.

It is generally only at this stage that the community or affected group has the influence to get such agreements in writing. A recent example of a monitoring program with subsequent provision for mitigation was negotiated between the U.S. Department of Energy, the state of Texas, and the Superconducting/Super Collider Laboratory. The process allowed for the payment of approximately $800,000 to local jurisdictions to monitor the impacts of the construction activity (Congress later decided to withdraw funding for this project).

PRINCIPLES FOR SOCIAL IMPACT ASSESSMENT

The Interorganizational Committee (1994, 1995) has outlined a consensus on the types of impacts that need to be considered (social, cultural, demographic, economic, social-psychological, and often political impacts); on the need for the SIA to include a discussion of the proposed action (i.e., the proposed facility, project, development, policy change, etc.); on the components of the human environment where the impacts are likely to be felt (affected neighborhoods, communities, or regions); on the likely impacts (generally defined as the difference between the likely future of the affected human environment with versus without the proposed policy or project); and on the steps that could be taken to enhance positive impacts and to mitigate any negative ones (by avoiding them if possible, by modification and minimization, and by providing compensation for any negative impacts that cannot be avoided or ameliorated).

As several SIA textbooks point out (Burdge, 1995; Taylor et al., 1990; Branch et al., 1984; Finsterbusch, 1980; Freudenburg, 1986) and as suggested by the CEQ *Regulations for Implementing the Procedural Provisions of NEPA* (1986), the SIA practitioner should focus on the more significant impacts, use appropriate measures and information, provide quantification where feasible and appropriate, and present the social impacts in a manner that can be understood by decision makers and community leaders.

The following principles augment the guidance provided in earlier sections. These principles are benchmarks for conducting an SIA (see Figure 14.2). They include the following:

1. Integrate SIA and public involvement in identifying and involving the diverse publics
2. Determine who wins and who loses as it concerns sensitive groups (impact equity)
3. Focus the SIA on the possible impacts identified by the affected publics and impacts identified through social science expertise
4. Identify methods, assumptions, and significance
5. Provide feedback to project planners
6. Use of SIA practitioners to do SIA
7. Establish mitigation and monitoring as a joint agency–community responsibility
8. Identify appropriate data sources for SIA
9. Plan for gaps in data

Involve the Diverse Public

A public involvement and conflict management program can beneficially be closely integrated with the development of the SIA process. A lack of understanding still exists among many decision makers as to how public involvement fits within the planning process. Public involvement can complement and fit within the SIA process by identifying potentially affected groups and by interpreting the meaning of impacts for each group. Public involvement plays an important role in recruiting participants for the planning process who are truly representative of affected groups. Public involvement should be truly interactive, with communication flowing both ways between the agency and affected groups. An executive order entitled Federal Actions to Address Environmental Justice in Minority and Low-Income Populations (Office of the President, 1994) requires additional efforts to include minority and low-income communities in the public involvement process.

- Involve the diverse public

    Identify and involve all potentially affected groups and individuals

- Analyze impact equity

    Clearly identify who will win and who will lose and emphasize vulnerability of under-represented groups

- Focus the assessment

    Deal with issues and public concerns that "really count," not those that are "easy to count"

- Identify methods and assumptions and define significance in advance

    Describe how the SIA was conducted, what assumptions were used, and how significance was selected

- Provide feedback on social impacts to project planners

    Identify problems that could be solved with changes to the proposed action or alternatives

- Use SIA practitioners

    Trained social scientists employing social science methods will provide the best results

- Establish monitoring and mitigation program

    Manage uncertainty by monitoring and mitigating adverse impacts

- Identify data sources

    Published scientific literature, secondary data, and primary data from the affected area

- Plan for gaps in data

    Identify missing data critical to an informed decision and use sound social research methods to fill data gaps (e.g., surveys, interviews)

FIGURE 14.2 Principles for social impact assessment.

Analyze Impact Equity

Impacts should be specified for differentially affected groups and not just measured in the aggregate. Identification of all groups likely to be affected by an agency action is central to the concept of impact equity. There can always be winners and losers as the result of a decision to construct a dam, build a highway, or close an area to timber harvesting, but no category of persons, particularly those who might be considered more sensitive or vulnerable as a result of age, gender, ethnicity, race, occupation, or other factors, should have to bear the brunt of adverse social impacts. The executive order on environmental justice requires a determination of disproportionate impacts to minorities and low-income communities specifically.

While most proposed projects or policies are not zero-sum situations, and while there may be varying benefits for almost all involved, SIA has a special duty to identify those whose adverse impacts might get lost in the aggregate of benefits. The impact assessment practitioner may be attentive to those groups that lack political efficacy, such as groups low in political or economic power, which often are not heard or do not have their interests strongly represented.

Examples abound in the literature of groups that could be considered sensitive, vulnerable, or low in power. The elderly have been identified as a category of persons sensitive to involuntary displacement and relocation. Children have suffered learning problems resulting from long-term exposure to various forms of transportation noise and local pollution (e.g., vehicular traffic and airports). Minorities and the poor are disproportionately represented in groups low in power; for example, low-income minority neighborhoods frequently were targeted in the 1960s as optimal sites for road construction and similar public works projects. Persons with some form of disability or impairment constitute another sensitive category with important needs. Farmers often are affected by transmission lines, water projects, or developments that take large amounts of land. The special impacts to those persons should be highlighted in an SIA, not lost in summary statistics.

Focus the Assessment

The assessment should focus on impacts identified by the public and by SIA practitioners. Social impact assessment practitioners must contend with stringent time and resource constraints that affect the scope of the assessment and how much can be done in the time available. Given such constraints, a central question emerges: If you cannot cover the social universe, what should you focus on? The answer is to focus on the most significant impacts in order of priority, and all significant impacts for all impacted groups must be identified early using a variety of rapid appraisal or investigative techniques.

Clearly, impacts identified as important by the public must be given high priority. Many of these will surface during the NEPA scoping process or earlier if a survey is used to identify the potentially affected populations. However, as noted earlier, some groups low in power that may be adversely affected do not necessarily participate in early project stages. It is essential that broadly based public involvement occur throughout the life of the SIA, but additional means (e.g., key informants, participant observation, and, if the expertise is present, surveys) often must be used to ensure that the most significant public concerns are addressed.

SIA practitioners have the expertise to help prioritize issues using a review of literature and professional experience. Often they will suggest the study of issues unrecognized by either the public or the agencies.

Identify Methods and Assumptions and Define Significance in Advance

The methods and assumptions used in the SIA should be made available and published prior to a decision in order to allow decision makers, as well as the public, to evaluate the assessment of impacts (as required by NEPA). Practitioners will need to consult the CEQ regulations. Definitions and examples of effects (direct, indirect, and cumulative) are provided in 40 CFR 1508.7 and 1508.8; effects and impacts are used synonymously. The CEQ regulations are clear that an EIS has to focus on impacts found to be significant.

Significance in terms of context and intensity considerations is defined in 40 CFR 1508.27. Context includes such considerations as society as a whole, affected regions, affected interests and locality (e.g., when considering site-specific projects, local impacts assume greater importance than those of a regional nature). Intensity refers to the dimensions presented under scoping, as well as consideration of health and safety, endangered species or unique human resources, precedents, and laws. While these criteria are helpful in judging significance, the SIA practitioner also needs to consult individual agency procedures for NEPA compliance. Some of these list additional social impacts that the agency must consider even if not always significant.

Provide Feedback on Social Impacts to Project Planners

Findings from the SIA should feed back into project design to mitigate adverse impacts and enhance positive ones. The impact assessment, therefore, should be designed as a dynamic process involving cycles of project design, assessment, redesign, and reassessment. This process is often carried out informally with project designers prior to publication of the draft EIS for public comment; public comments on a draft EIS can contribute importantly to this process of feedback and modification.

Use SIA Practitioners

The need for professionally qualified, competent people with social science training and experience cannot be overemphasized. An experienced SIA practitioner will know the data and be familiar and conversant with existing social science evidence pertaining to impacts that have occurred elsewhere, which may be relevant to the impact area in question. This breadth of knowledge and experience can prove invaluable in identifying important impacts that may not surface as public concerns or as mandatory considerations found in agency NEPA compliance procedures. A social scientist will be able to identify the full range of important impacts and select the appropriate measurement procedures.

Having a social scientist as part of the interdisciplinary EIS team will also reduce the probability that an important social impact could go unrecognized. In assessing social impacts, if the evidence for a potential type of impact is not definitive in either direction, the appropriate conservative conclusion is that it cannot be ruled out with confidence. In addition, it is important that SIA practitioners be conversant with the technical and biological perspectives brought to bear on projects, as well as the cultural and procedural context of the agencies in which they work.

Establish Monitoring and Mitigation Program

Crucial to the SIA process is monitoring significant social impact variables and any programs that have been put into place to mitigate them. As indicated earlier, the identification of impacts might depend on the specification of contingencies. For example, if the in-migration of workers during the construction phase is 1,000, the community's housing may be inadequate to meet the need, but if it is only 500, the impact may be accommodated by currently vacant units.

Identifying and monitoring infrastructure needs is a key element of the local planning process. Two key points are as follows:

1. Monitoring and mitigation should be a joint agency and community responsibility.
2. Both activities should occur on an iterative basis throughout the project life cycle. Depending on the nature of the project and time horizons for completion, the focus and long-term responsibility for monitoring and mitigation are not easily defined. Research shows that trust and expertise are key factors in choosing the balance between agency and community monitoring participation. Few agencies have the resources to continue these activities for an extended period, but local communities should be provided resources to assume a portion of the monitoring and mitigation responsibilities.

Identify Data Sources

Published scientific literature, secondary data, and primary data from the affected area should be consulted for all SIAs. Balance among the three may vary according to the type of proposed action, as well as specific considerations noted below, but all three will be relevant.

The SIA should draw on existing, previously reviewed, and screened social science literature that summarizes existing knowledge of impacts based on accepted scientific standards. Examples include journal articles, books, and reports available from similar projects. A list of easy-to-obtain, recommended sources is provided at the end of this chapter. Existing documentation is useful in identifying which social impacts are likely to accompany a proposed action. When it is possible to draw potentially competing interpretations from the existing literature, the SIA should provide a careful discussion of relative methodological merits of available studies.

The best guidance for future expectations is past experience; therefore, consideration of existing literature should err on the side of inclusiveness, as opposed to exclusion of potentially relevant cases. Caution is needed when the SIA presents a conclusion that is contradicted by the published literature; in such cases, the reasons for the differences should be explicitly addressed. Anthropological data on rural and ethnically and racially diverse communities is best for understanding the cultural context of the impacted community.

The best-known secondary sources of these data are the census, vital statistics, geographical data, relevant agency publications, and routine data collected by state and federal agencies. Examples of other secondary data sources include agency caseload statistics (e.g., from mental health centers, social service agencies and other human service providers, law enforcement agencies, and insurance and financial regulatory agencies), published and unpublished historical materials (often available in local libraries, historical societies, and school district files), compilations produced by booster and/or service organizations (such as chambers of commerce, welcome wagon organizations, and church groups), and the files of local newspapers. These secondary sources can be used in conjunction with key informant interviews, to allow for verification of informant memories and to be alert to potential sources of bias in other data.

Survey research, oral histories, and informant interviews are examples of primary data that may be collected to verify other data sources. If a social assessor concludes that community impacts will differ from those documented elsewhere, such conclusions must be based on the collection and analysis of primary data to show specifically why such alternative conclusions are more credible. Also, local residents often have important forms of expertise, both about local socioeconomic conditions and about the broader range of likely impacts. Because of its unique history and structure, each community may react to a development event or policy change differently than other communities.

Plan for Gaps in Data

SIA practitioners often have to produce an assessment in the absence of all the relevant or even the necessary data. The three elements of this principle are intended to supplement the following guidance already provided by the CEQ regulations at 40 CFR 1502.22:

> When an agency is evaluating reasonably foreseeable significant adverse effects on the human environment in an environmental impact statement and there is incomplete or unavailable information, the agency shall always make clear that such information is lacking....(a) if the incomplete information...is essential to a reasoned choice among alternatives and (b) the overall costs of obtaining it are not exorbitant, the agency shall include the information in the environmental impact statement.

Only if the relevant information cannot be obtained because the overall costs of obtaining it are exorbitant or the means to obtain it are not known is the EIS permitted a gap in relevant information. In such cases, however, the EIS needs to include: (1) a statement of relevance of the incomplete or unavailable information, (2) a summary of existing credible scientific evidence that is relevant, and (3) the agency's evaluation of the likely and possible impacts based upon theoretical approaches or research methods generally accepted in the scientific community (40 CFR 1502.22).

The following three elements are acceptable procedures to the social science community when there are shortages of resources necessary to do the desired data collection:

1. It is more important to identify likely social impacts than to precisely quantify the more obvious social impacts. All assessors should strive to identify and quantify significant impacts, thereby providing decision makers and the affected publics with information that is both as complete and as accurate as possible. In cases where this desirable goal cannot be met, it is better to be roughly correct on important issues than to be precisely correct on unimportant issues. Within the context of the social impact statement, there are two important differences between impact identification (what general categories or types of impacts are likely to occur) and impact evaluation (precisely how significant those impacts are likely to be). See the list of SIA variables in Interorganizational Committee (1994). Research has identified the social impacts of many types of actions, and the experienced SIA practitioner can identify plausible and potentially significant impacts relatively quickly and efficiently. On the other hand, an accurate evalu-

ation is a resource-intensive process and deals with the question of significance. Research on the decision-making process has found that experts and policy makers were particularly prone toward premature closure. Given a partial listing of potential impacts, experts tended to assume they had been given a complete list and, in most cases, failed to recognize the potential impacts that had been omitted from consideration. While empirical estimates can appear to be quite precise, demographic and economic projections have been shown by empirical analysis to have an average absolute error in the range of 50 to 100%. Therefore, the use of qualitative and quantitative measures of social impact assessment variables is desirable, and it must be realized that the evaluation of significance has an important judgment component.

2. It is important to be on the conservative side in reporting likely social impacts. The purpose of the EIS is to provide an even-handed treatment of the potential impacts, offering a scientifically reasonable assessment of the probable impacts in advance of the development event. This is a very different matter from providing solid proof of impacts after the impacts occur and all the evidence is in! All EISs and SIAs are by their nature anticipatory. Questions about the proof of impacts can be asked in an apparently scientific language but cannot be answered with true confidence in advance of the actions in question. In assessing social and economic impacts, accordingly, if the evidence for a potential type of impact is not definitive in either direction, the conservative conclusion is that the impact cannot be ruled out with confidence and not that the impact is not proven. In cases of doubt, in terms of statistical terminology, the proper interpretation is the Type II test for power or sensitivity, and not the Type I test for the strength of consistency of an association.

3. The less reliable data there are on the effects of the project or policy change, the more important it is to have the SIA work performed by competent, professional social scientists. Resource limitations will not always allow for SIAs to be done by experienced social scientists. The two following situations are ones in which it may be appropriate to proceed without professional social scientist involvement in an SIA: (a) cases where proposed actions are considered by agency personnel with social science training and by those in the potentially affected community as being likely to cause only negligible or ephemeral social impacts or (b) cases where a significant body of empirical findings is available from the social science literature which can be applied fairly directly to the proposed action in question and is referenced, summarized, and cited by the person(s) preparing the SIA section of the EIS. If one of these two conditions is not present, the absence of professional social science expertise would be imprudent for both the agency and affected groups and communities; any SIA would be speculative and not well grounded.

CONCLUSIONS

Social impact assessment is predicated on the notion that decision makers should understand the consequences of their decisions before making them. The human environment is more complex than other parts of the natural environment because it reacts in anticipation of change, can plan for change, and can adapt in reasoned ways to changing circumstances. In addition, people living in human communities interpret change in different ways, which, in turn, affects how they react. Perhaps because of this complexity or the political consequences of making explicit the social consequences of projects and programs, SIA has not been well integrated into governmental decision making. The principles presented in this chapter were designed to assist agencies and other institutions in implementing good SIA.

By recognizing that people adapt primarily through social, organizational, and cultural changes, social impacts become a legitimate and needed component for EISs. The challenge to social scientists, natural scientists, and NEPA managers is to think broadly and always consider the interrelationships between people, flora, fauna, land, air, and water. Put in terms of a real case example, it is not the increase in employment related to a radioactive waste site that causes people to worry but rather the perception of the effect the action will have on their future environment. The extent to which social scientists and NEPA managers consider the public's concern for social issues, as well as the range of possible social impacts and principles for SIA presented in this chapter, will determine the extent to which social impact assessment will increasingly be used by decision makers. If a well-prepared SIA is integrated into the decision-making process, better decisions will result.

SELECTED REFERENCES

Branch, K., D.A. Hooper, J. Thompson, and J.C. Creighton. 1984. *Guide to Social Impact Assessment.* Westview Press, Boulder, Colorado.

Burdge, R.J. 1995. *A Community Guide to Social Impact Assessment.* Social Ecology Press, Middleton, Wisconsin.

Burdge, R.J., G. Williams, L. Llewellyn, K. Finsterbusch, W. Freudenburg, R. Stoffle, L. Leistritz, C.P. Wolf, J. Thompson, P. Fricke, R. Gramling, J.S. Petterson, and A. Holden (Interorganizational Committee on Guidelines and Principles for Social Impact Assessment). 1995. Guidelines and Principles for Social Impact Assessment. *Environmental Impact Assessment Review* 15(1):11–43.

Burdge, R.J., G. Williams, L. Llewellyn, K. Finsterbusch, W. Freudenburg, R. Stoffle, L. Leistritz, C.P. Wolf, J. Thompson, P. Fricke, R. Gramling, J.S. Petterson, and A. Holden (Interorganizational Committee on Guidelines and Principles for Social Impact Assessment). 1994. Guidelines and Principles for Social Impact Assessment. *Impact Assessment* 12(2):107–152.

Council on Environmental Quality. 1986. *Regulations for Implementing the Procedural Provisions of the National Environmental Policy Act.* 40 CFR 1500–1508. U.S. Government Printing Office, Washington, D.C.

Finsterbusch, K. 1980. *Understanding Social Impacts: Assessing the Effects of Public Projects.* Sage, Beverly Hills, California.

Freudenburg, W.R. 1986. Social Impact Assessment. *Annual Review of Sociology* 12:451–478.

Interorganizational Committee on Guidelines and Principles for Social Impact Assessment. 1994. Guidelines and Principles for Social Impact Assessment. NOAA Technical Memorandum NMFS-F/SPO-16. U.S. Department of Commerce, p. 29; reprinted in Burdge, R.J. 1994. *A Conceptual Approach to Social Impact Assessment: Collection of Writings by Rabel J. Burdge and Colleagues.* Social Ecology Press, Middleton, Wisconsin, pp. 99–131 and *Impact Assessment,* 15(1):11–43, 1995.

Office of the President. 1994. Executive Order 12898. Federal Actions to Address Environmental Justice in Minority Populations and Low-Income Populations. U.S. Government Printing Office, Washington, D.C., February.

Taylor, C.N., C.H. Bryan, and C.C. Goodrich. 1990. Social Assessment: Theory, Process and Techniques. Studies in Resource Management No. 7. Center for Resource Management, Lincoln University, New Zealand.

OTHER REFERENCES

Atherton, C.C. 1977. Legal Requirements for Environmental Impact Reporting. In *Handbook for Environmental Planning: The Social Consequences of Environmental Change*. J. McEvoy, III and T. Dietz, Eds. John Wiley and Sons, New York, pp. 9–64.

Bowles, R.T. 1981. *Social Impact Assessment in Small Communities: An Integrative Review of Selected Literature*. Butterworths Press, Toronto, Canada.

Burdge, R.J. 1994. *A Conceptual Approach to Social Impact Assessment: Collection of Writings by Rabel J. Burdge and Colleagues*. Social Ecology Press, Middleton, Wisconsin.

Burdge, R.J. and F. Vanclay. 1995. Social Impact Assessment. In *Environmental and Social Impact Assessment*. F. Vanclay and D. Bronstein, Eds. John Wiley and Sons, Sussex, U.K., pp. 31–54.

Carley, M.J. 1984. *Social Impact Assessment: A Cross-Disciplinary Guide to the Literature*. Westview Press, Boulder, Colorado.

Elkind-Savatsky, P., 1986. *Differential Social Impacts of Rural Resource Development*. Westview Press, Boulder, Colorado.

Finsterbusch, K. and C.P. Wolf, Eds. 1981. *Methodology of Social Impact Assessment*, second edition. Hutchinson Ross, Stroudsburg, Pennsylvania.

Finsterbusch, K., L.G. Llewellyn, and C.P. Wolf, Eds. 1983. *Social Impact Assessment Methods*. Sage, Beverly Hills, California.

Finsterbusch, K., J. Ingersol, and L. Llewellyn, Eds. 1990. *Methods for Social Analysis in Developing Countries*. Westview Press, Boulder, Colorado.

Freudenburg, W.R. and R. Gramling. 1992. Community Impacts of Technological Change: Toward a Longitudinal Perspective. *Social Forces* 70(4):937–955.

Freudenburg, W.R. and R.E. Jones. 1992. Criminal Behavior and Rapid Community Growth: Examining the Evidence. *Rural Sociology* 56(4):619–645.

Freudenburg, W.R. and K.M. Keating. 1985. Applying Sociology to Policy: Social Science and the Environmental Impact Statement. *Rural Sociology* 50(4):578–605.

Gramling, R. and W.R. Freudenburg. 1990. A Closer Look at Local Control: Communities, Commodities, and the Collapse of the Coast. *Rural Sociology* 55(4):541–558.

Gramling, R. and W.R. Freudenburg. 1992. Opportunity–Threat, Development, and Adaptation: Toward a Comprehensive Framework for Social Impact Assessment. *Rural Sociology* 57(2):216–234.

Greider, T. and L. Garkovich. 1994. Symbolic Landscapes: The Social Construction of Nature and the Environment. *Rural Sociology* 59(1):1–24.

Gulliford, A. 1989. *Boomtown Blues: Colorado Oil Shale, 1885–1985*. University Press of Colorado, Niwot.

Jordan, W.S. III. 1984. Psychological Harm after PANE: NEPA's Requirements to Consider Psychological Damage. *Harvard Environmental Law Review* 8:55–87.

Leistritz, L. and B. Ekstrom. 1986. *Social Impact Assessment and Management: An Annotated Bibliography*. Garland, New York.

Leistritz, L. and S.H. Murdock. 1981. *The Socioeconomic Impact of Resource Development: Methods of Assessment*. Westview Press, Boulder, Colorado.

Llewellyn, L.G. 1981. The Social Cost of Urban Transportation. In *Transportation and Behavior*. I. Altman, J. Wohlwill, and P. Everett, Eds. Plenum Press, New York, pp. 169–202.

Llewellyn, L.G. and W.R. Freudenburg. 1990. Legal Requirements for Social Impact Assessments: Assessing the Social Science Fallout from Three Mile Island. *Society and Natural Resources* 2(3):193–208.

Meidinger, E.E. and W.R. Freudenburg. 1983. The Legal Status of Social Impact Assessments: Recent Developments. *Environmental Sociology* 34:30–33.

Office of the President. 1994. Executive Order 12898, President of the U.S. Order on Environmental Justice. U.S. Government Printing Office, Washington, D.C., February.

Public Law 91-90. The National Environmental Policy Act of 1969, as amended (PL 94-52 and PL 94-83) 42 U.S.C. 4321–4347.

Rickson, R.E., R.J. Burdge, and A. Armour, Eds. 1990. Integrating Impact Assessment into the Planning Process: International Perspectives and Experience. *Impact Assessment Bulletin* 8(1/2).

Rickson, R.E., T. Hundloe, G.T. McDonald, and R.J. Burdge, Eds. 1990. Social Impact of Development: Putting Theory and Methods into Practice. *Environmental Impact Assessment Review* 10(1/2).

Stern, P.C., O.R. Young, and D. Druckman, Eds. 1992. *Global Environmental Change: Understanding the Human Dimensions*. National Academy Press, Washington, D.C.

Stoffle, R.W. et al. 1990. Calculating the Cultural Significance of American Indian Plants: Paiute and Shoshone Ethnobotany at Yucca Mountain Nevada. *American Anthropologist* 92(2):416–432.

Stoffle, R.W. et al. 1991. Risk Perception Mapping: Using Ethnography to Define the Locally Affected Population for a Low-Level Radioactive Waste Storage Facility in Michigan. *American Anthropologist* 93(3):611-635.

FUTURE OPPORTUNITIES

THE MISSING LINK: EFFECTS ON COMMUNITIES, NEIGHBORHOODS, AND INDIVIDUALS

15

E.W. Cleckley

Twenty-five years ago, the Congress passed the 1969 National Environmental Policy Act (NEPA), which requires the federal government, in cooperation with state and local governments and other concerned public and private organizations, to use all practicable means and measures to create and maintain conditions under which man and nature can exist in productive harmony and fulfill the social, economic, and other requirements of present and future generations of Americans. The Congress also directed all federal agencies to utilize a systematic, interdisciplinary approach that will ensure the integrated use of the natural and social sciences and the environmental design arts in planning and in decision making which may have an impact on man's environment.

During the decade preceding the passage of NEPA, the conference reports and legislative history of the Congress show that the nation was experiencing haphazard urban and suburban growth, crowding, congestion, and conditions within central cities that resulted in civil unrest and detracted from man's social and psychological well-being. The loss of valuable open spaces, incoherent rural and urban land use policies, air and water pollution, diminishing recreational opportunity, soil erosion, degradation of ecosystems, deforestation, and extinction of fish and wildlife species continued. Infrastructure systems were faltering (e.g., transportation systems and public and private structures). Noise pollution, proliferation of pesticides and chemicals, radiation hazards, thermal pollution, billboards, power lines, and junkyards contributed to a declining environmental quality.

Title VI of the Civil Rights Act of 1964 and other related statutes were passed and require that no person because of race, color, or national origin be excluded from participation in, be denied the benefits of, or otherwise subjected to discrimination under any program or activity receiving federal financial assistance. The Highway Beautification Act of 1965 was designed to protect aesthetic values. The Highway Safety Act of 1966 sought to reduce death and injury. The Federal-Aid Highway Act of 1966 contained provisions aimed at minimizing soil erosion and preserving parklands and historic sites. The 1968 Federal-Aid Highway Act provided relocation assistance and required that economic, social, environmental, and other needs of each locality be considered in public hearings.

The 1970 Federal-Aid Highway Act required that guidelines be promulgated to assure full consideration of possible adverse social, economic, and environmental effects relating to any proposed project of the federal-aid highway system. Final decisions were to be made in the best overall public interest, taking into consideration the need for fast, safe, and efficient transportation; public services; and the costs of eliminating or minimizing the following adverse effects:

1. Air, noise, and water pollution
2. Destruction or disruption of man-made and natural resources, aesthetic values, community cohesion, and the availability of public facilities and services
3. Adverse employment effects, and tax and property value losses
4. Injurious displacement of people, businesses, and farms
5. Disruption of desirable community and regional growth

CREATING A DILEMMA

NEPA requires a "detailed statement" for all federal actions significantly affecting the quality of the human environment. The Council on Environmental Quality (CEQ) regulations were promulgated in 1979 to provide federal agencies with a framework for complying with NEPA. Section 1508.14 defines "human environment" to include the natural and physical environment and the relationship of people with that environment. The CEQ regulations interpret NEPA to mean that economic or social effects are not intended, by themselves, to require preparation of an environmental impact statement (EIS). When an EIS is prepared and economic/social and natural/physical environmental effects are interrelated, then the EIS must address all of these effects on the human environment. Case law has been interpreted by many to reinforce this definition, thus fostering the dilemma between considering the effects on communities, neighborhoods, and individuals in social settings equally with effects on the natural and physical environment. This means that human impacts alone could not be significant enough to trigger an EIS, public involvement, and the consideration of mitigation.

The CEQ regulations also require agencies to reduce excessive paperwork by integrating NEPA requirements with other environmental review and consultation requirements. While the CEQ regulations require agencies to consider the environment equally and contemporaneously with technical and economic concerns, this integration does not include requirements addressing human impacts such as individual displacement, community cohesion, neighborhood stability, etc. equally with those requirements addressed regarding the natural environment.

The findings of a 1991 CEQ-sponsored conference on NEPA integration noted that there had not been a change in official CEQ policy, regulations, or guidance, nor had the common practice of federal agencies changed. The findings indicated that "Congress designed NEPA to provide a flexible framework within which the goal of a high quality environment for all citizens can be achieved in balance with other essential needs of society. Federal agencies in cooperation with other authorities and interests are expected, through the provisions of NEPA, to manage for the long term those aspects of the human environment that are affected by their activities."

The basic objective of NEPA is straightforward—to integrate environmental quality objectives comprehensively into planning and decision-making activities. It is environmental quality as a public policy issue—a combination of technologic, socioeconomic, legal, institutional, and political challenges—that tends to complicate the nation's collective pursuit of environmental management objectives. In the public policy arena, environmental quality competes with other essential societal needs and values. Indeed, it was for the purpose of enabling environmental quality to compete on an equal footing with other important policies that Congress enacted NEPA. Experience with NEPA demonstrates, however, that environmental quality often suffers a competitive disadvantage for a variety of reasons, including an absence of agencywide methods and procedures which, consistent with Section 102(2)(B) of the act, will ensure that presently unquantified environmental amenities and values may be given appropriate consideration in decision making along with economic and technical considerations.

The operative provisions of NEPA were constructed around the concept of integration, which may be considered at two levels. At one level, integration contemplates merging under the NEPA "umbrella" all environmental laws and regulations that apply to a particular proposal. At another level, the merged environmental considerations or values must be "balanced" with other important policies and goals that flow from agencies' existing authorizations. The CEQ is assigned a leadership role in information gathering and reporting, program review, and policy development, all for the purpose of ensuring integration of environmental quality into the sociocultural fabric of the nation's system of free enterprise markets and democratic institutions.

NEPA is not a one-dimensional statute any more than environmental quality is a one-dimensional issue. Sound environmental management contemplates more than just "process." NEPA, read as a whole, clearly supports the need for a balanced approach, one that combines education, research, and practical management techniques, including a system of incentives, to integrate environmental and non-environmental policies. Striking that balance requires organizational initiative and resourceful, imaginative strategies.

DEVELOPING A SOLUTION

At the 1991 CEQ conference, the Federal Highway Administration (FHWA) indicated that sequential decision making to comply with environmental requirements at the federal, state, and local levels has lessened the importance of the NEPA process. This sequential decision making is rooted in legislation and agency regulations. As a result, the NEPA process does not balance competing policies as contemplated by Congress.

Agencies seem to have a single focus, considering one dimension at a time. Often, agencies responsible for the natural environment forget the human dimension. As a result, the executive branch of government should assess: (1) whether the intent of NEPA is still being accomplished and (2) what the relationship of NEPA should be to numerous environmental and non-environmental statutes, agency regulations, and policies at the federal, state, and local levels.

Not all agencies have practiced this piecemeal approach to environmental planning. In response to NEPA, the FHWA developed its procedures to make the NEPA process an integral part of its long-standing highway project planning, location, and design activities. The FHWA NEPA process is a comprehensive "umbrella" focusing on integrating numerous requirements of transportation and highway agencies; the requirements of NEPA; executive orders; and over 32 other federal laws, regulations, and policies (e.g., Section 404 of the Clean Water Act, the Farmland Protection Policy, the Endangered Species Act, the Uniform Relocation Assistance and Land Acquisition Policies Act, Title VI of the 1964 Civil Rights Act, public involvement, and consideration of impacts on communities, neighborhoods, and individuals). These requirements are integrated to provide the opportunity for the FHWA, state and local transportation agencies, and other federal and state review agencies' procedures to run concurrently rather than sequentially. Since October 1, 1983, the FHWA has actively pursued a strategic initiative with other federal agencies to institutionalize, within the highway area, the integration of all environmental requirements into the normal FHWA NEPA and related project development procedures and decision-making processes. The NEPA document captures the results and findings of that process.

As noted earlier, Title VI of the 1964 Civil Rights Act and related statutes require that no person because of race, color, or national origin be excluded from participation in, denied the benefits of, or subjected to discrimination under any program receiving financial assistance. It is FHWA policy to actively administer and monitor its program, procedures, operations, and decision making to assure that non-discrimination is an integral part of the project development process leading to location approval. The FHWA currently administers requirements which implement NEPA, 23 U.S.C. 109(h) and 128, and related statutes. These requirements address the following in the project development process leading to location approval:

1. Identifying, evaluating, and mitigating social, economic, and environmental effects
2. Involving the public and other agencies
3. Utilizing a systematic interdisciplinary approach
4. Considering reasonable alternatives

Specifically, the implementation of these procedures assures that the potential for discrimination is addressed. The identification, evaluation, and mitigation of adverse effects are addressed without regard to race, color, national origin, sex, age, or handicap. Operationally, the daily functions and responsibilities are administered in a manner to determine the potential for discrimination and to take actions to prevent it, recognizing that adverse project impacts in and of themselves do not necessarily constitute discrimination. For example, all comments on the draft EIS are addressed for all areas where the potential for discrimination is identified and no corrective action has been taken. Concurrence relative to the final EIS is denied if the potential for discrimination has not been identified and corrected. Non-discrimination is integrated into all training courses, policies, procedures, and guidance relating to FHWA's NEPA process and project development process leading to location and project approval.

EFFECTS ON COMMUNITIES, NEIGHBORHOODS, AND INDIVIDUALS

Communities and neighborhoods are places where people live and share daily activities. This sharing does not necessarily include oral interaction. Cohesion within a community or neighborhood would be the magnitude or degree to which people reside and share activities together. This magnitude may or may not be visible or measurable. Residential, ethnic, and neighborhood character; public and private facilities and services; residential behavioral patterns and linkages; and the values, attitudes, and perceptions of local residents are all forces that contribute to cohesion, stability, and a vital "sense of community."

As contributing forces to cohesion, it is evident that alterations to, displacement of, or removal of access to public and private facilities and services can adversely affect the daily activities of local residents. Negative impacts on other forces, such as residential behavioral patterns and linkages, neighborhood stability and vitality, and proximity and easy access to medical and shopping centers, neighborhood stores, schools, parks, churches, recreational centers, etc., can adversely affect cohesion.

The local residents who share daily activities with togetherness and pride represent the primary forces of community cohesion. When large numbers and key portions of local residents are displaced, this alters existing conditions in an area. Displacement of residents is probably the most severe social effect. While displacement may not have a significant effect on the natural environment, it is likely that it will adversely affect the person or persons, his/her family, and the community. It can cause families and individuals to endure personal, sociological, and psychological hardships that are in direct contrast to NEPA's goal of a "wide sharing of life's amenities." Certain groups and individuals may have special problems and require special consideration with respect to access to jobs, schools, churches, parks, hospitals, shopping, and various other community services. Examples of such groups are (1) the elderly; (2) school-age children; (3) the handicapped; (4) the illiterate; (5) dependents on public transportation; (6) non-drivers; (7) pedestrians; (8) bicyclists; (9) low-income groups; (10) racial, ethnic, minority, or religious groups; and (11) rural persons.

Even though the Secretary of Transportation had exhibited progress during the 1960s in identifying social and environmental concerns, and had established applicable planning and design guidelines, Congress still reported that it was clear that many costs and burdens on communities and individuals during highway construction were hidden and not fully understood (e.g., tax losses, temporary unemployment, relocation costs, loss of access, loss of public and private services, loss of potential land uses, and pollution costs). Congress required the secretary to issue guidelines for reducing these costs and burdens and to avoid or minimize any adverse effects. Congress also established that the provisions of NEPA concerning highways remained in effect until the provisions of the Federal-Aid Highway Act of 1970 became effective.

The 1970 Federal-Aid Highway Act required that guidelines be promulgated to assure full consideration of possible adverse social, economic, and environmental effects relating to any proposed project of the federal-aid highway system. Final decisions are to be made in the best overall public interest, taking into consideration the need for fast, safe, and efficient transportation; public services; and the costs of eliminating or minimizing the following adverse effects mentioned earlier:

1. Air, noise, and water pollution
2. Destruction or disruption of man-made and natural resources, aesthetic values, community cohesion, and the availability of public facilities and services
3. Adverse employment effects, and tax and property value losses
4. Injurious displacement of people, businesses, and farms
5. Disruption of desirable community and regional growth

Federal infrastructure actions or policies may cause many adverse effects on individuals, families, neighborhoods, and communities. If a decision maker is to know the extent to which an action harms a community's sustainability, the environmental impact analysis should assess employment effects; existing and future employment opportunities within a reasonable community area; and the type, number, and income of employees to be affected. Many industrial and commercial businesses solicit low-income, minority, ethnic, and elderly employees who incur more cost and increased travel time to work. When transportation and other infrastructure activities displace individuals and businesses, this could have a significant adverse impact on a community's well-being. Many displacees may encounter hardship in finding new employment, particularly in areas where unemployment is already high. Some may take new employment at reduced salary while incurring more cost and travel time. Some may move away from their families and community support systems.

The displacement of businesses and farms is closely related to adverse employment effects. Even though monetary compensation is provided for acquisition and related moving expenses by the Uniform Relocation Assistance and Land Acquisition Policies Act of 1970, businesses and farms can incur additional expenses, depending upon their status after displacement. By going out of business, monetary losses on stock and equipment could be encountered. Commercial businesses can encounter losses in sales due to changes in clientele. This change could be caused by population shifts, distribution, and diversification. Losses in sales may also be caused by highways bypassing businesses. In assessing effects on businesses and farm displacement, the number, type, kind, and owner of businesses/farms and their employees should be considered.

The relocation assistance program provides for compensation on acquisition cost and assistance in finding replacement housing. While this may mitigate the financial impact, the displacement of housing presents other problems and effects on local neighborhoods and communities. Even though the Uniform Relocation Assistance Act provides acquisition and related moving costs to the owner and tenants, other expenses may be incurred. Owners or tenants sometimes have to decide whether to move before legal compensation can be provided to get the replacement housing of their choice. The replacement houses may have higher rents, prices, and maintenance costs.

In particular, highway improvement requiring the acquisition of right-of-way can cause immediate tax base losses, including those related to the assessed value of properties acquired from displaced businesses, farms, and residences. These tax base losses must be replaced by other sources (i.e., raising taxes on remaining businesses or property owners, etc.). Adjacent properties may appreciate or depreciate in value. If depreciation occurs, the tax losses are magnified. However, adjacent properties may appreciate in value, consequently offsetting many tax base losses. Proximity and accessibility tend to increase the value of adjacent properties, whereas air and noise pollution and undesirable aesthetic conditions can decrease adjacent property values. Highway improvements may induce corridor development and economic, residential, and population growth if a comprehensive planning effort has been conducted by local authorities. This induced development can translate into beneficial effects on the tax base. To realize the short- and long-range tax base and property value losses or gains, close coordination must occur early during local transportation and land use planning.

ASSESSING IMPACTS ON COMMUNITIES, NEIGHBORHOODS, AND INDIVIDUALS

A methodology for assessing community, neighborhood, and individual impacts has been applied on several highway projects. It demonstrates how to address impacts on communities, neighborhoods, and individuals as part of the NEPA process and EIS preparation. The traditional EIS provided estimates of dwelling units, people, churches, businesses, and public facilities to be displaced by a project. However, the current methodology provides special emphasis to relate these estimates to the magnitude and severity of direct short- and long-range impacts on the displacees, current neighborhoods, and neighborhoods to accommodate displacees and the remaining residents and neighborhoods after the project is built. Some neighborhoods being traversed were comprised of low-income residents, the elderly, and blacks. They would have experienced special problems if relocated, thus requiring careful and comprehensive studies and plans to ameliorate adverse impacts and/or to provide possible benefits.

Various factors contributed to the cohesion (vitality) of the affected communities and neighborhoods (e.g., people, public and private facilities, churches, businesses and neighborhood stores, parks and recreational centers, etc.). The highway projects would have altered many of these factors. In addition, the projects would cause severe disruption and adversely affect adequate accessibility to public facilities and services. Available housing within economic means of relocatees, neighborhoods to accommodate potential relocatees, and the availability of facilities, services, businesses, and recreation were needed for relocatees in new neighborhoods. The types of issues that needed to be addressed were similar to the objectives of community development programs administered by the U.S. Department of Housing and Urban Development (HUD):

1. The elimination of slums and blight
2. The elimination of conditions detrimental to health, safety, and public welfare
3. The conservation and expansion of the nation's housing stock
4. The expansion and improvement of the quantity and quality of community services
5. A more rational utilization of land and other natural resources and the better arrangement of residential, commercial, industrial, recreational, and other needed activity centers

6. The restoration and preservation of properties of special value for historic, architectural, or aesthetic reasons

All of these issues were found to be appropriate in the case studies. The neighborhoods affected could only be addressed through a comprehensive planning effort. It was evident that the highway project was an urban renewal project without the necessary funding or comprehensive planning. Some key issues associated with these studies include:

1. Availability of housing and business sites
2. Impact (beneficial and adverse) of displacement on family situations, businesses, churches, public facilities, and neighborhoods to accommodate relocatees
3. Compliance with Title VI of the 1964 Civil Rights Act
4. The possibility of relocating residents twice

To address these key issues, household and business surveys were conducted, and the following data were collected:

1. Household surveys
   a. Total number of dwelling units to be displaced
   b. Total number of households
   c. Employment status and location
   d. Median family size and income
   e. Number of female heads of household
   f. Number of school-age children
   g. Behavioral patterns of household (where they shop, attend church, obtain emergency services, attend school, and participate in recreation)
2. Business surveys
   a. Ownership, type, and location
   b. Possible status after relocation
   c. Possible site for relocation
   d. Number of employees
   e. Racial characteristics of employees
   f. Residence of employees
   g. Area of service/patrons

Color-coded maps depicting the quality and type of houses to be displaced were developed. The maps depicted the location of businesses, schools, and public and private facilities and their interdependency with the neighborhood residents.

The survey approach that was used included the following elements:

1. Public meeting(s) with affected neighborhoods to inform them of the right-of-way limits of the preferred alignment.
2. Neighborhood members identified to assist in surveys.
3. Meeting with neighborhoods to review and comment on survey findings.
4. Analysis and presentation of data to city and state agencies for consideration during mitigation program development.

5. Preparation of a report for submission to FHWA. This report indicated additional data for mitigation purposes and to determine the availability of housing and business sites; the impact (beneficial and adverse) of displacement on family situations, businesses, churches, public facilities, and neighborhoods to accommodate relocatees; the impact (beneficial and adverse) of the project on remaining residents (noise, isolation, and vitality); and the possibility of relocating residents twice.

A comprehensive public involvement program had to be commensurate with this effort. The program was designed to ensure that citizens having the potential to be directly affected were identified and notified of their involvement opportunities to participate and aid in identifying social, economic, and other effects pertinent to them. This included informing and explaining fully to citizens the potential short- and long-range impacts and their consequences and developing procedures that afforded them involvement opportunities early in the study process to express their views and influence the course of the study(ies) and action(s) taken.

An assessment methodology also had to be developed to identify and address cumulative impact issues not normally considered by either the local, or state, or federal government. In one case study, because the city had overwhelmingly endorsed the project, it had to initiate efforts for funding, planning, and implementing the community development program. It had to provide a leadership role in promulgating a community development program and working cooperatively with HUD, the state, and FHWA to aid in administering the socioeconomic studies, public involvement, and development of mitigation and enhancement measures. Local officials and areawide agencies (including the city council, the mayor's office, city and county planning commissions, and other appropriate agencies and governments) needed to be involved in identifying, considering, and mitigating the potential effects.

Normally after a highway alignment is selected, development of the relocation plan commences. This plan only indicates inventories of estimates of family and individual needs and estimates of available housing. Because of the severe impacts and disruption, actual data and facts were needed. The information in the EIS for this case study indicating that various agencies would provide housing was not sufficient, especially since most of the issues essential to mitigation were associated with a comprehensive community development program. Building last-resort housing was only part of the mitigation needed. A new neighborhood, including stores, parks, and recreation centers, was also needed. Therefore, the city, state, HUD, and FHWA had to jointly develop comprehensive plans and provide funding not normally covered by FHWA funding. The FHWA included hardship acquisition to aid in lessening the adverse effects to relocatees. The findings of the survey, studies, and analysis and commitment for mitigation were ultimately included in the EIS and Record of Decision.

CONCLUSIONS

The President's Council on Sustainable Development (PCSD) recently addressed issues that contribute to sustainable communities (e.g., economic development and jobs; housing and land use; environmental justice; transportation and infrastructure; and social infrastructure, crime, and public education). It also examined case studies and issues such as public participation, planning and financing, and government policies that create barriers, drivers, and incentives for achieving sustainable communities. The PCSD used the following definition developed by Concern, Inc. in 1993: "A sustainable community uses its resources to meet current needs while ensuring that adequate resources are available for future generations. It seeks improved public health and a better quality of life for all its residents by limiting waste, preventing pollution, maximizing conservation and promoting efficiency, and developing local resources to revitalize the local economy."

A high-quality standard of living for all Americans in the future requires the essential resources—air, water, soil, and ecosystems—and the preservation of our neighborhoods and community values. Achieving economic growth that can sustain natural resources and neighborhoods for future generations represents the fundamental concept of sustainable development, which unites the protection of the natural and human environment with economic well-being.

The FHWA has built a framework of policies and procedures to help meet its social, economic, and environmental responsibilities while accomplishing its transportation mission. The FHWA is committed to the protection and enhancement of the environment. The term "environment" as used in the FHWA Environmental Policy Statement includes the natural environment, the built environment, the cultural and social fabric of the nation and its neighborhoods, and the quality of life of the people who live here. This quality of life is enhanced not only by economic security and ample natural resources, but by enduring community values and thriving neighborhoods where all citizens have access to safe, comfortable, and efficient transportation.

PUBLIC INVOLVEMENT UNDER NEPA: TRENDS AND OPPORTUNITIES

16

R.M. Solomon, S. Yonts-Shepard, and W.T. Supulski II

The National Environmental Policy Act (NEPA) was enacted during a period of public controversy and scrutiny of governmental actions caused by expanding public disillusionment with the Vietnam War and growing public awareness of environmental issues. In passing NEPA, Congress required federal agencies to acknowledge public procedural rights to voice environmental concerns prior to implementing public projects. However, in their efforts to implement the NEPA process, federal agencies have actually increased the public's power to influence, enhance, or prevent agency decision making. Thus, the NEPA process can be seen as another example of the public's desire to have a government more accountable to the popular will.

Founded on the constitutional principles of representative democracy and popular sovereignty, the United States has produced a history of public involvement which influences federal planning and decision making (Tipple and Wellman, 1989). Under the concept of popular sovereignty, a government is a creation of its citizens and does not stand above them. This mandates government representatives to demonstrate responsiveness to individual interests in order to gain public support for government actions (Rosenbaum, 1978). This form of government is influenced by: (1) personal values and individual choice, (2) opportunity for affected citizens to voice opinions through a fair hearing, and (3) public oversight of government actions. Possibly, it is this procedural opportunity to be heard and government responsiveness to expressed concerns that maintains citizen confidence and trust in government actions.

This expansion of public procedural rights of which NEPA was a part can also be seen judicially in the 1970 Supreme Court cases of *Goldberg v. Kelly* and *Data Processing Service v. Camp.* In *Goldberg,* the Court rejected the concept that welfare payments were a privilege and determined they were statutory entitlements like property. Since

TABLE 16.1   Perceptions of Environmental Problems for Selected Countries Throughout the World (Dunlop et al., 1993)

	Level of personal concern about environmental problems	
Country	A great deal (%)	A great deal/ a fair amount (%)
Brazil	53	80
India	34	77
Japan	23	66
Mexico	50	83
Nigeria	71	87
Norway	19	78
Portugal	46	90
Russia	41	78
United States	38	85

Goldberg, driver's licenses, travel abroad, and public education are considered liberties protected by due process. This landmark decision triggered the large expansion of procedural due process in administrative procedures. As the Supreme Court stated in *Data Processing Service*:

> Where statutes are concerned, the trend is toward enlargement of the class of people who may protest administrative action. The whole drive for enlarging the category of aggrieved persons is symptomatic of that trend (as quoted in Schwartz, 1991).

The public's expectation of involvement in agency decision-making processes has correspondingly increased.

Coupled with this procedural right is the public perception that risk to health and well-being from environmental degradation has been a problem and will continue to worsen. Citizens of the United States are more pessimistic and have higher expectations than most other nations in this belief (Dunlop et al., 1993). Table 16.1 shows the level of personal concern in some selected countries. This pessimism of impending environmental degradation, coupled with a desire to influence government decision making, created the political climate for NEPA and other environmental legislation of the late 1960s and early 1970s. In the United States, it will be the public who determines what changes are needed to NEPA in the future (Orloff and Brooks, 1980).

What has NEPA contributed to these trends and needs since its enactment? Case law on NEPA has focused on ensuring disclosure of effects to both the public and the federal agency decision maker and requiring consideration of those effects by the decision maker. In this manner, NEPA has been a catalyst in the total process of planning and implementing federal projects. It is this disclosure role that will be evaluated herein by exploring:

1. The trends in NEPA implementation that have had the greatest influence on charting a course of public involvement
2. Why these trends exist
3. The implications of these trends in fulfilling procedural rights

Ultimately, the following question must be addressed—is the public being given fair access to participation in implementing NEPA?

LEGAL REQUIREMENTS AND MANDATES

The legal mandates and regulatory requirements that set a baseline and establish boundaries for public involvement in the NEPA process are the Administrative Procedure Act, NEPA, and the Council of Environmental Quality (CEQ) regulations.

The Administrative Procedure Act (APA)

The principle of public "procedural rights" in the area of public policy and decision making was established in its modern roots with the passage of the APA in 1946 (60 Stat. 237). Among its requirements, this statute mandates federal agencies to observe established procedural requirements set out in law, including public participation when required; agency actions are not to be arbitrary, capricious, or an abuse of discretion by ignoring public input; and agency actions are not to be contrary to constitutional right, power, privilege, or immunity by formulating public policy without an opportunity for public comment or debate.

It is through the APA test of arbitrary and capricious action that NEPA litigation is ultimately decided; also, the legal adequacy of procedural rights to those affected is established (*NRDC v. Securities and Exchange Commission*, 606 F.2nd 1031, 9 ELR 20367, 13 ERC 1321 [D.C. Cir. 1979]; *Citizens to Preserve Overton Park Inc. v. Volpe*, 401 U.S. 402 [1971]; and *Baltimore Gas and Electric Co. v. NRDC*, 462 U.S. 87 [1983]). Without the APA, early NEPA case law and CEQ regulations would not have evolved as they did in defining the scope of public participation requirements.

The National Environmental Policy Act

The instructions in NEPA for public participation are not striking. They can only be found through careful examination of Section 102, which states:

> Copies of…[environmental impact] statements and the comments and views of appropriate Federal, State, and local agencies…shall be made available…to the public as prescribed by section 552 of title 5, U.S. Code [this section of the APA was substantially changed in 1974 by the Freedom of Information Act].

This requirement clearly states the intention that environmental information about proposed federal actions be made available to agency decision makers and the public before decisions are made.

The Council on Environmental Quality: Implementing Regulations

Although specific requirements of public participation are not in NEPA, the early CEQ guidance for implementing NEPA (36 Federal Register 20550–20563, 1973) and early case law between 1970 and 1979 (*Calvert Cliffs' Coordinating Committee, Inc. v. U.S. Atomic Energy Commission,* 449 F.2d 1109 at 1113 [D.C. Cir. 1971]; *Vermont Yankee Nuclear Power Corp. v. NRDC,* 435 U.S. 519 [1978]; *Citizens to Preserve Overton Park Inc. v. Volpe,* 401 U.S. 401 [1971]; and *Lathan v. Volpe,* 350 F. Supp. 262 [W.D. Wash. 1972]) established some principles and requirements that were eventually incorporated in the CEQ regulations of 1978. These regulations established expectations and agency responsibilities for public involvement under NEPA; examples include the following:

> 40 CFR 1500.1—Purpose. (b) NEPA procedures must insure that environmental information is available to public officials and citizens before decisions are made and actions are taken....Accurate scientific analysis, expert agency comments, and public scrutiny are essential to implementing NEPA.
>
> 40 CFR 1500.2—Policy. (b) Implement procedures to make the NEPA process more useful to decisionmakers and the public....(d) Encourage and facilitate public involvement in decisions which affect the quality of the human environment....
>
> 40 CFR 1506.6—Public Involvement. (a) Make diligent efforts to involve the public in preparing and implementing their NEPA procedures.

These regulations are limiting because they only specifically address public procedural involvement requirements and roles for environmental impact statements (EISs). This narrow scope has implications for more extensive public involvement, discussed below. However, other requirements for public participation in the preparation of EISs are explicit in many regards. For example, the regulations focus on requirements that:

1. Allow the public to help shape the content of the study by participating in scoping (40 CFR 1501.7(a)(1))
2. Give the public an opportunity to review the analysis and any underlying documents (40 CFR 1503.1(a)(4))
3. Require the agency to respond to public comments and make these comments available to the public in a final document (40 CFR 1503.4)

Summary of Legal Requirements

The NEPA legislation and the CEQ regulations require public involvement opportunities in the federal decision-making process; they establish basic expectations and procedures agencies must follow. This is well established for EISs because of the clear public involvement procedures outlined in the regulations. The legislation and implementing regulations leave most requirements for environmental assessments (EAs) or categorical exclusions (CXs) to the discretion of the agencies. This has further implications for NEPA's history of public involvement. It is clear through these regulations that agencies must provide for, and are accountable for, public participation opportunities. Agencies must ensure that divergent interests are heard and demonstrate that these interests have been taken seriously. Finally, NEPA documents must present information and rationale so the public, as well as the decision maker, can draw informed conclusions.

TRENDS OF NEPA PUBLIC INVOLVEMENT

There is no question that NEPA has opened federal agency doors. It has revolutionized the way federal agency decisions are made. However, the NEPA practices of some agencies during the last 25 years have established a number of trends which have reduced the level of public involvement below the desirable minimum. These trends have created an environment where the principles of public participation are difficult to achieve. Five trends have proven to be significant barriers:

1. Reduction in the number of EISs
2. Public involvement restricted to required CEQ procedural phases
3. Agency reliance on a limited array of public involvement techniques
4. An overreliance on the analysis of biological and physical components of the environment
5. A reliance on overly technical quantitative estimates of effects to explain risks and support decisions

Reduction in the Number of Environmental Impact Statements

The CEQ regulations emphasize procedural and substantive requirements associated with EISs; therefore, it follows that the impact statements would become the mainstay for federal agencies to effect public involvement in the NEPA process. It is through the EIS regulatory requirements of scoping and comment that the public is provided the greatest opportunity to exercise influence over federal decisions.

As shown in Figure 16.1, federal agencies have actually reduced their use of EISs, especially over the past 15 years. During this same period, discretionary domestic spending was relatively level or slightly increasing for some agencies.

There are several explanations as to why agencies have reduced their reliance on EISs (Blaug, 1992). For example, fewer questionable projects, in the public's mind, are being proposed by federal agencies. There is also a trend toward more programmatic EISs, which opens the door for increased use of EAs and CXs tiered to the programmatic document (40 CFR 1508.28). However, this reduced number of EISs has limited the opportunities for the public to access and influence federal decision making through the NEPA process.

After 25 years of implementation experience, agencies now have sufficient public involvement history to develop proposed actions which avoid the significance tests of NEPA (40 CFR 1508.27) because of the reduced environmental effects of their proposals. This reflects that public participation has successfully raised the environmental awareness of decision makers. Certain controversial projects (e.g., the creation of nuclear power plants routinely contemplated in the early 1970s) became unacceptable because of their unpopularity, thus forcing agency decision makers to change their decisions on how to or if they should implement these controversial projects. Additionally, proposed ac-

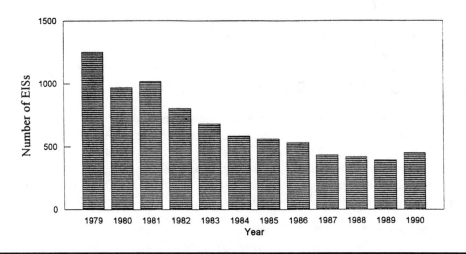

FIGURE 16.1   Number of environmental impact statements published per year (Council on Environmental Quality, 1992).

tions with reduced effects are more acceptable to most interest groups. The reduction of environmental effects should be considered a success in agency responsiveness brought about by NEPA.

Another important factor is that agency personnel and decision makers still believe the EIS path for NEPA compliance takes too long and is too costly to meet immediate needs. Therefore, they have modified proposals to ensure that significance criteria were not triggered and, in many cases, they accepted less ambitious results.

If the reduction in the number of EISs has meant a corresponding increase in the number of EAs and CXs, the opportunity for maintaining or increasing public involvement should be related to individual agency NEPA procedures for EAs and CXs and the associated level of public involvement required. However, no federal agency has provided the same level of public involvement for EAs and CXs as provided through the EIS process. Blaug (1992) reported that only 38% of the federal agencies have procedures for public participation in the EA process. Therefore, EAs and CXs are probably not providing the same level of public involvement opportunities as EISs.

It may be argued that this is to be expected, as NEPA and the CEQ regulations are aimed at focusing the environmental analysis and public involvement on those proposed federal actions that are truly worthy of in-depth analysis, i.e., projects that are major federal actions significantly affecting the quality of the human environment (40 CFR 1501.1). Ultimately, the preparation of fewer EISs, by itself, does not imply that the public is not being given participation opportunities or being denied procedural rights.

One measure of public satisfaction or dissatisfaction with the trend toward fewer EISs is to examine the level and scope of NEPA litigation. Litigation has declined correspondingly with the number of EISs (see Figure 16.2); however, this might be explained, in part, by fewer EISs to litigate. Another equally important factor may be the increasing number of NEPA-based lawsuits decided in favor of the federal agencies, thus suggesting

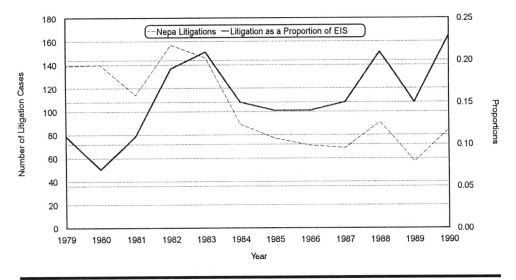

FIGURE 16.2   NEPA-based litigation and the ratio of litigation against the number of EISs produced per year (Council on Environmental Quality, 1992).

that agencies have learned from their court experiences and this litigation has helped to define NEPA requirements. Of interest is the relationship between the number of NEPA-based lawsuits and the number of EISs produced. This relationship increased from around 10% between 1979 and 1981 to around 20% between 1988 and 1990 (see Figure 16.2). The most striking statistic, and most frequently cited basis for complaints about the use of EAs, is the presence of significant environmental effects and the fact that EISs should have been prepared (CEQ, 1992).

These statistics indicate that not only is public involvement being decreased through the preparation of fewer EISs, but there is increasing concern among interest groups that federal agencies should be providing more public involvement opportunities to influence their decisions. It is uncertain whether this dissatisfaction is based more on how public participation is done or where it is done in the NEPA process. This dissatisfaction, coupled with limited agency requirements for public involvement in the EA process, can be interpreted to mean that public involvement in the EA process is not adequate.

Limiting Public Involvement to CEQ Requirements

To date, agencies have focused on the two required points in the NEPA process for public involvement, thus not realizing opportunities for increasing public involvement in the middle phases of the process. Recent case law surrounding the Federal Advisory Committee Act also contributes to this reluctance by agencies to engage the public in non-traditional public involvement phases of the NEPA process.

The CEQ regulations encourage the strongest efforts of public involvement at the point an agency decides to prepare an EIS; this entails the scoping process (CEQ, 1982). The regulations assume an agency has not advanced far in its planning for a project, so this would be the most advantageous and effective time to solicit the public for ideas and issues related to the potential action. It enables the agency to focus the scope of the analysis on the most significant issues raised by various publics.

In practice, agencies often have problems with their timing of public participation during their scoping phase. Two problems are typically encountered: public participation too early, before the proponent agency has a clearly defined purpose and need for the project, or too late, after the agency has de facto settled on a course of action before completing the necessary environmental analysis. Either problem leads to poor communication between the proponent agency and the public. While up-front involvement accommodates agency compliance with the legal process, it does little to raise public understanding and consciousness of the environmental consequences of the proposed action. This understanding and consciousness may be facilitated during the evaluation of the environmental effects phase of the NEPA process.

Agencies may also circumvent their scoping obligations because agency personnel prefer courses of action that avoid confrontation and conflict by minimizing public contact opportunities (Tipple and Wellman, 1989). Such an approach usually results in greater conflict and polarization of the public and leads to increased agency expense through post-decisional negotiation or litigation.

The other point where the CEQ regulations require public involvement is at the completion of the effects analysis; this occurs via public comment on draft EISs. Again, this is an important stage at which public concerns and positions can be solicited prior to a final decision. However, the question remains: Is this post-analysis involvement truly effective in meeting public expectations for procedural rights?

Decision points can also occur in the middle phases of the NEPA process between scoping and the review of draft EISs. Public involvement can play an important role in the middle phases, principally in the treatment of alternatives and the evaluation of environmental effects. However, the opportunity for involving the public during these middle phases of the NEPA process has largely gone unrealized by most agencies (Blahna and Yonts-Shepard, 1989). This unfulfilled opportunity may result in greater necessary attention by the agency at the end of the process through either litigation or conflict mediation (Bingham, 1986; Buckle and Thomas-Buckle, 1986).

Conceptually, Figure 16.3 demonstrates how frequent public involvement throughout each phase of the NEPA process can lead to more effective public participation and reduced conflict; such involvement builds the means for a cooperative relationship focused on resolving mutual concerns.

Ultimately, agencies bear the responsibility for engaging the public in the NEPA process. By doing so, agencies not only improve citizen confidence in the process, but also improve the public sense of community, quality of life, and trust in the agency (Wellman and Tipple, 1993). The concept of expanded public access to the decision-making process subscribes to the belief that the more opportunities for public involvement, the greater the demonstration by the agency of a cooperative role for the public and an illustration that citizens have been heard.

In summary, the public may have been provided minimum participation opportunities in terms of agency compliance with the letter of the CEQ regulations, and judges have not asked agencies to do more in public participation than these minimum requirements.

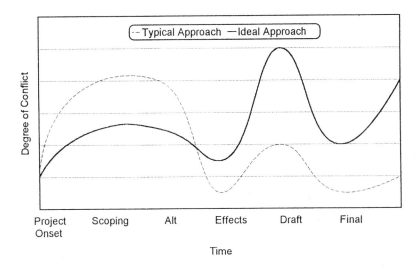

FIGURE 16.3   Theoretical degree of conflict during phases of the NEPA process.

However, if public involvement is to be truly valued under NEPA, decision-maker efforts to expand public involvement to all phases of the analysis process are needed, even though they may not be legally required.

Limited Array of Public Involvement Techniques

Despite an increasing awareness of the value of public involvement, there is limited success in truly integrating public needs, values, and issues into the NEPA and other planning processes (Creighton, 1983). Agencies have found mixed successes with their public involvement programs; this is in part due to their limited usage of techniques to solicit issues and dialogue with interest groups and affected citizens.

Agencies rely heavily on public hearings, information meetings, newsletters, written responses, and formal processes. As a result, public involvement has in many instances suffered by, at best, being ineffective and, at worst, by being confrontational (Blahna and Yonts-Shepard, 1989). Public involvement techniques should result in better disclosure and understanding; however, they have not necessarily increased cooperation between conflicting public interests. However, they have tended to become non-confrontational methods of one-way communication. While seeming least confrontational to an agency, they may not respond to public demands for more interactive techniques (Blahna and Yonts-Shepard, 1989).

Managers ultimately question the value of public involvement programs because of costs, time requirements, or conflicts; they may also disregard the results obtained through such efforts (Milbrath, 1983; Goldenberg and Frideres, 1986). In response, special interest groups view the agency public involvement program as non-responsive to their needs, and they may resort to other effective means of expressing their ideas, positions, or issues, usually by use of administrative appeal, litigation, or mediation processes. Therefore, this overreliance on non-confrontational techniques and underutilization of interactive techniques does not provide the most effective, efficient, or optimal public involvement.

Reliance on the Biological and Physical Components for Analysis

While all NEPA issues can ultimately be seen as human wants based on social values, beliefs, or attitudes which are often expressed in physical and biological terms, the agencies and the courts have kept them separated (*Metropolitan Edison Co. v. People Against Nuclear Energy,* 460 U.S. 766 [1983]). NEPA conveys ideals for integrating the biological and physical components of the environment with the social, economic, and environmental design arts. However, physical and biological aspects of the environment are supported by substantive environmental laws; in contrast, social attributes have not been mandated for analysis, unless they are interrelated with significant biological or physical impacts (40 CFR 1508.14). Substantive requirements from environmental laws such as the Clean Water Act, the Endangered Species Act, the Clean Air Act, and the National Historic Preservation Act have focused NEPA analyses and disclosure toward compliance with the legal mandates of these laws. Because of the specific requirements of these laws and their relationships to the NEPA significance criteria (40 CFR 1508.27), federal agencies have concentrated expertise, analysis, and discussion in NEPA documents to these biophysical components as opposed to social effects.

At the same time, document review by many interest groups focuses on the requirements of substantive environmental legislation that can serve as a basis for future litigation. These specific technical requirements of law are referred to as "show-stoppers" because they provide increased leverage to prevent implementation of a project through the litigation process (Thompson and Williams, 1992).

This emphasis on physical and biological impacts of proposed actions may diminish NEPA requirements for social and economic components as part of informed decision making for EAs and CXs. Only in EISs are social and economic effects required to be fully addressed (40 CFR 1508.14). With such a priority focus given to the physical and biological components of the environment, it could be expected that social needs and issues would be deemphasized. Yet, it is through the expression of social goals that society can begin to more clearly understand and articulate issues and impacts within the human context. As an example, Native American treaty rights, values, and needs have recently begun to be more fully evaluated. As society looks toward larger and more complex ecosystems, opportunities must be provided for greater public interaction that encourages learning by both communities and government entities in defining the social aspects of federal decision making (Shannon, 1991).

The public is not provided a full disclosure when the social dimensions of decisions are not fully described or taken into account by the decision maker. For this to happen, greater attention should be given to social impact assessments at the beginning of the NEPA process; this should occur by providing information on the social values, beliefs, and attitudes of those potentially affected by the proposed action (see Figure 16.4). Stakeholder analyses that identify impacts on and implications to specific affected citizens, groups, and government agencies should be documented and disclosed (Blahna and Yonts-Shepard, 1989; Thompson and Williams, 1992).

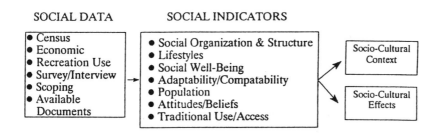

FIGURE 16.4   Key indicators for community structure/lifestyle model (Blahna et al., 1994).

Reliance on Technical Quantitative Estimates of Effects

Agencies devote considerable resources in quantifying environmental effects in technical terms and in displaying objective measures which succinctly display differing alternatives; this is done because of the belief that formal quantitative methods of analysis are the most efficient and effective. This information is typically presented in comparative form, an effort which is laudable and in keeping with NEPA's intent. However, it is questionable as to whether technical depictions of complex models, predictions, and assumptions are meaningful to most members of the public. Does the average person understand these models? Do these models and predictions depict the issues and effects in terms to which the average person can relate?

Agencies tend to deal with objective scientific information and interpretations that do not recognize or address the validity of public perceptions. As Slovic (1987) explained:

> Lay people sometimes lack certain information about hazards. However, their basic conceptualization of risk is much richer than that of the experts and reflects legitimate concerns that are typically omitted from expert risk assessments....

These quantitative methods, measures, and models may not be enough to facilitate public understanding, encourage public involvement, and resolve human conflict (Lawrance, 1993). Impacts must be displayed in terms people can understand regarding how proposals may affect their lives, and not just in the objective, analytical displays that typify most EISs. As discussed previously, incorporation of social analyses and stakeholder analyses could improve public acceptance of the NEPA process.

As part of these additional social analyses, public perceptions, as well as reality, need to be recognized and addressed. Peterson and Higley (1993) have stated:

> In our view, spoken and written responses to public concerns by experts often are inadequate, doing little to seriously address public risk perceptions. A traditional approach for scientists in both public and private sectors has been to respond to public concerns by comparing highly visible, well-understood risks with less-visible, less-well-understood risks.

Peterson and Higley (1993) suggested a framework for communication that includes principles such as responding promptly with complete openness, responding with simplicity and clarity, interacting informally with the public, and empathizing with and genuinely considering public concerns. Until citizen and group perceptions, values, beliefs, and attitudes augment the more technical quantitative components in the NEPA environmental analyses, the goals of procedural rights and popular sovereignty will be difficult to realize (Peyton, 1984).

EMERGING PRINCIPLES FOR PUBLIC INVOLVEMENT

Past trends are only part of the NEPA public involvement picture; of equal importance are contemporary trends that could change existing planning paradigms and the way public involvement needs are satisfied. Overall, the public has been afforded opportunities to influence public policy and decision making through the NEPA process, and this has been one of NEPA's greatest successes. However, this influence has not necessarily been at the most desirable levels. Two recent positive trends are particularly noteworthy: (1) changing attitudes about the role of the public in federal decision making and (2) expansion of the scope of analysis from a site-specific project perspective to programmatic analyses of greater spatial and temporal scales which cross multiple agency jurisdictions and administrative ownership. Both of these trends have great potential to extend and expand how NEPA is used in federal decision making.

Changing Attitudes

The M.A.D. (Make the decision, Announce the decision, and Defend the decision) method of decision making is rapidly becoming an unimplementable approach of the past (Freudenburg, 1993). Collectively, more and more agency decision makers are embracing NEPA as a front-end component for making good, reasoned decisions. This shift is accompanied by corresponding changes in management styles from ones designed to meet only process requirements to ones favoring more public involvement. There is also recognition by the courts by upholding agency decisions where agencies have demonstrated a reasonable compliance with the process. Secretary of Energy Watkins, during a recent congressional testimony, reflected this changing attitude when he stated, "Thank God for NEPA."

Increased interest in and practice of collaborative planning outside of the NEPA process is also enhancing shared planning and decision building among those interests that have the most at stake (Sirmon et. al., 1994; Cigler et al., 1994). Power is being decentralized. This change has the potential to bring the public closer to actual decision-making processes.

However, these initiatives and changing attitudes may be confronted with barriers. One such possible barrier is compliance with the Federal Advisory Committee Act (FACA), as evidenced by recent case law (*Northwest Forest Resource Council v. Espy*, 846 F. Supp 1009, 1010 [D.D.C. 1994], and *Alabama-Tombigbee River Coalition v. Dept. of Interior*, 26 F.3rd 1103 [11th Cir. 1994]). In these cases, agencies consulted with selected non-federal interests or groups while others were excluded or not provided the same opportunity to participate in the decision-making process. Expanding a closer working relationship with interest groups and selected citizens goes to the heart of expanding public participation goals under NEPA, but such close working relationships with a few most vocal interests must not infringe on or limit equal access or influence by all interested citizens. FACA provides the check to excessive influence by special interests, but in their implementation of FACA, agencies can inadvertently create administrative requirements that inhibit the candid exchange of ideas. These would be retreats to "safer" but less effective methods of public involvement for fear of FACA violations.

Changing Scope of Analyses

Expanding the scope of NEPA analysis beyond the physical boundaries of a project and including other non-federal interests are becoming more frequent occurrences. An example is the President's Plan for the Pacific Northwest (USDA and USDI, 1994). This plan represents a trend toward analysis of complex ecosystems comprised of interdependent plants, animals, and microbes and the coordination of federal, state, and local programs to achieve goals for sustainable development. The term "ecosystem management" has been used as an expression to describe this new approach to planning and decision making. Planning in this manner raises the complexity of the analysis and further increases the need for clearly and simply disclosing the problems and effects to various publics.

Federal agencies have struggled with preparing cumulative impact analyses since the 1979 issuance of the CEQ regulations. While the regulations require cumulative impact analysis, there is still no single, universally accepted, conceptual approach, nor are there general principles acceptable to most scientists and managers (Ritter, 1988). Issues of temporal and spatial bounds are at the heart of these disagreements. However, recognition of this problem and recommendations for its solution are now being explored (Clark, 1994). It is recognized that to fully address cumulative effects, public involvement, especially during scoping, will be critical to establishing appropriate spatial and temporal boundaries for impact studies.

The application and implications of NEPA to this new paradigm of planning can be profound. The CEQ regulations are most applicable to project-level environmental analysis; this was the focus when they were developed. The interpretation and application of NEPA to strategic planning and large spatial-scale programs will need modified regulations or case law. This new paradigm also offers tremendous opportunities to realize greater public involvement and influence in federal decision making, if such involvement is structured to be collaborative while achieving agency missions and retaining agency autonomy.

A number of suggestions can be made for expanding the scope of analysis. First, use social analysis information as a thread that ties management decisions together. Results from social analysis and consideration of social issues should be apparent for all alternatives. Second, assess individual or group beliefs about the uncertainty of outcomes or events—this involves telling not only what is believed, but also how much or how little is known on a particular issue. Third, use decision trees to demonstrate how an initial event can lead to other events or effects in the system. Each subsequent event leads to other possible final events or conditions. These decision trees can be used to develop logical scenarios and uncover uncertainties in the thinking and cause–effect analyses (Cleaves, 1994).

CONCLUSIONS

Over the last 25 years, has the public been given ample opportunities to participate in the implementation of NEPA? Has the public realized procedural rights in serving popular sovereignty and achieving reduced environmental damage? The answer to these questions is both yes and no.

On the positive side, the public has maintained procedural rights for targeted phases of the NEPA process, principally during scoping and comments on draft EISs. This role of the public has been clarified through the CEQ regulations and agency public participation efforts. Recent trends toward collaborative planning and attitude changes among agency decision makers are positive signs that public participation will increasingly influence the NEPA process, and decision makers will implement decisions that are more palatable to the affected public. Additionally, holding decision makers accountable to obligations contained in EIS Records of Decision will communicate to people that the federal agencies will do what they say they will do, and mitigation measures will be followed.

On the negative side, public participation has not been as extensive or influential as participatory democracy allows. Public participation has declined with the decrease in the use of EISs and limited public involvement during the preparation of EAs or CXs. The public's opportunities to be involved in the process have been primarily restricted to scoping and comments on draft EISs rather than a fuller involvement in other phases of the process, such as alternatives formulation and effects analysis. The limited range of public participation techniques and the focus on biological and physical components of the environment have also detracted from thoroughly addressing social issues that are of concern to the average person. Finally, reliance on technical quantitative estimates for effects analysis is often unclear to the public.

Given the new emphasis on greater responsiveness to state and local governments, there may be a legislative fix if agencies do not improve in their NEPA public participation process. In 1992, Congress passed Section 322 of Public Law 102-381, which amended the Forest Service's NEPA procedures for EAs and certain CXs that support decisions for projects and activities implementing land and resource management plans. Subpart b of this section established the requirement that after completion of the environmental analysis and prior to the decision, notice must be given of the availability to comment (for 30 days) on the preferred alternative and its supporting documentation. This notice must be given by both sending a letter to those who have participated or requested notification and by publishing a notice in a newspaper of record. Essentially, this legislated process has turned the Forest Service's NEPA process into one nearly identical to the process established for EISs. In the words of Senator Leahy, this was done so there would be a "process that gives the citizens of this country an opportunity to participate in the management of their National Forests" (Senate Colloquy, 1992).

Congress has also told agencies to be accountable to the public for actions that affect the environment, while not abdicating their responsibilities to make decisions. Congress expects agencies to be more open and responsive to public influence by expanding their traditional view of public involvement. The Forest Service legislation serves as an example of how Congress may expand the procedural rights of the public under NEPA, thus resulting in new levels of cooperation and partnership between the government and its citizens.

The use and interpretation of NEPA are at a crossroads. Its survival, application, and change will be based on public satisfaction, real or perceived. In the end, the public, Congress, and the courts will determine the appropriate level and influence of public participation in NEPA and federal decision making. Agency decision makers continue to be faced with meeting the spirit and intent of NEPA. Shrinking federal budgets and the loss of skilled employees require "practical" NEPA tools which may not satisfy all of the procedural and substantive requirements that have become accepted practice. The question will be: Do we want to do NEPA, or do we want to resolve the problem? If NEPA is going to be the vehicle for resolving environmental conflicts and airing differences, agency leaders and the public will have to come to a consensus on what the NEPA process should be addressing.

SELECTED REFERENCES

Bingham, G. 1986. *Resolving Environmental Disputes: A Decade of Experience.* The Conservation Foundation. Washington, D.C.

Blahna, D.J. and S. Yonts-Shepard. 1989. Public Involvement in Resource Planning: Toward Bridging the Gap Between Policy and Implementation. *Society and Natural Resources* 2:209–227.

Blahna, D.J., R.S. Krannich, and M.O. Roloff. 1994. Sociocultural Effects Model, Phase II. Department of Forest Resources, Utah State University, Logan.

Blaug, E.L. 1992. Use of the Environmental Assessment by Federal Agencies in NEPA Implementation. *The Environmental Professional* X:57–65.

Buckle, L.G. and S.R. Thomas-Buckle. 1986. Placing Environmental Mediation in Context: Lessons from "Failed" Mediation. *Environmental Impact Assessment Review* 6:55–70.

Cigler, B.A., A.C. Jansen, U.D. Ryan, and J.C. Stabler. 1994. Toward an Understanding of Multicommunity Collaboration. USDA Staff Report No. 9403. Washington, D.C.

Clark, R. 1994. Cumulative Effects Assessment: A Tool for Sustainable Development. *Impact Assessment Bulletin* 12(3):319–331.

Cleaves, D. 1994. Assessing Uncertainty in Expert Judgement About Natural Resources. General Technical Report SO-110. Southern Forest Experiment Station, New Orleans, Louisiana.

Council on Environmental Quality. 1982. Scoping Guidance. CEQ Guidance Paper. Washington D.C.

Council on Environmental Quality. 1992. Environmental Quality: 22nd Annual Report. U.S. Government Printing Office, Washington, D.C.

Creighton, J.L. 1983. An Overview to the Research Conference on Public Involvement and Social Impact Assessment. In *Public Involvement and Social Impact Assessment.* G.A. Daneke, M.W. Garcia, and J. Delli Priscoli, Eds. Westview Press, Boulder, Colorado, pp. 1–10.

Dunlop, R.E., G.H. Gallup, Jr., and A.M. Gallup. 1993. International Public Opinion Toward the Environment. *Impact Assessment Bulletin* 11(1):3–25.

Freudenberg, W. 1993. Personal Communication. Department of Rural Sociology, University of Wisconsin, Madison.

Goldenberg, S. and J.S. Frideres. 1986. Measuring the Effects of Public Participation Programs. *Environmental Impact Assessment Review* 6:273–281.

Lawrance, D.P. 1993. Quantitative Versus Qualitative Evaluation: A False Dichotomy? *Environmental Impact Assessment Review* 13(1):3–11.

Milbrath, L. 1983. Citizen Surveys as Citizen Participation Mechanisms. In *Public Involvement and Social Impact Assessment.* G.A. Daneke, M.W. Garcia, and J. Delli Priscoli, Eds. Westview Press, Boulder, Colorado, pp. 89–100.

Orloff, N. and G. Brooks. 1980. The National Environmental Policy Act—Cases and Materials. The Bureau of National Affairs, Inc. Washington, D.C.

Peterson, K.D. and L.G. Higley. 1993. Communicating Pesticide Risks. *American Entomologist* 39(4):206–211.

Peyton, R.B. 1984. A Topology of Natural Resource Issues with Implications for Resource Management and Education. *Michigan Academician* XVII(1):49–58.

Ritter, P. 1988. General Concepts for Measuring Cumulative Effects on Wetland Ecosystems. *Environmental Management* 2(5):38–44.

Rosenbaum, N.M. 1978. Citizen Participation and Democratic Theory. In *Citizen Participation in America*. S. Langton, Ed. Lexington Books, Lexington, Massachusetts, pp. 43–54.

Schwartz, B. 1991. *Administrative Law*, third edition. Little, Brown, Boston, pp. 257–258.

Senate Colloquy. 1992. Congressional Record, September 30, p. 515848.

Shannon, M.A. 1991. Is American Society Organized to Sustain Its Forest Ecosystems? In Symposium on Elements of Sustainability: Social Political Influences. Society of American Foresters Convention, San Francisco.

Sirmon, J., W.E. Shands, and C. Liggett. 1994. Communities of Interests and Open Decision-Making. *Journal of Forestry* 91(7):17–21.

Slovic, P.B. 1987. Perception of Risk. *Science* 236:280–285.

Thompson, J.G. and G. Williams. 1992. Social Assessment: Roles for Practitioners and the Need for Stronger Mandates. *Impact Assessment Bulletin* 10(3):43–56.

Tipple, T.J. and J.D. Wellman. 1989. Life in the Fishbowl. *Journal of Forestry* 87(3):24–30.

USDA and USDI. 1994. Final Supplement to the Environmental Impact Statement for Management of Habitat for Late Successional and Old-Growth Forest Related Species within the Range of the Northern Spotted Owl. Washington, D.C.

Wellman, J.D. and T.J. Tipple. 1993. Governance in the Wildland–Urban Interface: A Normative Guide for Natural Resource Managers. In *Culture, Conflict, and Communication in the Wildland-Urban Interface*. A.W. Ewert, D.J. Chavez, and A.W. Magill, Eds. Social Behavior and Natural Resources Series. Westview Press, Boulder, Colorado, pp. 337–347.

ALTERNATIVE DISPUTE RESOLUTION IN THE NEPA PROCESS

17

G. Bingham and L.M. Langstaff

T he emphasis and objectives of the decision-making process prescribed by the National Environmental Policy Act (NEPA) and the processes generally associated with alternative dispute resolution (ADR), when applied to environmental issues, are very similar. Both are designed to provide (1) improved exchange of relevant information, communications, and trust among affected parties; (2) better informed decision making; (3) greater acceptance and, therefore, "staying power" of decisions; and (4) decreased likelihood of costly and lengthy litigation. However, despite the complementary aspects of NEPA and ADR, this linkage does not seem to have been widely identified or utilized. More specific attention to the application of ADR techniques to the NEPA process, through increased awareness of proven ADR techniques and the use of neutral facilitators or mediators where appropriate, would enhance the ability of agencies to use the NEPA process as the decision-making tool it was intended to be rather than the onerous procedural burden it seems to have become.

A total of 112 lawsuits were filed under NEPA in 1992, a recent year for which data is available (Council on Environmental Quality, 1993). Dinah Bear, general counsel of the Council on Environmental Quality (CEQ), points out that "litigation is…a major factor in agency NEPA implementation strategies, executive branch policy considerations and in the Justice Department's litigation load" (Bear, 1995). During fiscal years 1991–93, NEPA litigation accounted for 18.9% of U.S. Department of Justice trial attorney's time and 14% of the appellate division's time (Bear, 1995).

Although many seek to avoid the high transaction costs associated with such litigation, it ought not be forgotten that litigation is an important tool to bring agencies into procedural compliance with NEPA. It is often the only tool with which parties can capture serious attention for their concerns over agency decision making. However, the results of litigation under NEPA do not necessarily translate into better decisions or improved environmental protection.

ADR processes have a valuable role to play in complementing NEPA and helping to achieve what it is intended to do—provide for more informed and, therefore, improved public decision making affecting the environment. The thoughtful application of ADR techniques to decision making under NEPA has the potential to focus energies on the substantive issues of concern early in the process, thereby decreasing the likelihood that issues of procedural compliance will be used as a means of blocking or delaying the implementation of decisions that are substantively unsatisfactory to one or more interested parties. Where legal action is initiated because the decisions being taken are, or are perceived to be, harmful to the interests or concerns of certain stakeholder groups, ADR processes ought also to help settle and thereby decrease the amount of NEPA-based litigation.

Throughout the NEPA process, there are points at which the thoughtful application of ADR techniques could enhance the process and increase the likelihood that decision making under NEPA is durable. ADR techniques lend themselves to productive handling of both existing controversies and contemplated actions for which the potential for controversy is anticipated. To help identify where and how NEPA might most effectively benefit from considered use of ADR processes, it is useful to think through parallels from the negotiated rule-making process, an area where ADR techniques have been deliberately and successfully applied to agency decision making in the regulatory arena.

WHAT IS ALTERNATIVE DISPUTE RESOLUTION?

The phrase "alternative dispute resolution" is used to describe a broad category of approaches with which the parties to disputes voluntarily seek to achieve a settlement of the issues. Most are "consensual" in nature, meaning that the goal is a voluntary agreement, or consensus on an action to be taken. Some approaches, such as dialogue and negotiation, are processes of direct communication between parties. Facilitation and mediation are terms for the assistance of a neutral person in such dialogue or negotiation efforts. Arbitration, both binding and non-binding, is an ADR process in which the neutral person is asked to hear facts and render an opinion concerning the terms of settlement. Although infrequently used in environmental matters, other litigation-related settlement procedures include settlement conferences, early neutral evaluation, and mini-trials.

Generally, ADR processes share several characteristics that can help shape strategies for using them successfully. Four in particular are key:

1. The voluntary nature of the process
2. Direct communication among stakeholders
3. Flexible design
4. Neutrality (or at least a "level playing field")

First, it is important to remember and preserve the voluntary nature of these processes. Parties have a choice about whether to participate in a consensus-building process and about whether to concur in a proposed course of action. Understanding this leads to greater attention to building on relevant incentives for parties to participate and, later, to reach agreements. This helps to ensure that consensus building is genuinely more likely to produce positive results for all parties than would confrontation in other forums.

Second, ADR processes all involve direct communication between stakeholders. Ultimately, successful resolution of issues requires stakeholders to exchange information, understand one another's interests and concerns, and develop options that address these concerns—in other words, to persuade one another to accept a proposed course of action. Basic principles of successful negotiation are essentially the principles of good communication—ask questions, listen carefully, and focus on interests rather than positions (Fisher et al., 1991).

Third, ADR processes are inherently flexible. Although mediation is a definable process, rarely are any two mediation processes alike. During initial consultations on whether parties are willing to participate in a mediated negotiation, questions about how the process will be conducted are often key. Clearly, who will participate, what the scope of issues (and alternatives) will be, whether meetings will be open to the public or closed, what deadlines apply, and what the consequences will be if an agreement is reached are all issues that link directly to parties' incentives to participate. One of the most important advantages of an ADR process is its flexibility to respond to the unique obstacles to agreement in each particular situation, whether that be a large number of parties, scientific uncertainty in predicting environmental effects, a long history of polarization, or a high level of political scrutiny.

Finally, ADR processes seek to create as level a playing field as possible. Mediators not only must refrain from taking positions that side with one party or another as part of their commitment to neutrality, but they must assess whether the fundamental assumptions structuring the process are detrimental to any party's interest. Such assumptions must be made sufficiently open that parties can either work together to change them or, if that is not possible, knowledgeably assess their risks. This is critical not only to the credibility of the process over the long run but also to whether sufficient incentives will exist for all parties such that the process will be worthwhile in the first place.

HISTORY OF ADR IN ENVIRONMENTAL MATTERS

Mediation was first formally employed to help settle a long-standing environmental dispute in the early 1970s. Since that time, the practice has grown steadily and positive results have been demonstrated in widely diverse situations. In the first decade of experience with environmental mediation, agreements were reached in approximately 78% of the nearly 200 cases documented, with no significant difference in success by the type of issues involved, whether air, water, land, chemical, or waste matters (Bingham, 1986).

The combination of parties to these disputes also has varied considerably, helping change old stereotypes that disputes have "two sides" and that they are between environmentalists and industries. Mediated negotiations have involved purely intergovernmental parties, such as the Columbia River Estuary Study Task Force in the early 1980s, in which the parties were four federal agencies, four state agencies, and four units of local government. Mediated negotiations also have been conducted among purely private parties and between environmental groups. Most commonly, environmental mediation efforts involve multiple agencies of government at multiple levels, including tribal governments; private sector interests, including manufacturing, agriculture, forestry, fishing, retail, and others; and public interest groups ranging across political perspectives, including consumer, environmental, and public health groups at the national, regional, or local levels, as well as local ad hoc citizen organizations.

Although most environmental mediation efforts have been convened on a case-by-case basis, since the 1980s efforts have been made to create more routine and systematic use of ADR in public decision making. The Administrative Conference of the United States adopted a resolution in 1982 recommending the use of and procedures for mediated negotiations in the federal rule-making process. This led to at least nine agencies building a body of experience with negotiated rule making on which, in turn, Congress passed the Negotiated Rulemaking Act in 1991, codifying procedures for its effective and appropriate use. In 1991, Congress also passed the Administrative Dispute Resolution Act, which was a more comprehensive effort to define ADR processes, establish guidance, and encourage their use through the requirement that all agencies identify an ADR official who would have the responsibility for developing a plan for the appropriate use of such processes in that agency.

Different agencies have emphasized different applications for ADR, and in many cases the focus has been on intra-agency applications, such as Equal Employment Opportunity and other personnel-related disputes, rather than on intra-agency or agency–stakeholder matters. State governments have also played a role in creating more of an institutional framework for ADR in public decision making. Some states have state mediation offices, while others have a variety of statutes encouraging or guiding the use of ADR in particular kinds of disputes (e.g., solid and hazardous waste facility siting).

Given this history and the possibly thousands of efforts from informal, facilitated workshops to formally mediated negotiations, the question persists as to why there has been interest but little action in integrating ADR into the NEPA process. In 1979, Nicholas C. Yost, then general counsel at the CEQ, was an early proponent (Yost, 1979):

> The Council issued its new regulations on November 29, 1978. They will come into full force on July 30, 1979. Every major affected group in the nation—from business to environmentalists to state and local governments—applauded the new regulations.
>
> Why this universal praise? I suspect it was, in part, because of the stress in the regulations, as in the process of their development, on seeking consensus...the new NEPA regulations will involve all those who are interested. The regulations make them part of the process. If all are part of the process, the Council believes, the process will be better. The results will be more environmentally sensitive and less subject to disruptive conflicts and delays...
>
> Don't wait, the new regulations say, until positions harden and commitments have been made to focus on the important issues and alternatives. Instead, involve all the necessary people from the beginning to see that the impact statement analyzes the information most significant to the ultimate decision. If the important issues receive attention at the outset, later squabbles about the need for more study and new information can be avoided, along with increased costs and substantial delay.

The scoping process, often including a scoping meeting, will provide a forum for using consensus-building techniques to insure that all essential information is gathered before the ultimate decision is made. Real opportunities exist for those skilled in facilitating consensus to aid diverse participants in exploring the issues and agreeing on those to be studied. Then, when a decision is made on a particular proposal, it can at least be agreed that the analytical groundwork was complete and developed fairly.

Why has this potential not been achieved to the degree hoped? Or has it? Perhaps the level of litigation is not high, if one considers the numbers possible. Many, if not most, environmental assessments (EAs) and environmental impact statements (EISs) do contain relevant information for decision making; most involve a scoping step. It is also possible that the assumptions above are too optimistic (i.e., that good information collection and analysis are enough to avoid conflicts).

Lessons from ADR suggest that how one involves people may also be a factor in NEPA-related decisions. The dynamics are very different if an agency, no matter how sincere about the NEPA process, is listening to information and concerns presented but waits until later to consider on its own what action to take than if it is seeking to reach agreements with stakeholders directly. Seeking to reach "agreement on issues to be studied" also may produce different results than seeking agreement on the alternatives to be considered or on the criteria to be used in choosing among alternatives. The dynamics of seeking agreement on the preferred alternative is likely to produce yet different results again. This is not to recommend one approach over another in all situations or even to suggest that these are the only possible variations—they are not. However, for NEPA to achieve its intended potential, it may be necessary to explore these and other opportunities for enhancing the process beyond more traditional notice and comment processes.

PARALLELS BETWEEN ADR IN THE RULE-MAKING AND NEPA PROCESSES

Both ADR processes and NEPA were initiated by persons with similar goals and objectives. Both represent decision-making processes with equivalent goals—more informed decision making. Two elements are key: (1) structuring the decision-making process and (2) providing good information.

The emphasis and objectives of ADR and NEPA are virtually the same. Both champion a process that promises:

1. Increased focus on relevant information (early identification of serious difficulties at an early enough stage where flexibility is still possible)
2. Improved communications among interested and affected parties
3. Greater "staying power" of decisions based on consensus (improved implementation prospects)
4. Decreased likelihood of costly and lengthy litigation
5. Improved prospects for future relationships among parties (ability to solve problems)
6. Better informed decision making and, hopefully, better decisions

ADR and NEPA also follow comparable procedural steps, as shown in Table 17.1. Differences emerge in how each step is accomplished, who is involved in the process, and who facilitates the process, particularly the extent of reliance on consensus (i.e., who decides). In ADR processes, such as negotiated rule making, most of the steps are accomplished collectively by the parties or stakeholders. In the NEPA process, stakeholders are involved in the scoping process and in the public comment phase, but are not active participants in information collection and analysis or development and selection of a preferred alternative. This may create a lack of receptivity and "ownership" in the decision that is at the root of many NEPA disputes.

Negotiated rule making represents a deliberate application of ADR techniques to a federal agency decision-making process—in this case, the rule-making process. Experi-

TABLE 17.1   Comparison of Negotiated Rule Making and NEPA Steps and Actors

Negotiated rule-making process		NEPA process	
What?	*Who?*	*What?*	*Who?*
Decision to promulgate a rule	Agency (legislative mandate)	Decision to take a proposed action	Agency
Convening • Identify parties • Identify issues • Assess willingness to discuss • Obtain agreement on process for consensus-based decision making	Neutral ADR professional, in consultation with all parties, including agency	Environmental assessment • Collect/analyze information • Decision to prepare EIS Scoping • Identify issues • Identify parties • Collect information	Agency (public involvement discretionary) Agency, with public hearings, written comments
Joint problem solving • Discuss issues • Identify information needs • Exchange information/ joint fact finding • Develop options/ alternatives • Evaluate options (using agreed-upon criteria) • Agree on preferred option	All parties (including agency) facilitated by a neutral ADR professional	Prepare EIS • Collect/analyze information • Develop alternatives • Evaluate alternatives • Select preferred alternative	Agency
Publish draft rule	Agency	Publish draft EIS	Agency
Comment period		Comment period	

ence demonstrates (and the negotiated rule-making statute ensures) that the ADR process supplements, not supplants, the traditional decision-making process. The final decision-making authority of the federal agency is not diminished.

A typical negotiated rule-making process is conducted as follows. The agency responsible for developing a rule seeks the assistance of a neutral convener in conducting a thorough stakeholder analysis to assess the potential for a successful negotiation process. The neutral convener interviews a wide range of potentially interested parties to consult with them about who should be involved, the key issues that need to be addressed, and preliminary recommendations regarding the advisability of and approach for moving forward with a negotiation process.

If sufficient agreement exists between the agency and stakeholders about whether and how to proceed, the agency publishes a notice indicating that it is considering the use of a negotiated rule-making process. The notice describes the interest groups and issues it expects will be involved. The notice should also invite comments on the proposed process, including appropriate representation and additional issues.

Based on the information gathered in the above activities, a multistakeholder committee is formed (typically a formal chartering process under the Federal Advisory Committee Act [FACA]). The group defines and agrees on procedural protocols, which serve as the ground rules under which it will operate. As required by FACA, all meetings of the group are announced in advance in the Federal Register and are open to the public. Most, if not all, formal negotiated rule-making processes have utilized the services of a trained facilitator or mediator who plays a neutral role on the substance of negotiations and whose role is to keep the negotiating group focused, productive, and moving forward. It is usually desirable to have the person who assisted in the convening stage serve in this capacity, as he/she will hopefully have developed effective communication and credibility with the parties.

The agency makes it clear from the beginning: (1) what its role will be in the process (generally an active participant representing its concerns, responsibilities, and constraints with regard to the issues at hand) and (2) what it is prepared to do with the consensus product, keeping in mind that the agency must be part of the consensus. The agency usually agrees to use the substantive agreement of the group as the basis for a proposed rule making. In many cases, the group develops actual draft rule language; in others, it reaches an agreement in principle, which is then drafted by the agency.

When agreement is reached, the agency publishes the consensus-based proposed rule as it would in a traditional rule-making process, and public comment is invited. Because the key interested parties have been involved in the development of the rule, the number of objecting comments tends to be less than in traditional rule making.

APPLICATIONS OF ADR TO THE NEPA PROCESS

What specifically should be the goal, and where in the NEPA process should ADR be targeted to maximize its contribution? The overriding goal, which ADR can assist in achieving, is meeting NEPA's objective for an informed decision-making process that improves the quality and durability of agency decisions. The other high-priority goal for agencies in the application of ADR to NEPA would be to avoid litigation. Yet another important goal may be to provide a potentially more attractive process as an alternative to litigation once a complaint is filed.

An effort to identify where in the NEPA process to apply ADR techniques in order to accomplish these goals may be informed by looking at the most common reasons for the filing of complaints under NEPA. For 1992 (a recent year for which data were available), these were (Council on Environmental Quality, 1993): (1) lack of an EIS (35%), (2) inadequate EISs (22%), (3) inadequate EAs (21%), and (4) lack of an EA (13%). All of these suggest that significant benefits could be achieved by using ADR in the earliest stages of the NEPA process, when a decision is being made about whether or not to prepare an EA, the scope of issues addressed in an EA, and the subsequent decision regarding the preparation of an EIS and what should be in it. Since each of these involves an agency decision, the extent of buy-in on the part of interest groups to each of these preliminary decisions can have a significant effect on the acceptability of subsequent decisions in the NEPA process.

The underlying concerns in these cases, particularly where plaintiffs claim that an EIS is inadequate, may often be related to a lack of sufficient involvement in or access to the decision-making process to ensure that stakeholder concerns are met. The common wisdom that "it must be the right decision, everyone hates it" is an unfortunate perception. Obviously, "win/win" solutions are not always possible, but solutions that solve real problems without creating major new ones are more feasible than commonly expected. The following brief description illustrates this point:

> The Tennessee Valley Authority (TVA) credited the process by which it involved stakeholders for the successful completion and public acceptance of its findings in the EIS prepared for its Lake Management Plan completed and adopted in 1991. The process produced a plan that successfully addressed issues of water quality, flood control, recreation, and hydropower production and effectively defused highly controversial policy debates regarding reservoir operating priorities that had divided agency staff and impaired TVA's relations with key stakeholders.
>
> TVA purposefully set out to use the NEPA process as a decision-making tool rather than an add-on to an agency decision-making exercise. It went beyond the minimum requirements for public involvement in a creative and expanded scoping process that included 11 public meetings as well as planning meetings with representatives of key interest groups. Through this process, TVA staff was able to share the identification of key issues and concerns and the brainstorming of creative options with the public and key interest groups. The scoping process flowed naturally into the development of alternatives for the EIS, which was ultimately received without controversy. While this was not a formal consensus process, TVA effectively applied ADR principles early and throughout the NEPA process to ensure the integration of public concerns and values in its Lake Management Plan.
>
> TVA found that it was able to use the framework provided by NEPA to support a level playing field on which all interested parties and individuals could voice their views and hear those of others and could work together to develop options to address their concerns. In accepting an award for this project, TVA Water Resources Projects Manager Christopher Ungate remarked that this process had been "designed not just to comply with NEPA but to achieve its purpose."

Integrating ADR processes into the EIS preparation process when the agency antici-
pates a high level of controversy—collaboratively defining the issues to be addressed (in
scoping), identifying alternatives, and selecting the preferred alternative (development of
an EIS)—creates the potential for a truly joint problem-solving process that would enhance NEPA's potential to promote better decision making and better decisions. In such
cases, an agency might consider the possibility of initiating a formal process, akin to the
negotiated rule-making process, for involving stakeholders in the development of alternatives to be considered or in the development and prioritization of criteria to be used
in choosing among alternatives. In one example, the San Diego County Water Authority
asked a mediator to convene a group, the Emergency Water Storage Working Committee, to build consensus on the criteria for siting a reservoir. The results of the committee's
work were tied into the alternatives considered in the EA prepared pursuant to that state's
NEPA equivalent (Emergency Water Storage Working Committee, 1993).

In cases where the degree of interest or potential controversy is uncertain or believed
to be low, early two-way consultation with stakeholders with a degree of formality
appropriate to the particular situation could help provide acceptance of agency decisions
regarding the development and content of an EA and, in the event of a finding of no
significant impact (FONSI), the decision not to prepare an EIS.

Finally, ADR processes may be useful in an effort to settle the litigation once a
complaint has been filed on NEPA grounds. This might involve referral to the CEQ for
informal mediation, early neutral evaluation for questions of law, settlement conferences,
or suggested referral to a mediator by the U.S. Department of Justice.

BARRIERS/CHALLENGES

Five key barriers or challenges to integrating ADR into the NEPA process deserve
attention: (1) lack of commitment to NEPA's goals, (2) hesitancy to involve others in the
decision-making process, (3) cost, (4) FACA, and (5) the large number of cases (lack of
screening criteria).

Lack of Commitment to NEPA Goals

While many value the benefits of the NEPA process, too often agencies have focused on
the procedural requirements of NEPA—particularly those aspects associated with the
preparation of EISs—rather than on NEPA as a tool for rational and defensible decision
making. This is not surprising, given the emphasis the courts have placed on procedural
compliance. The emphasis on procedural issues distracts agency decision makers from
considering and applying ADR techniques that would improve the effectiveness of the
decision-making tool at their disposal; this is perhaps due to the concern that the ADR
process would simply establish one more set of procedural hurdles.

Hesitancy to Involve Others in Decision Making

Another reaction that can be a barrier to the use of ADR is the perception that involving
others will result in loss of power or authority or will force unpleasant interactions with
project opponents. Experience with negotiated rule making and other forms of ADR

demonstrates that agencies are not giving up their proper decision-making authority—consensus cannot be reached without the agency's concurrence. However, ADR does require interaction with project opponents. This is its very purpose! Experience here shows that hostile interactions are more likely when stakeholders are excluded, or only given the minimum opportunity for comment required, than when they are invited into the process as partners. Differences do not disappear with ADR, but a well-constructed process makes the dynamics fundamentally more constructive.

Negotiation is a voluntary process. In some circumstances, parties choose not to participate. Generally, this can be linked to the incentives for participation. Either the design of the process is not perceived as giving adequate opportunity for a group's concerns to be addressed and/or the group may feel that it can win more through litigation. Not all issues can be negotiated, nor should parties be expected to forego appropriate legal recourse. However, opportunities for negotiation are frequently missed. Sometimes the questions for discussion can be creatively reframed based on the parties' underlying reasons for concern; for example, how a mine reclamation plan is designed may be the interest behind objections that an EIS should have been filed.

Cost

ADR does require an investment of time and money at the beginning. It is anticipated than an assessment of benefits for the costs incurred would result in some use of ADR. Still, this can be a real barrier for agencies in budget-conscious times and for some stakeholders. Although the investment of time and money up front may be difficult to make, it may help prevent even greater costs if a NEPA complaint is filed. Creative institutional management may be needed to achieve long-term cost savings within short-term budget cycles. Realistically, this is made even more difficult by the fact that future litigation costs may be borne by different parts of an agency's budget or by different agencies entirely. The establishment of an ADR program within the U.S. Department of Justice and in some state attorney general offices, however, suggests that a broad perspective is possible. On a similarly optimistic note, the U.S. Environmental Protection Agency (EPA), the National Oceanic and Atmospheric Administration, and others have paid the travel expenses of certain stakeholders to participate in consensus-building processes on policy matters.

Federal Advisory Committee Act

Currently, FACA is perceived as a major obstacle to creative federal agency use of consensus-building processes. Passed in 1972, FACA was designed to provide a process by which federal agencies could bring non-federal expertise to bear in agency decision making in such a way that would preclude the disproportionate influence of any one group of interests. FACA requires that: (1) the formation of an advisory committee be formally acknowledged in a charter describing its objectives and the scope of its activities; (2) committee membership reflect balanced representation of points of view; and (3) the process under which the committee functions is open, accessible, and transparent—meetings are announced in advance and are open to the public.

By and large, these requirements are consistent with what would be considered "good practice" characteristics of consensus-building processes. In other words, there is nothing inherent in FACA that is inconsistent with consensus building in most cases. However, in practice, FACA creates additional hurdles. First, the process for chartering a FACA committee can be lengthy and administratively challenging. Some agencies have established procedures for minimizing this administrative burden; others have not. Second, particularly in situations involving local site-specific discussions (as is often the case under NEPA), FACA may be perceived negatively by potentially involved parties as an attempt to "federalize" a process.

Finally, as a budget-cutting measure early in its tenure, the current administration issued Executive Order 5, ordering that the number of FACA committees be cut by one-third and that demonstration of a "compelling need" be required for chartering any new committees. Executive Order 5 has made it extremely difficult for agencies to obtain a charter for any new committees. Although subsequently, in Executive Order 14336, the current administration encouraged agencies to engage in partnering and collaborating with affected parties to develop rules and regulations, the effective use of consensus-building processes in compliance with FACA is currently stymied in many agencies. However, it should be noted that the experience of the EPA with the negotiated rule-making process has demonstrated that FACA does not have to be the ordeal that many other agencies perceive. If the ceiling on FACA charters could be raised or removed by revising or eliminating Executive Order 5, the other barriers could be overcome.

Large Number of Cases (Lack of Screening Criteria)

Realistically, the added costs of ADR mean that formal processes cannot be used in all of the thousands of decisions for which agencies comply with NEPA through an EA. Theoretically, it would be desirable to identify early in the process which cases are likely to be vulnerable to later controversy and litigation. However, this is not easy. Training of agency staff may be helpful, both in ways to integrate improved communication skills into the routine conduct of EAs and EISs and in criteria for determining the suitability of ADR and what form the ADR should take in a given case.

CONCLUSIONS

NEPA was designed on the premise that providing a mechanism for a better informed decision-making process would result in improved and more viable decisions with respect to actions affecting the environment. It was not intended to be—as it has become in many cases—a set of hoops for agencies to jump through after a decision has been made, without the benefit of the very process it prescribes. The negotiated rule-making analogy works (i.e., ADR can strengthen the NEPA process) when the agency wishes to use NEPA to improve the quality of the decision-making process and the decision made. ADR also can reduce possible litigation by helping identify issues early, thus giving the agency and stakeholders sufficient opportunity to address them.

SELECTED REFERENCES

Bear, D. 1995. The National Environmental Policy Act: Its Origins and Evolutions. In *Natural Resources and Environment,* Section of Natural Resources, Energy and Environmental Law of the American Bar Association. 10(2) Fall.

Bingham, G. 1986. *Resolving Environmental Disputes: A Decade of Experience.* The Conservation Foundation, Washington, D.C.

Council on Environmental Quality. 1993. Environmental Quality. The Twenty-Fourth Annual Report of the Council on Environmental Quality. Washington, D.C., p. 371.

Emergency Water Storage Working Committee. 1993. Report for San Diego County Water Authority Staff on the Emergency Water Storage Project. San Diego, California.

Fisher, R., W. Ury, and B. Patton. 1991. *Getting to Yes,* second edition. Penguin Books, New York.

Yost, N.C. 1979. New NEPA Regulations Stress Cooperation Rather than Conflict. *Environmental Consensus* 2(1) March.

CREATING A USER-FRIENDLY NEPA

18

P. Offringa

S enior federal officials manage millions of dollars on an annual basis. They are charged with carrying out the essential mission of an agency and implementing special programs and projects congressionally mandated with each budget cycle, as well as meeting their environmental responsibilities. The decisions made by federal officials regularly affect the quality of life and economic livelihood of every American; however, information to derive informed (better) decisions is often inadequate.

The decision-maker's task is not easy. The search for perfect information upon which to make a decision is elusive. Rarely are all the facts available; if available, they are seldom arrayed or presented to the decision maker in a logical, understandable framework. Assumptions must usually be made to account for unknowns and wide-ranging variables. Placing the facts, the assumptions, and the unknowns into an appropriately weighted decision matrix is a daunting challenge. This challenge is particularly acute in the public sector because it is more risk averse than for the private sector. In the public sector, the usual variables are compounded by the vagaries of public opinion and the weighting (trade-offs) is colored by political concerns. The decision maker stands clearly in the spotlight—with the press and the public ready to pass swift retroactive judgment.

Prominent in this decision context is the National Environmental Policy Act (NEPA), which was designed to ensure that potential environmental impacts have been thoroughly reviewed, considered, and incorporated in any decision. Although on the decision-making stage a relatively short time, NEPA has become a major player in public sector decision making. Virtually every major federal government action has an environmental impact statement (EIS) or an environmental assessment (EA) prepared as part of the decision-making process. Thus, the role of NEPA (and its strengths and weaknesses) in relation to decision making has had a significant impact on federal actions and, consequently, on the resultant quality of life in communities across the nation. If used effectively, NEPA can become much more than a simple environmental barrier; it can effectively reduce much of the public decision-making burden.

NEPA AND THE FEDERAL DECISION MAKER

In theory, the requirements of NEPA are relatively straightforward. The act specifies that federal agencies identify alternative approaches to accomplishing their mission and assess the potential environmental impact of each of these alternatives. This particular requirement was established as a result of congressional concern that mission-oriented agencies were not adequately addressing environmental concerns and that a mere "policy statement" (without something to force an action) would not ensure that agencies would properly account for the environmental impacts of their proposed actions. As a result, a key focus of NEPA is the "action-forcing" provision which requires federal agencies to prepare a detailed statement for any and all "proposals for major federal actions significantly affecting the quality of the human environment." At the heart of this requirement is the belief that if decision makers were presented with an array of choices and explicit trade-offs, they would choose the environmentally preferable path, if it did not hamper the ability to execute their mission. This basic paradigm is a common approach for sound decision making, as illustrated by the military decision-making process in Figure 18.1.

NEPA allows the decision maker to be ultimately responsible for the balancing of environmental effects with the achievement of a stated project objective and indirectly promotes an environmental ethic throughout agencies. Government officials retain the ultimate discretion to make the final decision, as long as they demonstrate that the potential environmental impacts have been thoroughly reviewed and considered in the formation of that decision. This discretion has been supported in numerous instances of case law (e.g., *Alabama v. EPA, Sierra Club v. Larson, Stryker's Bay v. Kariem, Vermont Yankee v. NRDC,* and *Brit v. U.S. Army Corps of Engineers*). Although the decision maker is not required to select any particular option, that decision maker must demonstrate that reasonable consideration has been given to the environmental impacts of the decision. Accompanied by such demonstration, agency decisions can only be reversed where the courts have determined that the agency's action was "arbitrary and capricious," making it extremely difficult to attack an agency's decision relating to substantive matters.

By contrast, the courts have required that decision makers strictly adhere to the procedural matters relating to the NEPA process. These procedural provisions were promulgated in regulations by the Council on Environmental Quality (CEQ), and the courts defer to the CEQ regulations regarding such requirements under NEPA. Most of the successful claims against federal agencies under NEPA have been based on such identified procedural shortcomings.

While case law has clarified the duties and responsibilities of a federal decision maker, it has unfortunately made NEPA a "compliance" issue rather than an aid to decision makers. This resultant focus on the procedural correctness of a NEPA analysis requires the decision maker to evaluate not only the facts and the analysis, but also to

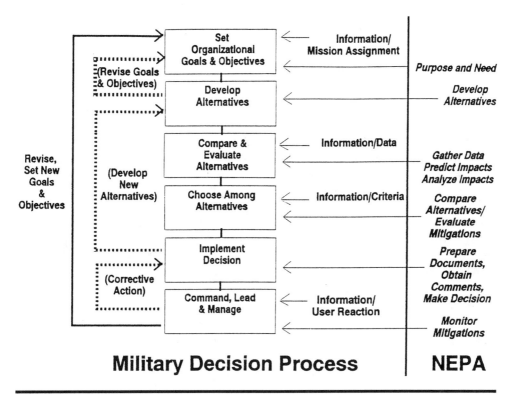

FIGURE 18.1   The military decision-making process parallels NEPA.

consider the correctness and completeness of the process which developed them. Often obfuscating the facts and analysis, NEPA process participants may become consumed with procedures rather than addressing the substantive aspects of NEPA and the information required to make complicated decisions. Documents thus become more important than analysis and decision making. In spite of this trend, the NEPA process can assist decision makers in the analysis and synthesis of issues. Notwithstanding the courts and the lawyers, creativity and risk taking must be introduced into the process for it to be a vital tool. Decision makers must embrace the value of the tool, not the "compliance" (realizing that compliance with law is the minimum standard and does not support a standard of excellence). Difficult decisions regarding alternatives must be clearly and logically identified in the NEPA process. Simple adherence to a mandatory process will not force the execution of sound decision making.

NEPA: AN AID IN DECISION MAKING

Importantly, NEPA mandates the use of a rational process, leading the decision maker through a structured deliberation. Although this structure, by itself, does not ensure good decisions, it does create a framework to guide the overall decision-making process. If used correctly, the NEPA process can create rationality out of chaos, thus showcasing sound analytical work such as cost–benefit analyses, risk assessment, and sustainability analysis.

NEPA requires better definitions of goals and objectives and encourages the delineation of facts (and opinions), often creating clarity where little previously existed. The process requires extensive research into the critical aspects of a proposed action, thus surfacing information that would otherwise remain unknown to the decision maker. NEPA provides a formal process that assures consideration of all environmental impacts before making a decision, partially filling a void in routine agency processes which are often lacking in intra-agency and interagency coordination. Although no organization acts entirely rationally and no decision maker ever has perfect information, maximizing the availability, definition, and clarity of factual materials is one of the key contributions NEPA can make in an agency's own internal decision-making process.

The NEPA process increases the knowledge of the decision maker and exposes the decision-making process to the affected public in an unprecedented manner. Public involvement is required throughout the decision-making life cycle, ensuring that senior officials are more accountable to the public. Although historically viewed as an unnecessary burden, public involvement forces public opinion into agency deliberations, thus ensuring that supporting and dissenting views surface early in the process. If decision makers are willing listeners, they will be sensitive to these views and incorporate them into the decision, thereby reducing the potential for political risk at a later time.

The requirement for public involvement can impact agency deliberations. How a proposed action will "play in Peoria" is often a key consideration early in any decision process, and public reaction to any proposed course of action is often ascertained early in the process. Projects clearly cannot be accomplished without public acceptance, and an old Army adage states that "bad news doesn't get better with age." Therefore, used appropriately, NEPA can become an important commercial mechanism for decision makers.

Through the public involvement process, NEPA has increased the environmental awareness of the average American, creating an open avenue for increased public involvement. Many concerned citizen groups have skillfully used this opportunity to present their views to senior-level public officials. The end result of increased public involvement has been a more informed public, providing the full spectrum of public perceptions early in the decision-making process.

For example, the public was integrated into agency decision making in the 1991 TVA Lake Improvement EIS. As part of this effort, TVA held 11 public meetings attended by over 800 people, gathered 60 representatives of key interest groups in planning sessions, and, in the end, identified over 500 alternatives for TVA to consider in reviewing its policies. The interaction between key public interest groups and TVA led to the identification of more creative alternatives which, in effect, "made the pie bigger," leading to a joint decision involving the people who cared about the lakes and their surroundings.

The engagement of citizens in a structured and rational examination process and the active listening of senior federal officials have elevated the importance of environmental issues in decision making. Many project decisions avoid or mitigate adverse environmental impacts and some decisions depend almost exclusively on the resolution of environmental issues. While there is still some risk that critical environmental considerations could be overlooked, without NEPA critical environmental and socioeconomic impact considerations surely would be overlooked or ignored.

MORE OF THIS OR LESS OF THAT

Trade-offs are inevitable in making complex decisions. NEPA can assist the decision maker in balancing competing demands, encouraging all viewpoints to participate in the decision. The public (including the environmental public) is not homogeneous, and for any given subject, there is usually a variety of perceptions and opinions. Environmental issues can often generate an increased number of decision options, and NEPA provides a mechanism for addressing the significant, important concerns within this plethora of opinions. Careful presentation and disciplined analysis can lead the decision maker to trust the NEPA analysis and documents and use them to support decisions. Good NEPA analysis should always clarify the trade-offs and identify the winners and losers among the stakeholders.

Trade-offs are often difficult for a decision maker. As an example, China, faced with a burgeoning population, was forced to decide whether to massively increase coal burning or develop the Three Gorges Dam on the Yangtze River. Three Gorges will produce 84 billion kilowatt-hours of energy, the equivalent of burning 40 million tons of coal. One choice requires massive resettlement of people; the other is known to cause chronic respiratory health effects. The environmental analysis in such a situation should help explicitly lay out the variety of impacts associated with these alternatives and, with appropriate public involvement, the best decision should be obtained.

Risk assessment tools have not been efficiently integrated into the NEPA process. Such tools could significantly enhance the decision maker's ability to deal with trade-offs and uncertainties. This need does not constitute a unique failure (on the part of NEPA) to integrate these types of concerns, as no integrated national system is available to help agencies address decision trade-offs on a national scale. A NEPA-type of analysis (with integrated risk assessment tools) of federal policies and programs would be useful in addressing the bigger picture.

THE GROWTH OF A PROFESSION

NEPA also stimulated the growth of a professional core of environmental specialists in agencies. Hard research and analysis must be done to aid the decision maker in disaggregating the valid from the invalid, and groups of environmental specialists have been created in most major public sector entities. NEPA requires many different disciplines to analyze information and draw conclusions. In the NEPA context, interdisciplinary requirements go beyond the inclusion of mechanical, electrical, civil, and structural engineers; such requirements also include biologists, sociologists, archaeologists, and a host of other disciplines which had typically not been involved in project planning and decision making. This core of professionals has added depth and dimension to agencies and has changed the culture of entire agencies. These experts provide the decision maker with necessary facts, analyses, and opinions for an informed decision, and the quality of decisions should be better now that this interdisciplinary approach is present.

In summary, NEPA can, if appropriately used, put discipline, logic, and information into the decision-making process, forcing a framework with specific milestones and publicly available credibility.

NEPA: SOME SHORTCOMINGS

In spite of its value as a decision support tool, current NEPA implementation does have some shortcomings which intimately involve key decisions and many different players with many different viewpoints, all implemented in a bureaucratic setting. As a process, NEPA can become solely a process—leading nowhere. There is a tendency to focus on process rather than performance in all bureaucracies. NEPA requires a series of steps in its decision support process, and it is natural for these steps to become bureaucratically complex until the process becomes more important than the product. When NEPA becomes a cumbersome process with a bureaucratic focus that minimizes results, NEPA loses credibility and effectiveness in the support of effective decision making.

NEPA is also extremely resource intensive. Too many EISs are still measured in terms of weight and thickness or fiscal expenditure. Enormous resources, often far out of proportion to the decisions being made, can be expended with little defendable rationale. A long document obtained at a high cost may destroy the credibility and defensibility of the process.

The NEPA process can require an extended time period. Some EISs have taken years to produce due to the conduction of extensive and costly studies. For example, the EIS process for the conversion of Camp Shelby, Mississippi went on for six years while virtually nothing happened. The process can take on a life of its own, relegating the decision (the original purpose of the process) to secondary importance. Some process participants have a vested interest in extending the process as long as possible. Often the tendency to "study an issue to death" negatively affects the decision-maker's perception of the process, and as a result, many shy away from NEPA rather than embracing it as a valued decision support tool. A tool that is not nimble and flexible will be cast aside in search of faster, cheaper ways to achieve the same goal. Time is, indeed, money, and the NEPA process can affect (and delay) many time-sensitive decisions. Sometimes the opponents of a particular decision (or project) are fully aware of federal budget cycles and their deadlines and will use delay as a tactic. The decision maker is often faced with a choice between a suboptimum decision and a timely decision.

Single-purpose players, who represent a single outcome and who are unwilling to accept compromise, have too much influence in some aspects of the NEPA process and often thwart NEPA's inherent ability to resolve conflicts and force federal officials to balance and compromise. Some single-purpose players will often attempt to make environmental studies vulnerable to legal review. At one public meeting on the Camp Shelby EIS, one single-purpose player stated, "We don't want to fix the EISs so they can't be challenged." Each of the valid players in the NEPA process is expected to weigh and balance the advantages and disadvantages of conflicting factors. The presence of uncompromising, single-purpose players inhibits the process, increasing conflict and forcing suboptimal decisions.

To work effectively, NEPA requires knowledgeable people to prepare, review, and manage both the analysis and the process. Although the body of NEPA expertise has grown, there is still an insufficient pool of skilled, available professionals. Additionally, agencies often do not assign their most effective and efficient personnel to NEPA tasks. Even though the head of the agency may be deeply involved in the trade-offs and the decisions affecting a proposal, the best and brightest, well-trained, super-skilled risk takers may be absent in the NEPA process.

The lack of in-house expertise (and the lack of commitment to hire it) has given rise to the growth of "NEPA mills." These private firms, responding to the needs of the marketplace, specialize in the preparation of EISs. Because the NEPA process is perceived as complex, many agencies will contract with these firms for NEPA analyses, often eliminating the primary benefits of NEPA. Contractors are even further removed from the key decision makers (and infrequently interact with decision makers). In the U.S. Army, environmental analyses prepared by in-house staff (and these have been rare) have been briefer, clearer, and more accurate representations of the proposals and the decisions being made. Although many firms are quite good, most resultant documents have enormous amounts of "boiler plate" surrounding minimal facts, analysis, and synthesis.

The requirements of NEPA are often unclear. Although the CEQ regulations are helpful to the NEPA analyst and provide needed flexibility, decision makers are not always clear on specific requirements of NEPA and its potential utility. Some language is vague, some intent is unclear, and agency staff often fail to articulate (to decision makers) what is required by law, what is optional, and what are potential benefits and undesirable consequences. This problem is particularly acute in trade-off analysis, a key ingredient of informed decision making. Clarity is a great aid to the decision maker, and NEPA can become a very effective tool to achieve it.

The current state of NEPA practice does not ensure that environmental protection (mitigation) actions specified in an EIS really are implemented. Most EISs, as documented in their Records of Decision, include mitigation actions which reduce the environmental impact associated with a given decision. In many cases, these mitigations are sizeable and costly, and in spite of the importance of these actions, there is often no mechanism to ensure their execution. Much of the mitigation may not be accomplished as specified, if it is accomplished at all. If this proves to be a systemic problem among enough agencies, the nation is given little environmental protection from the NEPA process.

Finally, and perhaps most importantly, there is currently no measure of cost effectiveness of NEPA compliance actions. The decision maker has no way to assess the costs of the NEPA analysis, the value of the benefits received, or the payback associated with NEPA analyses; however, this same decision maker may need to expend large amounts of money and time to support the process. An effective measure of value versus cost should be developed and included in the standard NEPA process and practice.

MAKING NEPA MORE DECISION-MAKER FRIENDLY

NEPA needs erstwhile decision makers and they need NEPA. The challenge for the future is how to make NEPA work as an effective decision-making tool. Eight modest suggestions are as follows:

1. *Make the process simple*—An easily understood process is more credible and supportable. Those parts of the act (or the CEQ regulations) that are unclear and confusing should be identified and clarified. For example, more clarity is needed to guide decision makers on when to produce an EA or when to produce an EIS. Does the mitigated finding of no significant impact serve the purposes of NEPA better than a complete EIS? The goal should be to eliminate the complexity and uncertainty associated with the current process. Attaining this goal would reduce the resources (money, people, and time) required for NEPA analysis.

2. *Reduce the influence of single-purpose players*—This action may be hard to achieve, but it is essential to the health of the process. Although single-purpose players may never retreat from their single purposes, their unwillingness to compromise should not be allowed to stalemate the process. The decision maker must ensure timely presentation, complete analysis, and full consideration of these views in the decision-making process.

3. *Develop and use more skilled people*—There is still a major shortage of in-house skills in agencies. Decision makers must focus the best and brightest personnel on the NEPA process, and in larger numbers. Sufficient skilled people will make agencies less dependent on outside resources. While it may be unrealistic to add new personnel to the federal payroll, those already on the payroll can be trained to do their own NEPA analysis. NEPA cannot be thought of as something "somebody else" does. It should be something supported and appreciated by everyone in the organization. The goal of NEPA process participants should be to provide better information to decision makers and their staff.

4. *Make NEPA trade-offs more explicit*—Decision making invariably requires trade-offs. Guidance and training are needed on evaluating risks and balancing trade-offs involving major environmental issues. CEQ should publish such guidelines and ensure federal executives are at least aware of common-sense methods for assessing risk. NEPA participants should be trained in conflict management, improving the implementation of the trade-off evaluation process. More NEPA analysis is needed for federal policies and programs, helping policy makers (as well as the NEPA analysts) explicitly cite priorities and explain the analytical bases for decisions. This would assist agency decision makers in addressing trade-offs at the national level, establishing priorities, and designing budgets based on these priorities. The proficiency of participants in NEPA analyses must increase, helping top-level decision makers assess risks and make necessary trade-offs.

5. *Develop a system to monitor predicted effects*—To be fully effective, NEPA must promote action, not just process. Tracking environmentally oriented activities over the project life cycle is essential to ensuring implementation of actions (mitigations) specified in Records of Decision. An effective follow-up mecha-

nism must be promulgated and implemented if decisions are to be meaningful and the commitments are to be honored.

6. ***Promulgate measures of cost effectiveness***—There is a balance point between the benefits and the costs of the NEPA process. This point is undefined, and, similarly, there is no way to measure the value of the NEPA process on a cost–benefit basis. A method should be developed and implemented to provide accurate measures of the value added by the NEPA process.

7. ***Better use of emerging technologies***—The NEPA decision-making process could be significantly improved through the incorporation of emerging technologies. Virtual reality, expert systems, decision support methodologies, and other emerging tools could be used to better define options and assist in the analysis of alternatives. NEPA practitioners should be as skilled in the complexities of decision making as the federal executive they are forcing to consider environmental factors. Agencies and the CEQ should promote better use of emerging technologies, and decision makers should expect or demand the same quality in an environmental briefing as they currently expect in a briefing covering the economics of the project.

8. ***Train the decision maker***—Many actual decision makers are still unfamiliar with the NEPA process. CEQ could offer NEPA training for executive-level decision makers or produce a NEPA decision-makers' guide. Steps should be taken to increase the number of NEPA-knowledgeable decision makers and inject NEPA into the mainstream decision-making processes of agencies.

These eight recommendations, if implemented, would make NEPA more friendly to the user—the decision maker. NEPA and the associated regulations would thus produce better decisions. Perhaps of even greater value, however, would be a credible and effective effort, viewed by all as an asset to the overall federal decision-making process, and NEPA would be embraced, not avoided.

NEPA AND TRIBAL MATTERS

19

G. Mittelstaedt, T. Williams, and K. Ordon

Indian tribes have a unique relationship with the government of the United States. It is therefore not surprising that the National Environmental Policy Act (NEPA) plays a different role for Indian tribes than it does for state and local governments, federal agencies, and private citizens. Why and how this role differs, and how it could be improved, is the subject of this chapter. An important precursor to this analysis, however, is an understanding of how two centuries of interaction between the federal government and Indian tribes was affected by the absence of a national environmental policy and review process.

It was, in fact, only 25 years ago that a national environmental review process was instituted. NEPA of 1969 had, as many scholars have noted, appreciable constitutional dimensions (Suagee, 1990). Its hallmark was its emphasis on direct citizen participation in federal decision making, as well as its encouragement of coordination among affected parties. From a tribal perspective, these two provisions were equally remarkable. If NEPA's substantive goals were met, it clearly would have the potential to become a cornerstone of tribal environmental protection efforts. This potential was furthered by the Council on Environmental Quality (CEQ) regulations that implement NEPA (40 CFR 1500–1508). These regulations require federal agencies to consult with tribes during all phases of the NEPA process. They also require agencies to identify possible conflicts between proposed actions and tribal land use plans. "(T)he procedural requirements imposed on federal agencies by NEPA and the CEQ's Regulations have established meaningful opportunities for state and local government agencies, Indian tribes, private citizens, and public-interest organizations to participate in federal agency decision making" (Suagee, 1990).

NEPA required federal agencies to develop internal procedures for fair and consistent public involvement opportunities. Some agencies were clearly more amenable to the task than others. While the Bureau of Indian Affairs (BIA) did take some actions to comply with NEPA, including the issuance of internal guidance and some efforts to build staff

©CRC Press LLC   CCC 1-57444-072-1 5/97/$100/$.50
St. Lucie Press is an imprint of CRC Press

capacity, NEPA compliance is not seen by the tribes as a very high-priority matter for the BIA (Suagee, 1990). This is reflected in the fact that at one point the BIA had designated fewer than 30 employees to address NEPA issues for over 550 tribes (Williams, 1995). Many tribes believe that agencies, including the BIA, are insensitive to the important distinctions between Indian tribes and the general public. In particular, agencies often fail to recognize the unique cultural and legal standing of tribes in U.S. history. Often, tribes are treated as simply one among many ethnic or socioeconomic groups. The establishment of reservations, however, distinguished tribes by limiting their mobility to a politically defined geographic area. Today, many tribes rely upon these parcels of land for livelihood and community and stand to lose more from environmental degradation than the typical more mobile American (Wenzel, 1992).

From a recent nationwide survey of Indian tribes, it appears that in the 25 years since NEPA's adoption, federal agencies have yet to fully comprehend or institutionalize basic distinctions regarding tribes, and some tribes have yet to realize the potential of NEPA to shape federal agency decision making. While NEPA implementation in Indian country is fraught with administrative, technical, and cultural barriers that diminish its utility, NEPA has been shown to be an effective tool in the protection of natural resources and should not be readily dismissed by Indian tribes. If NEPA's substantive goals, particularly the requirement of meaningful public participation, can be fully realized, then protection of tribal natural resources will be greatly enhanced.

HISTORY OF THE FEDERAL/TRIBAL RELATIONSHIP

Over the last 200 years, federal policies, new legislation, and court rulings have had a profound cumulative impact on both the environment and Indian tribes. For most of this period, there was virtually no systematic examination of the environmental or cultural consequences of federal programs, projects, or policies. Neither individuals nor institutions were able to fully appreciate the inextricable relationship between Indian tribes and the natural environment. As a result, the threads of tribal culture and economy, woven from a history of dependence on the land, gradually eroded. Tribal reverence for the natural environment has sustained itself throughout this period of history, yet many federally triggered events have fundamentally altered tribal economic dependence on the natural environment. To understand the impact of these events is to understand the role of Indian tribes throughout U.S. history.

The early relationship between colonists and Indian tribes was similar in form to "government to government." In general, tribal governments were treated as sovereigns possessing full ownership rights to the land of America.[1] As the U.S. government entered its formative years, however, the tone of the land acquisition debate changed significantly. Command and control became the paradigm of the federal government's Indian policies. "Although Congress spoke of liberality toward the vanquished and realized that some moderation of claims might be necessary to avoid renewal of fighting, its commissioners dictated the boundary lines and offered no compensation for the ceded lands."[2] In the 1823 "Doctrine of Discovery," Chief Justice Marshall wrote that "Indian tribes' rights to complete sovereignty as independent nations were necessarily diminished by the 'discovery' of tribes and their lands by European colonists" (Ordon, 1993).

Federal decision making was heavily influenced by this perspective, generally regarding tribes as a primitive form of social organization. In addition to potentially volatile relations between tribes, the federal government was insensitive to the fact that each tribe had its own language, religion, and social structure. Similarly, federal policies were also aimed at abolishing Indian tribes and assimilating Indians into mainstream society (Suagee and Stearns, 1994). From 1883 to 1909, the BIA conducted an allotment campaign of reservation property. Under the General Allotment Act of 1887, also known as the Dawes Act,[3] each tribal member of a given age was deeded an allotment of land. The object of the allotment era was to entice Indians to become Westernized, to assimilate Indians into mainstream American society, and to make them self-sufficient farmers. Allotments were often accompanied by mules, plows, and basic farm training. These federal government policies had a definitive effect on the relationship of Indians to their land and, by extension, the ecosystems upon which they once thrived.

One example of this approach took place in the Arizona desert with the O'odham Nation. The O'odham people, known as the Pima Indians, for thousands of years employed dry land farming techniques and sophisticated irrigation systems to raise crops in the arid climate. Their traditional lifestyles changed dramatically when the U.S. government began diverting water for neighboring communities. Natural food crops were soon rendered obsolete, and the federal government began shipping food commodities to the Nation in 1959. Canned, preserved, and artificial, the food commodities introduced high levels of sodium and glucose into the traditionally well-balanced diet of the O'odham people. Acute health effects were eventually observed (Simpson and Blackwater, 1995). Today, a profoundly high rate of diabetes affects the O'odham people, with approximately one of every nine persons on the reservation having diabetes.

EFFECTS OF FEDERAL AGENCY ACTIONS AND DIMINISHMENT OF TRIBAL TREATY RIGHTS

Many federal campaigns had profound, long-term effects, not only on tribal health but on the health of ecosystems as well. Ecosystems often reflect human activity that has evolved over many years, and the health of ecosystems is often dependent upon that human activity. For instance, many tribes helped maintain the health and diversity of ecosystems by managing fires that cleared out dangerous fuel loads and improved habitat for numerous plant and animal species. These fires also shaped the landscape for grasses and other vegetation important in the control of disease. Modern management of these ecosystems requires an understanding of how Indians managed them over hundreds of years (King and Rafuse, 1994). Federal agency actions and policies are gradually incorporating this tribal perspective. Holistic perspectives are, in fact, increasingly seen in NEPA scoping, public review, and cultural resources assessment.

Historically, however, the federal government's policies were responsible for degradation of tribal cultural and natural resources and, as a result, the diminishment of tribal treaty rights. This was due, in large part, to federal agency decisions being made in the absence of information on environmental consequences. Had there been a review of environmental and cultural impacts, technical and policy considerations would have received much broader attention. Instead, federal agencies were driven by implicit and explicit incentives to expand their land acquisition activities into Indian territory. At the time, such activities had few visible external "costs." Preservation of tribal culture specifically was not a highly visible consideration, and its inherent worth was notably undervalued in federal decision making. In general, society did not view elements of any cultural environment as having immediate or long-term practical value (King and Rafuse, 1994). Cultural resources were not considered non-renewable.

The federal government's limited cultural perspective resulted in policies that encouraged the overexploitation of resources while neglecting marginal resources such as tribal culture (Muzondo et al., 1990). The water resource policies of this era were exemplified by this problem. Water rights allocation decisions were typified by a short-term, political perspective, such as that which took place in the O'odham Nation case.

Another example occurred in 1982 when a tribe in Washington State brought and won a case against the Federal Energy Regulatory Commission (FERC)[4] for neglecting its federal trust responsibilities. In 1982, FERC issued five preliminary permits for hydroelectric projects in a highly productive river system of tremendous economic value to the Tulalip tribes. The tribes petitioned FERC to develop a comprehensive plan for hydroelectric development in the river system and specifically to establish guidelines and collect data necessary to evaluate the cumulative impact of its actions on the tribes' fisheries resource. Instead, FERC issued the five permits on a case-by-case basis and failed to consider the tribes' concerns. Ironically, because of the nature of the river basin, the most efficient and economical mechanism for evaluating the basin's current and future hydroelectric potential would have been to use the NEPA process. The NEPA process would have provided a framework to study the cumulative effects and to make strategic long-range decisions about power supply in the region.

The court ordered FERC to assess the cumulative effects in this case, yet many federal agency actions were not evaluated in this manner. Although the cumulative effects may have been difficult to assess, a NEPA analysis would have identified major impacts and possibly prevented some if not all of the detrimental impacts. In the FERC case, the NEPA process was conducted, but not adequately. In the case of the Pima Indians, there was no NEPA process. Had a proper NEPA analysis been conducted in either of these cases, the far-reaching effects of water rights reallocation would have been seriously contemplated. For many years, it was even unclear that NEPA was triggered by a tribe's proposal for major activities on its own lands. "Until the decision in *Davis v. Morton,* the BIA considered that the National Environmental Policy Act was inapplicable to Indian lands."[5]

From a historical perspective, consideration of alternatives and cumulative effects would have appreciably altered the course of history for Indian tribes. At a minimum, it is unlikely that the federal government's treaty obligation to protect fish and wildlife habitat, shellfish, and cultural resources would not have come to the brink of extinction. Instead, by the time NEPA required environmental impact analysis, many decades later, the treaty obligations and the fragile ecosystems they purported to protect were nearly decimated.

It was not one policy, or one agency, that was solely responsible for this situation, but the cumulative impact of multiple agency decisions and actions over many years. Previous court decisions maintained that the federal government has an obligation to not only protect tribal resources but to ensure that there is no diminishment of those resources. While the U.S. Congress is the only entity with the power to diminish or alter treaty rights, federal agencies diminish these rights simply by making decisions that are not protective of tribal treaty-reserved resources. Better agency coordination and assessment of cumulative effects will not only improve NEPA implementation but will have a definitive, positive effect on the environment, government-to-government relations, and the livelihood of Indian tribes.

BARRIERS TO EFFECTIVE TRIBAL PARTICIPATION IN THE NEPA PROCESS

Daily encroachments of land use, forestry impacts, water consumption, pollution, and agriculture bring continual impacts to tribal resources. With state and local regulations repeatedly failing to protect critical resources, judicial solutions are often sought as a safety net. Yet courtroom battles take significant time and financial resources, with incomplete results. The results are often not satisfactory and may precipitate additional legal wrangling. Cooperative approaches that prevent litigation by developing cooperative resource protection measures are equally frustrating due to lack of enforcement. In order to develop a strategy of protection which satisfies everyone's needs, compromise is key. Yet the present approach to environmental protection emphasizes control over compromise. When a federal agency acts as the lead in a project, it is also the final decision maker. For Indian tribes, this means that the "government-to-government" playing field is anything but equal. In order to level the playing field, tribes need a more effective decision-making tool. Such a tool would require federal agencies to seek consensus with Indian tribes before a final decision is made. Where consensus is not possible, it would require agencies to enter into dispute resolution with tribes to seek a mutually agreeable solution. An overarching federal mandate to protect the environment upon which treaty resources depend is needed. NEPA, if implemented regularly and consistently, may be the tool (Ordon, 1993).

Numerous factors affect the degree of technical skill and political influence that tribes bring to the NEPA process. Some of these factors are attributable to tribal action, but many are beyond tribes' immediate control. To fully understand the barriers to meaningful tribal participation in the NEPA process, these factors must be considered. While the requirements for NEPA participation are straightforward, the technical and political tools needed to participate effectively are far more complex. For Indian tribes, there are three primary tools. First, tribes need regulatory experience. This experience is gained primarily through intimate knowledge of the language, procedures, and requirements of the key federal environmental statutes. Next, federal agencies need to be culturally aware. The working relationship between Indian tribes and federal agencies is heavily influenced by the degree of cultural sensitivity among federal employees. Finally, tribes need jurisdiction. Recognition of tribal jurisdiction is challenged by many but recognized by few. Only Congress and the courts have the power to modify or alter tribal jurisdiction. If any of these three tools is absent, the effectiveness of tribal participation in any and all aspects of the NEPA process is hampered.

Experience

The CEQ regulations permit tribes to be cooperating agencies in any NEPA analysis which affects their reservations. Participation, however, requires experience with the NEPA process, substantial financial resources, and knowledge of the key federal environmental regulations. The FERC case, for example, required the Tulalip Tribes to acquire intimate knowledge of the Endangered Species Act, the Federal Power Act, and the Fish and Wildlife Act, all while trying to participate effectively in the NEPA process. When tribes are able to cultivate their knowledge, use, and implementation of environmental statutes, it can only serve to strengthen their role in the NEPA process.

For many years, the statutory language of the major environmental statutes exempted tribes' direct participation. Instead of tribes, it was states and federal regulatory agencies that were responsible for implementing national environmental programs. It was unusual for tribes to participate directly in environmental regulatory or grant programs administered by the U.S. Environmental Protection Agency (EPA) or other federal agencies (Ordon, 1993). Participation by tribal governments in various regulatory programs was limited to commenting on relevant projects, permits, or rules proposed by federal agencies. Only recently, through a series of statutory amendments, have tribes been authorized to seek delegation of various federal environmental programs. Specifically, Congress has acknowledged the role of tribes in statutes, such as the Safe Drinking Water Act; the Clean Water Act; the Comprehensive Environmental Response, Compensation and Liability Act; the Oil Pollution Act of 1990; and the Clean Air Act.[6]

Tribal capacity to implement federal statutes relies, however, on more than just a more permissive legal climate. Tribes, for example, must meet "state" requirements in order to obtain primacy for certain authorizations within the Clean Water Act, Safe Drinking Water Act, and others. Meeting "treatment similar to a state" requirements is just one of several obstacles a tribe must contend with to make self-governance a reality. While tribes develop "capacity," they must simultaneously contend with a variety of environmental regulations whose administrative and jurisdictional sources can come from any one of various federal agencies.

Cultural Awareness

NEPA can be a vehicle for bringing cultural awareness to agency decision makers. In many cases, the federal agencies responsible for implementing the environmental regulations are operating without a requisite cultural sensitivity or understanding of tribal treaty rights. As a result, regardless of the statutory language, many federal agencies have been either unwilling or unable to enforce environmental regulations on Indian reservations (Triad Associates, 1977). The personal beliefs and attitudes of agency staff are also a factor to the extent that, over time, they are gradually institutionalized into an agency's operating procedures. The inherent value of tribal culture, the sovereign power of tribes, and the sensitivity of subsistence lifestyles to environmental degradation are not the type of issues frequently incorporated into federal agency training programs.

In order to raise cultural awareness among federal agencies, training programs must be developed that explain the unique content in which tribal environmental management takes place. Tribal cultural and economic perspectives should be distinguished from the perspective with which mainstream society is evaluated. For example, development on

Indian reservations is in some cases inevitable and sometimes, though not always, desirable to tribes. Development presents tribal officials with opportunities to provide employment and business for tribal and non-tribal members, but also requires them to manage and preserve the tribal land base into perpetuity for generations yet to come. Tribal officials recognize that conservation of environmental resources is essential to conservation of tribal culture. Indian youth are taught by such officials to respect nature's "gifts." They are encouraged to take only that which is needed and to use all that they take. They are taught that these gifts of nature are essential to the survival of their culture and economy.

Federal agencies must also comprehend that tribal culture is often reliant upon subsistence use of natural resources. Despite significant technological and social changes, subsistence fishing is still an integral part of many tribal cultures. Observers note that such subsistence activities have symbolic, social, cultural, and economic value. They add that subsistence activities may enhance closeness to nature, self-reliance, and independence, as well as causing social and cultural ties through the sharing of resources. Federal agencies, in order to uphold their trust responsibilities and ensure effective tribal participation in the NEPA process, must understand cultural norms such as this through agencywide training.

Until such training takes place on a broad scale, federal agencies will continue to operate on old institutional norms. These norms are frequently observed by tribes that participate in the NEPA process. Tribal respondents who participated in a nationwide survey made several observations about federal agencies carrying out NEPA functions: (1) they found that implementation of NEPA is inconsistent from one agency to the next and sometimes within individual agencies from one region to the next, (2) they found that agencies do not adequately incorporate cultural resources protection as an important issue in the scoping process, and (3) they found that agencies address Indian tribes as interested parties rather than on a government-to-government basis. Tribal concerns such as those cited here can, however, be reasonably addressed through modifications in federal agency training procedures. Within each agency, the NEPA liaison specifically should receive treaty rights training. Environmental staff should be trained in the cultural differences and important values associated with different tribes. It should be emphasized in training that tribal governance structures, cultural attitudes, and economic and geographic characteristics vary widely; not all tribes can be treated the same. Finally, respondents in the survey noted that the senior-level staff of federal agencies should provide clear policy direction to their staff regarding tribal sovereignty. While it is apparent that senior-level staff are increasingly sensitive to tribal considerations, as yet there is no mechanism for institutionalizing this sensitivity throughout all levels of the federal government.

Jurisdiction

For Indian tribes, operating on a government-to-government basis without adequate regulatory tools is a daunting task. The task is rendered even more difficult, however, when tribes must contend with challenges to their inherent sovereignty. Federal agency recognition of tribal jurisdiction is paramount to effective tribal participation in the NEPA process.

Prior to the federal government's recognition of tribal sovereignty, it was unusual for federal agencies to operate on a government-to-government basis with Indian tribes. Recognition of tribal sovereignty by the president and Congress had a profound impact on the interaction of tribes and agency staff. In the early 1960s, President Kennedy publicly acknowledged the sovereignty of tribes. President Nixon, and later President Reagan, affirmed this position by establishing a Federal Indian Policy. Reagan's Indian Policy statement explicitly endorsed the twin themes of tribal self-government and tribal economic self-sufficiency.[7] Congress followed suit by enacting significant legislation in support of tribal self-government, including the Indian Self-Determination and Education Assistance Act of 1975 (Suagee and Stearns, 1994).

The judicial branch also affirmed tribal treaty rights during this period. In *U.S. v. Washington,* tribes were restored their treaty-reserved fishing rights. In this case, Puget Sound and coastal tribes joined forces with the United States to interpret the treaties and resolve battles between the state of Washington and Indians over treaty fishing rights. In 1994, a subproceeding in *U.S. v. Washington* clarified the treaties once more and declared that these same fishing rights apply to shellfish harvesting as well.

Restoration of tribal fishing rights was not, however, the hallmark of the Boldt decision. Rather, it was Judge Boldt's recognition that it would not be enough for tribes to have a fishing right if the fish had ceased to exist. Without habitat protection, Boldt argued, there would be no fishing rights. Truly progressive for its time, this reasoning is embodied in the Phase II aspect of *U.S. v. Washington.* Phase II anticipated that the fisheries resource would gradually be devalued in the state's economy and that high premiums would be placed on land uses other than those protective of fish habitat. In many ways, Phase II language reflected much of the treaty language to the extent that it recognized the direct relationship between conservation of natural resources and conservation of tribal culture.

The language from these cases and treaties is the springboard for government-to-government resource management between federal, tribal, and state governments. *U.S. v. Washington* forced the state to deal as a co-manager of fisheries resources with Washington tribes. In recent years, tribes and states have forged powerful alliances to bring about changes in management of forest practices, fisheries harvest and habitat protection, and water resources management. Through a series of compacts and cooperative agreements, tribes, states, local governments, business, agriculture, and citizens have worked together to seek solutions to contentious resource management issues which affect treaty resources. These agreements, along with the promulgation of NEPA and the amendment of major environmental statutes, provided tribes with a historic opportunity, as well as an enormous challenge (Suagee, 1990).

TRIBAL RECOMMENDATIONS FOR IMPROVING THE PERFORMANCE OF NEPA

NEPA is binding on all federal agencies and is therefore viewed as a potentially valuable tool for tribes. If used correctly, the procedural requirements NEPA imposes on federal agencies can create meaningful opportunities for tribes to shape federal decision making. It requires, for example, that "prior to making any detailed statement, the responsible federal official shall consult with and obtain the comments of any federal agency which has jurisdiction by law or possesses special expertise with respect to the environmental impact involved" (Suagee, 1990). In a recent nationwide survey of Indian tribes, the majority of respondents did in fact believe NEPA to be an effective and flexible tool for protecting tribal resources. Some also believed that regardless of its drawbacks, without NEPA, federal agencies would not consider tribal perspectives and would subsequently approve environmentally unsound projects.

NEPA could also create opportunities for tribes by creating a level playing field. The NEPA process can not only help federal/tribal relations but can help facilitate discussions between tribes and state and local governments and thereby help avert potential litigation. For tribes that do not yet have a tribal framework in place, NEPA can be an important tool in the protection of reservation and treaty-protected resources. This is especially true if tribes take specific actions to address or circumvent the "institutional norm" problems described earlier. For example, "tribes and others whose interest may be affected by actions taken by the BIA and other federal agencies should become involved early in the NEPA process. For actions that would require an EIS, tribes should participate during scoping, and they should consider becoming cooperating agencies. If the proposed action may adversely affect tribal interests, tribes should suggest specific alternatives and/or mitigation measures. If tribes lack the professional expertise to formulate specific alternatives, they may want to prevail upon their federal trustee for assistance, or they may want to build alliances with educational institutions, non-profit public interest organizations, and others who do have the expertise" (Suagee, 1990).

In some cases, it may behoove tribes to develop their own NEPA-type processes. A "mini-NEPA," or Tribal Environmental Policy Act (TEPA), can be drafted such that it meets the tribes' unique environmental and cultural resource protection needs. Due to its broad-based language, a TEPA can also serve as the springboard for a tribe to develop a more comprehensive regulatory framework. Development and implementation of a TEPA can, for example, help a tribe to identify and organize its technical, administrative, and legal resources. These resources can then be employed to develop other regulations, such as an administrative procedures act (APA), water quality standards, and clean air regulations. For tribes considering the adoption of federally delegable programs, it is in fact desirable to first adopt an APA. An APA ensures due process for non-Indians who may be impacted by proposed regulations and therefore protects tribes from potential litigation. Moreover, an APA establishes emergency and nuisance laws not otherwise found in media-specific statutes.

The performance of NEPA is not, however, solely a responsibility of federal agencies. There are a number of measures tribes can take to improve their participation in the NEPA process. A recent report by Americans for Indian Opportunity (undated) identified several of these measures. For example, tribes can further their relationship with federal agencies by ensuring that federal agency department heads and policy-level staff meet directly with tribal leadership. In doing so, they are furthering the commitment of the federal government to interact with tribes on a government-to-government basis. In addition, Indian tribes can assist federal agencies by developing a training module on cultural values, concerns, and perspectives that incorporates the contribution of tribal elders. Presently, there is no "inclusive, broadly understood definition of the cultural environment. As a result, important elements of the cultural environment 'fall through the cracks' between elements that are either defined in statute or broadly understood in practice" (King and Rafuse, 1994). In fact, a review of several EISs found that only two cultural considerations are routinely incorporated—historic properties and socioeconomics. The development of a cultural module for federal agency staff would elevate the idea that cultural resources protection should be a vital function of NEPA.

Other measures for improving tribal capacity involve action by Congress and the EPA. Specifically, they need to clarify and provide uniformity in regulatory language pertaining to environmental laws. A specific measure Congress can take would be to promulgate a National Indian Environmental Protection Act. The act, unlike all others, would specifically recognize and encompass Indian culture and values as a resource for protection.

In addition, tribal, state, and federal governments need to develop protocols for operating on a government-to-government basis. Memoranda of understanding and memoranda of agreement with county, state, and federal agencies should be sought in order to facilitate these relationships.

With specific regard to NEPA, respondents in the NEPA survey identified several ways to enhance tribal participation and provided policy, administrative, and practical recommendations. The policy recommendations include suggestions for improving NEPA implementation by developing uniform policy guidelines for agencies to follow. Most of the policy recommendations provided by the respondents can be implemented through policy guidance or rule making. Some, however, may require changes in the CEQ regulations in order to accomplish the objective. Regardless, improvements can begin simply by ensuring that NEPA is consistently implemented by and within all federal agencies. Moreover, the process should be streamlined such that agencies will view NEPA as a management evaluation tool rather than a formality. In doing so, agencies will be required to weigh the project benefits against the total cost of the project, including the cost of mitigating adverse impacts. Weighing project costs and benefits is a valuable tool of NEPA if used correctly. However, agencies attempting to balance "costs and benefits" must remember that these concepts are subjective and that tribes may define them differently than the general public.

Another of the key policy recommendations addressed how federal agencies can be not only the lead in NEPA processes but act as the final decision maker as well. This situation is a clear abrogation of the treaty-mandated government-to-government relationship between federal agencies and Indian tribes. Federal agencies should be required to seek consensus with Indian tribes before they issue a final decision. Moreover, in the event that consensus is not attained, the two parties should be required to reach agreement via a dispute resolution mechanism. The alternative dispute resolution method currently used by the BIA could serve this purpose, although other facilitation and mediation methods should also be explored.

Additional policy recommendations included ensuring the accountability of NEPA decision makers. Lead agencies would be accountable for treating tribes as governments rather than as members of the public. Lead agencies would have to respond to tribal input specifically and would prohibit balancing tribal needs with those of the public. In instances where more than one tribe was involved, it would be inappropriate to balance tribal interests against one another. Agencies involved in the scoping process would also have to address health and environmental equity issues thoroughly in light of the disproportionate impact to tribal communities.

Another integral step to improve the NEPA process would be to expand the definition of cultural resources to include more than physical or tangible resources. A mechanism should be provided to maintain the confidentiality of cultural resource information. This is particularly important in light of the fact that, despite elements of the cultural environment having their own protective legislation, "only NEPA provides a statutory basis for addressing and controlling impacts on the cultural environment in its entirety, and only NEPA provides a vehicle for presenting all statutory requirements to decisionmakers in a cohesive, comprehensive, and balanced manner" (King and Rafuse, 1994).

NEPA's performance would be significantly enhanced if federal agencies were routinely required to monitor impacts and conduct cumulative impact analyses of their actions. Other policy suggestions included providing a mechanism for tribes to receive advance funding to participate in NEPA and to further utilize EPA. For example, EPA has responsibility under Section 309 of the Clean Air Act to review all NEPA analyses. EPA could act as an independent third party and be responsible for reviewing all NEPA-related federal agency decisions that impact Indian tribes. If the review process were streamlined, a third-party review, other than the courts, would be feasible. Finally, EPA can assist tribal participation in NEPA by fully implementing the Indian Policy and helping tribes develop environmental programs and expertise.

These administrative recommendations pertain to purely process-oriented matters and can largely be accomplished through agency guidelines. Most of them pertain to the NEPA procedure; however, a few of the recommendations entail modification of how agencies coordinate and consult with tribes. Paramount, however, is that tribes be routinely involved earlier in the NEPA process so that their input can be used to help formulate alternatives, conduct the technical analysis, and prepare the documentation. The documents themselves could be simplified and the process requirements streamlined. The quality and style of the information should be improved to make it more culturally sensitive.

The administrative recommendations also identified the need to build in a long-term approach by which agencies can address cumulative effects, monitor and mitigate their projects, and apply adaptive management. An example of this was seen in the Boldt case, wherein tribal, state, and federal agencies were required to use the best available information and technology to implement the court's management decision. Yet, adaptive management has not always been used in implementing the Boldt case, as the court has had no mechanism for monitoring implementation of its decision. A NEPA requirement to this effect would provide for such monitoring. At the same time, a more open decision-making process should be established to avoid decisions being made during "pre-scoping" or for scoping to occur without tribal input. This latter problem can be remedied if notice provisions are mailed sufficiently prior to the comment deadlines. Efforts must also be taken to ensure that notices are addressed to the correct individuals.

These practical recommendations address matters that would significantly improve the role and level of participation by tribes in NEPA processes. While most of these recommendations are targeted at agencies in general, a number of these practical recommendations are targeted toward tribes as well. First, it is suggested that tribes be provided with specific training, as well as funds to attend the training. To institutionalize tribal participation, permanent funding should be provided for tribes to hire and maintain staff dedicated to dealing with NEPA processes. Training should also be made available for agencies to improve their communication and coordination with tribes, to better understand tribal governance structures, and to become more aware of cultural differences and needs. BIA staff should be provided with training in NEPA as well as receive funding to maintain staff dedicated to carrying out NEPA functions.

General improvements can be accomplished through better coordination and communication between and within agencies. Communication between agencies and tribes should be improved such that agencies can assist tribes with participation in the NEPA process. Tribes should also coordinate with other local tribes or tribal resource organizations to divide the labor and cost of participating in NEPA. An added benefit of this approach is that joining efforts allows tribes to forge a united viewpoint.

SUMMARY

In the CEQ effectiveness study of NEPA, tribal respondents assessing the effectiveness of NEPA found participation in the process a worthwhile but arduous endeavor with hard-won results. Their experience in the NEPA process is reflective of limited financial and staff resources, coupled with the historic inability of federal agencies to invite and empower tribes to participate effectively.

Despite process problems, the respondents envision continued participation in NEPA matters and made a number of recommendations which would enhance their ability to participate. The key recommendations include: (1) fostering a better government-to-government relationship with agencies, (2) providing culturally relevant NEPA training for tribes, (3) ensuring firm tribal funding to maintain staff dedicated to NEPA matters, (4) assuring consistent NEPA implementation between agencies, (5) broadening the definition of cultural resources and providing a mechanism to keep this information confidential, (6) providing agencies with training in tribal governance and cultural resource matters, (7) providing training and funding for the BIA so that it can more effectively carry out NEPA functions, and (8) encouraging EPA to assist tribes to develop and participate more effectively in environmental programs (Ordon and Mittelstaedt, 1994).

Most of the recommendations made by the tribal respondents can be accomplished by means other than policy changes to NEPA. However, policy changes must be made in order to provide agencies with guidance to achieve consistency in the application and accountability of NEPA decision making. Beyond NEPA, effective management of tribal environmental programs will require efforts by Indians and non-Indians alike and by tribal, county, state, and federal governments. Tribal capacity building cannot occur in a vacuum. Mechanisms must be established by which local, state, and federal governments can be introduced to the tribal perspective. Forums must be created through which all interested and affected parties have a guaranteed opportunity to comment. Agreements must be sought by which tribes can function on a cooperative, government-to-government basis with local, state, and federal agencies. Finally, a permanent, stable funding mechanism must be identified with which tribes can conduct long-term planning. Long-term planning is synonymous with capacity building, and without it, tribal efforts at effective participation in environmental review processes will remain impeded.

NOTES

1. Taken from Cohen, F. 1982. *Handbook of Federal Indian Law* (1982 ed.). Bobbs-Merrill, Charlottesville, Virginia, pp. 81, 109–121.
2. Prucha, F.P. 1962. *American Indian Policy in the Formative Years: The Indian Trade and Intercourse Acts 1790–1834.* Harvard University Press, Cambridge, Massachusetts; taken from Cohen, F. 1982. *Handbook of Federal Indian Law* (1982 ed.). Bobbs-Merrill, Charlottesville, Virginia, p. 34.
3. Act of February 8, 1887, ch. 119, 24 Stat. 388.
4. *Washington State Department of Fisheries, Washington State Department of Game, and Tulalip Tribes of Washington v. Federal Energy Regulatory Commission,* 9th Cir. Court of Appeals, 1985.
5. 42 U.S.C. 4321–4347. Taken from Cohen, F. 1982. *Handbook of Federal Indian Law* (1982 ed). Bobbs-Merrill, Charlottesville, Virginia, pp. 90–91.
6. O'Connell et al. Delegations of Federal Environmental Regulatory Authority to Indian Tribes. Environmental and Land Use Law Section Midyear #339. Washington State Bar Association, 1993.
7. Statement by the President, Office of the Press Secretary, January 24, 1983.

SELECTED REFERENCES

Americans for Indian Opportunity. Undated. Partners for the Protection of Tribal Environments. Final Report. Washington, D.C.

King, T.F. and E. Rafuse. 1994. NEPA and the Cultural Environment: An Assessment and Recommendations. Prepared for Council on Environmental Quality, Washington, D.C., September.

Muzondo, T.R., K.M. Miranda, and A.L. Bovenberg. 1990. Public Policy and the Environment: A Survey of the Literature. Paper prepared for the International Monetary Fund, Fiscal Affairs Department, June.

Ordon, K. 1993. Tribal Role in Growth Management. Environmental and Land Use Law Section Midyear #339. Washington State Bar Association.

Ordon, K. and G. Mittelstaedt. 1994. Indian Tribes Assess the Effectiveness of NEPA. Report for Council on Environmental Quality.

Simpson, K. (American Indian Environmental Office) and E. Blackwater (Gila River Indian Community). 1995. Personal communication. March.

Suagee, D.B. 1990. The Application of the National Environmental Policy Act to "Development" in Indian Country. *American Indian Law Review* 16:2.

Suagee, D.B. and C.T. Stearns. 1994. Indigenous Self-Government, Environmental Protection, and the Consent of the Governed: A Tribal Environmental Review Process. *Colorado Journal of International Environmental Law and Policy* p. 59.

Triad Associates. 1977. Tulalip Reservation Environmental Study. Bellevue, Washington.

Wenzel, L. 1992. Environmental Risk in Indian Country. Environmental Protection Agency, Washington, D.C.

Williams, T. 1995. Personal communication. March.

THE ROLE OF NEPA IN SUSTAINABLE DEVELOPMENT

20

H. Kaufman

What is past is prologue.

—Shakespeare,
in words from *The Tempest*,
carved into the base of the
National Archives Building

Most great ideas have been thought of before. A depressing notion perhaps, especially when one is in the midst of the incisive revelation of all time. But it is precisely because most great ideas have been conceived and even attempted by others that it behooves all visionaries to look backward as well as forward— learning from what has been tried increases the likelihood that a particular vision will succeed.

Such is the case with "sustainable development," the idea that society can meet social, environmental, and economic needs without trading off one at great expense to the other, now and into the future. Advocacy of the concept has mushroomed since the 1987 publication of the Brundtland Commission's *Our Common Future* (World Commission on Environment and Development, 1987) and the succeeding United Nations Conference on Environment and Development, held in Rio de Janeiro in 1992. All over the world, from villages to multinational institutions, proponents are ardently working to give life to the potentially oxymoronic term. In keeping with the sustainable development covenant signed at Rio, "Agenda 21," many countries have established blue-ribbon commissions to devise policies that will foster the integration of social, environmental, and economic needs.

The United States is no exception. President Clinton's Council on Sustainable Development (PCSD) is only one of many assemblies trying to chart the nation's way sustainably into the 21st century.

©CRC Press LLC CCC 1-57444-072-1 5/97/$100/$.50
St. Lucie Press is an imprint of CRC Press

But sustainable development is not a new concept in America. In the post-Rio enthusiasm to define sustainability, the fact that the country has had a sustainable development policy for over 25 years, comprehensively articulated in the National Environmental Policy Act (NEPA) of 1969, seems to have been largely forgotten. By reacquainting themselves with NEPA, sustainable development visionaries can learn from and build upon experience with this legislation.

The nascent teams of sustainability thinkers might consider the following questions: What should and could NEPA's role in U.S. sustainability be? What are its demonstrated strengths that could help reconcile environmental, social, and economic needs? What are its shortcomings? This chapter attempts to stimulate thinking about possible answers.

THE NATIONAL ENVIRONMENTAL POLICY ACT

As J. William Futrell (1994) states in "The Transition to Sustainable Development Law," "The most important step in the transition...will be a reaffirmation of sustainability as a prime national goal for...every development sector. In theory, Congress endorses the value of sustainability as a national policy in NEPA..." Indeed, NEPA is the only federal statute that requires agencies to consider the economic, social, and environmental consequences of their proposed actions:

> ...it is the continuing policy of the Federal Government, in cooperation with state and local governments, and other concerned public and private organizations, to use all practicable means and measures...in a manner calculated to foster and promote the general welfare, to create and maintain conditions under which man [sic] and nature can exist in productive harmony, and fulfill the social, economic, and other requirements of present and future generations of Americans.

The similarity between sustainable development as defined in the Nixon-era NEPA and by the Brundtland group is striking: "...development that meets the needs of the present without compromising the ability of future generations to meet their own needs."

Not only does NEPA establish sustainable development as national policy, it explicitly includes nearly all the sustainability provisions called for by contemporary sustainable development proponents. These include:

- Integration of human, environmental, and economic needs
- Public participation in decision making
- Intergenerational equity
- Use of environmental indicators and accounting
- Need for scientific analysis with recognition of its limits
- Recognition of the interrelationships among population growth and density, technology, industry, and other influences on the environment
- Incorporation of sustainability goals in all federal agency policies
- Consistency of policies within agencies
- Cooperation among agencies
- Cooperation among state and local governments, private entities, and the international community

Yet despite the foresight of NEPA's progenitors, the United States continues to witness a stunning lack of sustainability. Initiatives like "Sustainable Seattle" and the "Collaboration of Community Foundations for the Gulf of Maine" represent much of the positive action taking place locally and regionally toward making sustainable development a reality. For many engaged in the task at the national level, however, debate over the concept of sustainable development continues while environmental, social, and economic systems continue to decline. It appears that NEPA has fallen short of its sustainability goals.

NEPA'S POTENTIAL TO FOSTER SUSTAINABLE DEVELOPMENT

NEPA contains many provisions that could go a long way toward helping the United States promote human and economic development in an environmentally sound manner. The degree to which those provisions are implemented depends to a great extent on presidential will. Following are some of the additional reasons why NEPA's potential has not been fully realized.

The Statute versus the Regulations

Although a legislative vehicle for fostering sustainable development has inherent limitations, the primary reason NEPA has not succeeded in fulfilling its sustainable development objectives is because the *regulations to implement the statute are almost exclusively limited to one small portion of the law.* That portion calls for environmental impact assessments (EIAs) of proposed federal actions, such as building a dam or granting certain permits. Indeed, a major accomplishment of NEPA that bodes well for sustainable development is that it has resulted in an awareness of the need to minimize negative environmental impacts of projects when they are conceived. However, NEPA's broader sustainable development policy goals would have greater impact if the rest of the law were implemented as earnestly as the EIA provision. The most the regulations do to ensure that the entirety of the act is followed is to state that the "provisions of the act and of these regulations must be read together as a whole in order to comply with the spirit and the letter of the law." Thus NEPA has become synonymous with the EIA process, and the statute and the regulations are commonly considered one and the same.[1]

Integration of Human, Environmental, and Economic Needs

One of the many unfulfilled provisions of NEPA that is also a hallmark of sustainable development is the need to minimize competition among three of society's most pressing needs: human welfare, a healthy environment, and a productive economy. At the time NEPA was enacted, the environment was virtually neglected in federal decision making; economic and social concerns were more conventional decision-making factors. NEPA was key to elevating consideration of the environment.[2]

The emphasis on the environment is clear in NEPA's statement of purpose:

> To declare a national policy which will encourage productive and enjoyable harmony between man and his environment; to promote efforts which will

prevent or eliminate damage to the environment and biosphere and stimulate the health and welfare of man; to enrich the understanding of the ecological systems and natural resources important to the Nation; and to establish a Council on Environmental Quality (CEQ).

Conscientious consideration of the environment remains critically important when decisions are made that could affect it, but with NEPA *largely limited to analyzing project-level environmental impacts* of federally sponsored projects, its potential to help government and citizen decision makers contemplate what social, economic, or infrastructure development should take place in a region over time—a key to sustainable development—is diminished.

Conversely, the *consideration of the potential social, economic, and environmental benefits of conservation* is another untapped NEPA mechanism. NEPA regulations generally only come into play now when a decision or action is being contemplated (or virtually decided). Yet, the NEPA statute states that CEQ is supposed to recommend to the president national policies to foster the nation's conservation goals. Ideally, NEPA helps ensure that project development takes place in the most environmentally benign fashion, but as historically practiced, it does not take into account the societal need for non-development in certain places. NEPA's current project development construct leaves no room for assessing the values of leaving an area relatively untouched.

Citizen and Government Participation

One widely agreed-upon tenet of sustainable development is *public participation* in local and national decisions that affect people's lives and their environment. By virtue of the EIA process, NEPA exposed federal decision making on projects with environmental impacts unlike any previous statute and created mechanisms for public input. NEPA even states that every citizen is responsible for contributing to the sustainability goals the law embodies. Public disclosure and the opportunity for public involvement and influence on projects are among NEPA's greatest achievements.

Despite this success, NEPA's transparency requirements are not always sufficient and are compounded by *limited awareness of the statute.* For those citizens who know about the law, most do not long to curl up with an environmental impact statement for a good read. Many federal decision makers are unfamiliar with the range of NEPA's authorities and the intended roles of CEQ, as evidenced by several proposals to abolish the agency.

One avenue for improving awareness of NEPA and public participation is enhanced *CEQ consultation* with representatives of science, industry, agriculture, labor, conservation organizations, state and local governments, and others. Various advisory committees existed until early in the Carter administration, and the reestablishment of similar bodies, perhaps on an issue-specific basis, might enhance stakeholder participation and coordination among local and state agencies.

An opportunity to improve federal agency awareness and involvement is to invoke NEPA's *requirement that federal agencies review their authority, regulations, and policies to identify any deficiencies or inconsistencies* that prohibit full compliance. Reports on these reviews were due to the president on July 1, 1971. Not one agency reported any inconsistencies. Only now are several agencies writing sustainable development policies.

The existence of the PCSD is a chance for the administration and PCSD members—including the Secretaries of Commerce, Interior, Energy, Transportation, Housing, Agriculture, Education and State Departments and the Environmental Protection Agency administrator—to develop such policies for their agencies in the context of the long-overdue NEPA review. CEQ and PCSD could coordinate the effort to ensure that the required consistency with NEPA goals within agencies and cooperation among agencies are achieved.

The CEQ Annual Report to Congress is another underutilized existing mechanism called for by NEPA that could improve information dissemination and public participation. This document is sought by journalists and academicians for its national environmental data. However, most citizens and environmental practitioners have never heard of it. It could become a user-friendly, on-line, annual report card on environmental, social, and economic trends. These trends could be assessed according to regional- or sector-appropriate sustainable development indicators, and data could be aggregated at the regional, state, or ecosystem levels, rather than only at the national level as they are now. It could describe local, state, regional, and national sustainable development activities. It could be not only a data book, but a workbook that people and agencies could use to further their sustainable development efforts.

The annual report is supposed to include *recommendations for remedying deficiencies in existing federal programs.* The legislative recommendations could consist not only of suggestions for new legislation or regulations if warranted, but could emphasize suggestions for efficiency and effectiveness improvements in existing laws. The report could also recommend voluntary challenge programs, economic incentives, or other desperately needed new and creative means of achieving greater environmental protection along with social and economic progress.

Most importantly, the report could be a vehicle to implement a number of neglected NEPA provisions. For example, the federal government is supposed to inform and advise people about *environmental restoration.* Information on techniques, keys to success, and project descriptions could be provided. NEPA's recognition of the worldwide and long-range character of environmental problems, and the associated need to maximize *international cooperation* to mitigate them, could also be addressed. Status reports on U.S. activities that affect sustainability outside our borders could be included, such as progress on international treaties. In addition to being available through international computer networks, the report could be distributed to the United Nations Commission on Sustainable Development Secretariat.

CEQ could contract or coordinate with groups engaged in aspects of the reporting work described here, such as the World Resource Institute's previous *Annual Information Please Environmental Almanac*, the Worldwatch Institute's *State of the World* (e.g., a "State of the Nation"), and National Biological Service data. NEPA provides for such contracting.

A Multidisciplinary Approach

Another dormant mandate of NEPA is the direction to *integrate natural and social sciences and environmental design arts in planning and decision making.* The call for an interdisciplinary approach harks to an awareness that single disciplines and "rational" sciences do not produce comprehensive solutions to social, environmental, or economic dilemmas. Yet NEPA regulations are partly based on the premise that rationality, complete knowledge, and accurate forecasting for decision making are attainable. An over-reliance on science and other supposedly rational disciplines such as economics does not accommodate the fact that the ability to understand and foretell environmental, social, and economic consequences of proposed actions is limited.

An interdisciplinary approach is essential to carry out the section of NEPA which states that agencies must work with CEQ to ensure that *unquantifiable and unquantified environmental amenities and values are considered* along with economic ones. Paying heed to environmental externalities through the limited tool of full-cost accounting was mandated by NEPA yet is only recently becoming an acceptable factor in cost–benefit analysis.

WHERE NEPA IS NOT ENOUGH

Most of the shortcomings described above could be remedied by modifying the implementation of NEPA without changing the statute. However, even though NEPA eloquently articulates a national sustainable development policy and provides ways to implement it, there are at least two significant reasons why NEPA alone cannot serve as the nation's only road map to a sustainable society. NEPA must be implemented to work in concert with other policies and social institutions which together will redress these gaps.

One reason is that NEPA does not and cannot address social inequity and poverty. The other reason is that a law by itself cannot bring about sustainable development. As David Buzzelli, co-chair of the PCSD has said, "Sustainable development must become part of our culture and ethic....At the core of sustainable development is the search for a new regulatory system to rise above command and control policies...to include voluntary actions, market incentives, partnerships, and consensus building...this will happen when sustainable development becomes a social and institutional value."

The sustainable development concept has become virtually ubiquitous around the globe among people of all social strata because there is nothing objectionable about it. Nearly everyone can agree with the goal of a healthy environment and economic prosperity, without doing anything to achieve it.

But the value Buzzelli refers to may be starting to infiltrate American culture and influence behavior. The sustainability values that gave rise to and are expressed in NEPA are gaining popularity, probably in large part because of the increasing frequency and intensity of combined environmental, economic, and social crises, such as those involving diminishing salmon and redwood stocks. These crises have prompted broader recognition of the interdependence of and need to protect the environment, the economy, and human welfare.

ENHANCING NEPA'S ROLE IN SUSTAINABLE DEVELOPMENT: CONCLUSIONS

As this chapter points out, NEPA's limited implementation has prevented it from achieving its full potential to help the country develop in a sustainable manner. With the current attention to sustainable development at the federal level, a review of NEPA is imperative. This would avoid "reinventing the wheel" and ensure that the elements of success and failure in the status quo are understood, so that any modifications to the statute and its implementing regulations or other alternatives will have the greatest likelihood of success. The public and political leaders should take advantage of historical hindsight as they craft environmental, social, and economic policies appropriate to the 1990s and the coming century.

Before any new sustainable development policies or scenarios are drafted, sustainable development advocates should consider the following steps to help fulfill NEPA's potential:

1. Conduct a thorough review of the statute and the regulations with sustainable development goals in mind.
2. Determine what barriers to more thorough NEPA policy implementation may exist and how they could be overcome.
3. Increase awareness of NEPA and its goals among local, state, and federal agencies and the public.
4. Take fuller advantage of NEPA's participatory provisions through CEQ (e.g., the annual report), outside consultation, and international interchange.
5. Examine the role of the CEQ in light of its potential to fulfill NEPA's sustainable development mandates.
6. Create a mechanism to monitor the success of NEPA's renewed role in sustainable development and to make periodic adjustments in its implementation.

NEPA has clear limitations as a tool for sustainable development, but it does spell out an exemplary sustainable development policy for the country. If the policy were adhered to and CEQ had and used its authority to see that all sections of the statute were implemented, NEPA would more than adequately provide a sound, comprehensive, national framework for sustainable development.

ACKNOWLEDGMENTS

The author would like to thank Dinah Bear, Brandon Carter, Eugene Cleckley, Roger Dower, Janet Gille, Rose Hoffman, Keith Laughlin, Rhey Solomon, Harriet Tregoning, Lissa Widoff, Gary Williams, and Madelyn Yucht for their assistance with this chapter. Special thanks to Ray Clark.

NOTES

1. The Council on Environmental Quality under President Carter tried to include other substantive aspects of NEPA in the regulations. CEQ was prevented from doing so by other parts of the administration, including the Office of Management and Budget.
2. Trade-offs among environmental, economic, and social factors are assessed in the record of decision (ROD)—the agency declaration that the environmental impact statement prepared for a proposed project adequately considered environmental values.

SELECTED REFERENCES

Futrell, J.W. 1994. The Transition to Sustainable Development Law. Research Brief No. 3, Environmental Law Institute, Washington, D.C.

World Commission on Environment and Development. 1987. *Our Common Future*. Oxford University Press, Oxford, England.

NEPA'S INTERDISCIPLINARY MANDATE: REDIRECTION FOR SUSTAINABILITY

<hr />

21

<hr />

A.F. Euston

The National Environmental Policy Act of 1969 (NEPA)[1] embodies one underlying integrative challenge: to secure society's future sustainability and thus to redesign this urban civilization which, for now, is unsustainably redesigning this planet. Ours is an urban–rural industrial civilization. Its challenge, and that of NEPA, is to reconcile harmoniously the social, the economic, and the environmental (built and natural) components. Accordingly, NEPA's Section 102(2)(A), the interdisciplinary environmental design mandate, is at the heart of this challenge.

NEPA is a law ready to promote America's sustainability, an outcome dependent on the sustainability of the modern global, urban–rural, industrial civilization. Today, science questions such an outcome.[2] In the language of former World Bank economist Herman Daly,[3] our rapidly urbanizing world is already "full." Environment, ecology, trade, urbanization, population, resources, limits, and justice are now all interconnected. This means understanding their interaction and creating harmless outcomes, or it means overall decline. Section 102(2)(A) of NEPA, the interdisciplinary environmental design mandate, poses such an integrative urban and environmental design societal challenge.[4]

This examination of NEPA's first quarter century, therefore, concerns the full range of crises and complexities now at work in today's world. Where ecology is concerned, society's focus today is on environmental–economic systems integration. Thus, the emphasis falls on segmented industrial and consumer consequences. These are necessary to face, yet it is ultimately through addressing our overarching built environment choices that modern humanity can hope to steer itself along the path to sustainability. Becoming "sustainable" demands that NEPA's ecologically focused principles be applied in a deliberate process of integration for both urbanization and ecology. Doing so will mean mobilizing and informing citizens, specialists, lawyers, and leaders alike by the use and teaching of American society's wealth of interdisciplinary approaches.

<hr />

©CRC Press LLC CCC 1-57444-072-1 5/97/$100/$.50
St. Lucie Press is an imprint of CRC Press

Such outcomes will allow society to acquire a fresh consciousness about its true interests—an interdisciplinary consciousness. As it is, however, society remains blind in two potentially fatal respects. These can each be remedied. Both deal with the environment. We do not "see" ecology (the natural environmental systems), nor do we "see" urbanization (the built environmental systems). Consequently, we do not readily "see" that these two must and can become integrated. There is, of course, our tendency to ignore the future as well. Our communities are where we live. It is their changes and their consequences that in the aggregate are to determine our future's outcome.

As for "interdisciplinary" itself, this word often connotes orthodoxies or guilds of special competency and professionalism. These days there is even the term "transdisciplinary" for those offended by the confines of specialization and its exclusions. As introduced here, however, the key concepts of the "concerned interdisciplinary-minded citizen" and "interdisciplinary citizenship" transcend these limitations of credentialism and institutional hierarchies or of (white male) social pyramids such as may be found within academia, science, or bureaucracy. It can invoke any of these plus—plus ordinary people acting out of concern for complex interests within the contexts of open public discourse and decision making. It is in this informed, democratic, and creative sense that the use of interdisciplinary communication, and its NEPA mandate, offers the most strategic means for mobilizing America on to sustainability.

TOWARD THE INTERDISCIPLINARY REDIRECTION OF NEPA

Despite a near total public media embargo of news and commentary about this supremely profound set of events,[5] in 1992 the Union of Concerned Scientists (UCS), the National Academy of Sciences with its British counterpart, and other science groups declared their urgent warnings for civilization about the present ecologically disastrous course. The UCS released the following message:

> The "World Scientists' Warning to Humanity," signed by 1575 scientists from 69 countries...stresses that continuation of many destructive human activities may so alter the living world that it will be unable to sustain life in the manner we know....A great change in our stewardship of the earth and the life on it is required....No more than one or a few decades remain before the chance to avert the threats we now confront will be lost....Signers include 99 out of the 196 living scientists who are Nobel laureates.[6]

This is what our scientists have to tell us about our civilization.

Our species is nearing half urban now. The United States already has 90% of the human population living in metropolitan areas. The predominant technical, resource, and natural impacts of modern industrial civilization—both social and ecological—come from urbanization and the built environment. Far more can be done to curb these impacts and reintegrate the aggregated workings of the built environment within the dictates of the natural environment. This calls specifically for interdisciplinary urban and environmental design. Shaping the ecological outcomes and the human consequences ahead is nothing if not an interdisciplinary challenge. NEPA's challenge is a creative and hopeful call to action, however, rather than a negative, police-power call for reaction.

Integrating such complex matters implies the cultivation of an interdisciplinary approach in much of our daily problem solving. While the act applies to federal-level problems, NEPA Section 102(2)(A)—in effect a preamble to NEPA—is generic to our culture as a whole, if it is to sustain itself into the future. This section reads: "(2) all agencies of the Federal Government shall—(A) Utilize a systematic, interdisciplinary approach which will ensure the integrated use of the natural and social sciences and the environmental design arts in planning and decision making which may have an impact on man's (sic) environment." This chapter, in addressing the future potential of this mandate, is written as a complement to other chapters in this volume.[7, 8]

Everywhere are crises of overpopulation, and everywhere are crises of local to global ecology.[9] Take the cod. "Endless resources, free for the taking, are what made America possible, and it started with the cod. Cod spurred the settlement of the New World. They were its first industry and export. They fed the Pilgrims. And now, after 500 years, from Georges Banks right up to the Grand, they are all but gone."[10] In such contexts as these, NEPA will bear profoundly upon this ubiquitous urban civilization's future and the consequences of that for the human species. This will become especially true for NEPA's interdisciplinary environmental design mandate, once it has been aggressively mobilized.

In the words of NEPA's principal author, Lynton K. Caldwell, however, "What has been lacking and what is needed is the political will to enable NEPA to achieve its declared intent."[11] To his assertion could be added that NEPA (and its equivalents) can deliver on future sustainability only as society grasps that its future self-interest lies in reconciling both economics and urbanization within the dictates of their ultimate dependency on earth's natural ecological systems of support, when the shared and tragic costs of doing otherwise fully impact upon public consciousness, and when common cause is joined for the good of all—commensurate in America to our heroic response to Axis challenges in World War II—recognizing how urgent a factor time has become, if sustainability is the common goal.

Ultimately, the "domestic tranquility" of the Preamble[12] to the Constitution depends on the reconciliation of our socioeconomics (our politics) with nature and its ecologies. Doing so will not be easy, as NEPA temporizing by bureaucracy and society shows. Cordoned off, watered down, and handed down (to other bureaucratic levels) is NEPA's fate in many current federal contexts. For example, new and expanded federally aided roads have received abundant environmental impact statement (EIS) coverage, but once urban interstate highway battles were resolved in the 1970s, and prior to the Intermodal Surface Transportation Efficiency Act of 1991 (ISTEA),[13] little was asked in the process about alternatives to the investment in the new roads themselves. Federal mortgaging for hundreds of new subdivisions consisting of hundreds of homes has not been viewed as consequential. Federal and local strategies for prime farmland, open space, and wetlands conservation have had to cope with such a stance.

Is there blame for an imperfect NEPA first quarter century? Yes, no doubt, but it accords to society as a whole. Until recently, media, academia, leaders, and others have been largely somnolent about urbanization and its effect on future sustainability. What, then, needs to be different, if we are to grasp that our vital interests lay in the rebalancing of our own economics and urbanization with ecology?

First, the application of NEPA itself needs redirection. Emphasis today is on the EIS; hence, NEPA is thought of as strictly a police-power device, flowing from such constructs as the adversarial proceeding. Yet the act is one of far broader vision. If redirected, it can become pivotal in the guiding of positive and creative approaches to policy, administration, on-the-ground implementation, and especially to the elevation of public awareness and dialog.

Next, if the full genius of NEPA is to empower civilization toward a sustainable future, it should be employed for integrating the two systems of ecology and urbanization. Gradually, with the benefit of creative, inventive interdisciplinary processes, we can mobilize both our individual choice and concerted decision making. This we can do within businesses, industries, schools, tourism, and many other contexts. Meanwhile, local incrementalism is making a difference across the spectrum of disciplines and purviews of society within local government, industry, and citizen-based action.[14] Increasingly aided by electronics, this process offers great hope for success in the building of both results and enthusiasm for an ecological approach to the reinventing of modern urbanization.

Time, like the soil, is fast eroding. As ecological decline accelerates, society must rapidly find fresh decision-making approaches that employ interdisciplinary values, distinctions, concepts, inventions, and designs. Such approaches can be promoted broadly through public use and communications. Interdisciplinary-minded people are engaged in doing this locally already, redesigning our urban–suburban–rural future through sustainable community design.[15] Civilization's systems of power and politics will need to catch on, too, before it is too late.

SEVEN SOCIETAL PREMISES BASIC TO THE INTERDISCIPLINARY MANDATE

Today, America's experiment with democracy confronts its boundaries in ecology, in geographic expansionism, in economic competitiveness, and in matters of ethical fairness to its own citizens, to other peoples, and to future generations. Up to now, other large civilizations have succumbed one by one for many reasons, including ecological decline within their spheres of geographic influence. Typically, however, most human settlements were pretty well integrated with nature, but not today. With industrial civilization now omnipresent, its typically negative urban consequences happen everywhere. As asserted above, NEPA's great challenge to this civilization—to integrate our future urban systems with nature's ecological systems—means interdisciplinary decision making of all kinds and at all levels.

Seven premises basic to sustainability are, therefore, cited as a backdrop for NEPA's future. These premises are basic to modern culture and its future and, like NEPA, commend society's widespread use of interdisciplinary decision making:

1. *Premise 1*—As modern science has warned, very major changes in how civilization now behaves ecologically are required in less than one generation's span of time. This includes current behaviors related to our unbridled urbanizing and denaturing of the land.[16]
2. *Premise 2*—Ecology is to become the conscious bottom line of modern civilization's economic bottom lines.

3. *Premise 3*—When the human population has doubled (say 40 years hence, given present rates), urban population would then have quadrupled, and most of humanity should by then be metropolitan-scale urban dwellers, producers, and consumers.

4. *Premise 4*—Urbanization's infrastructures—its networks (roads, utilities, etc.), its in-fill (buildings, public spaces, etc.), and its natural support systems (farms, aquifers, etc.)—are this civilization's predominant industrial product, major source of impact on nature and people, and its primary driver of unsustainable consumption as a function of urban resource inefficiencies, technical deficiencies, consumptive lifestyles, low-durability products, sprawl development, etc.

5. *Premise 5*—Concerned and interdisciplinary-minded citizens, acting as specialists, educators, communicators, officials, and proponents, are modern civilization's hope and conscience for a humane and viable outcome in readapting this urban-rural industrial civilization back to the fixed realities of nature, if enough time remains.

6. *Premise 6*—In honoring NEPA: (a) at the federal level, an interdisciplinary mix of natural and social sciences must be creatively, that is inventively, brought to bear on society's larger enterprise of urbanization, and (b) at all levels of governance, an integrative process of planning, design, and investment must become normal to government, business, and to citizenship. Both outcomes are ones that electronics can help us make possible.

7. *Premise 7*—The majority of humanity seeking democracy must engage in understanding the consequences of societal actions affecting natural ecology, ultimately choosing to be concerned "interdisciplinary" citizens themselves.

FIVE CONTEXTS FOR NEPA'S INTERDISCIPLINARY IMPLEMENTATION

Nature's ecological systems are driving civilization's need for recasting our uses of NEPA. As with our Constitution, we are blessed to have this bedrock statute. As Caldwell's companion chapter states, this is new law; it is too new "to attain the importance and priority accorded such century-old political concerns as taxation, defense, education, civil liberties, and the economy." Even so, NEPA's objective of human compliance with natural ecology is destined to reshape within decades future taxation, defense, education, and the economy; if not, ecology will surely condition our stance toward civil liberties—and all the rest.

To focus upon what interdisciplinarity can become implies five contexts regarding future implementation of the NEPA Section 102(2)(A) mandate. A redirected NEPA must be driven by ecological reality and political conviction. Then a creative transition toward sustainability could result. The "how" is inferred by the following five contexts for interdisciplinary understanding:

1. *Context 1*—An interpretive framework is needed for legal, policy, and administrative understanding that broadly defines what "interdisciplinary" can mean in future NEPA contexts. As discussed further on, the expanding role of the in-

formed citizen is critical. Concerned and informed citizens perform a most vital part in shaping opinion and understanding. Education is essential for all citizens in a complex reality such as ours. Yet the lay person prepared to take a public stand, one indigenous to specific contexts at question, may have crucial insight and reference to bring to the issues. Beyond this, it is imperative that those claiming control over decisions be able to grasp what it is that motivates concerns other than their own. Then, both formal and informal interdisciplinary structures will be necessary. Teams, public or community design "charettes" (intensive, facilitated short-term choice-making efforts), visioning and studying processes, ad hoc structures to convene stakeholders, and many other formats could be utilized.

2. ***Context 2***—Conceptual frameworks are needed that suggest how technical and administrative venues for interdisciplinary problem solving, management, and strategic planning are inherent to NEPA Section 102(2)(A). An example can be taken from the concept of sustainable development infrastructures. Conventionally, the term "infrastructure" implies physical public works networks such as roads, utility lines, power plants, etc. Now, severe ecological consequences stem from all kinds of systems required to support modern urbanization. The need is to become comprehensive about addressing these consequences. Accordingly, six systems of infrastructure are important to consider: the natural ecological systems; the conventional physical networks; the in-fill between these networks of homes, parks, workplaces, etc.; the electronics and communications systems (tele-purchasing, -medicine, -commuting); regional resources of farms, lakes, etc.; and global resources.

3. ***Context 3***—Review of cases in law where some primal precedent setting has begun to array potential meanings of "interdisciplinary." We lack as yet a body of well-focused decisions. Interdisciplinary deliberations have involved suits such as: (a) *Trinity* (Church, New York City) *v. Romney* concerning stability "tipping points" for a neighborhood impacted by an influx of lower income housing units; (b) Three Mile Island litigation supporting claimants for compensation from the psychological effects of the nuclear plant ordeal there; and (c) the higher density housing implications at the new town-in-town of Cedar-Riverside in Minneapolis. A Court Master was introduced in the latter instance. The ebb and flow of laws and feelings that surrounds such issues as these cases raised during the 1970s will not desist. Understanding is an evolutionary matter. What constitutes meaningful expertise, special competencies, and informed citizen judgment will continue to confront our judicial process around society's reconciliations with the dictates of natural ecological systems.

4. ***Context 4***—Federal administrative answers that have been implemented consistent with, if not explicit to, NEPA interdisciplinary policy making. These examples are legion. In transportation, there have been public processes involving complex joint ventures such as the Boston Transportation Planning Review. It was a first in seeking to give a state options for public transit which would not be entirely dictated by Interstate Highway Trust Funds that focus on roads, even where they are not appropriate. The educational design charettes of the 1970s were instrumental in dozens of communities for the introduction of fresh dialogue

about both children's learning options and the future shape of their living contexts. Highly specialized research efforts, often involving those most directly affected, have been performed. Examples include *Boston Urban Wilds—A Natural Area Conservation Program* (1976), *Designing for Aging* (1980), Baltimore's comprehensive plan of 1981 (which brought capital budgeting directly into the service of rationalized uses of land and development), or the interdisciplinary strategies of many other communities, often with federal support, that enabled people's lives to be bettered through careful choices.

5. *Context 5*—An instance where federal agency NEPA policy has played a direct part in the administration of interdisciplinary follow-through (i.e., the regulations of the Department of Housing and Urban Development). These regulations quoted NEPA's interdisciplinary mandate, tied it in with the planning and eligible administrative functions the agency supported, and encouraged thereby an administrative philosophy of breadth and sensitivity where communities were prepared to ask themselves complex questions about their urbanization choices.

THE GROWING TREND TOWARD "INTERDISCIPLINARY CITIZENSHIP" TODAY

Overseas and at the United Nations, public dialogue is very much about sustaining the race.[17] In the United States, this is not so, nor is there significant understanding yet that we are consuming our inheritors' ecological futures, although the next generation's fiscal future is part of today's debates. Ideology and denial, rather than inquiry, often absorb the communications media. From the standpoint of biological resources, soils, water quality, or land as productive capital, our dialogue remains fragmentary, incoherent, and abstract.

Here the paradigm of "sustainability" enters. Its early voice was included in NEPA and whatever it may have invoked in its 1969 passage.[18] NEPA is our most grounded statutory bridgework into the real future of critical resource choices. Although NEPA is nowhere to be seen on the political or public media screen, as ecological information does its work and concerned local interdisciplinary-minded citizens mobilize to address sustainability, its omission will not be maintained. As it happens, on the 25th anniversary of NEPA, a new balance is underway politically. Into this rebalancing a place for complex judgments, complex information, and complex communications may yet step. These, of course, are "interdisciplinary" complexities, but ones which an increasing diversity of citizens are entering.

Communications bridges between America's urbanization and wider public understanding of its alternative consequences are being built. New links are being formed by information technologies and driven by increasing voter skepticism, awareness, and concern about the future. As this aspect of public dialogue grows, the interdisciplinary environmental design mandate of NEPA can serve our nation's transition toward sustainability as a fulcrum whose pivotal role is to center our debates on society's choices for the future. In this sense, "choices" are set by what people prefer; "decisions" are the expenditures and commitments made by those of wealth, power, and administrative authority. Meanwhile, privileged "decision making"—what senators, for example, have traditionally regarded as their own elevated provenance—may already be developing demographically into more pluralistic, grass-roots "choice making."

In 1992, multiple printings occurred of a book entitled *Changing Course—A Global Business Perspective on Development and the Environment.*[19] Its "Declaration of the Business Council for Sustainable Development" called for "appropriate information," "appropriate communications," "shifts in corporate attitudes," "changes in lifestyles" and other responses that are, in the words of the declaration, "best achieved by a synthesis of economic instruments designed to correct distortions and encourage innovation and continuous improvement." This is what concerned private sector individuals have begun to conclude about society's current reality.

Much earlier, the forecasting of the late Herman Kahn in 1967 (when NEPA was in gestation) offered many scenarios and few conclusions. Today, we are confronted by two contrasting scenarios posed by Kahn and Anthony Weiner in their book *The Year 2000— A Framework for Speculation on the Next Thirty-Three Years.*[20] These two scenarios are the paired alternatives of the "More Integrated Worlds" and the "Greater Disarray Worlds."[21] Unless the industrialized ("more integrated") world comes to its senses ecologically, hence redesigns itself and its urbanization, these concepts are but temporizing ones about current geopolitics and not about our civilization's future.

These early futurists did give impetus to America's willingness to think ahead. Now "futurists" are a discipline, and a potentially vital one for the cultivating of wider public consciousness. *The Year 2000* missed its mark on energy—particularly nuclear energy's place today, but it gathered many significant alternatives together into a somewhat coherent, if antesustainability, neoboosterism whole. One such contribution was a look beyond the year 2000 to the "Post-Mass Consumption (or 'Post-Industrial') Society." While ours remains very much an industrializing civilization, attention should be directed to three of several dozen possible attributes that the post-2000 world might evince: (1) "business firms are no longer the major source of innovation," (2) a "small world," and (3) a "learning society."[22]

On the first attribute, about business and innovation, it is the essence of NEPA, and of its small family of forward-looking federal enactments, such as ISTEA, that citizens are regarded as party to decision making and that, by this status, they too become potential innovators. Involvement of ordinary citizens is at the heart of interdisciplinary environmental design. NEPA's earlier years demonstrated such a promise.[23] It is a promise whereby Jefferson's informed citizenry do deliver the goods in judgment, balance, and invention.

On the second attribute, a "small world" is not only likely, it is ours today. Recalling Herman Daly's words, "Our world is full," today's rampant resource extraction, clear-cutting, and bulldozing are understood by such observers as human "overshoot," the precursors of possible human "die-back." The Central Intelligence Agency is already offering estimates for next year of tens of millions starving to death due to scarcity and the barriers to near-term food surplus distributions.[24] The Worldwatch Institute has pointed out that sea catches and grain yields leveled off in 1994, whereas no human population leveling is in sight.[25] These realities have a bearing on Americans pressing to have more say in that which truly affects us. Concerned citizens are increasingly conversant about choices that officials and special interests have held as strictly their own to determine.

NEPA's informed public has been increasing even as federal-level compliance and integrity have waned.

Concerning the third attribute, that of a "learning society," vast new access to quality information is on-line already via the Internet, and much more is to come. As citizens actively concerned about their own interest in where society is heading grow in number, influence, and awareness, the implications are of greatest consequence for interdisciplinary problem solving. Interdisciplinary-minded citizen involvement can be anticipated as a wave of the future. Three voices spanning our political spectrum point to such a possibility. For example, Max Singer, co-founder with Herman Kahn of the Hudson Institute, concludes, in his 1993 book, *The Real World Order—Zones of Peace/Zones of Turmoil,*[26] that "the danger of a big war in the future depends not on international politics and strategy but on the continuation of democracy in the great powers, especially in the United States."

Critical observer and pundit Kevin Phillips questions whether our popular democracy is working all that well. In his book, *Arrogant Capital—Washington, Wall Street, and the Frustration of American Politics,* he says that the public will have to be heard from during the 1990s. He decries "a special-interest ridden national capital and calcified government institutions tied to a tired party system, an overload of lawyers, speculators, and rentiers (the very wealthy owners), a depleted Calvinism, and a plague of debt."[27] His "Blue-print for a Political Revolution," with it nine proposals, would return power to the people. His prognosis is more favorable for this happening than it is for redressing the decline of this nation's collective fortunes. He does, for these purposes, identify a range of powerful trends to suggest that what is likely favors a significantly heightened popular say in future U.S. outcomes.

In between Singer and Phillips is author Sam Harris, founder of Results, a non-profit organization that promotes the end of hunger in the world. His recent book concerns redeeming public confidence in our system of governance. In his 1994 book, *Reclaiming Our Democracy—Healing the Break Between People and Government,* he reasons why increasing empowerment of citizens lies ahead. Yet he inserts in his introduction an interesting caveat by quoting a student in a college audience: "When it all seemed hopeless, we were off the hook, but if you're right, if individuals can make a difference with their government, that means we might have to do something. That's what is making us uncomfortable."[28]

A related interpretation from one highly seasoned observer, Lowell Weicker, the former senator and governor from Connecticut, is that the people themselves are behind. They have withdrawn in the hopes that governance could be left up to paid professionals. In a recent *New York Times Magazine* interview, he comments, "Why the hell are we tearing ourselves apart? That's different from saying we can't do better. We can, but right now the American people, as I've said before, just better understand that the problem doesn't reside with a few politicians. It resides with them—the fact that they've got to go ahead and participate. They've got to demand accountability, which could very well be a painful process."[29]

These diverse perspectives are those of concerned Americans. We may all crave doing the right thing, but there is poorly informed public discourse about what that could be when it comes to the complexities of sustainability.[30] This is the challenge of interdisciplinary communications.

CONCLUSIONS

The fate of the human family is dependent upon our making a conscious choice for its ecological sustainability. This choice is being posed now to present generations, and from here on it is to be maintained as a choice that is central to modern civilization. The state of today's information complexity and political confusion makes such a choice seems unreal to most Americans. This is changing as the non-partisan movement in America toward future sustainability begins to grow.

More a function of inevitability than of optimism, this appears to be a movement of concerned yet hopeful individuals. As they have grown in number, their identification of effective options for action has grown.[31] Their outlooks are integrative, or "interdisciplinary," in nature. Some people are engaged as part of their livelihoods, others as volunteers, and many others as indirect proponents or adherents. In what? In that which NEPA espouses, if it cannot effectively mandate as yet. Recognizing this broadly based movement, in 1993 President Clinton established a multisector civil dialogue on our nation's future by creating the President's Council on Sustainable Development.[32]

Underlying this movement are such trends as demand-side electric power management, cogeneration for power and thermal uses, industrial ecology parks to optimize efficiencies, and resource conservation or reduced agro-forestry chemical use. These trends and their technologies involve interdisciplinary problem solving. For example, efficient wastewater treatment today involves biology as much as it does engineering. Both disciplines must combine to secure the great efficiencies now possible. Lay people, including officials and citizens, play key roles in positioning the new natural wastewater treatment technologies. The media is learning how to explain such things to the public. It is in the nature of such activities that those involved become "concerned interdisciplinary citizens" in the process.

The arguments posed here concern NEPA's future and its effectiveness as a tool of government. The 1987 United Nations' landmark publication *Our Common Future* asserted that nations and states that have stronger environmental agendas are more prosperous and stable, and these assertions are being confirmed. Generally, society's hidden costs from ecological deterioration exceed the costs of creative alternatives. Today's heated question for government is how to temper the rigidities of conventional regulatory processes. One answer is to foster corrective and remedial invention. For industry, the question then becomes how to reap a reward for its up-front investments in sustainable alternative technologies. These often represent creative design challenges whose costs can offset those of negative legal challenges.

A wider public consciousness is growing in America, fed by a higher quality of information about alternatives that are more sustainable. However, public commitment gradually continues to grow for ecology as the new bottom line for the economic bottom line. Where all parties—government, industry, and the public—pull in the same direction, the "level playing fields" and "win–win solutions" will follow.

Is there a time frame for these possibilities to ripen? One thought, reinforced by the past quarter century since NEPA began, is that a trend continues in our culture, the 53-year Kondratieff cycle of economics, which indicates a resurgence of public expectations of many kinds. The year 2022 A.D. would be that cycle's anniversary for NEPA. By then, public concern could have culminated in a demand for across-the-board attention to sustainability in the United States. That may be altogether too late, according to science, but much can be done to pave the way for commitment and creativity by then.

Perhaps in another quarter century some type of a Marshall Plan, perhaps a "National Sustainability Mobilization Act," will be politically acceptable, if gravely overdue. Meanwhile, in every American community, our nation's interdisciplinary-minded citizens have their work cut out for them. Hopefully, during the National Environmental Policy Act's second 25 years, the law will make ample way for their contributions and approaches.

NOTES AND SELECTED REFERENCES

1. The National Environmental Policy Act of 1969, Pub. L. 91-190, 42 U.S.C. 4321–4347, January 1, 1970, as amended by Pub. L. 94-52, July 3, 1975, and Pub. L. 94-83, August 9, 1975, 42 U.S.C. Sec. 4371 (1976). Executive Office of the President. *Regulations for Implementing the Procedural Provisions of the National Environmental Policy Act.* 43 Fed. Reg. 55978–56007, November 29, 1978.

2. World's Leading Scientists Issue Urgent Warning to Humanity. Press Release, Union of Concerned Scientists, November 18, 1992, from Atlanta, Georgia, as circulated by Nexus, but carried by only five U.S. newspapers and a few others.

3. Daly, H.E. and J. Cobb. 1989. *For the Common Good: Redirecting the Economy Towards Community, the Environment and a Sustainable Future.* Beacon Press, Boston; Greenprint (Merlin Press), London, 1990.

4. Euston, A.F. 1990. NEPA and the Next America: Designing Our Transition to Global Sustainability. *Pace Environmental Law Review* 7(2). Article was a keynote address before "NEPA 20th Year" conference of CEQ (9/21–23/1989), held at the Department of State Auditorium.

5. The Union of Concerned Scientists' Warning (see note 2) was carried by the Nexus International News Service, but its records of several days following indicated only five U.S. newspapers addressed this extraordinary story. Similarly, the joint NAS/British Union warning of 1992 received scant domestic coverage. Members at a subsequent Washington (D.C.) Environmental Writers Association meeting were neither surprised by nor suspecting any machinations beyond journalism's prevailing view that ecology is not news if in competition with sundry alternatives (per personal discussion).

6. Quoted from the eight-page release (see note 2).

7. Caldwell, L.K. Implementing NEPA: A Non-Technical Political Task (Chapter 3 herein); Andrews, R.N.L. The Unfinished Business of National Environmental Policy (Chapter 6 herein).

8. Phillips, K. 1994. *Arrogant Capital—Washington, Wall Street, and the Frustration of American Politics.* Little, Brown, Boston.

9. Weiner, J. 1990. *The Next One Hundred Years—Shaping the Fate of Our Living Earth.* Bantam Books, New York.

10. Kunzig, R. 1995. Twilight of the Cod. *Discover the World of Science* p. 46.

11. Caldwell, L.K. (see note 7).

12. Sudia, T. 1989. The Gravity Bottle—The World as a Closed System. *We the People—Letters of the Institute for Domestic Tranquility* 4(6). "Discovering what the steady-state biological condition for any given place on earth is and adapting human activities to that end is obviously the most simple-minded direct way to utilize to its fullest advantage the tremendous energy of the equilibrating biological system" (page 5).

13. The Intermodal Surface Transportation Policy Act of 1991, Pub. L. 102-240, Stat. 1914, amended Title 23, U.S.C. It requires "a continuing, comprehensive, and coordinated transportation planning process in metropolitan areas and states."

14. Evidence of this action is vast. A sample of current reporting includes: *From Rio to the Capitols—*

State Strategies for Sustainable Development. Conference Report of the Commonwealth of Kentucky. May 25–28, 1993, 182 pp.; Hawken, Paul. 1993. *The Ecology of Commerce—A Declaration of Sustainability.* Harper Business, New York; Troxel, James P., Ed. 1995. *Government Works—Profiles of People Making a Difference.* Miles Press, Alexandria, Virginia.

15. Since 1986 within HUD, the author has worked explicitly with civic groups and local governments across the United States on sustainable community design and development interdisciplinary projects. A related estimate for the United States is that in 1995 all metropolitan areas, half of all cities, and a fifth of all townships had such activities underway. Reflecting this level of local action, hundreds of conferences; thousands of published articles, newsletters, and books; and citizens in the hundreds of thousands are already focused on the concept or paradigm of sustainability through specific local agendas, programs, and projects. Several dozen papers by the author are available on the topic from A. Euston, Room 7244, HUD, Washington, D.C. 20410.

16. See note 2.

17. The United Nations has conducted global summit conferences beginning with Habitat I of 1976 in Vancouver and including the Environmental Summit of 1993 in Rio, the Population Summit of 1994 in Cairo, the Social Summit of 1995 in Copenhagen, its women's summit in 1995 in China, and Habitat II of 1996 in Istanbul.

18. Related federal enactments of this tumultuous period reflect the ferment that accompanied concern for the environment. Major laws were passed for historic preservation (1966) intergovernmental cooperation (1968), flood insurance (1968), architectural barriers (1968), NEPA (1969), uniform relocation and clean air (1970), water (1972), endangered species (1973), historic and archaeological data (1974), and energy conservation and protection (1974).

19. Schmidheiny, S. 1992. *Changing Course—A Global Business Perspective on Development and the Environment.* Business Council for Sustainable Development, MIT Press, Cambridge, Massachusetts.

20. Kahn H. and A.J. Weiner. 1967. *The Year 2000—A Framework for Speculation on the Next Thirty-Three Years.* Macmillan, New York.

21. See note 20, p. 249, Table I.

22. See note 20, p. 25, Table IX.

23. Hundreds of NEPA-related complex multipurpose, multiagency, multidisciplinary citizen-based community processes occurred from the late 1960s through the early 1980s and since. A list of reports on these would include A Report on Community Environmental Planning Workshops, Lawrence Halprin and Associates, April–June, 1971, for San Francisco and Indianapolis; The Dallas Ecological Study, City of Dallas, 1973, Weiming Lu, AICP, project director, involving surveys by League of Women Voters volunteers, and consultation by Philip Lewis, ASLA of the University of Wisconsin; the NSF-funded Urban Design Role in Local Government, 1976, Weiming Lu, Kevin Lynch, Andrew Euston, et al.; HUD-funded Lessons from Local Experience—CDBG/ Urban Environmental Design, 1983, Rice Center, MIT, University of California, Berkeley; and R/UDAT—Regional & Urban Design Assistance Teams (a two-decade retrospective guidebook), 1992, The American Institute of Architects R/UDAT Program.

24. News releases during Winter 1994–95 on likely global famines.

25. Brown, L.R. 1994. Facing Food Insecurity. In *State of the World.* L.R. Brown, Ed. W.W. Norton, New York, Chapter 10.

26. Singer, M. and A. Wildavsky. 1993. *The Real World Order—Zones of Peace/Zones of Turmoil.* Chatham House Publishers, Chatham, New Jersey.

27. See note 8.

28. Harris, S. 1994. *Reclaiming Democracy—Healing the Break Between People and Government.* Camino Books, Philadelphia.

29. What, Us Worry? Conversation moderated by Todd S. Purdum. *The New York Times Magazine,* March 19, 1995.

30. Sustainability requires integrative values and actions. Our society's structural barriers to integrative thinking abound, including fragmentation in Congress (its myriad oversight committees) or

in local, state, and federal government (their myriad independent agencies); the rear-view mirror nature of law; overspecialization; our Western-world linear, left-brain dominance; absence of ancestral traditions and reverence for nature; media "sound bites"; information overload; etc. These barriers are falling as current reality educates us about the true costs for how we behave. Much is about common sense, too.

31. These are local activities being chronicled by organizations such as Global Tomorrow Coalition, Community Sustainability Resource Institute, Renew America, and many others focused on aspects of the overall picture, such as energy, waste management, alternative construction, agriculture, forestry, tourism, etc.

32. In addition to the PCSD, there are federal interagency working groups on sustainable development "indicators," on "sustainable redevelopment" (disaster impacted communities), on environmental technology (report *Technology for a Sustainable Future,* 1994), as well as preparations for the United Nations urban summit Habitat II in June 1996.

FORUM

22

The National Environmental Policy Act (NEPA) is praised for its prescience and condemned because it remains an unfulfilled promise. Those who have followed the debate have heard some environmental activists charge that it does too little to protect the environment and some developers charge that it favors the environment over equally important economic progress. Fortunately, the debate has not descended to a polarized, winner-take-all battle. Most participants in the debate are searching for the right tool that will help find balance and reason. The following panel—Bear, Caldwell, and Mandelker—three of the most articulate and nationally respected professionals, have written and spoken about the accomplishments and shortcomings of NEPA; they are interviewed by Ray Clark. The participants in the forum are:

> **Ray Clark** is the Associate Director for NEPA Oversight at the Council on Environmental Quality in the Executive Office of the President of the United States. He teaches a course in implementation of NEPA at Duke University.

> **Lynton Caldwell** is the Bentley Professor of Political Science Emeritus at the University of Indiana. He was a consultant to Senator Henry Jackson during the drafting of NEPA and is often thought to have influenced the shape and tone of the act more than any other individual.

> **Dinah Bear** is the General Counsel at the Council on Environmental Quality. She has served the Reagan, Bush, and Clinton administrations in that capacity.

> **Daniel Mandelker** is the Stamper Professor of Law at Washington University. He has written numerous books and articles on environmental law, including *NEPA Law and Litigation* published by Clark Boardman Callaghan. He also consults on land use and environmental issues.

Clark—What do you believe to be the most important accomplishments of NEPA?

Caldwell—I think there are three important accomplishments. First is its declaration of a comprehensive environmental policy for the United States. Second is its action-forcing mechanism in Section 102 and the full public disclosure provisions of the statute. Of course, these provisions interrelate to establish, by law, a national environmental policy.

Bear—I agree that opening up to the public access to information and analysis used in the decision-making process is one of NEPA's most important accomplishments. I also think that NEPA made consideration of environmental issues a part of the ordinary course of doing business.

Mandelker—Indeed, NEPA has substantially improved the environmental awareness of federal agencies, and that may be its most important accomplishment.

Clark—What is the full potential of NEPA?

Bear—The full potential is limited only by man's imagination and ability to creatively come to grips with living on the earth. In a slightly more down to earth sense, I think its potential is to be a framework in which American society wrestles with the question of how we treat the environment and other living things in relationship to our own needs.

Mandelker—The full potential of NEPA is to make environmental concerns an essential part of federal agency decision making. While I said earlier that NEPA has substantially improved environmental awareness, it has not yet forced all agencies to integrate environmental concerns in everything they do.

Bear—I agree with Dan. NEPA has unrealized potential for being used to authorize environmental research and to integrate other environmental review requirements.

Caldwell—The full potential of the act is deducible from its provisions, including Title II. NEPA has never been permitted to achieve its full potential.

Clark—Are there changes to either the statute, regulations, or administration of NEPA that you see are needed?

Caldwell—The Council on Environmental Quality (CEQ) regulations might be more explicit in some respects, although they are adequate in their present form.

Mandelker—The statute does not need revision. The strength of NEPA is its role in forcing full disclosure of environmental impacts through a decision-making process that must consider environmental problems. There could be some improvement of the administration of NEPA. There is some confusion, for example, about the level of environmental significance required before an impact statement must be prepared. This problem could be clarified through changes in the CEQ regulations.

Caldwell—The greatest need is unambiguous support at the White House. NEPA has been disappointing only in its marginalizing by a succession of chief executives.

Mandelker—One other thing a revision in the CEQ regulations could help to clear up is the confusion about the type of impacts that need discussion in an environmental impact statement (EIS), particularly indirect and cumulative impacts.

Clark—Have the courts helped or hindered NEPA's effectiveness?

Mandelker—The courts have become a "third arm" in the enforcement of NEPA, because they reinforce the role of organizations and other parties outside the decision-making process in enforcing the statute. I believe this judicial role is beneficial. The courts have played an essential role in interpreting the requirements of NEPA and making them enforceable.

Bear—Without the courts, I don't believe NEPA would have been implemented at *all*.

Caldwell—The judicial role has been ambivalent. The courts generally treat NEPA as procedural legislation. They have enforced conformity to the impact statement requirement, but generally decline to consider NEPA's substantive provisions. The courts find no constitutional basis for environmental protection.

Bear—I believe that the courts have been correct under American jurisprudence in their decision that the only *judicially enforceable* provisions of NEPA are the procedural requirements of Section 102(2)(C) and (E).

Having said that, I believe some courts have shown too much deference to the agencies in relationship to procedural and analytical rigor. In my opinion, the larger problem with NEPA in the context of American society is that many people have come to view the law as only that which a judge will enforce through injunctive relief. In other words, there are many sections of NEPA (e.g., Section 101) which are perfectly good law and which, in my opinion, we all have a legal and ethical obligation to try to implement, however imperfectly. But the bottom line for many is whether they can actually be penalized for violating it. It think we need to separate enforceability from obligation.

Clark—Has NEPA had influence beyond its requirement to prepare EISs?

Mandelker—Yes. Congress and federal agencies have incorporated NEPA's environmental decision-making process into legislation and regulations for numerous federal programs. The environmental decision-making requirements that pervade the federal highway and public transit programs are an example. Another is the public interest balancing test required by the U.S. Army Corps of Engineers in the administration of the dredge-and-fill permit program for wetlands.

Bear—And the CEQ is part and parcel of NEPA, and I believe the presence of a permanent institution in the Executive Office of the President representing environmental issues is extremely important. The information produced as a result of the annual report requirement is a major influence of NEPA. I would add that some agencies modify their proposals before the EIS is ever drafted.

Caldwell—NEPA has been emulated in various degrees by nearly half of the states and by an estimated 80 or more countries abroad, and that speaks directly to influence beyond the EIS.

Clark—Are there environmental research needs that could help further the purposes of NEPA?

Caldwell—As you know, Title II authorizes the CEQ to explore research needs. And I think there would be a national advantage to inventory, collate, and report on ongoing research to the extent that it is not now done.

Bear—I agree. It seems to me that NEPA mandates that agencies figure out what environmental research needs exist and then address them. I can think of areas where more environmental research is needed, like forest health, and where NEPA can be used as the legal authority to authorize such research.

Mandelker—We still don't know enough about how ecosystems function and how they are affected by actions that can damage the environment. More research on these problems would be helpful in the administration of NEPA.

Bear—In that regard, I suppose cumulative effects research stands out as important.

Clark—Has the passage of other environmental laws over the last 25 years made NEPA redundant?

Bear—No. If anything, some of the other laws are potentially redundant with NEPA if, and only if, NEPA's potential for both substantive and procedural integration was much further developed.

Caldwell—NEPA is a comprehensive policy declaration. Other statutes are needed to put its principles into practice.

Mandelker—Most environmental legislation is specific to a particular problem, and none of it requires the comprehensive environmental decision-making process that NEPA requires. NEPA also is the only environmental legislation that mandates environmental responsibilities for federal agencies.

Clark—In your view, should NEPA be used solely as an environmental analysis or should it be an integrating tool for all project planning?

Caldwell—NEPA was intended as an integrating tool for all project planning. Senator Henry Jackson declared that it amended the basic authorizing legislation of all federal agencies.

Mandelker—That may be so, but I think there is the danger that the environmental analysis requirement of NEPA would be downgraded if it were a part of an "integrated" planning process. I would not be willing to take that step unless I was certain that all federal agencies are serious about their environmental responsibilities.

Bear—I have mixed thoughts about this. There is a great deal of attractiveness in using NEPA as an integrative tool for everything. There is also the danger if NEPA becomes so burdened with every single aspect of decision making that environmental analysis takes a back seat. Having said that, I think much progress can be made toward integration before we reach any danger of the latter.

Clark—What changes, if any, do you see in the implementation of any of the provisions of NEPA in the next 10 to 25 years?

Bear—Hopefully, less duplication with the requirements of other laws and less paperwork. I would also like to see NEPA have a more direct relationship with the real decision making that occurs.

Mandelker—I would hope that there will be changes in the administration of NEPA that will clarify NEPA's role in decision making. I think this would help avoid unnecessary controversy and litigation.

Bear—I hope more agencies make more explicit ties to the policy goals of Section 101 of NEPA.

Caldwell—The answer requires more foresight than I possess. If oncoming generations are more responsive to environmental quality than the present adult majority, I would look for more rigorous implementation.

Clark—Thank you all for your generous time. Your contributions to an effective NEPA are well known and appreciated by many.

INDEX

A

adaptive environmental management (AEM), 164, 171, 174, 175, 176, 178, 179
Administrative Dispute Resolution Act, 280
Administrative Procedures Act, 25, 88, 187, 263, 307
administrative reform, 86, 89, 92, 95
Advisory Council for Historic Preservation, 205
Agenda 21, 94, 313
Air Pollution Control Act, 10
air quality models, 122, 125, 126
Alabama v. EPA, 290
Alabama-Tombigbee River Coalition v. Dept. of Interior, 272
alternative dispute resolution (ADR), 22, 277, 278, 279, 280, 281, 282, 283, 284, 285, 286, 287
American Ornithologists Union (AOU), 7
Atomic Energy Commission (AEC), 19, 87, 181, 199, 264
auditing, 164, 177, 211, 212
Audubon, John James, 4
Audubon Society, 8

B

Bald Eagle and Golden Eagle Protection Act, 143
biodiversity, 23, 79, 83, 141, 144, 149, 150, 152, 154, 156, 157, 158, 218, 226
Brit v. U.S. Army Corps of Engineers, 290

Brownlow Committee, 39, 40, 44
Bureau of Indian Affairs (BIA), 211, 299, 300, 301, 302, 307, 308, 310
Bureau of Land Management (BLM), 87, 91, 146, 155, 175

C

Cabinet Mountains v. Peterson, 184
California Environmental Quality Act (CEQA), 140, 142, 145, 148, 150, 153
California gnatcatcher, 139, 148, 158, 159
Calvert Cliffs v. Atomic Energy Commission, 40, 41, 166, 181, 189, 199, 264
Carson, Rachel, 10, 11, 16, 28, 37
categorical exclusions (CXs), 21, 77, 264, 265, 266, 270, 274
checklists (simple, descriptive, questionnaire), 118, 121
Citizens to Preserve Overton Park Inc. v. Volpe, 264
Civil Rights Act of 1964, 251, 254, 258
Clean Air Act, 68, 270, 304, 309
Clean Water Act, 68, 75, 140, 143, 149, 151, 254, 270, 304
community cohesion, 252, 256
Comprehensive Environmental Response, Compensation and Liability Act, 68, 230, 304
conservation, 5, 9, 23, 27, 28, 155, 306
Conservation Foundation, 28
cost-benefit analysis (or benefit-cost analysis), 17, 118, 167, 203, 318

Council on Environmental Quality (CEQ),
    12, 17, 20, 22, 25, 26, 27, 31, 34, 36, 37,
    38, 39, 40, 41, 42, 43, 44, 45, 46, 53, 55,
    58, 59, 61, 64, 65, 70, 78, 83, 86, 90,
    139, 178, 179, 193, 194, 195, 196, 197,
    200, 201, 202, 204, 208, 209, 210, 211,
    212, 222, 223, 253, 265, 280, 290, 296,
    297, 310, 316, 317, 319, 335, 337, 338
  guidelines, 115, 165, 198
  regulations (see also NEPA regulations),
    65, 115, 151, 153, 157, 159, 164, 167,
    168, 171, 182, 184, 185, 186, 189, 194,
    204, 209, 231, 241, 252, 263, 264, 265,
    266, 267, 268, 273, 274, 290, 295, 296,
    299, 304, 308, 336, 337
cumulative effects, 22, 92, 101, 164, 176,
    222, 273, 302, 309, 338
cumulative impact prediction methods, 128,
    130, 131, 132
cumulative impacts, 70, 71, 74, 116, 127,
    133, 135, 142, 156, 167, 185, 186, 192,
    201, 204, 209, 218, 226, 236, 273, 300,
    302, 309, 337

D

Data Processing Service v. Camp, 261, 262
Davis v. Morton, 302
decision-focused checklists, 118
decision-making process, 215, 216, 219, 226,
    231, 245, 282, 289, 290, 291, 296, 297
decision support systems or methodologies,
    216, 297
decision trees, 273
Dingell, John, 17, 29, 30, 31, 36
direct, indirect, and cumulative impacts, 73,
    115, 116, 127, 135, 241

E

ecological indicators, 134
ecological rationality, 51, 52, 55, 56, 57, 58,
    59
Ecological Society of America, 9, 165
ecological train wrecks, 139, 140, 141, 142,
    144, 147, 154, 158
ecosystem approach to management, 191,
    196, 203, 204, 209, 222, 273
ecosystem-level assessment and management,
    23, 83, 146, 147, 154, 155, 157, 175
ecotoxicology, 172

effects on communities, neighborhoods, and
    individuals, 252, 255, 257
Emerson, Ralph Waldo, 5, 6
Employment Act, 38
endangered species, 8, 32, 35, 63, 68, 143
Endangered Species Act (ESA), 10, 16, 33,
    140, 142, 144, 146, 149, 155, 185, 191,
    254, 270, 304
energy system diagrams, 123
environmental assessments (EAs), 21, 58,
    69, 77, 78, 83, 157, 163, 164, 166, 170,
    176, 179, 183, 184, 185, 186, 195, 196,
    199, 200, 201, 202, 203, 208, 264, 265,
    266, 267, 270, 274, 281, 284, 289
environmental audits, 178, 203, 209, 211
Environmental Defense Fund, 89
Environmental Defense Fund v. Massey, 190
environmental impact statement (EIS), 18,
    19, 20, 30, 40, 41, 42, 51, 53, 57, 64, 65,
    67, 68, 69, 71, 72, 77, 78, 79, 80, 81, 83,
    86, 88, 89, 90, 91, 92, 95, 99, 102, 148,
    157, 163, 164, 166, 168, 170, 176, 179,
    182, 183, 184, 185, 186, 187, 188, 191,
    192, 193, 194, 195, 196, 199, 200, 201,
    202, 203, 205, 208, 210, 211, 229, 231,
    234, 235, 244, 252, 264, 265, 266, 267,
    268, 270, 271, 274, 281, 284, 285, 286,
    287, 289, 294, 295, 296, 307, 308, 323,
    337
environmental index, 121, 122
environmental indicators, 134
environmental justice (EJ), 22, 23, 83, 168,
    240, 260
experimental methods, 121, 135
expert judgment, 237
expert knowledge, 235
expert systems, 118, 297

F

Federal Advisory Committee Act (FACA),
    267, 272, 273, 283, 285, 286, 287
Federal-Aid Highway Act, 252, 255
Federal Aviation Administration, 157
Federal Energy Regulatory Commission
    (FERC), 302, 304
Federal Highway Administration (FHWA),
    91, 253, 254, 255, 259, 260
Federal Insecticide, Fungicide, and Rodenti-
    cide Act, 11

Federal Power Act, 304
Federal Power Commission, 87
Federal Water Pollution Control Act of
    1948, 10
findings of no significant impact (FONSIs),
    21, 77, 78, 184, 185, 200, 202
Fish and Wildlife Coordination Act, 8, 89,
    304
Flood Control Act, 88
Forest Preservation Act, 16
*Foundation on Economic Trends (FOET) v.
    Heckler*, 188
Fritiofson v. Alexander, 185

G

General Allotment Act, 301
Geographic Information Systems (GIS), 219,
    220, 221, 222, 223, 226
Goldberg v. Kelly, 261, 262
Greenpeace v. Stone, 190

H

habitat conservation areas (HCAs), 146
habitat conservation plan (HCP), 144, 145,
    148, 149, 150, 158
Habitat Evaluation Procedures (HEP), 121,
    122
Habitat Evaluation System (HES), 121, 122
Highway Beautification Act, 252
Highway Safety Act, 252
Homestead Act, 5
human environment, 66, 67, 73, 230
human population and econometric models,
    123
hydrological models, 122

I

imagery (satellite and aircraft), 219, 221,
    222, 223, 226
Indian Self-Determination and Education
    Assistance Act, 306
Indian tribes, 82, 194, 200, 201, 205, 209,
    211, 231, 299, 300, 301, 302, 303, 305,
    306, 307, 308, 309, 310
indicators, 117, 118, 135
interaction matrices, 121
interdisciplinary, 321, 322, 323, 324, 325,
    326, 327, 328, 329, 330
interdisciplinary approach, 18, 22, 53, 152,
    156, 200, 230, 251, 254, 293, 317

interdisciplinary teams, 234, 241
Intermodal Surface Transportation Efficiency
    Act (ISTEA), 323, 328
International Association for Impact Assess-
    ment (IAIA), 42
Internet, 219, 222, 223, 225, 226, 329
Isaac Walton League, 28

L

laboratory testing and scale models, 118
Lacey Act, 8
Land and Water Conservation Fund Act, 10
landscape evaluation, 118
Lathan v. Volpe, 264
Leopold, Aldo, 8, 9, 16, 28, 153
life cycle assessment (LCA), 168

M

Marine Mammal Act, 143
Marsh, George Perkins, 5, 16, 28
mass balance calculations, 118
mathematical models, 135, 235, 271
matrices, 118
mediation, 279, 280
*Metropolitan Edison v. People Against
    Nuclear Energy*, 186
Migratory Bird Act, 8, 143, 146
mitigated finding of no significant impact
    (FONSI), 76, 77, 200, 202, 296
mitigation, 237, 238, 241, 242
mitigation measures, 21, 32, 62, 63, 66, 72,
    74, 75, 76, 77, 82, 153, 159, 163, 183,
    184, 203, 209, 211, 237, 295, 307
monitoring, 21, 78, 99, 107, 108, 109, 110,
    118, 158, 163, 164, 170, 173, 175, 177,
    178, 192, 203, 204, 206, 209, 212, 222,
    237, 238, 242
Muir, John, 6, 7, 8, 9, 16

N

Nash, Roderick, 4
National Biological Service, 317
National Forest Management Act (NFMA),
    146, 191
National Historic Preservation Act, 33, 270
National Marine Fisheries Service (NMFS),
    149
National Oceanic and Atmospheric Administ-
    ration, 218, 286

National Park Service (NPS), 16, 44, 87, 146, 155, 175

National Science Foundation (NSF), 177, 190, 191

National Trails Act, 10

Native American treaty rights, 270

Natural Resource Conservation Service, 155

Natural Resources Defense Council, 89, 148

negotiated rule making, 282, 283, 285, 287

Negotiated Rulemaking Act, 280

NEPA Analyst's Workbench, 225

NEPA regulations (see also CEQ regulations), 20, 21, 61, 62, 64, 65, 66, 67, 68, 69, 70, 71, 72, 73, 74, 75, 76, 77, 78, 79, 80, 81, 82, 83, 198, 316, 318

NEPANET, 205, 210, 222

networks, 118, 121

non-governmental organizations (NGOs), 206

northern spotted owl, 145, 146, 147, 191, 192

Northwest Forest Resource Council v. Espy, 272

NRDC v. Morton, 182, 183

Nuclear Regulatory Commission (NRC), 186, 189

O

Oil Pollution Act, 304

Organic Administration Act, 7

overlay mapping via GIS, 119

P

photographs/photomontages, 119

Pinchot, Gifford, 6, 7, 16, 153

pollution prevention, 23, 79, 83

President's Council on Sustainable Development (PCSD), 259, 260, 313, 317, 318, 330

programmatic EIS, 136, 150, 169, 265

project life cycle, 242, 296

public involvement, 23, 231, 238, 239, 259, 264, 265, 266, 267, 268, 269, 272, 273, 274, 292

public participation, 108, 109, 110, 216, 264, 265, 267, 268, 272, 274, 314, 316

Public Service Co. v. Nuclear Regulatory Commission, 189

Q

qualitative modeling, 117 ,119

quantitative modeling, 117, 119

R

Reauthorization Act, 230

Record of Decision, 76, 82, 259, 274, 295, 296

risk assessment, 23, 91, 94, 119, 164, 168, 209, 223, 293

Rivers and Harbors Act, 10, 151

Robertson v. Methow Valley Citizens Council, 184, 189

S

Safe Drinking Water Act, 304

scenarios, 119, 235, 237

scoping, 21, 65, 66, 68, 70, 78, 79, 80, 82, 90, 99, 102, 104, 106, 107, 108, 206, 231, 234, 240, 241, 267, 268, 273, 274, 281, 301, 307, 308

screening, 78, 101, 102, 104, 307

Seattle Audubon Society v. Lyons, 191

Sierra Club, 6, 7, 9, 69, 87, 89

Sierra Club v. Larson, 290

social impact assessment (SIA), 167, 230, 231, 232, 233, 234, 235, 236, 237, 238, 240, 242, 243, 244, 245, 270

social impacts, 230, 231, 234, 235, 236, 238, 242, 243, 244

Soil Conservation Service, 87, 218

species diversity indices, 122

strategic environmental assessment (SEA), 134, 135

Stryker's Bay v. Kariem, 289

surface and groundwater quality models, 122

sustainability, 23, 68, 71, 83, 156, 157, 188, 222, 321, 322, 323, 324, 325, 327, 329, 330

sustainable development, 61, 67, 68, 79, 94, 104, 146, 169, 196, 313, 314, 315, 316, 317, 318, 319

T

Tennessee Valley Authority (TVA), 87, 284, 292

Thomas v. Peterson, 185

Thoreau, Henry David, 5, 6, 9, 16

threshold concepts, 23
tiering, 66, 69, 82
training, 204, 209, 211, 297, 305, 310
trend extrapolation, 119
Tulalip Tribe, 210, 211, 302, 304

U

Udall, Stewart, 28
uncertainty, 164, 171, 172, 173, 179
Uniform Relocation Assistance and Land
    Acquisition Policies Act, 254, 256
U.S. Agency for International Development,
    231
U.S. Army Corps of Engineers (Corps), 44,
    75, 81, 82, 87, 91, 151, 155, 157, 185,
    189, 205, 337
U.S. Bureau of Reclamation (BOR), 44, 87,
    150, 155
U.S. Department of Agriculture, 86, 191, 199
U.S. Department of the Army, 190, 295
U.S. Department of Commerce, 8, 149
U.S. Department of Defense, 86, 205, 220
U.S. Department of Energy, 86, 237
U.S. Department of Housing and Urban
    Development (HUD), 86, 91, 257, 259,
    327
U.S. Department of Interior, 86, 139, 149,
    183, 191, 199
U.S. Department of Justice, 86, 285, 286
U.S. Department of Transportation, 20, 82,
    86, 199

U.S. Environmental Protection Agency
    (EPA), 75, 81, 86, 151, 157, 166, 199,
    218, 286, 304, 309
U.S. Fish and Wildlife Service (FWS), 10,
    81, 144, 148, 149, 155, 157, 175, 185,
    186, 205
U.S. Forest Service (FS), 7, 9, 44, 82, 87,
    91, 146, 155, 184, 185, 186, 220, 274
U.S. Geological Survey, 218
U.S. Park Service, 220
U.S. Public Health Service, 87
U.S. State Department, 86
U.S. Trade Representative, 86
U.S. v. Washington, 306

V

Vermont Yankee v. NRDC, 187, 264, 290
virtual reality, 297
visual impact modeling, 123

W

Wetland Evaluation Technique (WET),
    122
wetlands, 15, 75, 337
Wild and Scenic Rivers Act, 10, 16
Wilderness Act, 10, 16, 143
Wilderness Society, 9
Wright, Judge J. Skelly, 32, 181, 188, 189

Z

Zabel v. Tabb, 189